Walt's People: Volume 5

Other Books by Didier Ghez

They Drew as They Pleased: The Hidden Art of Disney's Golden Age (2015)

Disney's Grand Tour (2013)

Disneyland Paris: From Sketch to Reality (2002)

Edited by Didier Ghez:

Life in the Mouse House (2014)

Inside the Whimsy Works (2014)

Walt's People: Volumes 1-17 (2005-2016)

Walt's People: Volume 5

Didier Ghez, editor

Foreword by Mark Mayerson

Theme Park Press
www.ThemeParkPress.com

© 2016 DIDIER GHEZ

No part of this publication may be reproduced, distributed, or transmitted in any form or by any means, including photocopying, recording, or other electronic or mechanical methods, without the prior written permission of the publisher, except for brief quotations embodied in critical reviews and certain other noncommercial uses permitted by copyright law.

Although every precaution has been taken to verify the accuracy of the information contained herein, no responsibility is assumed for any errors or omissions, and no liability is assumed for damages that may result from the use of this information.

Theme Park Press is not associated with the Walt Disney Company, the Disney Family, or any of the individuals or companies associated with either or both of them.

The views expressed in this book are those of the author alone.

Theme Park Press publishes its books in a variety of print and electronic formats. Some content that appears in one format may not appear in another.

Editor: Bob McLain
Layout: Artisanal Text

ISBN 978-1-68390-011-5
Printed in the United States of America

Theme Park Press | **www.ThemeParkPress.com**
Address queries to bob@themeparkpress.com

To Enrique Alcala and Mark Linker:
Your friendship made work in Latin America feel like never-ending vacations.

Contents

Foreword ix

Introduction xi

    Hugh Harman *(Michael Barrier)* 1

    Nadine Missakian *(Dave Smith)* 7

    Ward Kimball *(Rick Shale)* 11

    Erwin Verity *(Rick Shale and Dave Smith)* 43

    James Algar *(Richard Hubler)* 69

    Winston Hibler *(Richard Hubler)* 81

    Bill Anderson *(Richard Hubler)* 93

    Bill Walsh *(Richard Hubler)* 101

    Bill Walsh *(Christopher Finch and Linda Rosenkrantz)* 109

    George Bruns *(Richard Hubler)* 123

    Buddy Baker *(Jon Burlingame)* 127

    Buddy Baker *(Jérémie Noyer)* 137

    Fess Parker *(Michael Barrier)* 153

    Walt Stanchfield *(Christian Renaut)* 175

    Marc Davis *(Richard Hubler)* 181

    Alice Davis *(David Oneal)* 183

    T. Hee *(Richard Hubler)* 197

    Maurice Noble *(Harry McCracken)* 217

    Al Dempster *(Christopher Finch and Linda Rosenkrantz)* 231

    Walt Peregoy *(Bob Miller)* 247

    The Saga of Windwagon Smith *(Floyd Norman)* 259

    The Making of The Jungle Book *(Floyd Norman)* 263

    Bill Evans *(Jim Korkis)* 273

    Jack Bradbury *(Alberto Becattini)* 289

    Lynn Karp *(Alberto Becattini)* 299

Dave Michener *(Didier Ghez)* 303
In Memory of Vance Gerry *(John Musker)* 329
Vance Gerry *(Charles Solomon)* 331
Vance Gerry *(Christian Renaut)* 339
John Musker and Ron Clements *(Clay Kaytis)* 343

Acknowledgments 373
Further Reading 379
About the Authors 381
More Books from Theme Park Press 385

Foreword

When a company starts producing quality work, it starts attracting quality people. The best want to work only with the best. Why should they settle for less? Creative people aren't just interested in trading their skills for a paycheck. They're burning with enthusiasm to do something interesting, and opportunities for that are rarer than they ought to be.

So the people who worked for Walt Disney throughout the studio's history were there for a reason: they could count on Walt to do something new and exciting that would provide them with an experience they couldn't get elsewhere. In exchange, they gave their considerable talents to Disney's service, allowing him to realize his dreams. We, the audience, were the beneficiaries.

And we're greedy, aren't we? We've watched the films and TV shows, traveled to the theme parks, read the comics, listened to the music, played with the toys, and we still want more. Not just more films, etc. We want to understand how and why these things entertained us and why they still have such a hold on us. We want to get inside the things we love by learning about the people who made them.

Didier Ghez and the interviewers have given us this opportunity. Some of us are looking for the behind-the-scenes anecdotes that add an amusing bit of background. Some of us are fascinated by Disney history and love the mix of personalities and events that determined how the studio developed. Some of us are professional artists, designers, and filmmakers looking for insight into how Walt Disney and his crew managed to create to such a high standard. None of us will be disappointed in this volume.

While Walt Disney was the magnet that drew these people together, they're still fascinating as individuals. They have different backgrounds, different personalities, and different talents, but all are fully engaged with their creations and happy to share their experiences. They're proud of their work, and why shouldn't they be?

Didier Ghez has now collected five volumes of these interviews, every one a gem. But I suspect as we plow through this volume, no matter how much we learn, no matter how much we enjoy it, we'll be wondering what will turn up in volume six.

'Cause we're greedy, aren't we?

Mark Mayerson

Introduction

"Pay dirt!" Those were my first thoughts when I managed to contact Jane Hubler through her son-in-law Louis Bremer. Jane Hubler was in her 90s and the widow of journalist and author Richard Hubler. She was therefore the holder of the copyrights of Richard Hubler's research. Among this research were some Disney historical treasures: the interviews that Hubler conducted in the late '60s for his aborted biography of Walt Disney. Jane Hubler accepted my offer to grant me those copyrights for *Walt's People*.

Richard Hubler had started his work on Walt's biography less than a year after Walt's death. Aside from Diane Disney Miller's biography of her father, which had appeared in 1957 and was, in reality, the work of Pete Martin based on a series of interviews with Walt, no other biography of Walt had ever been released by that time. It was only natural, therefore, that Roy O. Disney encouraged such a project after the death of his brother. By 1968, when Hubler's research was in full swing, Richard Schickel released his own interpretation of Walt's life, *The Disney Version*, which was perceived by the Disney family as highly critical and therefore increased the importance of publishing an official and approved biography of the "Mousetro".

Unfortunately, Richard Hubler approached the project to a great extent lacking the necessary historical perspective. His interviews with the Disney artists and Disney family members therefore lacked the sharpness and precision of later works by Christopher Finch, Michael Barrier, John Canemaker, Bob Thomas, and others. This probably explains why his attempted biography was never released and why audiences had to wait until 1976 to read the first official biography of Walt, which remains the approved "bible" to this day: *Walt Disney: An American Original* by Bob Thomas.

These considerations aside, however, Hubler's interviews retain great historical value for one key reason: Hubler conducted them at a time when many of the interviewees still had very sharp memories of the events they discussed. This allowed Hubler to stumble upon fascinating stories that no other Disney historians would be able to gather after him. But because the field of Disney history was mostly virgin in the late '60s, Hubler's interviews also contained a lot of information and questions that any of us today would consider as basic, almost childish.

In today's speech, the "sound versus noise" ratio was quite low. So whereas in earlier volumes of the *Walt's People* series I tried to deliver the interviews as uncut and uncensored as possible, I decided to follow a different route in this volume, offering you only the "meat" of Hubler's interviews: the stories, information, and anecdotes that you are unlikely to have read elsewhere or that are presented from such a different point of view that you will still enjoy reading them.

Previous volumes explored the interactions and creative processes of Disney artists. Since Richard Hubler's series of interviews was intended as the basis for his biography of Walt, it tries to answer a different question, the most puzzling question of them all for most of us: "Who was Walt?"

And so we are once more expanding our scope: Dave Smith's interview of Nadine Missakian, Walt's secretary at the time of his Laugh-O-grams venture is our first foray in the field of interviews with Walt's "family and friends" that will be at the core of Volume 6, thanks to Richard Hubler. In addition, meeting James Algar, Winston Hibler, Bill Anderson, Bill Walsh, and Fess Parker allows us to scratch the surface of the wonderful world of Disney television and live-action productions, another key theme that has been barely explored until now.

But there is more. I realized that Disney music, backgrounds, and overall design had not been discussed either. Volume 5 attempts to slowly fill these gaps, thanks to interviews with composers George Bruns and Buddy Baker, and rare testimonies by T. Hee, Maurice Noble, Walt Peregoy, and Al Dempster.

All those artistic fields, which have contributed significantly to the success of Disney movies while often being overlooked, will be explored again in future volumes. This is particularly true of the world of Disney music, since historian David Tietyen, author of *The Musical World of Walt Disney* (Harry N. Abrams, 1990), recently allowed us to get access to all of his research.

Which takes us to this volume's new contributors, starting with Rick Shale, the most famous specialist of the history of Disney during WWII along with David Lesjak, whose interviews allow us to dig deeper in a field which Dave Smith introduced in Volume 4 through his interview with Lou Debney.

To our delight, two other "heavyweights" have also decided to help the *Walt's People* project: Christopher Finch and Linda Rosenkrantz, a couple famous for having authored one of the "bibles" owned by every self-respecting Disney historian: *The Art of Walt Disney* (Harry N. Abrams, 1973).

And since the world of Disney research is more alive than it has ever been in years, thanks to the internet (see the introduction to *Walt's People: Volume 4*), new researchers are also joining the field. We are lucky to welcome three of them in Volume 5: music expert Jérémie Noyer, AnimationPodcast.com founder Clay Kaytis, and Dave Oneal.

Speaking of the internet, some of you may know that I launched The Disney History Blog (disneybooks.blogspot.com) in August 2006. Checking the blog is the best way to get a preview of the progress of the *Walt's People* project, to see photos that I cannot include in the series, or to read entertaining anecdotes about Disney history.

But despite this flow of exciting news, thankfully some things do stay the same volume after volume, and I like to start each new book with a look at the early days of Walt's career.

So, without further ado, let's pick up our story where we left it at the end of the very first interview of the very first volume of the series: let's meet one of Walt's very first artists, and let's find out how Walt himself decided to subcontract the production of a Silly Symphony...

Didier Ghez
Kruger National Park, January 2007

Hugh Harman (1903–1982)

Interviewed by Mike Barrier on December 3, 1973.

The *Walt's People* book series opened with an in-depth interview of Rudy Ising by JB Kaufman. Since Ising without Harman is almost like Laurel without Hardy, we owed you this interview with Hugh Harman, which took place on December 3, 1973, at the offices of Bob Clampett Productions in Hollywood. Joining Barrier were former Harman colleague Bob Clampett, and Mark Kausler, both of whom were close friends of Harman.

Hugh Harman: It seems we wasted so many years—and this goes for Rudy [Ising], it goes for Disney; it goes for all of us if we analyze it. We had to learn the craft the slow way. If any of us had in the beginning, as Orson Welles had, the essence of the stage and motion picture mastered, then on top of that learned the craft of animation, we could have made worthy things.

I remember when we were taking these foolish photographs in 1926 at Disney's, Rudy and my brother Walker and Walt and Roy [Disney] and me. We stood there in the evening, the sun was going down and it was very warm and nice and mild, and we were just talking generally. Walt said, "You know, I wish I had $10,000."

I said, "Why do you want $10,000?"

He said, "Do you know what I would do?"

"I haven't the least idea."

He said, "I would quit this business and go into the real-estate business. Think of the stuff up on Sunset Strip; that's going to be the most valuable property in the world."

I said, "That's all right for you, Walt, but that's not for me. I can see this cartoon thing developing to the point that we won't draw these silly characters, won't make silly stuff. Perhaps some day"—and I had no idea of sound—"we might, for instance, animate some of Shakespeare's plays, such as *Macbeth*."

He looked at me as if I had a hole in my head. I think he thought, "Well, Hugh means well."

Mike Barrier: When you were animating back in Kansas City, you said that you were given sequences of so many feet and you had the freedom to do pretty much what you wanted to do.

HH: Yes, it was all that way then. There was such freedom; in fact, invention was needed. It used to bewilder me that enough invention wasn't made in the story that we could go ahead and draw. It was so hard to sit there. It was easy to invent the little business, the little stuff, but to try to analyze certain actions at times seemed very difficult because we had no reference to live action. Our only study was the Lutz book,[1] plus Paul Terry's films. As Rudy has said, we used to get these at the exchange through a girl who worked there,[2] and being that there was no sound, we could treat these things rather freely and take scissors and clip out maybe 50 or 75 feet—they needed editing, anyway. They'd just run and run and run. If they had Farmer Al [Falfa] swimming, he would swim forever, and no stuff except to turn around and swim back the other way. We'd prune them pretty freely and keep these strips of film as studies. That's the way we learned a lot from Terry. Of course, none of us knew much at that time; we couldn't have: We had no instructors.

Mark Kausler: I guess that's why there's such a similarity between the early Alice films and Paul Terry's stuff.

HH: Oh sure, that influence was predominantly there. That did not change until we came to California.

MB: To what extent did Harman-Ising have training classes for its artists, like the ones Disney had?

HH: Same thing. About 1937, Bob Stokes and Lee Blair organized our own art classes. They wanted to do it on their own; they thought it would be a good thing, as Disney was doing it. I noticed, with amazement, the progression of these artists from that point on. We were trying to get finer drawing, to draw stuff that would look natural, instead of using the Bosko formula.

Looking back, I believe that from about 1935 up to the end of the war marked the greatest advancement of any period in cartoons. Not just with Disney, or with us, or with Warner Bros., but with all; it had moved ahead.

MB: Bob, I believe you mentioned that classes were held even during the Warner days.

---

[1] Edwin G. Lutz, *Animated Cartoons: How They Are Made, Their Origin and Development* (1920).

[2] According to JB Kaufman and Russell Merritt on page 64 of *Walt in Wonderland* (Edizioni Biblioteca dell'Immagine, 1992): "Nadine Simpson was hired as a bookkeeper and cashier, but her singular value lay in her connections. She had previously worked at one of the Kansas City film exchanges. Knowing that the exchanges regularly junked prints when they became too worn for theatrical use, she arranged to obtain the discarded cartoons."

Bob Clampett: In 1932. Hugh hired Stokes and he conducted some classes.

MB: How long did these classes go on?

BC: It seems to me they only lasted like six months.

MB [to Harman]: When you were studying film on your own, did you apply any of this directly in your work at Harman-Ising, or was it something that you used as background?

HH: No, I applied it; that was the whole purpose. I was particularly impressed by [Sergei] Eisenstein and his theory of juxtaposition of shots. I began applying this stuff particularly in those frog pictures, *The Old Mill Pond* and *Swing Wedding*. The composition of the scenes relative to their music, relative to each other—juxtaposition again; I applied the theory very definitely. I have done that in practically every picture I personally designed since. In anything that was theatrical, I always tried to apply these principles I absorbed from Eisenstein, particularly, and from [V.I.] Pudovkin, too.

Pudovkin makes a point—and it's a simple one—about films; if anybody starting to make films realized this one thing they'd know everything about films that's to be known. It is this: if you have a shot of a man walking down a rainy street, and on either side of him are houses, and he sees a light ahead of him, you immediately get the impression that this man is perhaps homeless, destitute, and he's seeking comfort. He comes to a door and the light is very cheerful inside; he looks in and he sees a woman placing a bowl of soup on the table. Well, there's the essence of picture making—you know that the guy's hungry, that he wants soup.

But suppose, on the other hand, we have the same introduction, but instead of seeing the bowl of soup on the table, he sees the woman first and she's in a state of incomplete dress, so much so that he stares at her avidly—immediately, it's another story. That second shot in juxtaposition with the first has told you one story, or it has told you the other. That's Pudovkin for you.

I've often wished that we had gotten Orson Welles into this business. What a find he would have been! What the business has needed is minds. With all respect for Walt and his vast achievements—he was the world's greatest promoter—to me he never had ideas for stories as, say, Chaplin did. I can imagine what Orson would have done. I had occasion to work with him for quite a few months at our studio. He and I went into partnership on a deal to make [Antoine de Saint Exupéry's] *The Little Prince* in 1943-44. I developed the greatest respect and regard for that guy; he wasn't, as the film business had him, a temperamental type, he wasn't that way at all.

He was going to play the lead in it, the aviator, and we were going to get a boy for the Little Prince. Our sets would have been a combination of drawn and live. There would have been animated characters within the scope of the picture playing with these live people. We studied and studied and studied that book, and I'm eager now to see the picture that is now being made,[3] to see whether they have viewed the thing as we would have. We didn't take it in its transparency; we took it for its deeper meanings. We read *Wind, Sand and Stars*, another one of the author's creations (it's a thing of such magnificent beauty) and after reading that I thought I knew what *The Little Prince* was about. It is juvenile fiction, and yet there is a depth to it that is amazing.

We had it all set and were ready to go when Orson became tremendously ill. We couldn't say a word about it, but he nearly died. He had a bad liver at the time; he went to Florida to recover and was gone for months. We didn't revive it after that and we lost the whole deal.

I think *The Blue Danube* is one of the few good pictures I ever made; I'd say that I made about three good pictures. I'm not kidding.

MK: What are your three favorites?

HH: My three favorites are *The Blue Danube*, *The Old Mill Pond*, because it's an impressionistic thing, and *Peace on Earth*, which was seriously themed, it had nothing funny in it. They tried to stop me from making that.

BB: What was their argument?

HH: That it was too serious. It made more money than any picture we ever made. Fred Quimby, who was sort of a business manager at MGM, tried to stop it. Then when it was finished, I think he wanted to take all the awards for it himself.

Peace on Earth was a tough one to animate and to write. We shouldn't actually have made that as a one-reeler, we should have made it in about three to five reels. We cut it and cut it and cut it; we didn't cut footage that was animated—nobody in his right mind does that, unless it's bad. But cutting the storyboard and switching around. It has some flaws. I just got tired of it near the end. That's always been a weakness with me: that I get so fed up with it at the end of a picture that I would just as soon turn it over to the Girl Scouts to make, unless it were a feature that would warrant going on with costs forever. I've observed that as a weakness in myself: that I often end up with a weak, insubstantial ending for a picture.

MB: How did *Merbabies* come about?

HH: Roy Disney called me one day, just prior to the completion of *Snow White*, and he said, "Hugh, will you come down and talk to me about *Snow White*? We're in a real jam."

---

[3] He is referring to the version directed by Stanley Donen.

I went down and talked to him and Walt. Roy said, "We have a Christmas release coming up and we've got all our money sunk in *Snow White*. We're broke, unless this thing makes it for Christmas." (It's within a few months of Christmas.) "We have to have the thing finished and we don't have enough people to finish it. Could you and Rudy let us have your entire inking department? We might want them for several months."

I said, "Sure, that'd benefit us, anyway, because we're keeping a staff and we'd like to slow down."

So we sent our inking and painting department over there. I've never seen people work so hard or long in this business. They'd work nights until those girls would drop. We had about 45 people at the time in our inking and painting department. These girls just slaved, along with their girls, to complete this thing. It must have gone on for three, four months.

In that time, I said to Walt, "Look, we're doing you a favor; you can do us a favor in return. You've got a lot of pictures to make and we're having a fight with Metro. I'd like to complete several pictures on a slow program until we wind up our fight with Metro and get a new contract. How about giving us, say, three pictures to make for your release? You have an open release for Silly Symphonies, for instance."

Walt said, "Sure, I'll do that. You're helping me. It's priceless."

The first picture was *Merbabies*, a thing Disney had on the fire for some time; he had a stack of inspirational sketches as they called them—just a lot of trash, actually. No story, no plot, no rhyme or reason to any of this stuff, except that it all took place underwater: pretty sketches of little starfish, half-human, and so on. That was the picture and we finished it.

Whereas Rudy and I had jointly worked on *Merbabies*, on the other two we thought we'd separate, he would make one and I'd make the other. We had those pictures well under way, with our own investment in them, when Walt called me and said, "Hugh, I'm going to have to cancel those pictures."

I said, "What are you trying to do, just wreck us suddenly?"

He said, "No, RKO has objected to any other studio than my own making the pictures."

"What reason do they have to object? That's none of their business, as long as they come out with your title on them." But it turned out that the pictures were canceled.

At that time, a former RKO executive came into our studio wanting to see me. He said, "I understand that your company is looking for money to finance a program of pictures."

I said, "That's exactly right. Who do you represent?"

He said, "I cannot tell you who my principals are."

I said, "I don't want to do business with people I don't know. We might as well just forget about that in its entirety right now."

So he left. I met this guy several years later, but he had, just prior to my meeting him again, sent word to me that he was sent over by his principals who were—guess who?—Disney's. In other words, Walt tried to knock the props from under us, pulling those pictures away, and then sending a man in to buy us out. This may be confirmed by this: all the time we were working on *Merbabies*, Walt and Roy were talking to Rudy and me about quitting our own operation and joining them. They naturally wanted us out of the way, because the competition was too heavy.

MB: Did you suspect that if you had gone with Disney, he would have fired you after a short time?

HH: No, he wouldn't have done that. He would have been very pleasant, been very fair.

I used to rather envy Walt in this respect: he had Roy paving the way for him all the way. I kept wishing Roy was with me. A guy of such honesty and such toughness, too; Roy was a very tough man, but such a gentle and gently spoken man.

MB: Rudy mentioned that each of you had started one on speculation…

HH: That's right. We finished those at MGM.

MB: Were these the two you had started for Disney?

HH: Yes. One was my *Goldilocks and the Three Bears* and the other was Rudy's *Little Goldfish*.

We were trying to get something very fine at that point; not just because it was a Disney release, but it was just our incentive at the time, because we were looking to making features. I wanted to get out of the shorts business and make features.

© 2007 Michael Barrier

Nadine Missakian (d, 1988)

Interviewed by Dave Smith on August 12, 1970.

The following is a transcript of part of a conversation between Mrs. Nadine Missakian, née Simpson, Dave Smith, and Jim Stewart held at the Disney Studio in Burbank, California, on August 12, 1970. Mrs. Missakian visited the Disney Studio to present the Walt Disney Archives with some photographs and letters relating to Walt's time in Kansas City, Missouri. Mrs. Missakian was one of the employees of Laugh-O-gram Films, Walt's Kansas City company, serving as stenographer-bookkeeper.

[Regarding photos that her husband, Baron Missakian, took of Walt in 1931].

Dave Smith: This was on a trip that Walt took back to Kansas City?

Nadine Missakian: Yes, he and his wife. They came to the hotel for some kind of meeting and then came by at the place where I worked at 17th and Baltimore, picked me up, and took me out to the [photography] studio. And Baron [Missakian] was going to make portraits of both of them, but he found out at the last minute that he only had four films on hand. That was during the Depression.

[Regarding photos of the Laugh-O-gram studio building]

NM: Here are some other pictures of Troost that I made. It hasn't changed at all. It's just the same.

DS: Is this right in the center of town?

NM: You see 31st and Troost. It's called Intercity now—it's close to downtown—because the city is growing out south so far now. These four windows were Laugh-O-grams.

DS: Did they have a sign up over the door or anything?

NM: No, they just had the name here on the windows. LAUGH-O-GRAMS.

[Regarding pictures of the Disneys' home]

NM: Now this is his home at 3026 Bellefontaine. It's changed a little bit. This is where he lived with his mother and father.

DS: Do you know when he moved out of the home with his parents?

NM: No, I don't. Of course, I didn't work for him then. That was before 1922–1923.

[Regarding other photos]

NM: Most of these were sent to me by Rudolf Ising, a fellow I used to date long before…

These were made at 1127 E. 31st, Laugh-O-gram. This is Walt, when they were making the picture *Martha* for Jenkins Music Co. And this is Mr. [Adolph] Kloepper, his manager, and this is Ub Iwerks. He had his hair all white with powder. At this time they used powder. And then he has a cigar in his mouth.

Now this is the old mill. This is the old Watts Mill where Walt and the boys used to go so much.

DS: I wonder if that's where he got the idea of *The Old Mill* that he made later.

NM: I'll bet it was, because they used to go out there. It is about 103rd and Morrow Road, off Indian Creek.

This is the Annunciation Church at Lynwood and Benton. They had an ice cream social there years and years ago when the boys were starving: Rudolf and Walt and them. And I gave them two dollars worth of tickets, because that's where I went to church. They had this ice cream social. They gave out tickets for prizes. I want you to know that they won a ham and all of the groceries. I think Monsignor Tierney must have just fixed that up so they could win. That's where they really struck it rich.

DS: What happened to the company when Walt left for California? Was that just the end of the company?

NM: Before that it was just dissolved. The story this Mr. Fitzsimmons wrote[1]…he said that they had the final wake at this meeting, October 16, 1923. And this was it. Well, these were the employees: Aletha Reynolds…

DS: What did she do?

NM: She was an inker. Ub Iwerks. Here was the sales manager [Adolph Kloeppper]. Carman Maxwell, Otto Walliman, Rudolf Ising, Lorey Tague, me, Dr. J. V. Cowles. I don't know who Mr. Hampton was. I don't remember him, but these were the people present on that day. And these were all the employees.

---

[1] According to Dave Smith: "Fred Fitzsimmons was a reporter with the *Kansas City Star* in the 1960s who was helping Nadine organize her autobiographical notes." We contacted one of Mr. Fitzsimmons' daughters and found out that her father's notes had not survived.

[Regarding the beginnings of Laugh-O-grams]

NM: [Walt] was just getting prepared because he did not have the money. He had this Dr. J. V. Cowles, who was an investor with an office at 1822 Main, over the Main Street Bank. And well, Dr. Cowles and one or two other gentlemen, that was their business to invest money in projects of this nature for the First National Bank of Kansas City. I don't know how Walt got acquainted with him, but anyway Dr. Cowles was his backer, financially. They had about four or five of these cartoons ready for sale and that was before they were popular in the theaters. In fact, they were unknown in the theaters in those days. And Mr. Kloepper went to New York and spent all the money they had for expenses.[2] They didn't have much, but he spent it all. And he sold this to Pictorial [Clubs] to be shown in schools and non-theatrical places, but instead of getting the cash, he got a note which was worthless. No money was ever received on it. Then Dr. Cowles wouldn't put any more money into the business.

DS: So, Laugh-O-grams started just about the time you went to work for them?

NM: Yes. I started in January/February 1922.

DS: It only lasted about one-and-a-half years?

NM: And then it dissolved, after about one-and-a-half years.

Jim Stewart: How long were you with them?

NM: Until they folded. They still owe me money. I mean they did. I just forgot about it.

DS: What were the offices like? How many rooms?

NM: Well, let's see... I had an office and my office was like a little reception room. And Mr. Kloepper would say "this space here was mine" and then over there was Mr. Kloepper's office, about that wide. He was sales manager. Then over here they had a partition and another room. It wasn't a full divider. It wasn't a full room. But in the next room was Walt's drawing board. And we could see him sitting there at the drawing board all day, drawing.

DS: What was your position?

NM: Stenographer-bookkeeper. That's what they called them in those days. Now they call them secretaries. But in those days they were stenos and secretaries...

---

[2] Michael Barrier notes: "According to contemporary reports, it was Leslie Mace, not Kloepper, who went to New York."

DS: How much did they pay in those days?

NM: $25 a week. That was good money, though, in those days. I mean, for that time it wasn't bad. I started out at $25 and ended at $25.

DS: Were the rooms well furnished?

NM: Oh, yes. They were very nice. There were really just two rooms there and then there was a hallway down between the offices and his drawing room. Then the other two rooms across the hall in the same building were where those pictures were made by Ub and all. Red Lyon was our cameraman. He died out in California trying to save the life of somebody out swimming.

Walt couldn't pay the rent at this rooming house, which was $3 a week, and they didn't have enough money to buy their meals. So I told Jerry, the fella who had the café on the first floor, I said, "Jerry, if you want me to type your menus up for you, I will, and then you can give…the boys can eat on that." 'Cause otherwise he would have to send them out to be typed. So I did and they ate down there at Jerry's. It was Jerry's Café, on the first floor.

DS: Did he have good food?

NM: Yes, he did. You know most Greeks do have good food. They're good cooks. He was a little fellow. I remember what he looked like. He was a very nice little fellow, small.

DS: And Walt was rooming at this time?

NM: Yes, he was rooming at this time and he couldn't pay the rent, so he slept at the studio, on the floor.

DS: In the room where he had his drawing board?

NM: In the room where he had his drawing board. And I know of many mornings I've gone up there—I remember this very distinctly—that he said, "I know there was a mouse in here last night. I heard him running around in here." So we have all attributed the birth of Mickey Mouse to that place and I still believe that is true. I guess it was characteristic of artists to like working when everything is quiet. All of the other employees have gone home and they're alone. I think they can concentrate and get a lot more done. I know he worked nights, and he was there all during the day.

DS: Did Walt do much of the drawing himself?

NM: He did all of it. The boys and girls did the inking, but he did all the drawings himself.

DS: What about Ub? Was he drawing at that time?

NM: Yes, he was. He was really good. I guess that's why he stayed with Walt.

© 2007 Disney

Ward Kimball (1914–2002)

Interviewed by Rick Shale on January 29, 1976.

In a way, one could write an entire history of the Disney Studio just based on interviews with Ward Kimball. It would be a very one-sided view of history, of course, but would cover every major subject of interest.

Rick Shale was researching his seminal book about Disney during WWII, *Donald Duck Joins Up* (UMI Research Press, 1982), when he met Kimball. Shale talked with Ward Kimball at his home in San Gabriel. After an initial conversation, which explained his project and how he came to choose this particular topic, Shale asked Kimball about *Victory Through Air Power*.

Ward Kimball: I think a film like *Victory Through Air Power* served its purpose at the time. It's not the sort of thing you look back on as a great work of art because, first of all, it's now dated, and secondly, they can't re-release it.

Rick Shale: It does not go with the Disney image.

WK: No, and it can't go out and make a pot full of money like *Snow White*. And even at the time it was controversial whether we should have made that picture because Alexander de Seversky was held in low esteem by our military arm because he had been beating the drum for winning the war with air power. And even though he might have been right with his theories, he was sort of an abrasive guy, and I think that antagonized a lot of the generals in the Army.

After all, the Army and all the major services were well known for their reluctance to observe new ideas or establish a new tradition. They're so steeped in "this is the way we've always done it; why change?"

I came up against that for the first time when I met Von Braun in answer to our desire to make a space picture for the Disney television series. He was having a hard time convincing the brass that we should be building rockets, and no one believed him. So he looked upon Disney's as a marvelous outlet for his ideas. He'd been writing in *Collier's*, but that reached just a small segment of the people. He realized also that our television show had a big audience. He said the same thing: he couldn't get anybody to listen, and they didn't listen until the Russians fired Sputnik. This turned the whole thing around.

Believe it or not, *Man in Space*, which won an Emmy for the best documentary that year, was shown in the Pentagon over and over for something like two or three weeks on Eisenhower's request.[1] Eisenhower had seen the film on TV on the Disney hour, and when he finally was convinced that we should be doing something about this, it was shown as sort of a primer for all these Army brass boys who didn't understand anything about it. There again, they were reluctant to accept any new-fangled ideas. But the Russians proved it could be done. So they ran our film. They flew them in from all over the country and foreign posts to see this film, because it was a first step to understanding what space was all about.

Alexander de Seversky in a way played that same role. He was trying to show, if we're going to win a war, we had to do it through air power. But I think by the time our film came out they were already convinced of that.

RS: When I talked to Erwin Verity the other day, he had many stories about Seversky's abrasive character clashing with some of the other military advisors at the studio at the time. He mentioned Jimmy Thach in particular.

WK: Yes, Seversky was a stubborn guy. He knew exactly what he wanted, and he would tolerate no exceptions. This ruffled the boys.

Primarily, Walt hunted down war work to do because he had a good reason: this deferred a lot of his talent. Hell, I'll be the first to admit I wasn't 1-A, because I was working on war work. Now, whether or not I actually put time in on war-related films for twenty-four hours a day or eight hours a day is open to question, but the main thing that Walt established was a blanket deferment for his top people, and this worked except, I think, for the cases of the guys who weren't married.

See, I was married. I had a family coming up, so it was easy to defer me. But I think it was a good move because it saved a lot of his talent from going into the service. I'll be the first to admit it. And I question whether what I did was really that—what should we say—necessary or important.

RS: Now you didn't work on the actual training films. You stayed in the entertainment?

WK: Yes, we stayed in the entertainment, and, there again, there's your blanket deferment. The draft boys never came down and said, "Hey Kimball, why aren't you working on a training film on how we're going to land on Iwo Jima?" No, I was up there laughing and living it up. And I was only classified 1-A near the end of the war during the famous Battle of the Bulge

---

[1] The TV show *Disneyland* won the 1955 Emmy for Best Action or Adventure series. *Man In Space*, episode #20 of that series, was nominated for an Oscar for Best Documentary Short Subject.

where, in that winter, the Germans broke through, and we got panicky, and the next thing I knew I was 1-A and I was down at the Pacific Electric Building taking my physical. Old Patton came through with his cap guns and his silver holsters and saved the day, and I went back in as a deferment.

RS: So you never had to…

WK: No. I got as far as the physical.

RS: That was one of my questions: why Walt went after so much military work. Because looking through the files he seems to have actively sought it out.

WK: Sure, because it kept his talent intact.

RS: Do you think just simple patriotism entered it at all?

WK: Yes, that has to be considered. But let's just face it, what is our freedom and our patriotism? It's the privilege to make a buck. And he never necessarily wanted to make a buck out of it. It was just the fun of making entertainment pictures, and this was just one way of more or less holding the good part of the talent together.

RS: It appears that shortly before Pearl Harbor the studio laid off quite a few people.

WK: Yes, we were in bad financial straits. I can remember that Walt called us all in, into the new theater at Burbank. I think this was just before the war. I'd have to consult all my diaries and records. I remember him sitting on the stage and saying, "We're in a bad financial way. We're all going to have to take a cut." This happened just about the time of the strike.[2]

RS: Before or after?

WK: I'm not too sure of that. But I can remember we all had to take a percentage cut. It might have happened just after the strike. I know we had some private meetings with Dave Hand and at Claude Coats' house. Our cuts were based on our salary as a percentage. And I remember I had the temerity to bring up the point at that time that what if our salaries were far below what we thought they should be at the time. Everybody took a dim view of my suggestion. Not necessarily because mine was, but I did feel there were people in the room who should be getting twice as much as they were getting.

RS: So little has been written about the strike. It's always spoken of in such hushed tones.

WK: Sure, it's a no-no. It's something we've swept under the bed. I kept a complete diary, a day-by-day record of the strike period, and I'm going to

---

[2] See *Walt's People: Volume 3*, page 70. The meeting happened before the strike.

sit down sometime and read it off into a tape recorder for [Disney archivist] Dave Smith because I think it's an important part of the Disney story. It was going to be part of a book I was writing, but I feel to be honest and treat this the way I would want a book written I would probably be sued for libel by a whole bunch of people. It's the sort of book that has to be written after most of us are approaching eighty and too feeble to hire a lawyer.

But it's a very interesting story, and from this diary I sent a weekly report to Walt Kelly, who had left the studio as the strike began and decided he wanted to go to New York anyway and do comic books. And he told me later that those were one of the biggest laughs he had, Kimball's weekly report on what happened during the strike.

But I'm going to have to put that down for posterity because I don't think anyone else kept such a detailed report of what occurred.

RS: By now, what happened during that period is clouded with legend. It's interesting that somebody kept records.

WK: Yes. I think as far as the war days are concerned, like every other business and part of the community, we had a different outlook—if you want to put it in a broad way—on life, because the psychology of a war turns everybody's minds to thinking of the present: to hell with tomorrow. You know, "Wine, women, and song, so drink today, for tomorrow you may be gone," and all that jazz.

Anyway, there was a great influx of female help at the studio, because the young Turks and lions had all gone off to Culver City to be part of Frank Capra's crew. That's the big thing I noticed: we really didn't take too many things seriously. You didn't plan for the future, because there was something about the feeling of the whole country that, "Who knows? We may not be here." It happens during every war, and Disney's was no exception. And we had weird people coming in there making films, and great stories.

I can remember the night that they were all up on the roof of the Disney Studio trying out some new flares that had been developed in Britain. What were they called? Very or Berry? It has a name that sounds like that. New flares that when they were fired would make a whole city block light up almost like day: very bright. So they were all up on the roof of the studio with Riley Thompson, Sr.,[3] the cop, and they fired one, and everybody kind of looked down at what is now the parking lot. It was a green grass, tree-covered...and here was this couple banging away on the lawn...and the surprise on their faces...they couldn't believe it. All of a sudden the sun comes up with no warning. And everybody looks down, and here is

---

[3] Riley Thomson Sr. and Jr. were known as Riley Thompson (with a "p") by their colleagues at the studio.

this guy with his pants down under a cork tree. Of course, Riley takes off to try and catch them, but they escaped.

RS: You say Riley Thompson, Sr. I notice he directed some of the films...

WK: That was Riley Thompson, Jr. Both of them had a drinking problem, especially Riley Thompson, Jr.

RS: Junior was the director?

WK: Yeah, director question mark. It was one of those things where the studio got so big that it was hard for Walt to keep track of some of the non-talent and what they were doing.

RS: I have one last question about the strike. Within six months after the strike, the studio and the whole country was wrapped up in the war. Did this, plus the influx of new employees and some older ones going off to be drafted, kind of smooth things over and lessen the bitterness and aftermath of the strike?

WK: Basically you have to go back and consider the fact that artists are apathetic toward unions and organizations. You take a guy who works in the Ford factory, or a shoe factory, or labor: he's gung-ho. Artists, I've found—I've came to this conclusion after years of working with them—they have so much personal ego drive that they're not joiners. They don't like to be ruled; they like to be loners, and that's why a union never is really successful amongst the artists or the cartoonists.

They have a union now, but it has no power. No union ever has, because you can't get the artists to go to a meeting. They want to do their own thing. Sure, they'd like more money, but they figure it's beneath 'em to get together and work hard for it, because they're in competition with the other artists. And it's an ego trip. This is why, if there was peace in the labor ranks after the war started, it was, I say, mostly because the makeup of the average guy in the film business is not one which holds for union organizations.

RS: I'm curious to get some personal recollections of the whole military presence then. When do you remember the military first showing up or the studio starting to become a war plant?

WK: The first thing that happened when we went into war work was that it became a big secret project. We all had to have identification tags. I still have mine. Unfortunately, the day I came to have my picture taken I forgot to shave. In those days I had a Richard M. Nixon five-o'clock-shadow-type beard, and I looked like something out of Murder, Inc. We were all screened, and we wore our badges at all times. But somehow my feelings, if I analyze the time, were all sort of make-believe, like we were playing soldier or playing with the military. These guys would show up with their brass, and every once in a while a guy like Jimmy Stewart or some ex-film great would show up, and there would be a murmur and a ripple of interest there.

A lot of the units were sealed off. You couldn't get into them. "This section is closed." You had to have your special pass. I never paid any attention to those, because I was merely going on with entertainment. You can call them propaganda films in some respect. We did things to make everybody happy about paying their income tax, because it was helping to defeat Hitler, like we had carried on during World War I with the Kaiser.

We made a film called *Education for Death*, which was based, I think, on a *Reader's Digest* article. I always remember that film, because all the other guys got stuck with that heavy sequence at the beginning with these mean-looking Nazi kids "Heil Hitlering" in this class, and I was lucky enough to get to work on the end of the film where Hitler and Germania do this opera thing. The big fat soprano was a caricature of Hermann Goering and I had all the fun. And guys still remember that Ward had all the fun on that particular film.

RS: Mentioning the income-tax films leads me to my next question. I have the filmography that Dave [Smith] compiled on you at the archives. It doesn't list that you worked on *The New Spirit*, which was the first one. It says that you worked on *The Spirit of '43*.

WK: What's *The New Spirit*?

RS: That was the first income-tax film where, at the end, Donald races across the country to hand deliver his income tax. That was the one, if what Il read was correct, that was cranked out in six weeks.

WK: I sometimes question the records kept on those things, because sometimes we jumped in and spent a day or two knocking out a little section in order to get it out, and I don't know how close their records were kept. I do remember working on one where Donald has a zoot suit on.

RS: Right. That's *The Spirit of '43*, which was done the following year, and it's got the zoot suiter as the spendthrift, and what looks to me very much like a precursor of Scrooge McDuck as the kind of Scottish thrifty person. He's Donald's conscience that suggests not to spend his money.

WK: Yeah, that old stuff with Jack King. That was the famous time that we worked Saturday; I worked clear through Saturday night to finish it. I had a scene where Donald Duck is standing on a corner in his zoot suit twirling his keychain, because that was all part of the costume then. And, to look real cool, I put his body on a held cel and just had him twirl his keychain, and he just rolls his eyes as somebody walks by and he has his hand in his pocket: A typical thing.

Now, I did that to show that he was cool. You know, just holds the pose and rolls his eyes. So I have the key action on one level and his eyes on another.

Well, Jack King, who always lived in great fear of Walt Disney, picks the stuff up Saturday night—it was going to be shot Saturday night—we had to get the film off Monday morning. He sees what I'm doing with this held cel with the guy's hand in his pocket, so he panics. Anyway, when I get the film back Monday morning to check it, here's Donald Duck standing there, twirling his keychain, and his hands are playing with himself in his pocket! He's moving it around like some sex pervert. And I blow up; I say, "What the hell happened here?"

I look at the exposure sheet, and I see the numbers are not my handwriting. I run up to Jack King and say, "Who the hell did this?" and he got embarrassed and confessed that he was afraid that Walt wouldn't like the fact that I held a cel, a body drawing, for that length of time, not realizing I did that on purpose. And so he had taken it upon himself to sit down there late Saturday night and put a cycle of this guy's hand moving in a rotary motion, and it was very suggestive.

I got real mad, and I said, "I'm gonna go tell Walt on you," and he said, "Oh no, no. Don't do that. Don't do that." So I tore those drawings out of the scene and threw them in the wastepaper basket.

RS: So they didn't end up in the final print?

WK: No. [Kimball chuckles.]

RS: I was going to say...

WK: Naw, naw, they were taken out. I tore 'em up. I mean, he was sort of a stupid director anyway. A good director would have called me up and said, "Ward, I'm worried about this being held. Can you do something about it?" Naw, he takes it, thinks he's going to sneak it through, and it turns out the Duck is playing with himself.

RS: You didn't work on *Der Fuehrer's Face* at all?

WK: If the records don't show it, I didn't. All I did was make the drawing for the sheet music for *Der Fuehrer's Face*, which shows Donald Duck has just thrown a tomato which has plopped in Hitler's eye, a big portrait, caricature of him, and that's as close as I came to it.

RS: Did you work at all on a film that ended up never becoming a film: *The Gremlins*?

WK: They tried to get that off the ground, but they just couldn't do it. It was cuter to talk about gremlins and things that happen, and nobody could decide on what a gremlin looked like.

RS: There's a huge file on *The Gremlins* at the studio, and everyone was writing in, suggesting what they thought a gremlin should look like.

WK: Walt never could decide in his mind what a gremlin should look like. It was as simple as that. Is it a little brownie? Of course, a gremlin today would be easy to design in our open-ended imaginative way of going about things, but in those days, with everything so confined to a certain technique and Disney style, it was impossible. I think Walt got frustrated and gave it up. I remember that.

RS: Apparently it was in the works for a few years; it just never got completed.

WK: It sounded great, but, pictorially, it was another bag.

RS: In the process of screening the entertainment shorts of that period, I've noticed that the animators and directors started to get screen credit in mid-1944.

WK: That was brought on by the union. That was one of the great things that occurred because of the strike. You have to understand that Walt Disney was regarded as some kind of deity amongst the public, and he was a super ego. He had to be. He might have put on a boyish air of embarrassment about the acclaim that he was getting, but he loved it. And he fought giving us screen credit.

After all, he'd given it to us on the features, but he wasn't about to give it to us on shorts. "Why do you want to take up all that damn time for? They're only six-and-a-half minutes long. Jesus Christ, it's another minute and a half giving you guys screen credit." But it came about.

RS: The other studios, such as Warner Brothers, seemed to have had screen credit right along.

WK: Well, it was this whole line of reasoning. You saw the comic strips signed by Walt Disney, and the things that appeared in *The Ladies Home Journal*[4] and different magazines all by Walt Disney; Sunday comics by Walt Disney, merchandise by Walt Disney; and you'd be surprised how a great percentage of the American public thought he *did* all this.

RS: Walt's been dead a little over nine years, and it seems all of our people that we elevate to that stature require a decade or so before they start to regain their humanness.

WK: Look what's happening to Kennedy. We find out he was seeing a prostitute. And President Harding had his mistress in a closet. I enraged Jim

---

[4] Kimball probably means *Good Housekeeping*.

Algar one day when they were planning the Hall of the Presidents for Florida, and they had our first preview of it. They had all these dummies standing out there on the stage. I hate that whole thing, because it's so lifeless and so unreal, I think, to use wax images like that and just have a few of them working like mechanical robots. Anyway, I suggested that Warren Harding in his little section of this tableau should have a secret closet door that opens every once in a while, and this female arm and bracelet comes out and beckons Warren to come into the closet, 'cause that's what he used to do. He used to take her into his cloak closet. Algar didn't think that was funny.

See, this is the problem. One of the one things, I suppose, that I disagreed on with the new Disney management was that they never understood the importance of satire. To me, what have you got in humor if you don't have a little bit of satire? Walt had a lot of it, even though it might have been veiled here and there. But after his death, anything that even approached the satirical was frowned upon. Then I realized that you can't make fun of institutions, I don't care how bad they are. If they're part of our American scene, you can't criticize them.

Now it was all right to criticize the Nazis, because they were our enemies. We could use satire. That whole opera scene was pure satire. I love that sort of thing. And we have it occur in a lot of our pictures, but even the award-winning *It's Tough to Be a Bird*, I know, they thought was too satirical.

RS: But it won an Oscar, so they probably accepted it.

WK: Reluctantly they accepted it. They didn't like the fact that when I received it, I extended my condolences to the unfortunate seagulls in Santa Barbara. Then I realized later that they got pissed off at that whole statement because Gulf Oil was one of the sponsors of our Disney Sunday show at that time.

RS: Did you work with any particular director? I'm not clear on how the whole process of theatrical shorts was done in those days. Were you parts of units?

WK: They had maybe four of five directors as high as... I guess I could sit down and remember the list. Sometimes a director like Jack Kinney, who did most of the Goof shorts, had his crew of Goof animators that more or less went from one picture to another, and if they weren't working on features, they worked on Goof shorts.

I, fortunately, worked with different directors like Ham Luske and Gerry Geronimi and Wilfred Jackson and got more of a variety.

RS: That was going to be my next question—if you specialized in any particular character.

WK: No. I was always known as an animator who could handle different assignments, but also, I suppose, I was favored for slapstick stuff or stuff they thought might be funny where I might get a different slant to it. Then there were crews that worked with Jack Hannah that did nothing but ducks. He was sort of the Duck director at one time.

RS: Was Norm Ferguson the Pluto...?

WK: He was the Pluto expert. I attribute to Norm Ferguson being the first animator to have a character think and reason, and I think it's a milestone in animation when he did the sequence of Pluto and the flypaper, which, when you look back on it, and at the time it was a blockbuster, because you could see the wheels going around in the character's head.

And we were more or less pulling out of that bouncing, dancing, musical age of Disney shorts, where all the characters with big smiles on their faces kept time to the music or played an instrument. Here comes a character that gets stuck with a situation and keeps building, almost like a Buster Keaton or Harold Lloyd or a Chaplin sequence. Like Chaplin's sequence with the automatic feeder in *Modern Times* keeps building. Well, this did. Norman did a breakthrough with animation, and he was one of the top animators, but I think when we gradually moved into more disciplined styles of drawing—moving illustrations—that Ferguson was kind of left by the wayside because he was not a trained artist. He was basically an animator who understood movement and who drew with very crude, simple lines the action.

He always had good assistants with drawing ability to follow him up and put Pluto's paws in the right perspective and claws and put the collar on, but he was wonderful at conceiving spontaneous action and worked very fast because he would draw Pluto with just a few lines. He understood movement and how far to move something in relation to the size of the screen or the field he was working with.

But we reached a point in Disney's development where Norman just didn't fit in anymore. And I never thought I'd live to see the day when they let him go, which they did.

RS: In another interview that I read about *Toot, Whistle, Plunk and Boom* you differentiated between stylized animation and limited animation. Are those just terms that somebody cooked up? Or are those legitimate terms?

WK: *Toot, Whistle, Plunk and Boom* was a mild breakthrough. When you look at the film now, I sometimes wonder what all of the hullabaloo was about, but this was almost regarded as sacrilegious for Disney at the time. Walt was in Europe, and we decided to try something different on this picture.

We had more or less dipped our toes in the waters of experimentation on a picture called *Melody*, which was the first 3D cartoon. Then we had used things on the backgrounds like old-time valentines and collages or used various techniques that didn't follow our usual Disney visual methods.

With *Toot, Whistle, Plunk and Boom* there was no basic plot. It was an educational documentary picture on the history of musical instruments. Walt wanted us to do a whole series on music. We were going to follow up this film with a film on the human voice. So, just on a lark, we decided to try to modernize the style of the picture a little. Get away from what I call the rubber-hose way of drawing. Get a few straight lines and so forth. And, of course, the die-hard people would stop by the room and comment, "You guys will never get away with this. Walt's not going to like this." Well, he came back from Europe and loved it!

RS: But you didn't do any more in that style?

WK: No, we sort of transferred the style to television then in a more subdued way, because my contention was there were certain types of comedy staging that were best done with limited animation. A *lack* of movement sometimes would put over a gag better.

There was never any attempt made to do a picture that was all limited animation. We had plenty of classic "full" animation in this picture, but there was an attempt also to get a decorative feeling in the movement by limiting certain parts of the animation. We wanted the cave man done in a different technique where we draw all the hairs on their faces and get crazy patterns on their skins they wore, and realizing that if you move this it would flicker and move. So we held them so you could see this texture and moved their mouths or hands. That wasn't done just to be limited; it was done because we wanted to get a flavor or a texture or a technique to the thing.

RS: In other words, limited animation would be an economy move where you would consciously strive for fewer drawings per foot.

WK: Yes, and this is best exemplified by the Saturday morning fare that Hanna-Barbera turns out, where you have three positions of the head: up, middle, and looking down. And each head has five mouth openings, and they use these five mouth openings to pronounce all the words. The character stands with his arms hanging at his side, and his body doesn't move, and he merely moves his head, so all of your acting is the same.

This is in direct conflict to the Disney technique where we developed the characters as actors. Alice had her way of reacting, the Mad Hatter had his way, Tweedle Dee and Tweedle Dum their own way. This you can't do with the new limited style that they're using on TV, which is done because of low budgets.

The new techniques in *Toot, Whistle, Plunk and Boom* were never conceived as solely a way to save money. They were done as an effort to develop a newer visual approach for doing films of an educational or instructional nature, and they were well received in the commercial box offices.

RS: So stylized animation would be simply that…

WK: Stylized animation doesn't mean it's limited. You see a lot of stuff by Murakami-Wolf where they draw with magic markers; it's full animation. Now that's stylized.

RS: So that would be an artistic rather than economic…

WK: Whereas some of the characters in *Robin Hood* are what you might call moving illustrations.

RS: In a lot of films they'll use newspaper headlines or a whole front page. Is that a photographic process where you would actually use a real front page from a newspaper?

WK: No, we had a print shop. We'd set up the type to say what we wanted.

RS: Nobody would actually draw the thing? It looks too real.

WK: No, they'd print that. See, all commercial artists would just order the type and paste it on. There might have been a little technique here and there to make the newspaper look like it had a folded edge.

RS: I know in *Victory Through Air Power* there's one sequence in that beginning part with a front page and a picture of Billy Mitchell, and the camera tracks into the front page.

WK: That was a fake page. That wasn't an actual thing. They took a picture of Billy Mitchell and glued it on the layout, and somebody might have done the headlines freehand, but any type would be ordered.

RS: Then he comes to life suddenly when they track into a close-up of the picture.

WK: On *Victory Through Air Power* I felt I was fortunate in having the most fun on the picture, because I got to do the historical stuff. I was fascinated with old airplanes. I've always loved old flying machines, and I just thought that it was a lark animating the first Wright Brothers' flight, and the early air battles between the Germans and the French.

There again was an early attempt at developing a different style with the drawing and animation of that stuff, to make the animation not follow the Disney tradition but to give you the flavor of something that was old and dated or antique—like the stilted way the pilots sat in their airplanes with the action following the customs of having a duel where the adversaries started out throwing rocks and ended up with pistols and finally machine guns. It was sort of an early ritual that I tried to catch with the stilted poses and stilted action in the sequence.

Even though that was done with a comedic flavor, I did a lot of authentic research. I poured through early copies of *Jane's Aircraft* books, and I put together little plane models. In fact, I had built a few of those same models when I was a kid—rubber-band models. So it was a fortunate choice in letting me work on this picture, because it was really fun. I did my own research, and I look back on it with pleasant memories.

RS: How did you happen to get that assignment? Did you just have a reputation for the humor? Why didn't they assign you to do the diagrams or the explosions?

WK: They thought I'd be the best for the job, which was a nice consideration.

RS: Was it possible for the animators to go and say, "I'd really like to work on this?"

WK: We've done that. I've done that. They would say. "No, Walt wants you to do this; he thinks you're more important to the picture." Or, "Walt thinks so-and-so should do it, because he's out of work and you're still working." This is something the outside world doesn't understand: that the logistics of casting depended a lot on the timetable. I have been assigned to animation that maybe I wouldn't have been assigned to, but I was out of work. And so-and-so, who should have been doing it, was still finishing up his job on another short. This happens quite a lot.

RS: I've been looking through the drafts that break the films down by scene, and it was a revelation to me to find that, say, in the space of twenty feet of animation, there will be half-a-dozen different animators credited. Was it such that you would finish up one thing, and somebody would say, "Hey, came over and help me finish this scene?" It seems to skip around so much.

WK: We've even had pictures where... I think in the crow sequence I would just merely indicate where the little mouse would be in the tree, and I think Fred Moore would finish it up after I did my crow animation. We did a lot of that: co-animate a scene where one guy's sequence would overlap into the next guy. Or, we've had situations where one guy did all the Duck, and another guy did the other character, and that's why they might change quickly in the sequence. They might be cutting back from one to another.

RS: You mention Fred Moore. Some animators seem to be linked. You and Fred Moore seem to be linked frequently. Frank Thomas and Ollie Johnston often work together.

WK: We always called Frank and Ollie the Siamese twins. They went to school together, grammar school. They went to college together. They lived together. We used to kid them about it. I think they were the last ones to get married. Even after they were married, they both bought a duplex, so Frank and his wife were on one side and Ollie on the other. It was the gold-dust twins. It was just one of those things.

Now, Fred. We were on *The Reluctant Dragon* together.

RS: I have a copy of one of the drafts and I wondered if you could explain some of it to me. I notice that, instead of an artist's name, it frequently says "music room".

WK: That meant the director would be responsible for that. You notice that the first one is "The History of Aviation: Opens to a title". That means he will take care of it; maybe go up on the sound stage and shoot a book opening, and he will have his layout man make sure that the first pages in that book will tie into my scene. That's something that an animator wouldn't be worrying about.

RS: So "music room" doesn't really have anything to do with music?

WK: No, "music room" was our director's room. That was our title. Because, you see, all of our pictures started out as musicals. You look at all the Mickey Mouse pictures, all the Silly Symphonies. They're musicals. Everybody's dancing and singing. They did that for four or five years, until it became old hat, and Walt was wise enough to start working up plots. That's where the term came from.

George Lewis[5] had one music room, Frank Churchill in another, Leigh Harline in another, and they were called music rooms, but they were actually a director's room with a piano, and the musical director of the show would sit in with the director in the same room, and they would decide on how many bars of this, and they would play it, and the director would say, "Yeah, that's what I want." He would mark the sheet. So it means director's room.

Now you see "Wright Brothers' plane at camp in Kitty Hawk". The book opens and shows it. We move in maybe closer, and that's my scene. I take that same setup, and I bring it to life.

RS: What would the N.P.'s and the N.S.'s mean?

WK: "N.S." means new scene. ["N.P." ("New Page"), here] means "page turns to blueprint of plane". "S.A." means "Same as" the setup or background, same as scene one. So we go down "new scene, new scene, same as", or, if the thing was to occur on the same background but a different action, it would say "same as whatever the last scene that this background was used for".[6]

---

[5] Ward means Bert Lewis, who became music director when Carl Stalling left.

[6] JB Kaufman notes: "N.S. and N.P. are designations that appear in the background column of the draft. They both designate new backgrounds; N.S. means it's a still background and N.P. means it's a pan (which means it has to be painted on a long piece of background paper). Ward is right about S.A."

RS: If it says 5F or 6½F, that's the field?

WK: Yes. In those days our first camera was a five-field camera. It was smaller, and we used smaller paper. We began to see there were certain things where we had to use a larger field, larger paper to get more detail in. So that was called a 6½ field.

There was a time when you run across that in the records where the director would decide whether it would be a five-field camera using the small paper or 6½. Course, now it's all 6½. It was only a matter of time to get away from that cumbersome...

RS: Is that standard in the industry, the 6½ field?

WK: No, no, Disney has its own set of pegs and own field size. All the rest of the industry has another. It took us so long to get around to using hundredths of an inch, for instance. Our system is really cumbersome compared to the industry as a whole. The rest of the industry on drawing boards had sliding bars top and bottom.

I fought like hell to get our boards installed with those conveniences that would save time. This has been the record as far as technology was concerned on the lower levels—not on Walt's level—of being reluctant to instigate changes. Most of the boards you're now looking at with the sliding bars and bottom bars—the lightweight system—a lot of those I instigated.

I fought for it, because I kept my eyes open, and I saw how convenient some of those things were, working on the outside. In fact, I was doing some commercials once during the fifties, and I was loaned a board with the Acme system, and it was so beautiful to work, so simple.

Here again, Ub Iwerks was a technician: he went to Montreal for Expo and saw the computer-operated cameras and tried like hell to get some system...aw, they fight you. Same way with the sound system. They're using crystal mikes in there—all other studios and recording places have new Telefunkens, all the new equipment—simply because so many of the heads of department were allergic to change.

RS: It's been particularly interesting to screen both Warner Brothers and Disney's films from the war period because so many of the Warner Brothers films were topical. They had so many references to things like the rubber shortage and the war itself, and it seems so few of Disney's...

WK: Gasoline A stickers...

RS: Yeah.

WK: Walt never went too much for that unless he had to, like in the income-tax picture. Closest he ever got was the topical thing with the Nazis. Maybe in retrospect he was right, because you date your picture.

RS: I wondered if that was the principal motivation.

WK: It gets back to why you don't see *Victory Through Air Power* and why *Snow White* will be run forever. There's nothing in our product that dates it. Like haircuts or dresses. When you see an old show on TV, you can almost guess the year that it was made by how the dresses look, whether there was any cleavage showing, etc. But Disney pictures are timeless. He had this intuition about that. Whether he did that with calculation, I'm not sure, but that's the way it turned out.

RS: When you screen the films and you actually do see a topical reference—for instance, there's one called *Donald's Tire Trouble*. He has a flat tire, and at one point in the film he squawks about the "doggone rubber shortage". It happens so infrequently in these films.

WK: That's a good picture, and it holds up in spite of that reference. It's a very funny picture. I think that's a good example of milking a gag completely. I mean, how many other tire gags could you think of after that? It's a pretty funny picture.

RS: Another one, one of Jack Kinney's Goofy pictures, *How to Be a Sailor*, goes on just as most of the Goof pictures did, until the end when Goofy becomes a torpedo and is suddenly fired out of a ship and crashes through all these Japanese battleships with the Rising Sun in the background. I think that is the most atypical of all the shorts of that period because of that specific reference.

WK: It still would hold up, because 99% of the picture is dealing with sailing. Now, there are exceptions. But your comparison of our product with Warner Brothers and the rest of them points to the fact that we were less topical.

RS: Disney people did the animation, or at least part of it, on the maps and diagrams in Frank Capra's *Why We Fight* series. Do you know anybody that worked on these? I know Frank Thomas said he and Ollie Johnston did one scene and it never got used. Most of the animation consists of maps with arrows.

WK: I think the only pure instructional film that I worked on was at the beginning before we'd gone in the war, but Britain was in. It was the *Boys Anti-Tank Rifle* [aka *Stop That Tank*] for Canada, and Ub Iwerks was the director.

Now that's a weird combination of Ub Iwerks coming back into directing on a *Boys Anti-Tank Rifle*, which looked like a BB gun to me—that's before the Germans developed the super armor plating—and me showing how not to use the rifle.

See, you can get comedy into that. Guy comes in and does everything wrong. But I don't think I worked on the section where you break the rifle down and become technical.

RS: That film is so interesting because the first part has the humor: the soldier popping out of the horse or up in the trees shooting Hitler and everything, and then it does go into the more didactic, X-ray animation of the cross section of the gun. Most of the military films, the training films that the studio did, are pretty dull. Apparently, Walt and the people at the studio tried to inject humor, and it was the military brass that refused.

WK: Of course, because you've got the whole Army going to land on some island, and this is not to be taken lightly.

RS: But yet to screen something like the *Boys Anti-Tank Rifle* film: the humor works well enough so you're not put asleep before you get to the important part.

WK: Well sure, but, there again, the humor can only be used in a negative way to show how *not* to do something. How can you be funny when you get to the serious part? They might not take it seriously. They may put it together wrong or blow themselves up.

RS: A whole series of films done for the army by the Warner Brothers animators, the *Private Snafu*... Have you ever seen any of those?

WK: No.

RS: It was not for civilian audiences. It's the same principle. He's a fumbling character who does everything wrong, so they teach by showing his poor examples. There are some slight references in the files that Disney was offered this *Private Snafu* contract first, and then apparently Walt was told that someone had underbid him, and that someone must have been Leon Schlesinger.

WK: It was always our problem at Disney's: the overhead charges, which put us out of a lot of business.

RS: Do you remember when Hank Ketcham worked at the studio?

WK: Sure. He was one of my assistants before the war. I also had Dave Swift, who became a director and writer, as my head assistant, along with Tom Oreb. Doing in-betweens for us was Hank Ketcham.

I have an amusing story to tell about him. He was bound and determined that he was going to sell gag drawings to *The New Yorker* and *Collier's* and all the rest of them. But he got nothing but rejects. He would bring in his drawings and ask me what I thought about them—why he got so many rejects. And I would say "maybe you've overstaged this" or "maybe "you chose the wrong angle here", and we used to laugh about Hank, because he was so damn tenacious.

He wasn't as good an artist then as he is today. Next thing we knew, he enlisted in the Navy. Of course, the rest of the story is history. He got a job on the Navy magazine as some sort of sub-editor or art editor where no one could reject his work. So he started publishing regularly, and this is how he developed as a gag artist.

He gained confidence and experience. And when he got out of the Navy, due to this experience he had of submitting his own gags—to himself, he broke into syndicated work—through Walt Kelly, I think. The next thing you knew, he was doing *Dennis the Menace*. A big success!

RS: Let me run through a few of your films and ask some scatter-shot questions. I notice in one, Jack Kinney's *Hockey Homicide*, all of the hockey players have the animators' names. Did this sort of in-joking go on constantly in those films?

WK: If you had a situation like that, they used the guys' names. That was done on a lot of pictures. They would use the names of the guys working on the picture on the side of a boat or "Wanted for Robbery". You knew you were in the clear and you wouldn't be sued.

RS: Let me toss out a couple of names to you. Carl Nater: did you work at all with him?

WK: I had really no association with him or had any cause to discuss any studio matters with him until I started working on the space pictures. He was just someone off in the distance. And, at that time, he was head of the 16mm department.

I remember Carl because he came up and we had finished *Man in Space*, which had won an Emmy;[7] *Tomorrow the Moon*, which was a lot better but didn't win an award; and we were working on *Mars and Beyond*. Now, here is a studio employee who knows damn well that we made a picture called *Fantasia*, which in artistic montage, shows you evolution: when that first one-cell animal in the sea finally comes up and tries his legs on land. We go through the age of the giant reptiles and so forth.

He comes up, and he's looking over the board that we have. We have a much shorter, much more abstract suggestion of evolution to show why man can exist only in a certain temperature range, the conditions we have on this earth. If it gets too low, he freezes; if it's too hot, his blood boils. And there's just a very narrow temperature band, and this happens to be coincidental with the position of the earth and its distance to the sun.

And we have a short section of evolution, done very artistically—hell of a lot more abstract and realistic than *Fantasia*—to lead up to the point: here is man. Then we discuss man and his body chemistry and show why the chances of finding life as we know it on other planets in our solar

---

[7] The *Disneyland* series, not the episode *Man in Space*, won the Emmy.

system is nil, but it could exist in millions of other situations where the temperature is the same.

He [Nater] comes up, and he says, "Ward, I'd like to discuss something with you. I'm serious about this. Is there any way we could eliminate this sequence here?" And I said, "You mean the evolution sequence? No, this leads up to a very important point." "Well, you know I'm stuck with these films after they're made and releasing them to the schools, and to infer that... This is admitting that the theory of evolution is valid, and I don't think we should do that. You know, this is against what the Bible says."

I look at him like, "Who the hell is this freak?" And I said, "Carl, we did this much more realistically in *Fantasia*, and did you read *Life* magazine last month?" Remember that issue of *Life* that had it much more explicit than *Fantasia*? They were calling nuts and bolts on that.

He says, "No, no, I never read those magazines." I said, "What do you read?" I found out the only thing he reads is the *Christian Science Monitor*. Then I found out he was a devout Christian Scientist. But for him, as head of the 16mm department, to come up and request that I take this out of a picture because it would be wrong for the kiddies to see it in the schools when they finally got it in 16mm was just beyond my comprehension.

Now, I said, "Well, it's nice of you to give me your opinion, Carl," and so forth.

The next brush I had with him was when I did a picture called *Eyes in Outer Space*. It was to show how the first weather satellite would work. This was before Sputnik, mind you. We were pretty damn close to the way it really happened. Of course, we had the benefits of the likes of Von Braun, Stuhlinger, Willy Ley.

So the picture goes out. It gets down to the stage where it's to be packaged for 16mm. And he calls me up one day, and says, "Ward, how would you feel... Would you feel disappointed—we're getting this ready for release to the schools—if we took out that sequence: the hydro-cycle, the little drip?"

That's a section I had explaining how moisture comes back to the earth in the form of hail, snow, rain. How it's evaporated, goes up, and forms clouds. We call it the hydro-cycle, and Mr. Crick, who was quite a well-known weatherman had worked with us a bit, and he said, "For the first time you guys have explained this so everybody can understand it."

I got letters when it appeared on television from school teachers who commended us on for the first time we were able to explain to the kids how this all worked. And we did it with a little jazz thing, little talking thing. It was cute. It was done in cartoon. It was the one light section of the picture, except how we felt about rain and moisture. Here's this guy calling me and wanting me to... And I had to go down the whole line of testimonials to Carl as to why that should stay in there.

It was the most important part of the picture, and finally I got there. I said, "Why do you want to take it out?" "Well, you know, it's a little flippant. It's a little, you know, it's just not... I don't think it's the sort of serious fare that these children should be exposed to." I couldn't believe this guy!

RS: Did you have any contact or work with a man named Robert Spencer Carr?

WK: He was one of the jokes. I think I have a great collection of his pink slips. I saved a lot of them. To me, one of the great sources of humor, I figured out, in the days to come would be the inter-office memos. Some you wouldn't believe.

RS: I believe them. I've read plenty of them.

WK: Bob Carr, or Robert Carr, came in there. Nobody knew exactly what he was supposed to do. But he came into the story department and actually, I think, he decided on what sort of activities he would follow. It would be sort of a gag analysis or story analysis, and he would maybe roam from one unit to another and make critiques on whether he felt it was going to work or not.

I mean, after all, this was the prerogative of Walt Disney. Anyway, Bob Carr, when he got an idea, he had a little clothesline in his room on a pulley, just like the tenements in New York when you hang your washing out. And he would pin these with a clothespin on this line and wheel them down to the end.

When he got another idea, he'd put it up, and these things would be hanging in his room like a clothesline, and his legendary inter-office communications—lots of people remember them. I saved all of them; I have them filed away. He was one of those self-appointed efficiency-idea experts that Lord knows how he got in there or who hired him. But he didn't last long.

RS: I see his name on a lot of memos. But very few of the people who are still there could pin down any information...

WK: He came in there like so many people come in, and they have some wild ideas. And, instead of playing it cool and finding out how the place operated, especially how Walt operated, they would dive right in with their own ideas, and they would finally come in this clash with Walt Disney. He'd say, "Who the heck is this guy? Get rid of him, boy. Don't bring him to any more meetings."

We'd be right in the middle of a story discussion. Walt would be there. I think this was one of the first confrontations. And here it is twelve o'clock. Time meant nothing to Walt. If we were rolling along, getting ideas, hell, he might go 'til 1:30. Bob jumps up, claps his hands together, and says, "Well, twelve o'clock. Shall we break for lunch?" [Kimball laughs] Walt turns and goes, "Who the hell is this?" You get the picture of Bob Carr?

RS: The story conference returns me to an earlier question about content that I didn't pursue very far. Suppose somebody in a story conference decides, "Well, let's put some topical reference in. Let's gag up something about the rubber shortage or the gas shortage." Would Walt be present at all of these conferences?

WK: Walt okayed every story. Period.

RS: In other words, if somebody decided to get rather topical and Walt objected to it, he'd be there?

WK: First of all, the story guys would get an idea. They would sit around and say, "Hey, let's do one on Donald changing a tire." "Yeah, that'd be a good idea." And they would do a rough outline and send the idea up to Walt, and he'd say, "Yeah, sounds interesting." He'd either say, "Go ahead with it," or "No, you guys get over on something else. I don't think it works."

Anyway, if he okayed the idea of their going ahead, they would do a storyboard, a rough storyboard, and, at a certain stage, Walt would be called in to see right away whether it was going to work or not. Walt would sit down with them, and he might cut it to pieces, but he would definitely either say "shelve it" or "go ahead".

So then they would work another week—or three months—or so refining it and putting all the suggestions he had made at the meeting. He was the world's best gag man. And he would be the leader in all those story meetings. They would do the final board. Then he would come in, and at that final meeting they would get the word whether it was okay for the project to go to the director and into animation.

The director would have the layout men design the backgrounds, and when he finally got a rough of the pencil animation tests, then Walt would be called in again. So Walt had another critique session to make suggested changes in the animation.

When he finally okayed the picture to go into animation cleanup and inking and painting, he would have been in on the development of the picture five times at least, so *nothing* went through the plant without his okay.

This was part of Walt Disney's genius. It was his attention to the minutest detail. He tried to delegate responsibility, which he did. He had a big organization. But he knew when to come in for the nuts-and-bolts session, and he would come in at the right time. He didn't tell us how to animate and didn't tell a guy how to paint a background, but he would certainly let us know the feeling he wanted. And he would even pantomime sometimes how he wanted a character to act, or how he saw a character.

He would be in on the choosing of voices. For instance, when the thing would go to the director to be made, the director then would go out and test voices and pick one out, and Walt would listen to those voices. So he was in on every phase of that, whether it was a short or a feature—just like he was on Disneyland.

Disneyland was a huge success because he was down there every day with his boots and straw hat and telling people to move this plant more to the right and this tree to the left, so the people standing here could see the steamboat coming around the bend. Nothing escaped his eye.

This is what killed him. Trying to do thirty-two hours of work a day and his constitution wasn't able to handle it. That, aided and abetted by the smoking problem. He had what was called rampant cancer. It happened in just a couple of month's time.

He was broken down physically, trying to do everything his increasing responsibilities demanded. This is important to consider: here is the same man who had just built Disneyland, had been in on every phase of the multiple problems involved, who was sitting in his office okaying and reading scripts far into the night, going to people's rooms and looking over their story work, making decisions on film, making decisions on a corporate level, laying out the new Florida complex, plus the decisions on the Lake Buena Vista EPCOT city of tomorrow, making personal appearances, greeting visitors, and keeping an eye on all the film productions.

I once sat down and made a list of what he was trying to do in a twenty-four-hour day. I was a rather active guy who organized my work. But I couldn't even consider accomplishing one eighth of the things he was doing. He was stubborn. He wouldn't admit that physically and mentally, he couldn't handle this daily schedule of responsibilities. And he wouldn't really admit it to himself, and his body just gave up. There's no reason for Walt Disney to die, because he had a record of longevity in his family, except for accidents, like his folks getting caught in the fire.[8] That's what killed Walt Disney: too much responsibility, and it was increasing every day.

RS: I wanted to bring up a couple of films, both directed by Gerry Geronimi: *Chicken Little* **and** *Education for Death.* **We've already mentioned** *Education for Death.* **You did Germania?**

WK: I did the opera sequence between Hitler in the knight's outfit and the Hermann Goering-Germania doing the duet: his trying to get her up on the horse, and the whole works.

RS: That's a funny scene.

---

[8] It was not a fire. Fumes from a faulty furnace killed Flora and put Elias in the hospital.

WK: Yeah, it still holds up today. And they made... You know where they're doing this: he's going "aw-haw", and she goes "oo-woo". "Aw-haw." "Oo-woo." It's a back-and-forth thing; all of a sudden, "woo-HOO", just like she's being goosed. Which is funny, but I caught it.

It got tremendous laughs. They made me cut down on her expression, because they didn't really want people to think she got the finger or something. It was all suggestion. So, she was laughing "aw-haw", then all of a sudden: "Wooo." She comes up with that expression [Kimball acts out the expression], and I had to kind of keep the same laugh in. You know, it's more of that damn reluctance.

Gerry was one of our stupid directors. Nobody had any respect for the guy. He was put into the job because he was a failure as an animator. Walt had this way of playing one guy against the other. He knew Gerry didn't like the animators, and the animators didn't like him. He figured that's a way of getting good work out of us.

But Gerry grew up on the Lower East Side of New York, and he was small in stature, and he was probably beat up every day of his life. He had this tough, Lower-East-Side way of talking. I could list you stories of this guy you wouldn't believe.

We had no respect for him; we tolerated him, and those pictures turned out—and maybe this was Walt's secret—in spite of Gerry, because we had to fight harder to make 'em work as animators.

Finally, it got to the point where no one would work for him anymore. Word got back to Walt, so Walt took him out of the studio and sent him to Germany to do a series of television shows, and, of course, Gerry was a concentrated Archie Bunker. He was very racist. And the fact that he was in Germany: they were krauts. They were the Kaiser's krauts. He didn't know how to get along with them.

Finally Walt had to fly over there, and that's when Walt said he was going to fire him, because there was nothing he could do. The animators had boycotted him.

RS: Who were the directors that *were* held in high respect?

WK: [Wilfred] Jackson... I think he was held in the greatest esteem. Ham [Luske], who was sort of a bumbling guy, but we knew he was sincere. He was a good director who paid attention to work. We respected him. Jack Kinney, because you couldn't criticize success. The Goof pictures were that way. But Jack was a good director. When a guy became a director, it was because—in the early days—he was put out to pasture. Walt was the director, really, because he okayed everything, but the director was the follow-through guy.

RS: You worked on *Reason and Emotion*, with the little people inside the head.

WK: That was our first trip into psychology. [Kimball laughs.]

RS: Were you modeling each other? Are the characters representations of the animators?

WK: The character of Emotion was supposed to be a caricature of Ward Kimball. I weighed a lot more then—I think maybe one hundred and eighty pounds. I had sort of a bluish, Nixon five o'clock shadow, more hair—it was black—and in those days, partly through basic insecurity in my character, I was a little gruff with people. I'm the nice old man now, but in those days I was sort of a curmudgeon character, so they patterned Emotion after me.

I can show you caricatures done at that same time that are supposed to be me that are just like that. Tom Oreb or I had made a model sheet of Ward Kimball. It was passed around as a gag, showing all the different emotions I was acting out in the model sheet. This is sort of the basis of that character.

Leo Feeley,[9] an ex-cartoonist of the Cleveland *Plain Dealer*, was more or less the model for Reason, the milquetoast. I put him in that category, but he really wasn't [garbled]. We had him in mind when we did [Reason].

RS: I've screened that film a couple of times, and it fails for me, at least the message. Because Reason is supposed to triumph over Emotion, and Emotion, as it's portrayed in the film, is so much more likable.

WK: He's the one with ideas. It's the people who are emotional and crazy that make the world progress, that think of the ideas. We condemn them, because they don't conform, but all the crazies keep the world going. They're the ones that think of all the inventions, make all the discoveries.

RS: I haven't screened it, but apparently a film offered by the educational division, *Man Is His Own Worst Enemy*, is almost the same film.[10]

WK: This is really weird stuff. This is some of Carl Nater's and a group around there that thought that we should go out into the world and moralize and show the world what was right and wrong. And with the name of Walt Disney on the picture, people might sit down and become morally perfect. This was a big mistake. We did a thing with Uncle Scrooge on money. Can you imagine doing a whole program on saving money and nothing in there about money being the cause of conflict and the root of

---

[9] JB Kaufman notes that the name might actually be "Leo Thiele".

[10] *Man Is His Own Worst Enemy* is a television compilation with Ludwig Von Drake which includes *Reason and Emotion*.

all evil? That was totally ignored, because, there again, we whitewashed the issue. When we get into areas of psychological subjects, all of them are terrible. They're just so wrong.

RS: Did you animate Scrooge in that film?

WK: Yeah. It's the only example of a character that developed first through the comic books.

RS: Did Carl Barks create Uncle Scrooge?

WK: Yes, and it's the only character that went backwards into film, where all the other characters emerged from films.

RS: Is it possible to take the famous Disney characters and actually say who created them? Or was it more of a group effort? I mean, Walt created Mickey.

WK: Sure, but Ub Iwerks drew it. It was Walt's decision to go ahead and approve the character, so you can say he did. It's always a joint effort. I was supposed to be the guy who did the Cricket. I went through that whole metamorphosis of this awful character, which I think is the most abominable thing I ever did.

From a real cricket with sawtooth legs bent in the wrong way like a grasshopper to this little blob that has an egg head with no ears. That's because all along the say Walt says it's not cute enough. So the more of the insect quality I eliminated from the Cricket, the more he liked it. So it's a blob; it's not a cricket.

RS: It's not a cricket at all.

WK: You see, Geppetto is a real man. He's believable. Pinocchio is a real puppet. And the Blue Fairy is a beautiful lady, five fingers, the works, a slight suggestion of breasts in the true Disney style of minimizing sexual parts. But what is a cricket?

Same thing can be said of Mickey Mouse. They'll say, "What happened to Mickey?" He was the one character in our whole cast that was not believable because when you saw Donald Duck you accepted him as a duck. He was three feet high or two feet high. Pluto was a real dog. Goofy, you accepted him as a man. He might have had ears, but he was a man. But what the hell are you going to do with a mouse that's three feet high where his ears just float—they don't turn in perspective—has this funny black-and-white division, has garden hose legs.

This is what happened to Mickey. What spelled the demise of Mickey Mouse was that after he stopped keeping time and dancing and playing instruments—he was still an acceptable symbol in "The Sorcerer's Apprentice"—but we could never figure out what to do with him. Who is Mickey?

What does he like? Is he mean? Is he happy? Is he a Boy Scout? Does he play with himself? No one knew. And so he finally just became a symbol… 'Cause he's three feet high, and he's a *mouse*!

RS: I know the animation feature they're working on right now is *The Rescuers*, which apparently has been in the works for quite some time. I wondered if you had done any work on it yourself?

WK: They were contemplating that picture at the time, and it was going to be an anti-communist picture.

Getting back to *Chicken Little*. When you first brought this up, I forgot to mention that we used the word Fascist two or three times in the picture, because, after all, we were fighting Fascism. Gunther Lessing, who was a darn Fascist, homegrown, and gave all this bad advice to Walt Disney during the strike, went to Roy Disney and said, "They're using the word Fascist in there." At that time, they were using the word Fascist in reference to our own homegrown variety here in this country. It was sort of a no-no word. Just as the scenes were being inked and painted, they came to Gerry and said he'd have to take out the word Fascist, which is "Faa-shist", two positions of the mouth, basically. I had that on the fox. I had to take it out and substitute in place the word totalitarianism. That takes four times as long, so we had to go back and open up that scene, and here's the fox saying totalitarianism: "to-tal-i-tar-i-an-is-m". It burned me up. Along with the work involved in changing those, was the reasoning behind taking out the word Fascist, which went right to the point—which is the only word we use today—and putting this compromising word in there: totalitarianism. In other words, if we called him Fascist, we should also kind of make it sound like we're condemning Russia, too.

RS: It looks like the final version of *Chicken Little* that reached the screen was toned down, because the draft calls for the fox, I think, to read a copy of *Mein Kampf*. Specific references.

WK: That was taken out. It was deflowered. There again, that's a no-no at Disney's: controversy. Nothing controversial in your pictures. They have to be bland: controversy or satire were two words that were no-nos.

RS: Speaking of satire and controversy, a project I guess you initiated or worked on was *Play Now, Work Later*. Did anything ever come of that?

WK: No, and, to me, of all the things I ever worked on, I thought that would be the most wonderful picture of all. Mind you, we were taking advantage of a technique that Walt used many times: a combination of cartoon and live action. We designed a funny dog called Bingo, and he was a cartoon. He was the only cartoon in the whole picture.

I shot all the scenes with real dogs where he's talking to them, and they react, and he's printed in with them. When you see those scenes, which are now put away somewhere, they're so great.

We had Stan Freberg, who was a great expert at satire. He took our script and put a lot of cute things in it. He normally doesn't do that. I talked him into doing that. He normally doesn't go around recording for anybody. He's got a big million-dollar business. But he was intrigued by this idea of a cartoon dog realizing that a crisis has been reached.

The picture opens with our dog following commands: "Lie down! Sit! Speak! Roll over! Play dead!" and he's going through all this thing, and you hear the master's voice, and we added a few more things: "Sit Up! Turn sideways!" Then all of a sudden it starts getting faster and faster like a tape [Kimball mimics a tape at high speed] and he's still trying to keep up, and it's just a blur, and BOOM!... It stops, and he's flat on his back... That does it.

He walks over and turns off the tape machine. It's been left there while the master's away. So he goes out [whistles] on the front porch—a real house—and we have a bunch of dogs coming from all over the neighborhood. One dog comes out of a cellar door. One goes right through a screen door. It was so great. They all come by and, "All right, c'mon, let's go, c'mon, move faster," and he gets them all in the house—and you know Stan Freberg. He says, "You in the back there, come in closer. Watch out for the polished floors," and all that kind of stuff.

He says, "Gentlemen, I called you all together because we got a crisis." And the whole thing is how the dogs have been neglected by the owners, because they're all going out and having vacations and motor homes. He tries to explain it to them. He tells one of the dogs to go pick up...it says home movies. "We're going to look at some. Wait till ya see some of these..." So he tells the old poodle dog to pick up the film can and thread up the projector, and he runs home movies. That was another satire—on home movies—all the horrible things we take. And he builds this case.

The studio didn't like it, because, here again, I'm attacking leisure time—the fact that people like it. We show how they leave a beautiful lot, maybe like this, and go to Carpenteria Beach where they have twenty feet of sand. And there are row after row of these campers. We showed all the campgrounds *clogged*, and the debris and the pollution. He's doing it by showing these home movies.

This was a little trick I thought was great. It was satire, though. I was attacking the American institution of the right to go camping. I was criticizing a man for neglecting his dog. I was making fun of this. But it got great laughs, and we had great, great dreams for that picture.

RS: So the picture's been shelved?

WK: It was shelved and, to me, it was going to be my greatest thing. I realized then… It was no climate for me as a creative person to just knuckle under and go through the paces of being employed under conditions that were totally against my way of working. So we had an agreement, a parting of the way. And to ease the thing, I asked first for a leave of absence. We were both trying to say the same thing, you know. Bingo was my last attempt. It was too satirical. And, unfortunately, to me it was one of the most imaginative of anything I've ever done.

RS: The other film I wanted to ask you about was *Escalation*.

WK: That isn't a Walt Disney picture.

RS: Is *Escalation* the only film you did outside the studio?

WK: Yes. It's recognized as the first animated editorial cartoon. And it was an underground film, believe it or not.[11]

We were getting involved in Vietnam…500,000 troops. And like so many other people, I'd just come back from Europe, and all my friends in the different studios, in Copenhagen, Paris…were all asking, "Why are you doing this in Vietnam?" And I didn't know.

Everybody said it was wrong. I said it was wrong. So I decided to do a cartoon on my own. First time I'd ever done that. I did it all with my own money: a three-minute picture. It was all shown underground, because this was before censorship had been lifted. And to compare the growing of Johnson's nose to an erect penis, which it finally achieves at the end, was shocking. It was all done to "The Battle Hymn of the Republic". The first chorus was sung by Johnson. Paul Frees did it in his twang and where he pronounces the word sword: "swwword" [w is heard] and an out-of-tune guitar [is heard] into the voices. We used a big choir like the Mormon Tabernacle: it was Los Angeles City College. Finally, the brass is added to the trumpets.

But every time the word truth… We come to that bar where you say the word truth, which he says at the end [whistle sound like a censor's bleep]. Remember they used to have on TV if you mentioned the other guy's product, you have a cuckoo. Even with the big brass ensemble at the end, it stopped for that little cuckoo. And it just tore up audiences.

It was first run down at the [Cinema?] Theatre in Hollywood. I had it run there so it'd be accredited to go into the Academy Awards. It was a facetious [garbled]. The guy called me up and said, "You ought to come down here." They were running the Newport Jazz Festival film. And he had run it three times the night before. I came in in the middle of a show—full house—and it just tore them up.

---

[11] *Escalation* may be seen on YouTube.com.

Now, the film is rather conservative for our moral standards. The openness in treatment you now have: scenes in bed and everything... But it's still recognized in the industry as the first editorial animated cartoon.

RS: What year did you do that?

WK: It was released about three months before Johnson decided not to run.

RS: So that would be '68?

WK: Yeah. It would be in the latter part of '67, first part of '68. Here's an interesting thing about this film. I had asked certain guys to help me, like my cutter who worked with me on Disney TV. He didn't want to touch it. He thought he'd be harassed by the IRS or something.

Well, this has all come out in Watergate: The pressure of using agencies to put the heat on you. I didn't give a damn, and I got some other guy to cut it for me. Everybody donated their talents, and when I put it up for the Academy Award, for the first screening with a group we have which picks out a certain number of films out of this avalanche of films, it tore them up. They fell down laughing, and it went into the second group.

The second group pares it down into three pictures. It was mysteriously withdrawn, because they all came to me and said how everybody laughed at this thing, just made them scream. Somehow, it didn't get into the finals, and I figured it was an embarrassment to the academy.

RS: Probably the same feeling as at the studio.

WK: Yeah, so I never pursued the thing. I had done my work. It went out on the college circuit, and people still come up to me, young kids, and say, "You're not the Ward Kimball? I saw that film, blah-blah-blah." It was just a thing done on the spur of the moment.

I got this idea. I'd been a charter subscriber to Paul Krassner's *Realist Magazine*, and in that *Realist* I had read something about Johnson's preoccupation with his genitals. And, uh...such things as a reporter saying when they were on the presidential yacht on the Potomac, instead of going to the head, he just walks over to the side and takes out this twelve or fifteen inches worth of cock, and turns to the reporter and says, "Let me know when it hits bottom." Things like that... And other things.

When he was in the Senate, if he had the vote of a certain other senator or congressman, his reference was, "I've got his prick in my pocket." These are well-known Washington reporters quoting. So I said, "Well, now I can tie this in with his nose." The nose explodes at the very end.

We go cinema verité—impressions, all different: Aunt Jemima to Daddy Warbucks. Finally, the medals come forward, and the last one's the Purple Heart, and then this bust of Johnson disintegrates at the very end. As the end title comes, you hear this [whistle-bleep] once more.

That's all it is. It tore 'em up. It was something I had to do. When it was shown at the studio, interestingly enough, the conservatives laughed their asses off. They thought it was great because I was making fun of a Democrat. The liberals at the other end of the spectrum just roared, because it was a satire on our whole involvement in Vietnam.

RS: From looking at the drafts, it appears that in *Saludos Amigos* you animated Pedro, the little plane that flies over the Andes.

WK: I call that a sissy picture, as Jonathan Winters would say. "Pedro, little Petey-boy. Petey-boy, c'mon, you can do it." You know, the little engine that could. So you can strike that out. Was that the picture where I also did an interesting dance sequence with the Duck dancing, doing the samba? Or was that in…

RS: I think that's *The Three Caballeros*.

WK: Because I point to the animation of the song in *Three Caballeros* as the one bit of animation that I'm still proud of, that I can look back on and say it's still funny and it holds up.

It was a song where I was given no story business or action instructions by the director. I had this long singing sequence—five minutes, or so it seemed—with little idea on how to stage it. It involved three characters: Donald Duck; Jose Carioca, the parrot; and Panchito, the rooster.

In desperation I decided to think of business that would interpret the words of the song literally, like if they sang the word "serape", serapes would suddenly appear. If "rain" was said, it would rain, or sombreros. This cinema verité approach to rapidly appearing objects or changes of action based on key words of the song was the key to the action and to the comedy.

Another idea I had that gave the sequence a good climax was the extension of the long-held note by the rooster at the end of the song. Gerry Geronimi [the sequence director] didn't like the gag, but that's what makes the sequence. It's where Donald and the Parrot try to stop the Rooster from holding the pose with the note. At the time these ideas were very new and progressive and had never been tried.

Gerry didn't want to show the sequence to Walt because he thought it was too awkward. In other words, the Duck would run out on the right of the screen, and he'd come back from the top—all that rule-breaking, magic stuff that is done all the time now. He wanted me to change it before Walt saw it. I said, "I'm not changing a thing. Stuff it up your ass." And he had to, because Walt said, "I want to see everything tomorrow."

So, reluctantly, Gerry had to run the sequence along with the rest of the picture. Walt howled. He just thought it was so great. He said, "Jesus, this is it." And Gerry says, "Well, of course, we're going to change it. There are some bad hookups." Walt says, "Shit, Gerry, don't touch it. Don't you know when something is funny? It's OK." Walt gave him hell for even thinking of changing something that worked so successfully. In desperation I had to think of all those gags in the *Three Caballeros* song, but it all came out to the good. I like that sequence.

RS: I appreciate the time you've taken to talk to me. Maybe one last question. You've told me the directors that were held in high esteem. I'm curious to know who were the animators that through the whole history of the studio have the best reputation.

WK: Well, as I look back when I came to the studio, it was Fred Moore and Norman Ferguson that were the top animators... Later on there was Bill Tytla that was sort of a chieftain.[12]

© 2007 Rick Shale

---

[12] After the tape ran out Kimball mentioned Frank Thomas, Ollie Johnston, and Milt Kahl in addition to Moore, Ferguson, and Tytla. He also added John Sibley.

Erwin Verity (1914–1992)

Interviewed by Rick Shale and Dave Smith on January 19, 1976.

Despite evidence to the contrary, it is often hard to imagine the Disney Studio, synonymous with "entertainment" in the mid-twentieth century, becoming a production factory for training and propaganda films for four years. Strangely enough, however, as explained by producer Erwin Verity, Disney's artists' experiences at creating great entertainment made them better at creating great training films. Whatever the purpose, good storytelling was tremendously useful in making even the driest movies effective.

Erwin Verity was born on August 8, 1914, and joined the Disney Studio on February 1, 1937. By February 1938, he was serving as assistant director on various projects, including a few sequences in *The Reluctant Dragon* and, of course, a great many of the war movies that he discusses extensively in this interview. Verity was also the unit manager for most of the various health and educational films that the studio produced for 16mm distribution in Latin America during WWII.

By the mid-50s, Verity had become a producer on the True-Life Adventures and the People and Places series as well as quite a few live-action movies. His credits in that capacity include *Siam* (1954), *Men Against the Arctic* (1955), *Secrets of Life* (1956), *White Wilderness* (1958), *Grand Canyon* (1958), *Nature's Strangest Creatures* (1959), *Big Red* (1962), *The Incredible Journey* (1963), *Ida, the Offbeat Eagle* (1964), *Charlie, the Lonesome Cougar* (1967), *The Footloose Goose* (1975), and *The Secret of the Old Glory Mine* (1976).

He retired in 1976 and passed away in 1992.

The interview begins with Verity examining a photograph.

Erwin Verity: The gentleman in the center there—the military man—is one of the most distinguished men we had at the studio during the war: Commander John S. "Jimmy" Thach. His nickname was Jimmy. He was a great guy. He was second from the bottom in his class.

When the war broke, he was a fighter squadron commander: Fighting One, F-1. Navy, of course. He was one of these swell officers—great personality, plenty of glory, plenty of guts.[1]

The reason I'm questioning you on our shorts production was that Walt got hot on a subject called *Victory Through Air Power* [by Alexander de Seversky], which infuriated this man. Literally!

Rick Shale: Because air power would not have been in the Navy's interests?

EV: The multi-gun bomber, which Seversky advocated, was certainly not in the Navy's interests.

RS: This man [Thach] was a flyer, right?

EV: That's right. His philosophy was that we have to hit the enemy with every weapon we've got, and we don't know which weapon is going to be the most effective. We do know that no horizontal bomber has ever sunk a capital ship. Now, you think about that a minute.

RS: Was Thach here when Seversky was here?

EV: You bet he was. But, you ask me again about the capital ship: Thach issued a challenge to Seversky. And the thing that really infuriated Thach was when Seversky called an aircraft carrier flight deck a "postage stamp".

RS: There's a sequence in the movie where he goes to some length to show how ineffective it was.

EV: When Thach saw that in the storyboards, he issued an open challenge to Seversky that he, Thach, would take on Seversky's multi-gun bomber with live ammunition: His fighter plane vs. the multi-gun bomber—one fighter plane—on one condition. And that was that Seversky would be in it. [Everyone laughs.]

RS: It sounds like a pretty serious challenge.

EV: He was, boy, he was deadly serious. And at the same time, we had an RAF fighter pilot here. He flew Spitfires, and he was shot down in the desert and horribly burned. Stocky Wright was his name. He was here in connection with the *Gremlins* story. He heard about Thach issuing this challenge to Seversky, and he said, "And if Thach is sick, I'll take his place." [Everyone laughs.]

---

[1] See Lou Debney's interview by Dave Smith in *Walt's People: Volume 4*: "Commander Thach had a fighter squadron. He was in the Navy—I think he ended up being a captain—but he was their top instructor. He developed what they called a "Thach weave," for instance. He was the first real hero that I can recall coming on the lot. Here was Commander Thach; you read about him in *Time* magazine. He was working in this next unit; that unit was locked off. He had story sketch men working with him—laying out what the Thach weave is, lining back and forth, how to throw your men off, etc."

Oh, this infuriated them. But seriously, Jimmy felt that we should hit the enemy with everything—anything—even an axe handle—whatever—just to make a point.

RS: So, it wasn't that those other flyers didn't believe in air power—but they objected to Seversky because Seversky thought air power was the only method? Is that what you're saying?

EV: Seversky felt that we would completely destroy the enemy by virtue of the long-range, multi-gun bomber. Did we?

RS: Somebody made the point when they were arguing against—I think it was a newspaper critic reviewing the film—and he says that shows us how to conquer another country; it doesn't show us how to occupy it. You don't occupy it with a long-range bomber, and Seversky doesn't really go into any of the questions of occupation or anything like that. How do you control a country if you've conquered it? So I suppose that may be the other side of the argument.

EV: Or the other side of the argument might be that the long-range, multi-gun bomber didn't win that Japanese war.

RS: I haven't read Seversky's book yet, but my impression was that Seversky thought the war was going to last an awful lot longer.

EV: I think he did. Well, of course, that would just simply indicate that he didn't have any knowledge of the atom bomb, which is fine; he shouldn't have. But after all, we developed that island-hopping technique and the multi-gun, long-range bomber didn't have a hell of a lot to do with that. That was the carrier landing: carrier transport.

RS: Seversky didn't think much of that theory. Before we get too far into our conversation, just for my record I would like to get what your capacity with the studio is right now, either your title or essentially what you do.

EV: I'm production manager.

RS: Of a particular area? Film, TV, live action, animation—everything?

EV: We switch around here. But basically, I'm production manager of nature films: Films that have animals in them. And yet I'm not exclusively in that capacity, because John Bloss, he's a production manager and he produces films, or handles films for producers who have animals and people in their subjects as well. I'm also getting ready to retire.

RS: The other half of the question is what was your capacity or title at the studio during the war?

EV: I was an assistant director.

RS: Did you have a particular area, either in the training films, or strictly Army or strictly Navy?

EV: Well, I'll tell you. The real beginning of the training film program here at the studio occurred on Pearl Harbor Day when Walt Disney received the strange phone call, and it turned out it was an officer from what was then known as the Bureau of Aeronautics. He said, in effect, "Mr. Disney, as you very well know, we now have a war on our hands, and I would like to ask you if you would be interested in having your company make a contribution to the war effort." Walt's reply: "Of course. Why, certainly. I think every red-blooded American has got to do something, and do it in a hurry." And this officer said, "Well, Mr. Disney, we would like to have you produce 20,000 feet of training films for $100,000 to start off with." And Walt said, "My God, I've never made anything so cheap as that in my life!" "Well," that boy said, "this is for the war effort, you know, and we've got to do our part here."

And Walt said, "Well, all right. We'll do our best." And the officer said, "Thank you very much, Mr. Disney. I'll have you know that we have recorded this conversation, and at 9:30 tomorrow morning your office will receive a visit from a Lieutenant Commander Chambliss, who will introduce you to this 20,000 feet of training films that we'd like to have you begin immediately to produce." And sure enough, at 9:30 the next morning, he was here.

Dave Smith: What was the name of the officer that called Walt, do you remember?

EV: No, I wouldn't know. But the name of the officer that came in was Chambliss. And when I came to work Monday morning, that morning, I received a phone call to be in a meeting at 9:30, and we had the job: Four or five of us. Ub Iwerks was to head it up.

DS: This was WEFT?

EV: This was the WEFT series.

RS: We screened one of the first films in the series.

EV: Which I personally wound up finishing directing myself, because before we really got under way producing—and there were scads of those things to be named: wings, engine, fuselage, tail. That was the system we had to follow. And already we had begun to realize, "Hey, now, wait a minute. You're not going to have time to methodically identify an enemy aircraft that's coming in on you head on!"

DS: We were wondering about that.

RS: When we screened the film we wondered how they would have time.

EV: It was a ridiculous system. You have to learn to identify an aircraft by the flash method—quick flash cards. But we couldn't convince anybody of that. The Service: "Oh, no. This had to go out. These were great!" Well, probably they did do some degree of teaching. We didn't think so, but I'm sure that some farm boy that was suddenly drafted and hadn't seen but two or three airplanes in his life learned to identify a P-38 from a P-51 Mustang.

DS: Had you had some military experience before this that you brought into the project?
EV: No.

DS: This was all brand new to you?
EV: Oh yes, certainly. We were just green. But it was a picture, and we know how to make pictures and the subject was the fascinating thing: now this was identification of aircraft. Incidentally, we *made* the series, too. We got everybody off of it, and I was the only one...practically the only one left on it was the film editor.

And we made budget! And we made schedule. The Navy was tickled to death, and Walt was very pleased that we could turn out such a series. He didn't think the series was worth a damn, though, really.

RS: It was the Navy that imposed the method of showing that.
EV: Yes. Oh my, yes. WEFT System, they called it, and they had pamphlets that supplemented the films and all that stuff. But I swear to you, surely that series must have been dead by the time we'd finished the last subject.

RS: Was there any way to measure? I've read in a couple cases that they felt that training films increased the learning speed with which someone learned the material by 40 or 45 percent. Did the studio or your military contacts have any feedback at all to find out how effective these films were?
EV: No, nothing that was ever translated into percentages.

RS: In other words, there wasn't any way they could say at one point, "This film isn't doing what we thought it would, so let's stop it—or change the method"? They didn't have, really, a way of judging its effectiveness?
EV: Depending on the rank and the influence of the technical advisor, he had the authority to do that, certainly. But the effectiveness of the films can best be illustrated by this story. It wasn't very long after the war started that this Commander Jimmy Thach arrived.

DS: He wasn't on the WEFT series?
EV: Oh, no. We got word that this bloke was coming in, and he was hot! He was fresh from combat. And we were tickled, because—with all due

respect to Commander Chambliss—Jimmy Thach was fresh from combat. Actually, he led his fighter squadron into the battles of Midway, Coral Sea, and he'd been out there while it was maneuvering around Wake Island.

Jimmy Thach had won, at that time, two Navy Crosses and a Distinguished Service medal. Now, he won the Distinguished Service medal for inventing a system of fighter tactics, though the principal one's the "Thach weave".

He invented the two-plane section, and the four-plane section, I believe it was also called. They all stuck together: whatever happened, they were all together. Then he would develop tactics, where the two-plane section would split under certain circumstances. For example, they're meeting a Japanese Zero head on. Thach's tactic was: the two-plane section splits, and whichever plane of the two-plane section the Zero chose—he exposed himself to the other, broadside, and flew right into his bullets and was shot down.

RS: So this would be why he was against Seversky's method—the idea of using two planes or a squadron as opposed to a single plane.

EV: Oh yes, of course. He was heavily indoctrinated in the Navy. Jimmy Thach, in my personal opinion, was a spokesman for the admirals and at one time during the war, a great story hit the press: "COLIN KELLY SINKS BATTLESHIP *HARUNA*!"

The details were that Colin Kelly had the hell shot out of his B-17 and he was mortally wounded, and he literally dove that 17 right into the stack of the *Haruna*! It was a great morale story, except it wasn't true.

It electrified the American people. After all, we were down. We'd just had our whole fleet destroyed in Pearl Harbor, and then we had a boner out there in the Pacific when we lost five cruisers or something like that due to the fact that they weren't up to steam. Hell, they couldn't even move out of another harbor against the Japanese attack! We really needed a shot in the arm, and of course, what we didn't know was that the Services were getting ready to begin the island campaign with the eventual invasion of the Gilbert Islands.

But it was Jimmy Thach who stood up in Madison Square Garden, right after the Colin Kelly incident, and in front of about 5,000 people he stated flat out: "The exploit of Colin Kelly is not true." And, oh my God, the congressmen went after him, just as they did in later years, after one of the Crommelin Brothers—it wasn't Dick Crommelin; it was one of his brothers—also stood up and shot off his mouth to the public about what was going on.

Jimmy Thach was a spokesman, I think. Well, that really turned Congress nearly upside down when the Navy staunchly supported the statements that Thach made.

It's because we knew this man, and because we knew he had made that statement... We kept track of every Japanese ship that was sunk, and the battleship *Haruna* was sunk in the second battle of the Philippine Sea at the end of the war. And Jimmy Thach came into my office and jumped up and down and said, "We got her!" I said, "What do you mean?" He said, "We got the *Haruna*!"

DS: But several years after it was supposed to have gone down.

EV: It was at least two years.

DS: What film did Thach come in here to work on?

EV: This boy was hot, and we immediately read him. Oh boy, when he lit a cigarette, his hand shook so badly...he'd get a cigarette over like this, he'd quick-like light the match, and if he had to he'd hold the match on against the wall, too—because his hands shook so much from combat. He came in with what I shall refer to as a "blank check", and authority. He had a pipeline to Washington.

The president of our company, Card Walker... Again, to digress, Card was a cadet, an ensign.

RS: In the Navy?

EV: Yes, on a tin can. And Jimmy Thach came into my office and said, "Say, Disney had an employee by the name of E. Cardon Walker, and he's now on a tin can in the Caribbean. Do we need him?" That's the authority this man had.

RS: What was Thach's rank?

EV: Lieutenant commander. We shortly had a problem because he got a promotion to commander, and he couldn't ever find another stripe. We found one for him at Warner Brothers' wardrobe. [Everyone laughs.] Also the scrambled eggs on his hat. He was happy then.

Thach later became a vice admiral, and I tried to go in and see him a couple of times, when I was back there and they were having a conference. My God, he had a Marine guard there. But here, this man who was second from the bottom in his class at Annapolis, and who admittedly said, "I just barely made it," became—well, he would've become one of the admirals in the war, if the war had continued—I'm sure he would have.

His mind was so active all the time that he invented the cross-pollination system when he became vice admiral in charge of the anti-submarine defenses for the entire country.

RS: How long was he actually at the studio here?

EV: Oh, perhaps over a year.

RS: This would mean he came in...

EV: Maybe two.

RS: This would be '42 to '43, or something like that?

EV: Time goes by so rapidly, it could have been. Yes, he would have been here in... I'm sure he was here within six months of the start of the war. And I believe he would have been here at least a year and a half. So, if he was already in his forties, he wouldn't be going back into combat.

He did his stint, and they wanted him right here, putting all his knowledge at our disposal so that we could translate it in terms of film.

RS: Which film was he advisor on?

EV: A series of films. They were called *Fighter Tactics and Fixed Gunnery*.

DS: This was the Mooney project?

EV: No.

DS: That was different?

EV: Mooney was a "methods"—aircraft manufacturing methods. This was a hot project. We used to be overtime whenever we wished and could use it effectively.

DS: Were you pulled off WEFT and put on this?

EV: No, WEFT was finished.

RS: By the time you started the *Fighter Tactics*...?

EV: There might have been one or two others that slipped in, but it wasn't very long after WEFT that I went right on the *Fighter Tactics* project.

DS: In conjunction with WEFT you also did some on warship identification.

EV: Yes.

DS: Was that about the same time that you were doing the aircraft identification?

EV: Yes. I remember now: I moved off of that because we had another project that came in called *Rules of the Nautical Road*.

I started to say something awhile ago, and we got sidetracked. That was in answer to, "Was the teaching effectiveness of these films ever measured percentage wise?" And I said, "I'll answer that by a story." This is the story.

During the *Fighter Tactics* film series, a delay was experienced in the laboratory. At that time, Commander "Butch" O'Hare, who was the hot Navy fighter pilot, the war ace who shot down four planes or five enemy planes in one flight, was in San Diego. He [Thach] invited me to go to San Diego and observe the films that we had made as they were being used.

RS: Being shown to the pilots?

EV: Well, shown to Butch O'Hare's squadron, for example, and also some of the *Rules of the Nautical Road* films were being shown to the training section of the Navy, and so forth. At that time, there was a great question, because the Navy had educators, and certain educators recommended that at the end of every training film there'd be, let's say, a three-minute review.

RS: That's still how the Army operates its education.

EV: We were against it. And we weren't popular with some of these educators as a result, I might add. So I asked Commander O'Hare, "I'd like to know: is this three-minute review at the end of the subject effective?" And he said, "Hell, no! All you have to do, Verity, is send us more prints. You see, the one thing the educators have overlooked is that we are trying to learn how not to die. We don't need any reviews." He said, "I can't tell you how many times we screen these films. We seldom miss a day, I'll tell you that."

DS: A review is necessary if you only see it once.

EV: Sure.

RS: So did this get back to the studio so you would not have reviews even though...

EV: No, they still insisted that we stick the review on. I said to him, "Well, Butch, you may still get stuck with these reviews because we get instructions from the Pentagon that they're supposed to be on. But we'll see that you get enough prints, and if you run out of a print, Commander, you just call me up. And if we've got one here, we'll either have a screening for your pilots or we'll send it down there." I think that's the best answer that anybody could give on any training film and how effective it was.

Of course, a second thought here now. If they're films like these films were, [which were] directly to the point and a direct application to what these pilots were doing—all aspects of their flight from the time they left the carrier deck. We covered with—I don't like to call them training films—instructional films on the assembling after takeoff for the combat flight.

We showed...here's why they came to Disney: we showed with tricks, cartoons; we used animation; we used little tin airplanes, warships...

RS: Actual three-dimensional models?

EV: Yes, three-dimensional. And with a vertical crane, we showed the combined attack on an enemy squadron the way it should be properly made, including with dive bombers, torpedo bombers, and fire planes, and in detail. It was one of the best scenes that I think was ever produced for the war, and I'm sure that some people back there thought it was real. And we had shrapnel breaking. It was one of the carrier films we made.

DS: *Carrier Rendezvous and Breakup* was one.

EV: I would guess it was in that.

DS: I've just made up this list of all the training films we made.

EV: You see, this boy Thach was hot, and this was very stimulating to our people, because... Well, for example, Ub Iwerks was our top technician, and when Jimmy Thach explained that he would like to show the scene, this master scene, the attack, so that he could position and have the path of the attack and assembly again just exactly the way he wanted, that was a challenge to our Ub Iwerks.

DS: And he loved a challenge.

EV: He loved challenges. And this was the greatest challenge you could give him. And then, man! Jimmy jumped up and down when he saw the scene! That was what we were good at.

RS: You mentioned Iwerks first as with the WEFT series. What was his capacity? Did he work as technical advisor on all of them?

EV: He was the director on them, along with a couple of other men. He figured out a way to do this line over the leading edge of the wing, and erase it, and bring it on backwards; simple, little animation tricks. He then moved on to other things, one of which was... No, I guess that was before Pearl Harbor. The Canadian bond films: you'd have to get the production dates on those. Those were earlier than '41; I worked on those with Ub.

DS: What about the *Boys Anti-Tank Rifle (Stop That Tank)*? Was that before Pearl Harbor, too?

EV: Yes. That was the same time the bond films were made.

RS: We screened that.

DS: That's a nice film.

RS: Yes, it's very good. We were talking with Mr. [Harry] Tytle earlier: he said that the Disney Studio ran into a lot of resistance about putting any humor in the films. From the ones that Dave and I have screened, that *Boys Anti-Tank Rifle* film is the best because it has an opening humorous sequence, and then it gets into the serious part. It seems not just entertaining, but it seems like a good educational film to use it. And Mr. Tytle was suggesting that that's what the studio tried to do, and it's what Walt wanted to do, and that the military people didn't want any humor at all in the films.

EV: For the most part, they didn't. Though I must admit, Butch O'Hare had a pretty good reason. You see, they weren't interested in jokes or funnies.

RS: That's right; they didn't need to be entertained.

EV: And they didn't screen the films after lunch, either, when half of their audience would go to sleep. He hit his squadron with films in the morning, right away. Of course, it's just about like anything else that America does: We overdo it. Just as we geared up production on all sorts of war implements, production was geared up on training films.

We always laughed, and a lot of us are still laughing, about the Hal Roach Studios in Culver City. When the war broke out, they happened to be half-vacant or something of the sort.

And Frank Capra, the famous live-action director, and incidentally it's a name you should never forget in the whole overall story of training films.

RS: Right. I've screened the *Why We Fight* series.

EV: That was a base over there, and the Hal Roach Studios name was changed to "Fort Roach". [Everyone laughs.] But Capra used that as his headquarters.

Frank Thomas, one of our top animators, single man, never had a chance at getting out of the service when the war broke out. My God, he was practically in the first call. And here's this fabulous guy with the wonderful hands, and you should meet Frank Thomas, and you'll understand because he's slump-shouldered, and long arms, and he's got these beautiful hands that have spent a lifetime doing nothing but drawing. Now, how the devil is a guy like that going to do very much in a war? Fortunately, they grabbed him and assigned him to Fort Roach, and he worked on films.

RS: Did he actually do the animation in the *Why We Fight* series?

EV: Some of it, yes. But Capra made so many films. He made…they called it "captured" film, incidentally. I had a little laugh at that. "Captured" film, and our boys were not only capturing the prints, they're capturing these dupe negatives, too.

Yeah, the Germans *wanted* us to capture them. It was terrific propaganda. But nevertheless, we used it and turned it round on them. And Capra had all this film, and then anytime he needed animation he would call on us, although they did have a small animation unit over there.

Of course, everything would be here, and everybody had film units all over. Some of them were producing junk, and others were producing pretty good stuff. We naturally tried to get the hot projects; they were the ones we wanted.

For example, I think one of the outstanding films we made was a film in animation: it showed a torpedo, after firing, arming itself on the run. And that's quite a technical film.

RS: The kind of thing that could never be shown by live action.

EV: No. As I say, this studio quickly transformed itself into a—oh, I believe at least 95% of our production was for the war effort. And as soon as the Seversky film was finished, we were *all* war effort.

We had a Marine combat photography unit here. We not only went over cameras that were going out into combat—Ub Iwerks and his staff of technicians: [Eustace] Lycett, John Hench, quite a few of the boys—they freely gave them technical information we knew on the cameras and so forth.

We had combat films come back from Italy that were made into more-or-less "reporting" films. I don't know what they did with those—possibly they were used as reports to the president, and the Senate and Congress.

RS: Yeah, they have lots of those films in the Army; they've retained them.

EV: Films showing a line of men advancing through an olive grove and dropping, one by one, and no kidding about it: very rough stuff.

RS: Do you know how the work that the Disney Studio was doing compared with other studios in Hollywood in terms of training films?

EV: No, not accurately, because we were so busy that...

RS: Busy enough with this work you didn't know what the other studios were doing.

EV: All the key units that we had were working six days a week, and if it was some hot project that should be finished by a date that was rapidly approaching, why we went right into overtime. Some men we had worked so much overtime that they fell asleep at their desks.

RS: We're trying to track down some information on films about the Norden bomb sight that have been done here.

DS: I can't find that title on that list anywhere. Do you know under what title that was worked on?

EV: Well, it wasn't about the Norden bomb sight.

DS: It wasn't?

EV: No. It was a C-1 autopilot.

DS: Oh. That we've got on the list.

EV: Yes, I worked on that project. You see, that was a hot one. Now, that came to us with a technical advisor by the name of Colonel Garland. There was also a Colonel Garland Project, too.

DS: The C-1 autopilot was for Minneapolis Honeywell.

EV: Yes. They all were, actually.

RS: How about that one titled *High-Level Bombing*?

EV: That was Colonel Garland's.

RS: But you don't think that was the Norden bombsight?

EV: No, I don't think there was a film on the Norden bombsight. At least if there was, I didn't work on it.

RS: That's been a mystery we haven't been able to solve.

EV: But I was on the autopilot film, and I was on the Honeywell project. That was one of the boys that made a landing over at Grand Central Airport. We'd been up over the valley; a young technical advisor had taken us up in a twin-engine Beechcraft with an auto pilot. And one by one we'd switch—go down into the bombardier's section—it was a military version of the Beechcraft. And we literally fly the plane from there; it was a great experience.

We finished our exercise and came back and made a landing at the airport, which was camouflaged—this pilot had not made a landing there before. When we hit the runway, about ten thousand people stopped work and watched us bounce down the rest of the runway; it was kind of hairy.

I was beginning to wonder whether we were gonna run out of runway or not. And it was damned close; we were clear down past the tower at Grand Central. There's a fence down there, I always remember. But we were pretty close, and he spun it around... Oh boy!

RS: Was this a common experience, when you'd be working on a technical film, to take the crew that was doing the film up either in the airplane, or take them to a ship, or whatever?

EV: I'd say yes. Not always, but...

RS: When it was possible?

EV: Oh yes, whenever possible. They had men go down to the submarines, and a couple of boys went out on a carrier that was taking on a load of planes. And we filmed all the planes landing...occasionally, one cracking up. They were new pilots, on their way out, you know. And flying bombers, B-17s.

Our autopilot crew flew in B-17s. We started with Beechcrafts, went up to Spokane, that was a big B-17 base there. We went on training flights there. Now that was all spearheaded by Colonel Garland. He was a West Point graduate, and as I recall, he'd had his share of combat when he came in.

I'd like to make a point: every time you had a man who came in from combat, there was no doubt about his ability as a technical advisor.

RS: Because he'd proven himself?

EV: He knew exactly what we should do.

DS: Who was Major Geisel?[2]

---

[2] Theodor "Dr. Seuss" Geisel was part of Capra's unit during WWII.

RS: You took the question right out of my mouth. [Everyone laughs.]

EV: Major Geisel was a tall fellow... I don't think he was here very long.

DS: We never found a title. There's a Major Geisel project.

EV: I would guess that Geisel had something to do with the Mooney project.

DS: Oh.

EV: We made a lot of films, which I didn't pay any attention to, actually, as they were so very dull, on aircraft manufacturing procedures.

DS: Riveting and welding and blanking and punching.

EV: Yeah, riveting and welding and all that stuff. However, there's a lot of sense behind it, because those were filmed records of illustrations... shortcuts in manufacturing. Now those could be taken right under the arm, then into other aircraft plants: "Now, this is the way Lockheed is doing this procedure." They were always changing. We had a crew, if I recall, on that project for over a year, shooting film, and traveling around to various plants.

DS: They put a lot of footage on...moving around.

EV: Oh, my goodness, yes.

RS: What would be an average number for a traveling crew? Are you talking about two or three people, or a larger group?

EV: No, I'm talking about what we referred to in those days as a "minimum union crew" (they didn't have directors because they were technical; there was no director that could quite be that technical), so one of our own technicians was usually in that capacity. He had a cameraman and an assistant. And you'd have one or two grips. That's about it.

RS: They would go out, for instance, to get the live action where you'd have the planes or something, and then would the unit—the unit was larger than just that crew—there would be the animators and stuff?

EV: Yes, you'd have the unit here that was viewing the film as a team.

RS: Now, how large would that be, just on a typical film?

EV: There was the chap who was going to direct the film, a writer, a key animation man. You see, as we got into these films, we found out that you didn't need animation, per se, one hundred percent. You could use a simplified form of animation (three drawings instead of twenty) and you could still make your point. We went the simple way.

RS: Is that also why you went to models and stuff, because you could do that faster than animation?

EV: That's correct, yes.

RS: I've looked at a weather film, I think it is *The Cold Front*, in which it looks like they took just straight live-action footage and traced over it so it's animated, but it's so realistic.

EV: Yeah, they animated lines over it, and so forth, to emphasize points being made by the narrator. I'd have to look over the list to refresh my memory, but right off the top of my head, after all of these years: that series that you've just mentioned, the *Weather* series, Commander Thach *Fighter Tactics*, *Fixed Gunnery*, the *Torpedo* series...

RS: Are you saying Thach was involved with the *Torpedo* series?

EV: No, not involved at all.

RS: Was there a specific military man here for the *Torpedo* series?

EV: Yes. I don't remember his name. If I recall, he was a Navy chief with a jillion years of service...sub service. He knew torpedoes like crazy.

The Colonel Garland Project, which I call...when I say Colonel Garland, I call it the high-level bombing, precision bombing, which involved the auto pilot as well. I would say off-hand those were the outstanding projects we made.

RS: Are there any other names like Major Geisel on there that we haven't come up with?

EV: You've got to have a name down there: Captain Thorn. He was on the auto pilot. "Thorny", as we called him, was a whiz, and he had been in combat over the hump—Asian theater. And probably by plan, Thorn was sent out there to study the results that bombing squadron, or that base, whatever it was, was having with their bombing.

Apparently, there were quite a few things wrong. First thing was they were not using the auto pilot. They'd lost all confidence in the auto pilot, and Thorn showed them that they were wrong, that that was a great aid to accuracy.

Then he came back here and was a technical advisor on the films. And we went right through the procedure that a bombing crew went though when they were making their run or getting ready to make the run. They're on a mission, in other words, and they're about ready to make the run on their target... At what point they did this and that, and so forth—of course, emphasizing the use of the auto pilot.

Thorn went back and had the films with him and used them as a teaching aid and personally led missions. That was the most convincing thing he did. They learned facts that way when Thorn led them right out into the mission.

RS: That would restore their confidence. I have a couple of names that I've been running across in files that I wondered if you could help me identify or place as to what function they had. Carl Nater?

[Tape runs out.]

EV: …the military.

RS: For a particular branch, or for all branches?

EV: All branches.

RS: Now, is he the one who would go and actively seek the contracts and say, "We can do it for this?"

EV: Yes, for the most part. It got to be such an avalanche of paperwork that we separated it: I took the Navy… We even had the coordinator coming in there, too. It wound up I had all military, I think, and Nater went over to the Coordinator of Inter-American Affairs films.

RS: How about Bob Carr? Does that ring a bell at all?

EV: Bob Carr was a writer.

RS: Did he work on the military stuff at all?

EV: No.

DS: Looks like you're remembering a funny story. [Everyone laughs.]

EV: Yes, as a matter of fact I am. Bob Carr was a rather gullible individual, and it didn't take us very long to find that out. I guess he was probably the first writer that came in here and had a terrarium. He had a turtle in there, and at times he'd comment to the fellows about how his turtle was thriving on this particular feed he was giving it.

It didn't take very long for that turtle to be identified, and we got half a dozen turtles, larger in size [everyone starts to laugh] and graduating up to a pretty good size. And periodically, we switched turtles on him, and that guy was going crazy! He thought he'd made a great discovery of this special feed he was giving his turtle.

At that point, then, we reversed the trick, and they went shrinking back down. Oh, that was kind of cruel, but we had the dig on him.[3]

Bob Carr, to my recollection, made no significant contribution to our military training film effort at all.[4] In fact, he even came in here afterwards, if I recall correctly, and he wasn't here at the studio very long; he left us, did a couple of articles in the *Saturday Evening Post*, and I've never heard of him again.

RS: Are there any names that I'm ignoring? I don't mean the military

---

[3] According to Bill Justice, this trick was played on Walt. See Bill Justice, *Justice for Disney*, p. 123.

[4] JB Kaufman mentions: "Carr did suggest a number of ideas for propaganda films and other war-related theatrical pictures."

advisors that would come in, but studio people that played a very important role during these years?

EV: I'll tell you one thing: [pointing]: don't ever ignore Walt Disney. Because here and there he would become very impatient with a certain training film we were making. For example, with Jimmy Thach's training film called *Fixed Gunnery*, there was a formula the fighter pilots had to use, and they had a gun sight, and so forth, that they used in following this formula.

The relationship of knot speed to mil lead was 3 to 2, and that was what they had to calculate before they'd fire. "Mil lead": millimeters of lead coming through the sight. "Knot speed" is the speed the target... Well, that was complicated; that was mathematics; that was fact. Walt couldn't make any contribution there.

But here and there, on other films, oh boy! He'd go right through them! I'll tell you one thing he did: he did his best to shorten up *The Rules of the Nautical Road*. When I had made this investigation down in San Diego for Walt, I came back and reported to him that those instructors down there were showing *The Rules of the Nautical Road* training films to recruits after mess.

RS: Were they getting any recruits with that sort of procedure?

EV: To new recruits. They were a captive audience, but they were a sleeping audience. Sure didn't help to see their heads dropping.

DS: It's good we saw that at ten o'clock.

RS: Yeah, we'd have been in trouble if we'd tried to screen it at four.

EV: As compared to a Butch O'Hare screening, which I saw and nobody knew who I was or anything of the sort: the pilots walking in, pulling off their goggles and helmets and their Mae Wests, sitting down, and then Butch would talk to them for five minutes and say, "Let's roll the film now." At times he would talk right over the film: "Now watch this!" That's the way they were using the films, which was certainly very impressive.

DS: He found them useful, then?

EV: You bet. I'll tell you something that isn't commonly known—and it gave all of us a tremendous charge—that was that we had a meeting here at Mickey Mouse Studio of the five fighter squadron commanders of our carriers: the *Lexington*, the *Saratoga*, the *Essex*... There were names like Lieutenant Commander Mike Sanchez and Jimmy Flatley.

These are great names in Navy fighter tactics/fixed-gun history, great leaders. When they survived the combat, why, they eventually went right on into captain and admiral. And they went into a room over here, closed the door, locked it, and left a secretary outside: "Not to be disturbed." And the only thing she did outside of that was to keep serving them coffee.

Once in a while they'd run out of cigarettes, and she'd get more cigarettes for them. Some of those boys came in from Guadalcanal; and there was a B-17 parked over here at Grand Central, with a full crew standing by. And boy, if they weren't attracting attention! Because that whole Lockheed bunch over there was wondering, "What in the hell is going on? That plane came in from combat!" Jeepers.

These officers started at about nine o'clock in the morning, and at about three o'clock in the afternoon the door opened, and Jimmy [Thach] came out. I happened to be right near. I knew something was popping. And he turned to me and said, "We've got it! We are in complete accord. Now we've got our doctrine that we're going to follow." Meaning the complete doctrine of fighter tactics that we were going to use for the rest of the war.

Then we went right ahead, and there was never a question about, "What are we gonna do?" or anything. Jimmy answered the questions.

RS: That was midway—you'd started production on this fixed fighter tactics—on *Fixed Gunnery*, when they brought them in and made sure that the rest of the series was…

EV: Yes. Jimmy made certain that he wasn't going off the deep end: That the boys were all in accord with him. In other words, he wasn't jealous about it at all. He wanted to make certain that this was right, this was it. Those films, you see, did a job, every damn one of them. They really did a job. Oh, boy!

DS: Was 1943 our busiest year during the war? It seems to be, from the titles and the number of films.

EV: Does it really? I never have looked at it to see.

DS: And also it seems that most of the work for the Navy was '42–'43, and then the Army was mainly '44 and '45.

EV: Incidentally, there is another man, an officer here that we had during the war, his name was Hutchison; Harry [Tytle] undoubtedly mentioned him to you.

DS: No, he didn't.

EV: Lieutenant Hutchison. He was a chap who arrived shortly after Lieutenant Commander Chambliss. But he was a Bureau of Aeronautics man. He wasn't a flyer; he was just a—I don't mean this disrespectfully—he was a bureaucrat, a civilian who was on military…

RS: What was his function here?

EV: He was their liaison for the Bureau of Aeronautics. He could report to them directly any confidential information he wanted, on the conduct of the Navy officers that were here. Every project we had had Navy officers. But you see, some were academy men and some were not.

DS: Oh, that was the story: they tried to get Hutchison to get Farwell out of Walt's office, and Hutchison was a lower rank than Farwell.

EV: Yeah, that's right. You know, accommodations were tough, really, in Los Angeles, and they had to be here every day. In our little penthouse club upstairs, we had a couple of beds, and there were officers quartering themselves up there. And along came Commander Farwell. So Walt generously let him have part of his office, which consisted of a bedroom, and so forth.

The only thing Walt couldn't stand in him [was when] old Farwell washed his clothes in a bucket. [Everyone laughs.] And then there came a time when accommodations were opened up, and naturally, Walt would have liked to have had his office back completely—and he couldn't get him out!

RS: That was comfortable there.

EV: Oh yeah, it was comfortable, and the price was right, and so forth.

If there's a lesson to be learned in the production of training films, it is that you must always get the producer, a technical advisor with combat experience—actual experience—or the next thing to it.

RS: The technical advisors that were here: did they have the authority, or when these films were in production, did you have to always check with Washington first? Or was there someone right here at the studio that could say, "Yes, we'll do it," or "Yes, it will be longer," or shorter, or more expensive?

EV: Seldom.

RS: Seldom here?

EV: It was left up to the producer. By that time, you see, we had a contract and had worked up a budget, and we were rolling. So if there were any questions about costs, why, they arranged that...

RS: That was all worked out beforehand, when the bidding was taken?

EV: Oh, yes. We didn't even want to bid on anything unless it was fixed; it was all set. If they'd made up their minds: "Yes, this is the doctrine we want to use, make it *this* way." We had certain officers whose projects got fouled up as they unfolded.

Maybe the first subject had been finished and the second was on its way... bang! There'd be a repercussion from Washington. This officer then would have to give us changes and so forth. Colonel Capra had that problem.

Colonel Capra had several problems, and I have a lot of respect and admiration for this man. Sure he was a great director in Hollywood—for my money, I don't think there was ever a better director than Capra—but you see, he would run into criticism of some of his subjects from agencies that he probably didn't even know were involved. [Chuckles] What was the CIA called—Office of Strategic Services, was it?

RS: Yeah.

EV: That's what the CIA was called in those days. They might come in; some tactical group might want a couple scenes cut out. I'm ad-libbing. The Navy didn't want the area even shown on the screen, which would betray the fact that we at least had knowledge of it, we at least had knowledge of that area, you see. Then there was another problem that Capra had, and that was the accuracy of the material.

We had a campaign in Burma. That's a good red-hot subject anytime. If you start talking about the campaign in Burma, why, you've got one! Some historians, probably British, will record the victories, when in truth, they got the hell kicked out of them by the Japanese.

Story sketch artists worked here with at least two Army advisors in visually preparing a story sketch board. Our old cartoon method of making a funny was ideal to make a training film. Story sketches worked out perfectly. And here we had this room; you could sit there and just read the copy under each sketch, and you could follow the campaign in Burma, and so forth.

We got all finished, and had this meeting with Capra. Capra came in and a couple of officers, majors, and so forth with him, Army captains, five, six officers, a fair amount of rank. They came in to go over this story we'd prepared. Not a word was said to Capra, and he said, "Why, this is a whitewash!" I knew what was going to happen then. He said, "This is a far cry from the truth."

He turned and he said, "Fellows, correct me. There is very little in this whole story that I find is accurate. Do you agree or disagree? Let's hear it." They agreed and shelved it. He refused to make it.

I don't know what Washington thought about it, but *we* never made the picture, I know that. I admired the man for taking that position. Of course, he had fellow officers there that agreed with him, but he was a high-caliber man, and he felt that it would jeopardize the entire series of films to put something up there that was so completely false.

RS: There's one question I want to ask on a totally different subject here, which you may be able to answer with your experience in the nature films. I've read somewhere that someone was making the supposition on how Disney got into the nature films in the first place, and this person suggested that some of the live-action footage they took down on the South American trips was sort of the initiating force, that from that grew the idea of the True-Life Adventures. Does that sound true or false or anything close to how it happened?

EV: No, it's not true. I don't think it was.

DS: What about *The Amazon Awakens*? Did you have anything to do with that?

EV: Yes, I had a great deal to do with that.

DS: That didn't grow into the True-Life Adventures?

EV: No, I don't think so. If it had, we would have made the True-Life Adventures immediately after *The Amazon Awakens*, you see.

DS: It was about five years later.

EV: *The Amazon Awakens*, interestingly, I believe is the first 16mm color teaching film, or "awareness" film, let's say, that was ever made.

DS: Well, maybe that's the way. I think Ben Sharpsteen[5] said in an interview once that this sort of led into the True-Life Adventures.[6] Now, maybe that's the way in which he was referring to it, as being the start of 16mm training.

EV: Could be. Incidentally, I worked with Ben longer than anybody else in the studio, so Ben and I share all these memories. Ben didn't work on the *Fighter Tactics* film, for example; he was on *Fixed Gunnery*, and so forth.

I want to tell you another story, and this is pertinent. Ben Sharpsteen was an animator: as a young artist, he gradually became an animator here. Ben retired some fifteen years ago, at the age of sixty-five. Ben was one of our key people who came up through the animation business, and he was a director in animation: Shorts—a lot of the Goofy's—*Hawaiian Holiday* was a short subject that Ben developed and directed.

And it happened that the auto pilot project was assigned to Ben. It so happened also that we had an animator by the name of Wolfgang Reitherman, and Woolie Reitherman was over there in the Asian theatre. He was flying the hump, as a matter of fact, as a transport pilot.

Woolie came back to the States on leave, and of course he, like a sailor going to a park and renting a rowboat on his pass, Woolie came back to the studio. And who does he see, of course, but Ben, with whom he had worked for years as an animator when Ben was a director.

---

[5] See *Walt's People: Volume 3*.

[6] JB Kaufman, who researched *The Amazon Awakens* for his book on the Latin American films, notes: "It struck me that the *method* of producing *The Amazon Awakens*—sending a cameraman or camera team into the field, having them shoot great quantities of film, then applying Disney expertise to reshape the raw footage into a polished production—was essentially a blueprint for the way the True-Life Adventures were made later on. Maybe that's what Sharpsteen was talking about."

Woolie said something about the auto pilot. I believe it was to the effect that he actually wanted to learn how to use the auto pilot, but he'd never had the time and probably was never going to get such an assignment because they kept him flying those C-54s (four-engine jobs) over the hump, to support that operation that was going on.

And Ben very casually said, "Well, look. You want to learn how to use the auto pilot? I'll show you. It won't take very long: fifteen minutes, Woolie." And Woolie said, "Ben… What do you mean *you* are going to teach *me* how to use the auto? You can't even fly an airplane! What are you talking about?" And Ben said, "Well, come on, I'll show you." And he did.

Now, Woolie never got over that, and some educators that have heard that story have never gotten over it either.

Many people besides educators and some of us here wondered what was that ingredient that we had that we could learn how to use an auto pilot and we couldn't fly an airplane. And we learned it well enough to teach it to a flyer who came back! And more than that, we taught him how to use it in fifteen minutes!

I've often felt that maybe there was some product that came out of the discipline we'd gone through to learn the continuity of a picture. You know, you can't talk about the picture that you're making until you can talk about the continuity. When Walt could talk the continuity of *Snow White and the Seven Dwarfs*… Oh boy! We went like crazy to finish that picture up! There was no doubt how it was going to be made, and we made it.

But, possibly by going through that process of becoming instilled in the continuity, there was an ingredient that we had that you could absorb this stuff. It didn't make any difference how technical it was. How did Wilfred Jackson, our cartoon director, absorb the "complexities" of the piece out of *Fantasia*, "Night on Bald Mountain"? And yet, he did. And he methodically knew where those notes were going to fall. Of course, music is mathematics, and once he had the mathematics of Mussorgsky's music, he had it, you see. It gives you a little food for thought.

RS: Yeah, it's food for thought right now. It's not so much the content, but you had the method from pre-war experience that you could apply.

EV: Yeah. Aldous Huxley visited us years ago, when we were at the old studio, and he said to Walt (I happened to be in the projection room), "How do you come up with your humor: the jokes? I'm interested in learning the process that you use to do that."

And Walt said, "Oh, just good hard work, that's all. We get together and sweat it out, that's all. We talk it all over, four or five of us in what we call a story meeting or gag meeting. We try to think up some funnies that'd be appropriate." Huxley said, "Have you ever tried alcohol as a stimulant?" And Walt said, "Yeah, we tried that, too. We had the funniest, the damnedest, greatest story meeting you ever saw in your life, but the next morning, that stuff was lousy." [Everyone laughs.]

RS: Do you think most people working at the studio felt proud or satisfied to be working on these government war film contracts?

EV: I think so. There were exceptions.

You know, one or the other of you interrupted me on a Card Walker story back there, and I didn't get to finish it. He was on a tin can in the Caribbean, and Commander Thach said, "Do we want him?" I used that as an illustration of Thach's authority. And I said, "Let me give you the answer, Jimmy, in about fifteen minutes. I know a way to get an answer. I know we don't need him because he's in the camera department, but let me check on this. I feel this boy wanted combat, Jimmy." And Jimmy said, "Well, he's sure as hell not going to get much combat down there."

I came back to Jimmy fifteen minutes later or so. I'd checked with a close friend, and he'd confirmed my opinion that Card wanted combat. And Jimmy closed the subject by saying, "Well, he sure as hell isn't going to get any down there, as I told you." And I said, "Well, he's just going to have to hope for it, then." Do you know that within two weeks Card was transferred from that tin can to Norfolk!

He became the flight deck officer on the *Bunker Hill*, which was one of our carriers that really saw combat, tremendously. And Card was on the carrier until she came back.

DS: Are you implying that Thach had something to do with this?

EV: Yes, I am. You bet. I know damned well he did it.

RS: You know he did it?

EV: I know he did it. You just didn't move ensigns around like that. And Card, of course, turned out to be a fine officer and had a tremendous war record.

I think it's not of much consequence, but it surely will occur to you: surely Disney must have really suffered from the draft. Quite true: we did.

Frank Thomas was an example of it. At a point where it looked like quite a group of us were going to go, the Manning Table came out. The Manning Table was some kind of a formula that a corporation could use in retaining a nucleus of its staff.

RS: Key people?

EV: Yes, key people particularly. The Manning Table prevented the obliteration of a company by having all of its people drafted. The Manning

Table saved quite a few of our key people. I was not on the Manning Table, but our artists were. That really did help us. [The artists] would never be adapted to it. You could never have trained them to do things like that [like use a machine gun]. Their hands…look at Milt Kahl and his hands: so delicate, long fingers…

We were talking about the Colonel Garland Project, and I didn't get a chance to say this at the time, but when our first two or three films were made, they went to the 8th Air Force and the colonel went with them.

He used the films in instruction over there, and then we received letters, comments—unsolicited comments—from pilots, navigators, and so forth—right out of the 8th Air Force: what they thought of the film, and how they thought it could have been better, and so forth.

Boy, that was a great psychology for the production crew, to receive those letters.

I didn't answer your question about the birth of the True-Life Adventure films.

RS: That's right.

EV: I'm certain that well before the war was over, Walt began to think about what we were going to make. Walt was very concerned, wondering, "What am I going to do with this staff?" Naturally, he came up with several different ideas that he wanted to exploit.

One that really fascinated him was Alaska, and he was talking about how Alaska is the most northern part of the United States, and she sits up there on top of the world: we bought her for a song, and probably no man has any idea how rich Alaska is in natural resources, and so forth. And we ought to know more about Alaska, because in the scheme of things—the global scheme of things, he used to say—Alaska is going to be right there.

It happened that a couple by the name of Alfred and Elma Milotte knocked on the gate, and they had some 16mm film. We didn't know them, and we'd never had any contact with them. But they had some film, and the cop called upstairs to Sharpsteen's office.

Ben and I were working together. He said, "I've got a couple down here that has this film, and they'd like to show it to somebody." Ben said, "What is it about?" He said, "Well, it's about Alaska, and the salmon industry and so forth." Ben put his hand over the receiver and said, "We can take time to look at some Alaska film, can't we, boy?"

So we saw it, and it was beautiful. It was beautiful. This man was a tremendous photographer, and it didn't take Ben very long, of course, to notify Walt. He came in: same reaction. He really thought it was just fine and talked with these people and liked them. We sent them to Alaska. I think this was about December of '45, and they were up there almost all of '46.

They had two directives that Ben and Walt had conferred about. One: they had to photograph the fur seals on the Pribilof Islands. Number two: they had to photograph the life of an Eskimo family, winter and summer. And the rest of the time, they could photograph what they wanted to. Having come from Alaska, they had spent quite a bit of time at Ketchikan, and although that's the Panhandle, they had traveled around Alaska for a bit. They had a portrait studio in Ketchikan, of all things. So away they went.

They shot—I'll always remember this—they shot 48,300 feet of 16mm film.

RS: Thanks very much for taking the time to talk with us. You've given us some fascinating details about how the studio operated during World War II.

EV: You happen to be talking about a period in my life that was extremely critical, the war effort. I always get a great sense of satisfaction that I was on the team.

© 2007 Rick Shale

James Algar (1912–1998)

Interviewed by Richard Hubler on May 7, 1968.

We met James Algar thanks to Robin Allan and Dr. Bill Moritz in *Walt's People: Volume 3*. This interview, conducted by Richard Hubler, focuses on the latter part of his career, while revealing a few more interesting details about how it actually started.

Richard Hubler: What did the Disney Studio appear to be like when you joined?

James Algar: To me, personally? It's almost hard to recapture the excitement of that time, and yet I have never completely forgotten it. For example, I was working on the hometown paper and I got this letter from Ben [Sharpsteen] on a Friday afternoon. I was on the train the next night headed for Los Angeles. This was when the Southern Pacific was still running the Owl and the Lark, which they have just taken off. And I recall buying a magazine for the trip down, and in it there was a piece about the Walt Disney Studio.

Of course, I'm built up with huge hopes. I arrived in town and I had two friends who lived in Hollywood and were going to art school. I knew their address, so I went out there. The landlady had a spare room and could put me up. This was a boardinghouse over near the old City College, and the two in question were Frank Thomas and Ollie Johnston. They hadn't come to the studio yet.

I think I got into town on a Saturday afternoon, and on Sunday I got a city map: I found Hyperion on it and I somewhat foolishly set out to find the studio on foot. So I walked from City College, which is on Edgmont near Santa Monica and Vermont, way down Vermont to Silver Lake Boulevard, out around Silver Lake Boulevard and onto Hyperion. It must have been about two miles or three miles. Anyway, I sort of reconnoitered the battlefield, shall we say. I sneaked up on the old studio and here was a sign that said "Silly Symphonies". There is a picture of that old studio now down on the first floor, and that to me was the Fantasyland castle in Disneyland. You know: that was it! Of course, the next morning I managed to find out how to get out on the bus and didn't walk.

I think the tryouts were one week, and I remember that while the tryouts were going on before it was decided who would stay and who would not, I got a telegram from the hometown paper that asked was I coming back or not? I said to hold just a little longer. When I was taken on, I got just half the money that I was getting up in the hometown, my salary was a cut from $25.00 a week to $12.00 a week, but I was pleased to be here.

RH: What was your impression of Walt?

JA: My impression of Walt was that he was a very interesting, sort of handsome, dapper man in those days. You know, Walt was always a somewhat frustrated actor and he could have passed as an actor in Hollywood in those times. His enthusiasm was completely contagious.

RH: How would he express his enthusiasm?

JA: Walt was a great one to talk the story problem of the moment and to think in terms of the story that was to be told, to literally pantomime and act out the parts. I found that Walt never particularly theorized or philosophized much. It was just that Mickey was the good guy and Pegleg Pete was the bad guy, and we'd get into these situations and these were the things that happened. He was a very pragmatic workman; he thought in terms of the camera, the screen, and the audience.

RH: What would be an example of that?

JA: It was not long after that we were beginning to get into *Snow White*. I can still see in my mind's eye the scene in *Snow White* where the little girl has gotten lost in the forest. And all the little animals come out and form a circle around her, wondering who this is, and the little birds come up, and fly above her. Walt used to literally do the little birds. He would talk it and he was the little birds, acting the whole business out.

Now I can give you a kind of an amusing sidelight of that incident. Walt would talk the scene, how the little birds would come out and "hoover" above her. Now, we all have blind spots about the pronunciation of words, and this was one of Walt's: He always said "hoover". (My own is "larynx", which I mistakenly learned as "larnyx".)

Now the second half of this episode came about twenty years later, at least. I wrote a little lead-in for Walt on one of the television shows and unthinkingly I dropped in the ward "hover". Frankly, I've forgotten when the show was, but one day after lunch Walt agreed to come down on the stage and record the narrative for this lead-in. He was reading along something "hoovered over us". And I am in the monitor booth and I have to push the control button and my voice comes booming out on the inside there like a voice coming out of the heavens, and I'm in a delicate moment. I have to correct the "boss". I said, "Walt, gosh, I'm sorry to interrupt you, but that should be "hovered" not "hoovered". And he kind of snorted and said "Oh, you and your damn college education… Besides I'm a Republican."

That was part of the byplay. Walt always knew that I had come out of Stanford, and I think he valued such brains as I had when he had me in the right slot, shall I say. But there was a kind of running gag that went on between us about the fact that he hadn't bothered to go to college and I had. One day in his office he said, "I'll tell you what I'll do: I'll match you degree for degree." And I said, "No takers, Walt, you've got me hands down." After all, he had an honorary degree from Harvard, and he had one from Yale and he had one from UCLA, and I don't know where-all. Anyway, that was one of the fun sides of him.

RH: How did the True-Life Adventure films get started?

JA: During the war period, we had been committed to so many documentary and training-type films around here. Walt had it in his mind that there might be a documentary type of story in Alaska. And this is sort of interesting because this was a forerunner to our finally doing a story on Alaska just this past year. But this was long before the 49th state had been established. Anyway, we found a couple of photographers, Alfred and Elma Milotte, who had had a photo shop in Ketchikan, Alaska. They had had pictures printed in the *Sportsman's Magazine*. They looked like likely people to go up and document Alaska. So they were sent up. They shot miles of footage on the industry and the timber and the salmon fishing and the railroads and the cities and the sportsman's hunting and Mt. McKinley, and the whole thing, including a side trip out to the Pribiloff Islands where these fabulous herds of fur seals were.

When all this material came back, we were in charge of looking it over and finding some kind of a documentary report on Alaska. This was in 1945, actually.

I think what Walt had in mind about a story in Alaska was that we would tell a story about the last frontier. In other words, here was a kind of romantic outpost of civilization, and we would kind of show the pioneer efforts. We covered that valley out of Anchorage, where the huge vegetables are grown: Matanuska Valley. You remember just prior to that there had been the colony of settlers. I guess it was in the late '30s that the colony of settlers had been sent up in the Roosevelt Administration. Here was a new part of our nation to be carved out of the wilderness and so forth.

The upshot was that the footage did not turn out to be as exciting as we hoped. For some reason the sawmills, the salmon canneries, the fisheries, didn't come up to our hopes. But there was this marvelous material on the fur seals, the vast herds of fur seals on the Pribiloff Islands. There we had a natural photographer's bonanza; heavens, the man just had to be on the island and to turn the camera on and get exciting material: the natural story, the mystery and the migration, the fact that they come up out of the sea and they breed on these beaches and then vanish into the sea. We had a natural, tailor-made tale to tell. So it was agreed that instead of a feature-length documentary, we would do a two-reel short subject, which we called *Seal Island*.

The curious sidelight to all that was the later success of these shows. I think we have to remember that we didn't have eight or ten True-Lifes at that point, we had just one. And we had just thought of this name, True-Life Adventure. This was Walt's selection. He thought that these stories, or this story, ought to be known as a true story.

He never liked the word "documentary" because of the sins that had been committed in its name. And that's why the Alaska thing didn't pay off: it was a little too nuts and bolts as we say; it was kind of mundane.

RH: Did Walt send the photographers back to do more shooting on *Seal Island*?

JA: No, they had covered it so thoroughly that we had what we needed. After which, the Milottes were sent out on an assignment to do *Beaver Valley*, then they did *Prowlers of the Everglades*. Then they were sent to Africa, and they were in the field for two years and three months with a studio-supplied Dodge Power Wagon. This was in 1954. We were making *African Lion*, and Walt turned to me one day and said, "Well, if you're going to write the narration for that thing, maybe you ought to get over there and see what it's like. Do you want to go?" And I said, "Try me," and off we went. He sent my wife with me and this was a great, grand gesture on Walt's part. It was sort of my "25-year pin", you might say.

RH: How long did you stay over there?

JA: About nine weeks. We were in Africa six weeks, and the other three weeks we were doing some PR work in Europe, because *Living Desert* was just then being released in London.

RH: How did the music come about—the musical accompaniment which provides an extra dimension to all these films?

JA: In the cartoon medium it's a simple enough matter: You write the music and you mathematically draw the drawings to match it. When we came on down to the True-Lifes, the music came afterward: you shot the footage first.

But then in the True-Life stories, whenever we saw a chance, we tried to take rhythmic natural action and edit it in such a fashion that a music score could accompany it and lend it the dimension you speak of. In *Water Birds*, the flight of the birds is set to the second *Hungarian Rhapsody*. In *Beaver Valley*, the croaking of the frogs had been set to the sextet from *Lucia*, as I remember.

In *Living Desert* we had the material of the scorpions in their little mating ritual where they walk back and forth and circle. And the more we looked at that, the more it obviously felt rhythmic and the more we saw the chance of creating something interesting. This is one time where we actually created the music, and we set it to a square-dance routine. Now people tend to marvel, "Gee, how do you get those animals to perform to music?" where in truth you get the musician to perform to the animals. It's not quite as mysterious as it might seem. Take something like bird flight: after all, you have marvelous natural rhythm just in the motion of wings to a certain beat. And the croaking frogs: we had some material of some frogs whose throats would balloon out and puff up and puff in, and puff up and puff in...

RH: What is your favorite True-Life Adventure?

JA: In terms of my own personal satisfaction and pleasure, I always enjoyed *The Vanishing Prairie*, for a couple of reasons. I'm a sort of westerner, a Californian by birth. I'm a western Americana history buff. I kind of savor the tale of the plains, the buffalo, and all that business.

During the making of *Vanishing Prairie*, I had a fun adventure. I went up on the Crow Indian agency in Montana and I got in on a buffalo hunt. I personally rather enjoyed the sort of re-creation that *Vanishing Prairie* was: the idea that it portrayed what the prairie once was. Later, when I went to Africa—this was one of the thrills—there in Africa was what the American plains were 100 years earlier with the vast herds of animals wandering around. In another generation they're going to be wiped out, as we wiped them out here.

Anyway, what with the buffalo and the bighorn sheep and the prairie dogs, we were into a set of creatures that I found most intriguing.

RH: Would Walt have the ideas for these films? Or would you present him with the ideas? Or would you send out crews with the expectation that they would bring back something?

JA: Well, a little of both ways. After *Seal Island*, it was Walt himself who came up with the idea to do a story on beavers. Now where he got the idea I really don't know, but it was he who said, "Why don't we do a thing on beavers?" When the Milottes were sent up into Yellowstone and Montana and Wyoming, they ran into a curious problem—a photographer's problem. They found that they were dealing with an animal who didn't come until after dark. This required a long period of patient preparation where Milotte would go and sit out by the beaver pond. By after dark, I mean 4:30 in the afternoon before the beavers start to come out. They're a twilight animal. They don't come out at noon, normally. Milotte managed to get them so accustomed to his being there that they didn't worry about him.

RH: What about *Living Desert*?

JA: *Living Desert* came about in this way. A young man from UCLA came in and showed us about 10 minutes of film that he had made as a thesis. Because it had to do with nature and we were then making nature stories, he brought it here. This was a boy named Paul Kenworthy. And this was one moment when Walt spotted a thing instantaneously; it sounded very exciting. Kenworthy's sequence was the story of the wasp and the tarantula. It was a very well-covered, very well-photographed, thorough-going account of how this wasp stings the tarantula to a state of paralysis and lays its eggs inside the body of the tarantula. The tarantula is in a state of preservation, and when the wasp's young hatch, they then feed on the tarantula and become new wasps and fly off. This was a little complete short story right out of nature, and the boy had done it well. And Walt said, "Let's get hold of this young man and set him up out there and see if we can't find out more such stories about the desert and build a thing about the desert." And this is what happened.

RH: And *Vanishing Prairie*?

JA: By *Vanishing Prairie* we had begun to realize that these stories seemed to work best if we could pick a large environment for them to happen in. The desert automatically created a setting and a cast of characters who lived in this situation. I can't recall quite who said, "Why don't we make one on the prairie?" I don't know that anyone did. We would bring these up, and we would kick them around with Walt and kind of investigate the possibilities. I think we had seen some rather exciting footage on some buffalo that we liked, and that got it started.

If you go across the board and review the features of the True-Life Adventures, you'll discover that we did the desert, we did the prairie, we did the Arctic, we did Africa, and we did the South American jungle. By that I mean this is the theatre, the arena in which the stories were told.

We attempted Australia, and we came up a cropper for a curious reason. Again the Milottes were sent to Australia. They actually stayed with these nature films for 10 or 15 years.

RH: How many crews did you have at any one time?

JA: I would say that half a dozen was the general

RH: What would they consist of: a husband and wife, usually?

JA: Often it was a husband-and-wife team. We had Herb Crisler and his wife, who went up into Alaska to do the *White Wilderness* story. Al Milotte and his wife used to travel as a team. We have also used men like Kenworthy, Jack Couffer, Hank Schlass, and Chuck Draper, who didn't normally take their wives out.

The secret to the whole thing is to go into the field. One of the reasons for going with 16mm is the fact that you can shoot so much more footage and bear the expense. This 16 equipment is lightweight, portable. You can get into some rough situations. But since it is to be a time-element program, testing the cameraman's patience, as well as your budget, you can afford to float him out there in the field for seven months if the crew is small and kept small. The crew is generally composed of a cameraman, a director, a production man or two, and some help with animals, if it's a story where animals need to be worked in a compound.

RH: Did you have any failures, or things that Walt turned down out of hand?

JA: Australia. The attempt to do a feature True-Life on Australia failed in that the material that came home didn't seem strong enough to hold for feature length. Walt agreed with this and recognized it... Actually what happened, I realized afterwards, was that we had all read about Australia and all these amazing biological specimens that are there: duckbill platypus and the koala bear and the spiny anteater and the wild dog that's called the dingo, and so on and so on. Australia is a curiosity among continents because it's cut off in just such a fashion that all this life there is peculiar to Australia. But what happened was that when Milotte started to shoot these animals, nothing much happened. We didn't get any action or excitement, or "business" as we call it. We didn't get any dramatic conflict to speak of, and the reason was this: item one, most of the creatures are rather tiny, nocturnal, and rather furtive and shy, and don't do much. And then Australia is a cutoff continent without any of the large-scale predators. You don't have any of the lion family, or the tigers or mountain lion, or the bobcat or the lynx, or any of those heavies that give us menace in other shows. Yes, you do have the wild dog, which will prey on other creatures, and you have something called the Tasmanian Devil, whose name is more impressive than he is. So anyway, the upshot was that Walt was a great one never to give up on a thing just because it didn't come off as a feature. We could fall back and make a couple of short subjects of it, which we did.

RH: Was Walt always looking for story, even in True-Life, or did he simply attempt to put together interesting sequences?

JA: He was always looking for the story, the actual, factual story. You might say the prescribed story in all of the True-Lifes is the story of survival. And the interesting way that can get told is to watch how different creatures solve that story and problem. How they protect themselves, how they raise their young, what they eat, who their enemies are, and how they escape them. This was the story that Walt always searched out and was interested in, and was the one he felt the audience could be interested in.

RH: Could you do one on man? The survival of man?

JA: We could. But Walt was not too interested in a story about primitive man. He was fascinated with animals. For example, before we sent the Milottes down to Australia... We often would meet very interesting people who had very interesting film. Occasionally, we would pick up things by purchasing film from them. And a man came in with a very good film on the Australian aborigines, who are the most primitive people on earth. As I remember, they have spears and they have fire, but that's about it. They don't grow crops and they don't build buildings and they don't possess any animals. And they eat hand to mouth, and they eat such species as an ant that fills itself with sugar and gets as big as a grape. But Walt's response in that case was that they were not appealing enough to tell a story about. He had rather uncanny instincts about audiences. Intellectually, they would be fascinating, but emotionally there wasn't much there to tell a tale about. I'm filling in a little of some of my own surmise here, but I think this is perhaps Walt's way of thinking. Walt was never particularly intrigued with film on the African tribes like the pygmies, for example. They didn't particularly entice him.

RH: Did you go down the Colorado?

JA: Yes.

RH: Why didn't that picture come off? It seems to me that that would have been an exciting picture.

JA: It was, in its best parts. As you know, this was the reenactment of the Major Powell journey down the Colorado from 1869 to 1871. Again we went to tremendous effort to give it authentic flavor, even to going down the river ourselves, and this was at Walt's insistence that we not do it on a soundstage. We really got out there and shot the Grand Canyon and the rapids in the Colorado River, and it became a terrific problem in production. That is, the very logistics of the thing... The journey down the river was made first with a very small second unit, and I got to go on it. It was a very exciting adventure, I have to say. We got some quite impressive footage of actually going through the rapids. Later we came back and took the so-called first company with the actors, and we did the dialogue and then dramatized the bits and the campsites and so forth up near Moab, which is still near the river but not literally in the Grand Canyon. But it's the same kind of country and it all blended in perfectly.

I think the Powell show suffered a little for an audience. It was called *Ten Who Dared*, and it was about ten men and four boats attempting a very big adventure. But, for one thing, it wasn't a woman's picture. There were no women in it to make it a man's picture, on that score. And possibly the energy we put in to make it authentic and proving we were there even gave it a kind of documentary cast that maybe took a little of the romance off.

I think Walt looked on the Powell story as a show that had certain values, that if we could bring them off, might make it a little different from something else. He sort of personally relished the flavor of adventure that it had: The sense of bucking the unknown and conquering the impossible and climbing the mountain. I believe he hoped for gripping conflict out of the clash of personalities that cropped up as the script unfolded. But I think one thing that he would have agreed didn't come off as well as we hoped was the very fact that in dealing with ten different personalities in a feature and in trying to make each figure in the story have his moment and come through as a characterization, the story tended to take on a kind of diffused quality. You weren't really pulling for anybody. You were pulling for ten men when you were supposed to be zeroed in on Powell emotionally.

RH: Did Walt always go for the identification to the good guy and the conflict with the bad guy?

JA: Yes. A show, for Walt, was successful if he could get wrapped up in it, get caught up with it. I do remember one line he actually said. We made a True-Life story called *The Legend of Lobo*. It was based on the old Ernest Thompson Seton story. We showed the first half of the story to Walt one day. We did have some marvelous family footage on wolves and some cute action on the wolf pups. We had found out that the wolf is a very devoted provider and father to his litter and that he defends them and protects them. A wolf father is a much better father than a bear father who will actually kill his off-spring if he can get at them, has to be kept apart, and so forth.

We got about half way through this thing and we hadn't got any ending yet. Walt turned around and said, "If you kill this wolf off, I'll never forgive you." I do remember he said literally that.

Now in the Seton story the wolf does die; in our show he does not. In our show, he bundles up his family and goes off over the hill in a very beautiful shot.

RH: Did you ever do one on the coyote? How did Walt feel about those?

JA: Yes, we did. I think he liked them because I think he rather admired the coyote. In other words, Walt was always on the side of the creature who was doing something for himself and was fending off whatever was threatening him and outsmarting enemies. The coyote is a very intelligent animal, capable of pulling tricks on people, and I think Walt always admired that in a creature, because I think he kind of read himself into it. That's what he would have done if he were a coyote.

RH: Did you have advisors on these pictures?

JA: Oh, yes. When necessary I did an awful lot of the reading and the research for the early True-Lifes, but we would call in people like Ken Stager, from the L.A. County Museum, or the head of the zoo over here, or the San Diego Zoo.

When I was in Africa, I had an interview with Colonel Stephenson Hamilton, who was then still alive, and who had been the founder and the first warden of Kruger Park. I also met Merwin Cowie, who was head of the national parks in Kenya. And we went to Conrad Wirth, who was then head of the national park system.

RH: Did you use people like Frank Dobie?

JA: We used his book and we read his works, like his marvelous book on coyotes. I also heard him speak once at a Westerners group, but I don't remember that we ever talked to him personally.

RH: Did Walt ever add his own things or ask for sequences that were not faked, but staged?

JA: In the True-Life beginning, one of the things Walt did insist on was that there never be a script sent into the field with the cameraman. The cameraman was to go into the field, and he was to sit out there and get close to the animals and watch them and shoot and shoot and shoot and record what they did, and get on film everything he could possibly get. Then, out of that would emerge the story. Walt had a very sharp and good reason for refusing the scripts. As he put it, "If we give that cameraman a script, he will be so close to it and have his nose so deep in it, trying to shoot what we've written on the typewriter, that he will be missing all these marvelous happy accidentals that were going on all around him." And in truth, Walt was correct. Furthermore, we found more and more that there's an awful lot of nature lore that gets preserved in books and in print that scholars themselves tend to preserve even though it's false. In other words, they read each other's books and they digest each other's reports.

This is what lifted the True-Lifes out of the rut over most previous animal stories: these moments of tremendous, amazing accidents. Like when Milotte in Africa caught the leopard up in a tree and the herd of wildebeest came down under the tree and the leopard dropped onto one of the calves, and the great hubbub and turmoil and chase around in the dust... When it cleared you found he had caught it. That was the real thing and as much as it might hurt to watch the calf lose its life, you realized this is the way nature was. This was literally true.

Now there has been a little transition go on as we've entered the TV era. A couple of things happened with the television nature shows. In the first place, you can't afford to let the cameraman sit out there for a year and a half. The budget won't permit it. So we try to shoot the material for a television show within the span of, say, a summer—a shorter period of time. But since it is shorter you have to be a little better organized, and since the stories have gone over into more of a fictional handling, what we've done is to come away from a generalization about a species, and we now pick up a specific animal that we give a name to and we involve him with people. And we got into scripted adventures.

RH: A television show, like say *A Day at Beetle Rock*: is this not just done by shooting?

JA: *Beetle Rock*, curiously, is more nearly a hark-back to the True-Life Adventures, where the camera was an observer. But, for example, I made a television show a while back called *The Coyote Who Wasn't*, and the premise was that an old Navajo Indian found an orphan baby coyote, raised it, and trained it to be his sheep dog. We actually were lucky enough to get a coyote who learned to work sheep and this was the whole twist of the thing. We didn't force it, we didn't fake it. The coyote did actually learn the signals and did learn to keep the sheep in line. There was one marvelous moment when the coyote went way out and picked up a single ewe and chivvied the animal clean back into the herd just like a sheep dog.

One of my best animal stories was *Incredible Journey*, about five years ago. It was the story of two dogs and a Siamese cat that make a journey across Canada trying to get home.

RH: Walt said something about it on a Canadian broadcast, I recall.

JA: Walt loved the animal action. It was some of the best we ever brought off. Walt's whole summary about *Incredible Journey* was that he loved the animals, but he didn't care for the people. Now this comes back to a side of his nature. I think, in truth, Walt did love animals, but didn't care too much for people. You know what I mean? He always felt that the director Fletcher Markle didn't get a good performance out of the people. I don't think that was true, though Walt said it was. At the same time, he was correct in that the appeal of this story is in the animal action.

RH: What was the story about Lincoln?

JA: The Lincoln figure was the most sophisticated audio-animatronic we had ever attempted. As the deadline approached for the New York World's Fair, we were rehearsing this Lincoln thing down here on the sound stage, and there were electronic bugs cropping up in it. Even the sound engineers and the sound experts were into areas that had never been attempted. We were daring the equipment to do more than it had ever been designed for. We were putting, as I remember, fourteen overlapped channels on a piece of tape that were bleeding through and sending signals across. And Lincoln would shudder and his eyes would go back and forth as though the sheriff was right behind him. It was the most nerve-wracking period I have ever spent. It got down to about two weeks before Fair time. Walt had to go on back because the other shows were being opened, and he would be on the phone every night to find out how we were doing. We were holding out until two in the morning. What was so staggering was we couldn't get our finger on the problem. Fuses would blow out and wires would get crossed, and the character would do the wrong thing at the wrong moment, and finally one night when all this happened, Marc [Davis] turned to me and said, "Do you suppose God is mad at Walt for creating man in his own image?"

© 2007 Jane Hubler

Winston Hibler (1910–1976)

Interviewed by Richard Hubler on April 30 and May 7, 1968.

Winston Hibler, "Hib" as he was known at the Disney Studio, is probably best known as the voice narrating the *True-Life Adventure* and *People and Places* series. His contribution to Disney goes well beyond his voice, though: he also served as a writer, director, lyricist, and actor, and influenced quite a few of the live-action projects produced in the '40s, '50s, and '60s at the studio.

Born in Harrisburg, Pennsylvania, on October 8, 1910, Winston was the son of Louise and Christopher Hibler. The youngest of four children, Hibler was the only one to go into show business.

He planned from the time he was 12 to seek his fortune in the theater and admitted that he might have been influenced by his mother, a concert singer of some note in Philadelphia, and his maternal grandfather, Elias Whitehail Eisenbeis, a Yankee captain in the Civil War and owner of a showboat that traveled the canals of Pennsylvania. Young Hibler was gripped by the desire to act, though he worked for a while at a packing house and held a clerk's job in the state capitol building during and immediately following high school.

In 1930, he graduated from the American Academy of Dramatic Arts in New York. That same year he married Dorothy Johnson in Greenwich, Connecticut. He spent most of the following year performing on Broadway and in summer stock in Massachusetts and Pennsylvania. A year later, he moved to Hollywood to pursue a motion-picture career. He drove out to Los Angeles in a Chevy roadster, lured by a promise of a job from a New York director who was working at Paramount. When he arrived, he found out that his sponsor had not had his option picked up and was heading back to New York. The young couple could not afford to go back and decided to stay.

Hibler's landlady, Mrs. Norton, was Darryl Zanuck's mother. She introduced him at Warner Brothers, where he made contacts and got some acting calls. His wife became a skater with Sonja Henie and appeared in several movies. She later toured with the St. Moritz Express, a road show on ice.

Hibler kept acting through the thirties and, to supplement his income, started writing freelance articles for magazines and radio in 1938. In 1940, he founded the Hollywood Academy of Dramatic Arts and served as its owner/director for two years.

In 1942, he joined The Walt Disney Studios as a camera operator, and soon began writing and directing armed services training films that were being produced by Disney during World War II.

His first pure entertainment work was writing the "Johnny Appleseed" segment of *Melody Time*. Walt took notice of his talents and assigned him to work on the stories of such animated features as *The Adventures of Ichabod and Mr. Toad*, *Alice in Wonderland*, and *Cinderella*.

Along with his writing partner Ted Sears, Hibler also composed lyrics for Disney songs, including "Following the Leader" from *Peter Pan* and "I Wonder" from *Sleeping Beauty*.

In 1946, when the studio began producing nature films, Walt cast Hibler as narrator of *Seal Island*, after having heard his voice in the test recording that had been created by Hibler to check story continuity. Hibler then went on to write and narrate other True-Life Adventures, including *The Vanishing Prairie* and *The Living Desert*, among many others. He also narrated Disney's People and Places travelogue series.

He combined his talent for writing, narrating, and directing on *Men Against the Arctic*, which, like *Seal Island*, won an Academy Award, as well as *Operation Undersea*, which won an Emmy in 1955. In total, Winston Hibler shared credit in nine Academy Awards and an Emmy. Among his other credits, Hibler co-produced such films as *Perri*, *Those Calloways*, *The Ugly Dachshund*, *Follow Me, Boys!*, and *The Island at the Top of the World*, as well as numerous shows for the *Disneyland* television series.

Winston Hibler died on August 8, 1976, in Los Angeles.

Richard Hubler: When did you start at the studio?

Winston Hibler: In 1942. I started in the camera department as a cartoon camera operator. After that, I became a "technical director" on the war films. I also worked on educational films: pilot-training films, Norden bomb-sight film, etc.

RH: What did you do before?

WH: My background was always in the theatre, Broadway. I was an actor and a writer. At the start of the war I was working at Lockheed. A friend of mine worked here and suggested I come here for an interview.

RH: What kind of writing did you do before Disney?

WH: Magazine stories, radio scripts.

RH: How did you get into film work?

WH: I submitted rewrites on technical stories such as the training films.

RH: What was your first entertainment film?

WH: *Johnny Appleseed*.

RH: When was the first time you met Walt?

WH: I passed him in the halls and I was always in great awe. I think the first time we actually met was in test camera. Walt would come around and greet everybody: "Hi, how's everybody doing in here?" And then he would look at what you were doing. Walt would always recognize the new guys and would comment, "You're new here." The next time he would call you by name.

RH: How did Walt dress?

WH: Very casual: sports jackets and sweaters. [Here Winston Hibler brought up a booklet called *The Ropes at Disney*, a brochure he wrote with Hal Adelquist in 1943. The booklet starts: "This is a slacks and "no tie" place..."]

RH: You did the narration on the *True-Life Adentures*, all of them?

WH: Yes, all of the original series through *Jungle Cat*. I was working on cartoon features stories when Walt came upon the True-Life idea.

RH: How did you become the voice?

WH: Somebody suggested I make a temporary narration track because I used to be an actor and Walt saw the *Seal Island* footage with my voice. Later we recorded a professional commentator, but Walt apparently liked my voice better.

RH: Do you remember your first conference with Walt?

WH: I went into his office with Ben Sharpsteen. I think we were preparing an approach for a project with Ford. I was awed to be in Walt's presence. But I was young and brave: I said what I thought, which was a wise move. Walt could always tell in a moment if you were telling him only what he wanted to hear.

RH: Did anyone try to "con" Walt?

WH: Oh, sure! You had to prove yourself with Walt. With a new writer Walt always tried to find out if he was leveling or was putting him on.

RH: What was Ben's role?

WH: A producer with a fine record in cartoon feature work. When I first worked with him he headed up industrial-type films, then more cartoon features like *Johnny Appleseed* and *Pecos Bill*. He broke me in.

RH: What kind of guy was Ben?

WH: He was very tough, a strict disciplinarian, but I liked him very much. He taught me a great deal.

RH: How did you react when Walt changed your ideas?

WH: Well, you took the things that Walt said and you found something in them that inspired you.

It was best to listen and not take notes with Walt. Walt with very few words could project creative thoughts and ideas that inspired people to create better. Walt in a single hour could transmit more ideas to a writer than I can in a whole day.

RH: What was the length of a conference with Walt?

WH: Usually a half hour. An hour was a long time. Walt was always apprehensive that he would lose his perspective by getting too close to something. Once in a while he would hand you a page of yellow paper and say, "I think it should go something like this."

RH: An example?

WH: *Calloways*. Walt would change something he thought was wrong no matter what the cost or time factor involved. For *Calloways* we had started production. All the schedules were set. We presented Walt a final shooting script: it only had a few stage directions changed from the previous script. The first day of shooting, we were on the set and Walt came over and said, "I like the script very much. There's only one thing: you can't kill Cam." I nearly fainted. That meant changing the whole ending of the show: about ten pages. I gulped and said, "Walt, I don't have an answer." Walt said, "I know you don't, but I have a couple of ideas." So I went over them with him and in three days Lou Pelletier, the writer, and I had a new treatment.

RH: How did Walt criticize?

WH: He never gave a negative criticism without a positive solution, or if he couldn't find a solution he would say, "This isn't working for me," and drop the project. Or he would say, "There's lots of stuff I don't like in this," and you would get a script back with blue slashes and checks that only Walt could interpret. He would go over the script with you. Often he would reminisce about a script, finding something in it from his own life.

RH: Did you argue with Walt?

WH: If I believed in something, I would argue. Maybe twice I would try to bull it through. Then I would do it his way. Try to develop and add my own creativity to the image he was projecting. For example, if he suggested a segment I didn't think would work, I would voice my criticism. Sometimes he would see my argument, but if he didn't, then I would try to develop his idea as best I could. Then I would bring it back to him to see if it was working.

RH: Do you remember any wrangles?

WH: You didn't wrangle with Walt, ever. You could discuss or disagree with him.

[Hubler again presses the point about disagreements and Winston Hibler cites a problem with *The Ugly Dachshund* that had arisen in production after Walt had approved a shooting script.]

Walt said, "Look, I'm busy, are you producing this or aren't you?" Later that day, Walt called and asked what we were doing in the back lot. I said, "That's where the dog-show sequence is going to be shot." Walt said. "I think it should be shot inside," and mentioned the time of year, etc. So that's where we shot it.

On the first shooting day of the dog show, I was on the set and Walt came up, tapped me on the shoulder, and asked, "What's it doing out there?" Sure enough, it was raining. Walt just had a good common-sense judgment about everything in picture-making.

RH: Did you have anything to do with the first Christmas television show in 1950?

WH: Oh, yes. That was when the avalanche hit. I do remember that when this avalanche of work hit the studio, we augmented the staff by adding additional writers. We used our nature photographers, of course. We started moving them out on new projects.

How the Mickey Mouse show was tooled up is a whole Bill Walsh thing, but we had to get ourselves into high gear. From a program that would include maybe three, four, five features a year, plus a few nature pictures, plus whatever we were doing in cartoons, to the prospect of 26 shows a year.

RH: What did Walt say about that?

WH: We never sat down and discussed it. He never said, "C'mon boys, we gotta have a team effort here and get out that work." Assignments were passed out. All of us began to "double" in positions we had never been in before. For instance, a group of us immediately entered the Directors Guild so that we would be in a position to direct our own television shows, which would include our lead-ins and anything else we were doing on the sound stage.

RH: Did Walt just say, "This is it," in essence, or did he come down and talk with you about problems?

WH: Oh no. We would talk about certain shows, but he would talk more organizationally with guys like Bill Anderson and whoever was the team that was shaping up the program for that year and years to come. I was not part of that team.

But I was pulled in on specific projects. At that time, actually, I wasn't a producer. I was writing and doing dialogue direction and story work on cartoon features, as well as working on the nature shows. When we moved into television, I produced some of the nature shows, as well as writing and directing some of them. In our all-out effort everybody spread out, took their assignments, and attacked the problems.

I can't remember really what I attacked first. I know that in those early days we made a lot of documentary films, which made us a good number of programs. For example, the Geophysical Year in Antarctica: We got at least three shows out of it.

RH: What was Walt's interest in the Geophysical Year Show?

WH: Walt was steering and guiding this whole deal. He was in on everything. He shaped the shows, picked the shows, aimed everybody at a project.

RH: Did Walt ever disagree with you?

WH: Oh yes. In the casting of the Indian in *Nikki*, he wanted an Indian for a role, a real Indian. I went to Canada and came back and said, "Walt, I just can't find an Indian who is a competent actor." Walt said, "Oh, Hib, lots of times somebody tells me they can't do something and it just isn't there. But," he said, "it's there. Why don't you go back and find the Indian?"

So I had interviews with Mohawks, Sioux, etc. No one was right. I found one man who belonged to a tribe that I had never heard of, but was common to Canada, I guess. He was a Montagne. And then I found a middle-European, who was not an Indian but had classic Indian features. I brought these two screen tests out and showed him the first one, who was not a good performer but was an Indian. And Walt said, "He's not an Indian," and I said, "Yes, he is. He belongs to the Montagne Tribe." Walt said he had never heard of the Montagne Tribe. The next guy came on and he said, "Now there's an Indian!" I didn't know whether to say he is not an Indian, but I said, "Walt, he is really not an Indian." Walt said he looked like one and I told him he was middle-European, that he might have some East Indian in him. Walt said he was an Indian and would be good for the part.

So we used him and he was good for the part. Damn good.

RH: Do you have any other stories like that that you can tell about? How about scripts?

WH: We were casting for *Alice in Wonderland* and for a long time we had been trying to get Margaret O'Brien. Walt was very high on her, but we had real trouble making arrangements. She was either committed or she was somewhere else. Meantime we had been auditioning girls and came up with Kathy Beaumont, who eventually played it, and Walt liked her very much. While we were playing the audition, Hal Adelquist, who was running animation in terms of management at that time, said to Walt, "You know Margaret O'Brien is available right now." Walt said, "No, she's in England." Hal said that her agent had called him and that she was back in New York now. Walt is listening to little Kathy, you see, and he looked at Hal and said (with emphasis), "She's in England, Hal." So we got the message and we cast Kathy Beaumont.

RH: Did he ever have a lot to do with scripting, in the sense of "over your dead body"?

WH: Not in this way. Walt couldn't and didn't want to work with a "no" man, a negative man. I don't mean he wanted a "yes" man. He just wanted to get a point over to the producer, the writer, whoever, and then he wanted that person to work with him. You knew he wasn't going to lay all of the bricks and spell it all out right there in one meeting, but he had an idea he wanted to communicate to you.

What he wanted you to do was (with emphasis) get on the train with him! Not make a snap judgment on what was going to work. When you kept working against him, when he was knocking himself out trying to be helpful, he just got upset and angry, and if you kept it up he would just stop the project. And that would be the end of it.

It wasn't a question ever of him saying, "This is the way I want to do it." At least I don't remember that, but he could impress that on you in other ways. What he was really saying was, "Now I'm convinced I have the right way to go; now you find the way to make this work."

RH: Would he delay working on a script until his mind was jelled and he had a complete concept?

WH: No, he would toss ideas around with you. Make snap judgments and toss them out. Sometimes he would get enthused in his office and get up and act out a line or two. He might cast it out, and then say, "No, this isn't working." Or if he was sure of a line, and you brought it back to him the next day and he was wrong, he would say so.

RH: What was the toughest script, one you fought with a long time?

WH: They were all tough. But some were tougher. The toughest one I ever had to make was *Follow Me, Boys*. That script was in work over a year and *Horse in the Grey Flannel Suit*, too, was in work for a long, long time.

Walt wasn't in on the final stages of that. He had died before we got to the final stages. He had seen only the story outline and had approved it, and we were about a third of the way through the screenplay when he died.

RH: What about *Follow Me, Boys*?

WH: Walt had a big part in that story. He liked it because it was that small-town America that he loved so much.

RH: What would he say?

WH: The "letter from Whitey" sequence, for example: Whitey was the adopted boy in the family, and Walt began to reminisce and he said, "You know, you never know how much you mean to your children and how they feel toward you until they go away. I remember when Diane went away." (I guess it was to college.) She wrote a letter to Walt and Mrs. Disney and expressed, apparently in an appealing and emotional way, how much they both really meant to her. Walt never forgot this and it touched him very deeply.

He said, "When Whitey goes to Europe, why don't we have Cam and Vera Miles get a letter from Whitey?" That in effect expresses that same feeling. So that was the thing we put in the show.

Many times in creating this kind of script, if things were close to events that had happened in Walt's life, they would find their way into the script, because he knew them so well and these were the things he loved so much. They were very warm, touching things.

RH: What were the other films you worked on?

WH: *Big Red, Nikki*. Here's another example of a complete change in an approach which changed a whole picture. In telling the story of Nikki, in the wilderness section where there is just narration and it is telling the story of how they survived in the wilderness, Nikki, the dog, is out on his own and surviving by hunting and looking for food. I wrote the narration, and wrote it in a rather grim battle-for-survival way. "He stalked an elk," and so forth. Walt said, "This is too grim, and really that's not what is on the screen. It's not the film you have. This can be funny."

It was all done, polished and complete, but he said, "Take another shot at this thing, at this particular section, and approach it with a humorous narration." And we did. There was no killing in it. But Nikki did attack a bull elk. Nikki took a dive for him and the elk side-stepped and picked him up on his horns and tossed him into a snow bank. And it was humorous fashion. We explained in narration that he picked on something too big. He should try for something smaller. So he tries for a rabbit and it eludes him, and then he tries for a mouse in the snow and we had a funny scene where he can't touch the damn mouse. It keeps burrowing under the snow and comes up under his stomach and so forth. So in the battle for survival he never is catching anything, and it became very funny. We simply stated that Nikki did learn to hunt and survived on small game. So here was a section that began "downbeat", but by Walt's changes became "upbeat" and much warmer and much more interesting.

Conversely, in writing narration of the early nature films, we talked down to the animals and made wisecracks and treated them like puppets. This annoyed Walt very much. "Dammit, nature facts are interesting. I want to know the name of that animal. I want to know why he burrows a hole in the ground. I want to know the nature facts. You tell the facts and put your funny stuff in later." We have stuck by that ever since. We do put funnies in it, but the story goes through first.

I think the greatest accumulation of footage we ever had was on *Perri*. We had something over a million feet of film. I don't know if it was 16 or 16 blown into 35mm, but it was a million feet. We figured that if we sat in the projection room 24 hours a day, it would take 7 days to run all that film.

Much of *Perri* was filmed in nature, but we did keep some squirrels to photograph in controlled scenes. During the two years it took to complete the project, I have no doubt that some of these squirrels died, but this was certainly not due to a lack of proper care and feeding.

The truth is, our nature photographers are devoted to the animals with which they work. Whenever the animals are controlled or contained, there is always a vet available. Indeed many of our wildlife people have become vets in their own right. For example, when we were working with controlled eagles, for *Ida, the Off-Beat Eagle*, a blight spread through the wild eagles along the Snake River and somehow contaminated our own flock. We were able to develop methods and medicines to treat and cure the disease. The government people came to us for help and our nature photographers made a sizeable contribution to saving the wild eagles in that particular area.

RH: How much attention was Walt paying to television at the end? Was he satisfied that it was a going concern and needed minimum attention?

WH: Walt never was satisfied that anything was taking care of itself and he wouldn't have to worry about it. As his interest grew in Disneyland and Disney World, he leaned more and more on us, as he felt he should. He wanted us to "steer our own ships".

And when he built the producers group he told us very plainly that we were supposed to be producing our own pictures and not running to him with problems. In fact, that's another one of his quotes, "Bring me pictures, not problems."

He always said "Don't bring me any story (in other words, a producer working with a writer) that you don't believe in yourself."

RH: Did you ever have borderline cases that you brought to him?

WH: Oh, yes, sure.

RH: What would be an example?

WH: I suppose the key reason [for bringing Walt borderline stories] would be I felt there was something in it—this was a good story for us—but perhaps I hadn't been able to get it out and I wasn't satisfied with it and I brought it to him hoping that he would find that missing ingredient and make it jell.

Now you're going to say, "What did that happen on?" I would say it happened on *Calloways*. His answer to that was very simple. I had taken the book, which I liked very much and I wanted to produce it. But, with the writer, we had strayed rather far from the book, contriving and constructing the plot, changing the progress of action, etc., and we brought this to Walt. I wasn't that sure of it. It was at attempt, an approach, a treatment. He said, "You're way off base. I don't see this at all. It's forced and contrived. You've got a book. Why not make the book?" And we pretty darn near did. This was the same picture I told you about in which he changed the ending at the last moment on the stage. For the most part, that was the only major change from the book, except for Lou Pelletier's beautiful dialogue.

RH: Did you ever have a property that you felt enthusiastic about, but Walt turned down?

WH: Yes. I was enthusiastic about a couple of Audubon scripts I did. He was never satisfied with them.

RH: That seems to be an appropriate subject.

WH: Walt felt we never found the answer to it. I tried in live action; I tried to do it in cartoon. Yes, you would certainly think it would be appropriate, but he was never satisfied with it and I never knew the reasons why. We had a couple of good scripts. I think he probably felt that they were too contrived.

RH: Were you going from the naturalist standpoint?

WH: Yes. We tried to make a real screenplay, a feature. Actually, it was constructed for television, but we had approached it on a feature-treatment basis: The story of his life fictionalized and made into a sort of adventure story. Because he [Audubon] was a remarkable man: a master fencer, he played violin, was once a swimming teacher. His life was multi-faceted. You would certainly think here is a great character.

RH: Now Walt would turn it down and say, "Don't do it." Would he say, "Put it on the shelf and we'll try it again"?

WH: He would say, "Let's let it rest for a while." We couldn't think of the answer, so he would say, "We're a little worn out on this. Let's let it rest a while."

RH: Would he ever discard it?

WH: Forever?

RH: Yes.

WH: No. He would never say, "Forget this thing and throw it in the ash can." We might attack it at a later date. In fact, we did attack it at a later date.

RH: Was there any film that he rested for one year, two, three, five years?

WH: Lots of the cartoon features.

RH: I meant in live action.

WH: Yes. I'm trying to think of the one that we rested and brought to life and proved successful later. One that we have done many treatments on, many approaches, and still haven't produced is *Woodcutter's House*. That's been tried by I don't know how many writers, but always turned down. I still would like to do it.

RH: Would Walt ever give a reason why?

WH: Yes. Sometimes he would just become baffled himself and say, "I'm worn out. We're not making this. Let it rest for a while." Sometimes, "If we could get an ending on this thing we could bring it off." That doesn't mean you would give up right away. You would work your head off for weeks or months. It was when he felt he had put as much time, money, and effort into it as he wanted to at that time that he could cut it off.

RH: Walt had a sort of unconscious kind of humor and an unconscious kind of wit. I'm anxious to get samples of this. Is there anything he said that particularly sticks in your mind?

WH: I know there are a lot of inside jokes.

RH: Tell me a few.

WH: One of our writers, Dick Huemer, who is still here... Dick was in one of these story rooms. It was early in the morning. He had just come in and had his electric shaver and was giving himself a shave in front of this little hand mirror, when the door opened and Walt walked in. Dick takes the razor and put it in his pocket and couldn't get it shut off. Walt started to talk and stopped a moment and said, "Make my milkshake vanilla, and then shut that thing off."[1]

---

[1] Here is how Dick Huemer remembered the story in his interview with Richard Hubler on February 27, 1968: "One of the famous stories of the studio is about me using one of the first electric razors. Walt was supposed to have come in, and I put the shaver, still buzzing, in my pocket. That didn't really happen. He did walk past the office while I was using the shaver, however, and he came in. He wanted to know what it was. `Sounds like somebody making malted milk in here,' he said." In the same interview, which only contains this other interesting anecdote, Huemer also recalled: "Walt never wanted his men to grind or to be chained to their desks. Some of the men would be lolling around and would jump back to their desks when Walt came in. Walt got mad. "I don't care if you're stalling. Everybody gets tired. Get some fresh air and you'll feel better. But don't let me catch you jumping back to your desks."

Harry Reeves and Homer Brightman had presented their storyboard to Walt, and Walt had cut them up pretty good and didn't like them at all. These guys had spent a lot of time on it (like we all did) and Walt turned and stalked out into the hall, and as he started down the hall, Harry said, "Godammit," and took a kick at the storyboard and drove his foot right through the beaver board. He had got it in up to here [indicating about halfway up his ankle] when Walt had another idea and came back and Harry is hanging there with his foot halfway through the storyboard.

Nothing was said. Walt knew exactly what had happened, of course. Walt was in hysterics. He just busted up laughing and turned around and walked down the hall.

© 2007 Jane Hubler

Bill Anderson (1911–1997)

Interviewed by Richard Hubler on April 9, 1968.

One of Disney's most prolific film and television producers, Bill Anderson was without a doubt part of Walt's later inner circle.

A native of Smithfield, Utah, born October 12, 1911, Bill followed his boyhood dream to become an actor, arriving in Los Angeles in 1929. During the Depression, he obtained minor roles on local radio stations and went to work for an auto financing subsidiary of Ford, where he rose to regional sales manager.

Casting calls weren't steady, though, so he landed a job at Firestone Rubber Company and used his small salary to enroll in pre-law at Compton Junior College and later the University of Southern California.

In 1943, in the midst of World War II, Bill was hired by Disney when the studio's artistic community was dedicated to producing training films for the U.S. Armed Forces. He started in the studio's production control department, then was tapped to oversee the reorganization and expansion of feature animation's ink and paint department, which subsequently led Bill to a position as assistant to the studio's production manager.

By 1951, Bill was named production manager for the studio and, five years later, vice president in charge of studio operations. After the death of Walt Disney in 1966, he was selected to be part of a small group of producers who would guide studio motion picture production over the next decade. From 1960 to 1984 Anderson also served on Disney's board of directors.

Among film and television contributions, Bill served as associate producer of the Disney live-action classic *Old Yeller* in 1957 and went on to produce other memorable motion pictures, including *Third Man on the Mountain* (1959), *Swiss Family Robinson* (1960), *The One and Only, Genuine, Original Family Band* (1968), *The Computer Wore Tennis Shoes* (1969), *The Barefoot Executive* (1971), *The $1,000,000 Duck* (1971), *The Apple Dumpling Gang* (1975), *The Shaggy D.A.* (1976), and *The Treasure of Matecumbe* (1976).

For the small screen, Bill produced 58 episodes of *Zorro* during the late 1950s, as well as popular programs for *The Wonderful World of Disney*, including *The Swamp Fox* series (1959–60), *Texas John Slaughter* (1959), and *The Scarecrow of Romney Marsh* (1964). His feature film co-producing credits include *Moon Pilot* (1962), *Savage Sam* (1963), *The Fighting Prince of Donegal* (1966), and *The Happiest Millionaire* (1967).

Bill Anderson died December 28, 1997, in San Francisco, California.

Richard Hubler: Why did Walt start doing live action?

Bill Anderson: The cost of animation kept growing [because of] the length of time it took to produce an animated feature. Live action also broadened Walt's scope, and the kind of stories he wanted to do. He could invest less money and make more tales.

RH: What about the money tied up in England?

BA: Walt used Disney dollars and RKO dollars tied up in England (to do *Treasure Island*, *Sword and the Rose*, etc.). It was 50-50 on costs and profits. RKO said, "You make the pictures you want to make, Walt."

RH: What about *Sword and the Rose*?

BA: Walt always said we didn't make the right kind of picture—we started with the wrong story. Walt was more interested in adventure, not in love stories. *Sword and the Rose* didn't quite come off; it was an Errol Flynn type and we didn't have Errol Flynn.

RH: Wasn't *Parent Trap* a love story?

BA: Not really a love story. It was a family story. There has been romance in our pictures, but all incidental.

RH: Why did Walt use animation in *So Dear to My Heart*?

BA: First, it was expected of him. Second, he felt he could give it more nostalgia, more basic appeal.

RH: Did RKO insist on it?

BA: No, but the critics asked, "Why not stick to animation?"

RH: Did Walt have any qualms in going into live action?

BA: Not qualms, but he sought opinions and information on where he was going. Often peoples' reactions touched something off in Walt.

RH: For example?

BA: In *Blackbeard's Ghost*, Walt knew he had an intriguing story. He was looking for the right person to play Blackbeard. Walt wouldn't let anyone *sell* him anything—he would pull away from you if you tried. We mentioned a lot of people, but Walt never bought them. Ustinov was mentioned, but Walt said no. Then one day at lunch, someone from the outside suggested Ustinov. It clicked with Walt.

RH: Was there a way to sell Walt?

BA: The most successful way was to think out an idea as well as you could, then give it to him without a high-powered pitch. A memo was the best way—a simple approach. Give him time to think about it then find an occasion to mention, "How about so and so?" Then you could explain your idea to him, and drop it if he didn't spark to it, once he had made up his mind.

RH: Any particular picture as an example?

BA: *Old Yeller*. That was my first picture as a producer. The story was serialized in *Colliers*. I thought it was a great story and called Walt. I said I had found an idea, a story about a family and a wonderful dog. I sent him the serialized version, but through some mix-up, he didn't read it all, and I didn't hear from him. Eventually, it turned out to be one of the most complete stories we ever bought, but Walt said he didn't see anything in it: "Wouldn't even make a good TV show." You couldn't fight with Walt, but you could disagree. Walt knew I was puzzled by his reaction. One Sunday morning about 8 or 8:30 I got a call at home. Walt had read the story and was so enthusiastic about it he wanted to get started right away!

RH: What was the average cost of story material?

BA: It varied: As little as $5,000 to over $100,000.

RH: How did Walt express approval [about stories?]

BA: His general reaction was, "Yeah, this is something for us. We can have some fun with this."

RH: What was the ideal Disney story?

BA: Basically, a good situation or story, like *Old Yeller* or *Darn Cat*.

RH: That had the best planned chase sequence.

BA: Walt had a great facility for laying out a story so it was simple—no problem for people to understand. He could lay out a story so people didn't have to struggle to follow it.

RH: What about *20,000 Leagues*?

BA: Bill Walsh suggested it to Walt. It was a vague story. It was a great adventure, but an obscure story. Walt had to work like hell to get a story an audience could follow.

RH: And *Swiss Family Robinson*?

BA: I was interested in making it. But the book is not really a story; it's a series of events. It didn't add up to anything. Walt said, "If we don't whip this, we'll go to several segments on TV." So I re-read the story. In the beginning, there's a mention of pirates, but that's the last of them in the book. I suggested involving the pirates in the story, and called Walt. He said, "Sure, maybe that's the way to go." I suggested Lowell Hawley, and he came up with the storyline. The whole process involved months of effort.

RH: What did *Swiss Family Robinson* cost?

BA: Walt said we could have made it less expensively. He thought there was "too much scope". Everything was shot in Tobago. We played it for the big production values. Walt was always interested in the more personal vignettes.

RH: *The Shaggy Dog*?

BA: It was a short story by Felix Salten, based on an old tale from Italy about a man being changed into a dog. Bill Walsh developed the storyline. Walt wanted a family comedy for TV, but ABC didn't want it. Out of this mish-mash came *The Shaggy Dog*.

RH: What was the determining factor as to whether a story became a feature film or TV?

BA: With many things in the story stage, we didn't know which way to go. First, price was a factor. Walt was practical. If something was going to cost a lot, it had to be a theatrical. Second, the development of the story. Often Walt said, "Let's try it; we'll make up our minds later about where it goes."

RH: Before or after production began?

BA: Usually before production, but sometimes after.

RH: For *Treasure Island* the endings of the book and the film are different.

BA: That was Walt's decision.

RH: Why?

BA: That was Walt's approach. He never liked straight heavies or brutality. He felt heavies had greater audience identification if there was also a good side to the heavy.

RH: Walt never considered stories as sacrosanct?

BA: No. He felt he could change them.

RH: Where was *Treasure Island* shot?

BA: In England, at the old Denham Studios. They have old lagoons and an area that's very tropical. That's where Walt felt *Swiss Family Robinson* should have been shot.

RH: What about *Rob Roy*?

BA: It was the least successful of the four films we made in England because of the Scotch accent—we've always had trouble with the Scotch accent. Then, too, Cinemascope came out about then, and *Rob Roy* was a little-screen picture.

RH: Richard Todd?

BA: Walt liked his happy-go-lucky attitude, his natural look.

RH: Fred MacMurray?

BA: Fred MacMurray and Walt had a wonderful relationship. Walt thought he had a great sense of humor. For the kind of things we were doing, Fred was right. Only when he went straight character he didn't come off. Apparently, the public doesn't accept him that way.

RH: Who's to blame for *The Happiest Millionaire*?

BA: I guess I am as much as anyone. We lost the story idea. It ended up with a romance, the story of a boy and girl.

RH: *Family Band*?

BA: Walt liked the characters: the father and the relationship of the father and daughter.

RH: Was Walt sick at the time?

BA: Walt wasn't sick at the time of the story development. I guess we were all caught up in the success of *Mary Poppins*. We thought the music and dance would make it.

RH: How were the effects done in *Absent-Minded Professor*?

BA: Wires, pulleys, shock springs, etc. People say Walt was a perfectionist, but he would compromise. He just wanted it acceptable. He often said, "Don't redo, we're only going to use one foot of it."

RH: Can you describe the procedure involved while planning a picture?

BA: Live action never went to storyboard. There's a treatment first. Take *Old Yeller*. First, we brought in the author [Fred Gipson] to write the screenplay. He had worked with another writer, then we brought in a screenwriter to break down the script.

RH: How did the story evolve?

BA: Walt and I had blocked out the story in our minds…the things from the book we thought would make good visual treatment. The author came in and wanted to write the screenplay. Walt said, "No, let's get the story right. Let's get a treatment." Then we had meetings, discussions, and another treatment.

RH: When would you go to the screenplay?

BA: When the story was straight in Walt's mind.

RH: What were some of the elements?

BA: Fun, direct, simple to follow, no great character studies.

RH: What was the toughest story to lick?

BA: Walt spent the most time on *Mary Poppins*.

RH: How many treatments were necessary?

BA: A number; storyboards as well as treatments. It was going in three different directions at one time: Bill Walsh on story, Don DaGradi on visual, and the songwriters, the Shermans.

RH: Once Walt got the details straight in his mind, when did he cast?

BA: After the screenplay.

RH: Would Walt revise a screenplay?

BA: Oh yes, right up to the day of shooting. He would revise both story and dialogue.

RH: Did he ever second-guess himself?

BA: Oh yes. Nothing was too precious for Walt to change, including his own ideas.

RH: In *Mary Poppins*?

BA: I remember one story meeting on the chimney sweep dance sequence. Peter Ellenshaw came up with the idea. Walt and Ellenshaw did the dance in the middle of the story meeting. Walt could act out every part, especially if he loved a story and could identify with the characters. He was a frustrated actor at heart.

RH: Tell us about *Darby O'Gill*.

BA: Walt loved it. He could identify with Darby, the character.

RH: How did it do financially?

BA: Not too well. The Irish dialect was difficult.

RH: What did Walt say?

BA: He wanted it the way he thought was right. He thought the special effects and charm could overcome the accents. Now we're re-doing four or five of the voices to re-issue it. We're re-doing the voices so they can be understood.

RH: Did Walt say anything about the accents in Darby?

BA: The marketing people mentioned the problems of a dialect film. Walt got Albert Sharpe for Darby, and Walt talked to him: "Now Albert, we have to understand you." But Walt was more interested in Albert's performance. Walt liked him as an actor.

RH: How did *Tonka* do?

BA: There was some question in Walt's mind about *Tonka* when he did it. It started out as TV material. Walt soon recognized that it had to have location work, the outdoor, broad feeling. Walt realized he had to go theatrical to get enough money out of it. *Tonka* did all right.

RH: Who did *Ten Who Dared*?

BA: Jim Algar. Walt wanted to make it. A number of us said it was too expensive for TV, and not enough entertainment for theatrical. Walt wanted to make it. He was fascinated by the adventure. Algar and Bill Beaudine [director] were involved. Walt wasn't happy with the results.

RH: Walt said he didn't like sequels. Why a sequel with *Son of Flubber*?

BA: Because of the public response. Walt laughed about it: "We don't make sequels, but we'll make one here!"

RH: In animation, Walt could produce exactly what he wanted. You can't work that way with actors. Did Walt accept this?

BA: Oh yes. He was a practical man. It's the same thing with directors. You can't control once the camera starts. Bob Stevenson made a career out of understanding Walt, and giving him what he wanted.

© 2007 Jane Hubler

Bill Walsh (1913–1975)

Interviewed by Richard Hubler on April 30, 1968.

Walt's foray into TV and live-action production would probably have been very different without the seminal contributions of producer and writer Bill Walsh.

Bill Walsh was born in New York City, on September 30, 1913. He lived there about two weeks, then grew up in Cincinnati, Ohio, with his aunt and uncle, Agnes and William Newman, who were in a tent show.

Walsh traveled with them during the summer and whenever he could sneak off during the school season, selling tickets, candy and peanuts, playing small parts, and helping pack the tent after performances. His formal education suffered, but he learned a lot about the back roads of Ohio, Kentucky, Indiana, and Tennessee.

Walsh was 13 and attending Purcell High when he got an afternoon job as sports reporter on the *Cincinnati Commercial*, since defunct. He also found time between classes to play football and write songs, including Purcell's stirring anthem *Onward Cavaliers*.

Walsh entered the University of Cincinnati on an athletic scholarship. Although he promptly sank to the bottom of his class scholastically, he wrote a show during his freshman year for the Fresh Painters, a campus musical club, and got reviews which were as laudatory as his grades were poor. At the same time (1934), Frank Fay and Barbara Stanwyck, stars of the New York stage who also were popular in films, happened to be barnstorming their footlight musical *Tattle Tales* through town en route to Broadway. They read the reviews of Walsh's show and invited him to join them as rewrite man and script doctor at $12 a week.

The show closed just five weeks after reaching Broadway, and Barbara Stanwyck and Frank Fay invited Walsh to follow them when they left New York for Hollywood.

On the West Coast, he was employed for 15 years as a press agent for the Ettinger Co., publicizing the Brown Derby restaurants, Technicolor, and such stars as Irene Dunne, Loretta Young, and Edgar Bergen.

As a side job, he began writing jokes and gags at the suggestion of Edgar Bergen, and got his first job with the Walt Disney organization in 1943 as a writer for the *Mickey Mouse* comic strip.

Within a few years, Walsh phased out the press-agent side of his career and went to work for Disney full time, helping to write and produce the Walt Disney Christmas shows of 1950 and 1951, and serving as producer of the *Davy Crockett* television series.

Meanwhile, Walsh had brought *20,000 Leagues Under the Sea* to Disney's attention, had written a film entitled *The Littlest Outlaw*, and helped cut the pattern for *The Mickey Mouse Club*.

Shaking himself free of television, Walsh then produced the film *Westward Ho the Wagons!* in 1956, followed by *The Shaggy Dog*, *Toby Tyler*, and such hits as *The Absent-Minded Professor*, *Son of Flubber*, *Bon Voyage*, *That Darn Cat*, *Lt. Robin Crusoe, U.S.N.*, *Blackbeard's Ghost*, *Mary Poppins*, *The Love Bug*, *Bedknobs and Broomsticks*, and *One of Our Dinosaurs Is Missing*.

Bill Walsh passed away on January 27, 1975.

This interview, conducted at lunch, began with a general conversation about some of the pictures Walsh had worked on. Hubler praised the chase scene in *That Darn Cat* as being one of the finest he had ever seen, and Walsh answered that it was a good idea and "we pursued it". Hubler asked where the idea for the Volkswagen picture (*The Love Bug*) came from, and Walsh said it was from a school teacher in the San Francisco area by the name of Gordon Buford.

Richard Hubler: In what year did you come to work for Disney?

Bill Walsh: 1945. I started doing an ad campaign, some publicity and comic-strip gags.

RH: What did you do before?

BW: Radio writing, gags for Bergen and McCarthy, publicity. I can't remember not trying to be funny.

RH: What was your first live-action experience?

BW: I went to England to do a promotion on *Robin Hood*. I got a beat-up old cameraman and we shot odds and ends. We put together the *Riddle of Robin Hood*: a 12-minute reel. We had gone back to Shakespeare and visited Nottingham and the whole idea was: was there or wasn't there a Robin Hood?

RH: How did you end it?

BW: We left it up in the air.

RH: How was it used?

BW: We put it on television. That was 1948 and stations were unsophisticated. Many used it and even schools began to use it.

RH: How did you get involved in television?

BW: In 1950 I wrote Walt a passionate memo on why not to go into television. The next day I saw Walt in the hall and he said, "You're the producer of the Christmas Show." We got Charlie McCarthy and Walt told stories. We took hunks of various pictures: *Snow White*, *Bambi* and *Alice in Wonderland*. That was a plug because *Alice* was about to be released.[1] I think that was the first time Walt saw TV in its true light: as a promotion device for the studio. He saw it as the world's greatest promotion device, so we did the same kind of show again the following year.

RH: How much did the Robin Hood promotion reel cost?

BW: I think about a thousand pounds, but you can't measure its value.

RH: What was the cost of the first television show?

BW: We built a beautiful set and I think the cost was about $110, 000. Or maybe that's what we got for it. Walt always told me, "Don't worry about money, just worry about what we're doing."

RH: Tell me about the early television show.

BW: We did 26 shows a year. I thought it was the hardest thing we ever could do. We didn't have a staff geared for that. The first show was a big promotion for Disneyland, the second was *Davy Crockett*. It was just a story about some guy shooting at Indians, but all hell broke loose. I can't understand it.

RH: Did you ever analyze its success?

BW: No. I thought it might have been the song, which was an accident. We had a lot of footage coming in, but it looked dull to me. We needed to keep the show going. I had a talk with Tom Blackburn [the writer] and George Bruns [musician], and they came back in 20 minutes with the song. It was short and had to be repeated over and over, but that was part of the success.

RH: What other kinds of shows were there during the first year?

BW: We were doing *20,000 League under the Sea* at the time and Hibler put a promotional film together with six or seven minutes of animation at the beginning. That *trailer* won an Emmy award and it wasn't for the best show promoting a picture either! By that time Walt was quite pleased with the television show. So was ABC: it had become the third major network.

RH: What did you do after that?

BW: Well, one day Walt came to me and said, "I have a surprise for you. We have a new television show and it's not just an hour a week. It's going to

---

[1] The show was named *One Hour in Wonderland*.

be an hour every day on film." That was *The Mickey Mouse Club*. It was an hour every day, ostensibly for children. It starred the Mouseketeers and "everything went". We had crews all over the world finding us newsreel footage. It was so popular I used to go into bars while the show was on and all the drunks had mouse ears on, singing that song. It was a big thing for a while. Then the Mouseketeers started to grow up.

RH: Annette?

BW: She had a figure like this [holding up a knife] at first, but it kept getting more like this [holding up a spoon]. We kept putting looser sweaters on her.

RH: Did the studio have any arguments with her?

BW: No.

RH: How long did you work on television?

BW: One year on the *Disneyland* show and three years on *The Mickey Mouse Club*.

RH: What did you do next?

BW: Walt had an idea. He had a story called *The Hound of Florence*, which was part of a package he had bought from Felix Salten. It was a mystical story. You couldn't read straight through it. Walt kept seeing something in it. We came up with the modernized teenage thing and broached the idea to ABC as a series. They said no. Walt got mad and said he would make it as a feature. It was cheap to make, and it made an enormous amount of money. It brought Fred MacMurray back as a big star. [Bill points out that this basic concept—a boy, his family, his father, the dog— is now the basis of MacMurray's show on television, *My Three Sons*.]

RH: Was *The Shaggy Dog* [based on *The Hound of Florence*] your first live-action picture?

BW: No, I did the *Littlest Outlaw* with Larry Lansburgh.

RH: It was another chase picture.

BW: That's the classic form. Look at *Gone With the Wind*. Chase is implicit in the title.

RH: Where did you shoot the *Littlest Outlaw*?

BW: All on location and everything was shot in two languages.

RH: What about casting for *The Shaggy Dog*?

BW: Walt liked the idea of using kids from *The Mickey Mouse Club* in features. Annette was getting an incredible amount of mail. The kids identified with her.

RH: How would you explain trends like that?

BW: You hit a certain mood, a feeling, an identity. You're always throwing things out and hoping they'll catch on.

RH: Where did the idea for *The Absent-Minded Professor* come from?

BW: Sam Taylor had written some "Letters to the President" in *Liberty Magazine*. There were several—one about a rubber device, another about a flying car, and a third something about milk. Walt had bought the stories a long time ago and it was an old idea that came back to him. He adapted what he had bought for his current needs.

RH: How long was the usual incubation period?

BW: Probably several years. The Professor stories were bought during the war.

RH: What did Walt see in Fred MacMurray?

BW: He loved him as a comedian. After *The Shaggy Dog*, Walt looked for another vehicle for MacMurray. The idea of *The Absent-Minded Professor* came to him.

RH: What about the technical effects in *Absent-Minded Professor*?

BW: We hired Professor Julius Sumner Miller from El Camino College. We used him as a lab advisor. He worked the details out so they would be authentic. Then we used a basketball game to dramatize flubber. Walt said, "Maybe we're overlooking something...sports." No other studio was doing movies relating to sports, but Walt saw that this was our kind of audience: kids, teenagers, the family.

RH: How did you do the technical effects? Did you use wires?

BW: There were 18 sets of wires. It was terrifying. Art Vitarelli is a great second-unit director. We used the same idea later in a football game in *Son of Flubber*, and in the track meet in *Blackbeard's Ghost*.

RH: How did Walt develop ideas?

BW: Walt's strong point was conceiving the whole package: figuring out how to adapt the whole thing, deciding what elements would make it right for a "Disney" audience.

RH: How would he conceive the whole thing?

BW: Walt had the basic elements floating around inside his head. He was thinking of everything: promotion, television, is it a story that can be sold on television, is it suitable for American audiences and not foreign? He could stand far back and look at the whole thing while I would be face-up against the story.

RH: Did you start with a treatment?

BW: Yes, and then we would meet with Walt. He would say something like, "There's a lot of talk here." He liked visual things. He didn't like "jokey" dialogue. Walt liked character-comedy dialogue.

RH: The next step after the treatment?

BW: We would get a sketch artist to develop the idea visually. The artist had worked on storyboards with Walt [on cartoon features]. That's how Walt brought Don DaGradi and me together. Walt thought Don could develop my ideas into pictures, but Don turned out to be a terrific story man himself. Don was used to developing storyboards.

That's how we work with Bob Stevenson. Storyboards are shooting scripts. Bob breaks it down: every camera shot, every angle. In the long run, it's an enormous savings because he only shoots what he has worked out on the boards.

RH: How many storyboards for a feature?

BW: We have 42 boards with 40 drawings to a board on *Love Bug*. With storyboards we don't have to build a full set. Stevenson has worked out his angles so he is shooting on 1/4 of the set. That saves an enormous amount, but it means the director has to come in a lot earlier on the production. Stevenson comes in eight to ten weeks before the picture starts.

RH: Who else uses this technique?

BW: Stevenson is the foremost practioner. Another original Disney technique.

RH: How close would you work with Walt during this development?

BW: We would stay very close to Walt in the early phases. Walt would go through a script page by page and line by line. He would go through it methodically. You would never hear "I don't like this" or "I don't know what's wrong". Walt would work with you to solve the problems. This is the hardest kind of work on a picture.

RH: What were Walt's typical comments?

BW: "Too long."

RH: Then he was always cutting?

BW: He was concerned about the pace: always keeping it moving. And the believability. The more we got into the fantasy area, the more Walt emphasized believability.

RH: How can fantasy be believable?

BW: Everyone thinks "everything goes" in fantasy, but that isn't true. It must be believable. That's the great thing about Fred MacMurray.

RH: An example?

BW: *The Absent-Minded Professor*. Professor Miller talked about serendipity: "Set up a climate in which things can happen logically." Walt got fascinated with the word. He had the Shermans run upstairs and write a song about it. Then we started developing the story. Walt said, "If a man's son turned into a dog, who would most hate dogs?" It was a mailman, of course. So MacMurray became a mailman, and that made the whole idea much funnier than if he was an insurance man or a stockbroker, etc.

RH: Where did Walt first see Hayley Mills?

BW: In her first picture, *Tiger Bay*. She played it straight in that. But we found she had a marvelous ability to clown. Julie Andrews was very funny, too. Walt always sought this out. Often he changed a picture to suit [the personality of an actor]. He would find something in an actor and would find a way to use what was best in him.

RH: What was the most difficult live-action picture?

BW: *Poppins* was the most *complex*. [Bill did not think "difficult" fitted the description of any picture he worked on.]

RH: Did Walt interfere with shooting?

BW: Never. Walt was primarily concerned with one, story, and two, casting. During a picture he would never come down and breathe on you. He assumed you would solve small details. But he saw the dailies every day and could keep up with what you were doing.

RH: Was *Mary Poppins* difficult?

BW: No. It was a breeze. It was cast with people Walt liked and that was halfway home with him.

RH: After a picture was cast, what if Walt disliked the way an actor was performing?

BW: We had very few problem that way with actors. Occasionally they would want more money. [The train incident with Kirk Douglas] is the only funny thing I can remember. Fess Parker was upset because of the buckskins.[2] He wanted to be an actor. Now, of course, he's back wearing buckskins.

RH: [Expressing surprise that *Mary Poppins* didn't have any difficulty.]

BW: It was a breeze in the sense that everything worked. "The feeling was there." After a picture is going a week or two, it has a certain feeling. It's like a forest fire, a fire of its own. By the second week of *Poppins*, the word

---

[2] See interview with Fess Parker in this volume.

was out. Every studio in town wanted Julie [and before they wouldn't consider her].

RH: Why did Walt cast Julie Andrews?

BW: He had an instinct. He sensed things in Julie even though she had never done a picture. We did a make-up test and it was only on the screen three seconds when Walt said, "We're home!" She had a certain empathy. He knew he was right about it.

RH: What about *Darn Cat*?

BW: Only a little with Hayley. She was beginning to feel she was a grown-up lady. We had to make her like the script. The story was about a 12-year-old but we had to write it as a 17- or 18-year-old.

RH: About the format of *The Mickey Mouse Club*: was it anything goes?

BW: It was like the original *Disneyland* show: it was divided into different segments. *The Mickey Mouse Club* had five segments. One was circus, two was Guest Star Day, three was Anything Can Happen, four was Western Day, five… Each day was divided into four segments: newsreel, special acts (like the FBI series), a serial, and a musical with the Mouseketeers.

RH: Did Walt keep track of all this or did you have absolute control?

BW: I don't like the word "absolute", but I guess you could say I had near-absolute control. After a while, the mothers and the agency men were driving me crazy. Walt backed me up and said I didn't have to talk to the mothers and agency men any more.

RH: How did the Mouseketeers do after the show went off the air?

BW: Cheryl married Lance Reventlow. Annette got married and has a baby. Some of them have been on the Lawrence Welk show, [like Bobby Burgess].

RH: Why did it go off the air?

BW: After three years we felt we had run out the string. It was a wild way to do a show. We would discuss an idea in the morning. The songwriters would write songs that day and we would shoot that afternoon. We had to work quickly.

© 2007 Jane Hubler

Bill Walsh (1913–1975)

Interviewed by Christopher Finch and Linda Rosenkrantz on June 27, 1972.

The transcripts of the interviews conducted jointly by Christopher Finch and Linda Rosenkrantz do not mention who between Christopher and Linda asked each specific question.

Christopher Finch & Linda Rosenkrantz: You came here originally as a gag writer for the *Mickey Mouse* comic strip?

Bill Walsh: That's correct.

CF&LR: How did you get from there into producing and writing live action?

BW: God knows. It all seems sort of strange. See, we were going to make movies in England at that time.

CF&LR: This was about 1949?

BW: Yeah, about then because we had no money to make movies in Hollywood, but we did have some frozen pounds in England. So Walt began to brood about the frozen pounds, which was money over there, but it wasn't over here, and he decided to do films in England. The first one was *Treasure Island* and the second one was *Robin Hood*. At the time of *Robin Hood*, I bumped into him on the street, and he said, "Will you come along with me?" I said, "What do I do because I'm still doing the *Mickey Mouse* comic strip?" He said, "Well, we'll think of something when we get there." So we go there and sure enough, there was nothing for me to do. I had to think up something.

What I thought up was to do a kind of little documentary behind the scenes. In those days, behind the scenes really wasn't going on anywhere. I was sort of intrigued by the story of Robin Hood because I talked to a couple of the old geezers who were technical advisors on *Robin*. A little guy with a beard (I've forgotten his name) told me there was kind of a thing up in the air whether there was such a person as Robin Hood, or whether he was just a fake or whether it was something somebody thought up. I thought that was kind of a good idea for a documentary, so I wrote this little kind of behind-the-scenes thing called *The Riddle of Robin Hood*, in which you present the facts on one side of the argument and the facts against. Such as there's the old tree in Nottingham called the Trysting Tree where Maid Marian and Robin used to court, according to the story, and the name Robin kept turning up in a couple of Shakespeare stories. It turned up also in Walter Scott. Then other people say it's a phony, there was no such thing. I marshaled one side and the other, used a lot of scenes from the film, and used the actors like Peter Finch (it was his first film).

CF&LR: That was his first film?

BW: Yes. We have a lot of first guys like that. *Kidnapped* was Peter O'Toole's first film, *Darby O'Gill* was Sean Connery's first [significant] film. We got these guys up and they weren't working at that time.

So these guys were kind of helping and we were putting together this funny, goofy little thing. I remember the cameraman cost me two pounds a week. We were known as the fifth unit. And then I went to the British Museum. I documented the stuff and gradually we put together some kind of a story. I brought it back to America and we shot it here, pulled all the bits together and then the next thing was what to do with it?

In those days, naïve was the word for the TV people. They didn't know what to do. They had to fill up a lot of time all day long, but they didn't have all the stuff. So we planted this film with a lot of TV stations all over the country, planted it with schools, cause it had kind of a documentary feel about it. Nobody knew what that word meant at that time. Pretty soon we were getting a lot of mileage out of this goofy little film. And Walt was sort of enchanted by that, all that free space promoting the film. So the next year was the year the networks came in and wanted Walt to do a TV show, and he was sort of spooky about it because I think he had had a bad experience on radio using the voices like the Duck and the Mouse. Nobody could understand it and the show wasn't successful. So he was a little leery about doing a TV show. But now he began to think TV could be useful promoting the films, as a result of this experience.

Then the first thing they wanted was a Christmas show. He wanted us to use the same technique, using a lot of old film. It had Edgar Bergen and Charlie McCarthy and Mortimer Snerd in it. He had kind of an office party and we got the old voice in the mirror from *Snow White*. The face in the mirror conjured up the old films and we got a lot of footage on that promoting films that were going to come out pretty soon. That got a marvelous rating and again it was kind of stuck together with glue and chicken wire, very cheaply. That somehow gave Walt the idea maybe I was a producer. Now what that meant I don't know, because I remember going in at the time and he said, "Well, you can write the show and you can produce it." I remember going in and saying, "I don't know how to produce a TV show," and he said, "Who does?" I gave a pretty good answer: "Okay." I stayed with it for a while and did the next year's Christmas show. The first year was Coca-Cola, the second year was Johnson & Johnson, and then was the point when they started to think TV-wise around here. Because the year after that they came back for a regular show and Walt was sold by that time.

It was also a way to sell the theatrical product. I think he always thought of TV that way because he used it to promote Disneyland later on, to promote everything. Everything that moved around here he promoted. He never let anything stand by itself. Something always had to help it. It was always a family job. He would help the park and the park would try to help us, with the films or with giving jobs to the Mouseketeers and things like that.

The network people came to Walt for the regular program that first year. Again he hauled me in and said, "You take care of the show." Again I said, "I don't really think we know how to do it here." He said, "Forget it. Go right ahead. See what happens." So we did a first show, which was kind of a trailer of what all the shows would be that year. It was the first time we'd gone into more or less sustained theatrical product week after week after week. We'd done a film maybe once every two years. Now it was week after week and it was kind of spooky. So we did a preview of the first year's product. It was just bits and pieces of old movies. Some of them were animated films. We were going to do a series on American folk heroes, like Johnny Appleseed, Davy Crockett, Daniel Boone, Wind Wagon Smith, Big Foot Wallace...

And the first one we picked out, by dumb luck, was Davy Crockett, who nobody at that time had ever heard of. He was just one more frontiersman. We shot that down in Tennessee. We didn't have enough footage, so we got the film back and we thought, well, we're shy for three shows. Walt said, "Why don't you take these drawings and stick them all together and give them an idea of what the show's going to be about?" We put the drawings together (sketches of Davy's life) and he said, "That looks kind of dull. Maybe we can get a song." So we got the guy who wrote the script and he said, "I never wrote a song before in my life." We said, "Well, try it." He and the composer of the score for the film went down the hall, and they came back in 20 minutes and they said, "This is not much." We said, "How does it go?" And he said, "Born on a mountaintop in Tennessee..." I said that sounds pretty awful. He said, "That's all the time we got. Let's go." They kept repeating that phrase over and over again. I don't know what happened the first year. The whole country came unglued.

We realized we were in big trouble, because in the third show we had to knock Davy off. Walt said, "My God. We've just created a marvelous thing and we have to knock him off." I said, "Every schoolboy in America knows that Davy dies at the Alamo and now we're getting petitions from all the school children saying please don't let Davy die." I said, "No, he's got to die. What the hell can we do?" Walt said, "We'll do something called *The Further Adventures of Davy*, then we'll kick him off at the Alamo the way he's supposed to go."

Then they took all those films and made a theatrical film out of it, and that made a lot of money. By now, Walt was getting fairly interested in the live-action part of the business. It created the money to build Disneyland. He was originally going to build it across the street there on that little strip of land. The money started rolling in from *Davy* and he raised his sights very quickly. He started looking for this new area with all the acreage down there. And then things started to roll quite a lot. Hib, Winston Hibler, did a film, a TV show, which was the backstage stuff on *20,000 Leagues Under the Sea*. Everybody said you can't do an hour of a trailer for a movie. Walt said, "Why not?" So we did it and it won the Emmy as the best show of the year. From there on, everybody was very exploitation minded and we did quite a lot of it. The next year, Walt said, "I'm taking you off the evening show." I said, "Thank God, I'm exhausted!" He said, "There's a new show. It's called *The Mickey Mouse Club*. That's an hour every day." I went flat on my face. He said, "You can do two or three years of that. If we get by, you'll never have to do any more TV." "Fine, it's a deal." He stuck to his point. I never had to do any more TV shows.

CF&LR: On *The Mickey Mouse Club*, that must be a very different problem from producing segments for a weekly show. Is that a question of getting a format and then working within that format?

BW: It was a question of just trying to survive from day to day. We didn't know. We just knew we had to go on the air in two months with a show that had to go on every day. We were just kind of making it up. We had to find kids who would do it. I remember Walt saying, "Don't get me those kids with those tightly curled hairdos—tap dancers—get me kids that look like they're having fun. Then later we'll teach them how to tap dance or sing or whatever it is." He said, "Go to a few schools and a good way to try to find them is watch the kids at recess and pretty soon you'll find there's always one kid you're watching, whether he's doing anything or not, because you're interested in that kid." And he said, "That's the kid you find." We used that technique and we found these kids for the first year of the *Mouse Club*: Annette and Darlene and Cubby and Karen and the bunch, and for some reason or another they all became popular.

CF&LR: You just went to schools?

BW: We prowled around, we went to dance schools and things like that, but mainly we went to ordinary kids. These were fairly ordinary kids.

CF&LR: You didn't use casting agencies? You didn't look for show biz children at all?

BW: That way you'd wind up with what used to be the old-fashioned kind of theatrical kiddie, which was death, apparently. He said to get kids that look like they're having a good time and then we'll put them on the show and other kids will watch them and enjoy them and that will give them the image that they're having a good time, too. That was the original formula for the *Mouse Club*.

CF&LR: And then you developed the dramatic episodes.

BW: As we were on the air, by simply force of being there, we developed various techniques of segments of music, little things of the kids going down to the FBI, seeing how that's done, the San Diego Zoo... Then we had to establish a newsreel unit and the newsreel went all over the world. We sent kids to the political conventions, the Republican and the Democratic. Mouseketeers covered that and everything the kids could do, they did.

The key was really Annette Funicello, because for some reason or another, from the very first week of the show, Annette got all the fan mail. Nobody understood what the heck was going on. There were many kids on the show and some of them were very good, very talented, but for some reason Annette got all the mail. So everything was more or less keyed to Annette. We didn't know why, but we knew it was happening. The first time Annette came in, she had a figure like that. The second year we had to get a little looser sweater, third year a very loose sweater, the fourth year there wasn't a sweater that loose. So we said, "Well, that's the end of *The Mickey Mouse Club*." Walt said, "Maybe we'll go on to something else."

CF&LR: Was it still getting good ratings when you ended it?

BW: It was getting marvelous ratings. We were getting bigger ratings than most of the evening shows. So that was just fine. But my God, what a lot of work it was. You must try that some time: an hour every day.

CF&LR: It sounds like a lot of fun.

BW: It was kind of hysterical, it was like a Chinese fire drill, but it was fun, because we'd have meetings in the morning with the kids, then we'd have the writers, then we'd have the guy who did the sets and the costumes, so everybody would have to have a big meeting, who goes this way, who goes that way, then we'd meet after lunch. By now the set designer's gone to the back lot and found some pieces, the wardrobe people have gone to the wardrobe and got some pieces, and the kids have learned how to sing the songs, and about three o'clock that afternoon, we'd shoot it. But it was at least fresh: you didn't have time to get over-rehearsed.

CF&LR: How far ahead did you shoot that?

BW: I think we were just within a whisker of getting murdered: At no time were we more than two months ahead. At times we were less than three weeks. It was kind of like riding on a bicycle.

CF&LR: You didn't shoot more than one show at a time? You just shot one show a day, did you?

BW: Generally, we shot one show a day. But it happened all kinds of ways. We'd shoot six shows one day, we'd shoot a half a show. You just did the best way you could. That thing was always pressing you from the rear. It was hysteria, but as you say it was fun. And the kids were marvelous. Even the parents were good, they were cooperative. They had a little area where they'd go and knit, talk to one another, try to avoid talking to us as much as possible. It wasn't easy: it's against nature not to talk about your children and the fact that he learned to do a cornet solo this weekend or something.

CF&LR: Or this afternoon.

BW: Yes.

CF&LR: After the show you went into movie production entirely?

BW: Yes. As had been promised me, and was my due. I was a little hysterical by that time. We went to Mexico for a film, so I disappeared there for a little bit. Then I came back and did things like *Shaggy Dog* and *Absent-Minded Professor*, which was a whole different kind of thing. It was kind of fun. We were well into features by that time.

CF&LR: If it hadn't been for this whole thing of the frozen money in England, do you think Walt would have ever gone into live action?

BW: I wonder. After all, animation was his first love. But it was a critical time for the studio in which money was very short, and being an extremely logical man, there was all that loot lying loose over there and he needed it, the studio needed it, and that was one way of converting it into cash over here. It was almost obligatory. They just needed the money.

CF&LR: Did he get very involved with live-action production at that point? Was it something new that really excited him?

BW: Yeah. The first big film we did over here was *20,000 Leagues Under the Sea* and he got quite involved with that. I think it excited him. It was a period where he was more interested in doing that, but he gradually swung back to doing the animation thing, which was really his first love. He was fascinated by live action.

CF&LR: Did you work on *20,000 Leagues*?

BW: I was involved at the beginning. Card Walker and myself were the ones who conned Walt into doing it. We were doing a series of films here at the studio called True-Life Adventures, which didn't cost much money to do. So we conceived the idea of doing a True-Life Adventure under the sea, with fish and things like that. Then, from there on it was a step to thinking, "Why not use the Jules Verne story," which was kicking around and was a good title, big title, good international title. I remember we did a great big billboard, a phony billboard which we stuck in Walt's office, because Walt was kind of down on the whole idea. He didn't see any reason for going into a full-length feature at that time. It cost a lot of money. But we stuck that billboard in his office and kept it there and every morning he came into his office and saw that billboard. It started to prey on his mind.

Eventually he said, "Well let's develop this a little bit." There were two young men working for Stanley Kramer at that time: Dick Fleischer and Earl Feldman. Earl was a writer, Dick was a young director, and they had done some B pictures at RKO which were quite good, quite tight. I thought they'd be very good, talented people for us, because we didn't want to spend a lot of dough. At that time, Mr. Kramer had had a falling out with the Columbia people about his commitment there, so Earl and Dick were free. I got them over here for the picture, and we started working on the project. Walt bought the rights from MGM, and then he sort of looked at me and *now* he says, "You don't know enough about producing. I think you need more seasoning." I said, "Okay." So he sent me to Mexico to do this film about a bullfighter's horse. I was down there almost a year, and in the meantime they started *20,000 Leagues*, which turned out very well.

CF&LR: Was it all shot here? The big sound stages were built at that point?

BW: Most of it. They did some location work down at Montego Bay with Kirk Douglas and Peter Lorre and Mason. Then they came back and they did the squid sequence here on Stage 3, in the big tank stage. I'd say 80% of it was done here.

CF&LR: Was there a big outdoor tank built here as well?

BW: No. It was on Stage 3.

CF&LR: Because there were some photographs in publicity that looked as though there was an outdoor tank.

BW: I think they shot a few shots, where the submarine went down, at the 20th Century Fox tank. We never built any outdoor tank ourselves.

CF&LR: That's what I wondered. Because you couldn't see where it was, but there was an outdoor tank and it looks as if it was the boat that was used at the beginning of the movie.

BW: They shot some stuff down in San Diego.

CF&LR: So what was the first major feature that you shot? That you personally produced? Have you written everything that you've produced?

BW: Mostly. I wrote quite a bit with a fellow named Don DaGradi and I've done a couple by myself. The first one really was *The Shaggy Dog*. Don wasn't on that. It was sort of an offshoot from one of the TV shows. It was done in black and white. Cost very little money and it made a lot of dough. We brought Fred MacMurray back from doing Class C westerns. At that time he didn't know what the hell he was doing here, but from that time on, Fred has never stopped working, or stopped making money because that was a whole new career for him.

CF&LR: What year was that?

BW: It must have been about '55 or '56.

CF&LR: So *My Three Sons* started soon after that.

BW: It started precisely after that; the same dog, the same kids. Some smart cookie in TV said, "Well, a house doesn't have to fall on him." He got Fred and a couple of kids and a dog and he was back in business. And *My Three Sons* kept running up till last year. A way of life for Fred, God knows. He invented a way that he didn't even have to go to work very much, just worked a few days a year, just doing entrances and exits. Then we did another one with Fred called *The Absent-Minded Professor*. Then we did a sequel to that called the *Son of Flubber*.

CF&LR: Were those things existing stories or were those original scripts?

BW: We get stories in a strange way here. We don't literally get stories as stories: we get springboards or ideas and we develop the story around that. Like for the *Shaggy Dog*, which was based on a book by a guy named Felix Salten, who was a Viennese author: kind of a nutty little thin book called *The Hound of Florence*. That was always on the shelf here and nobody knew what to do with it, because it was kind of nutty. It was about Michelangelo's apprentice, who got mixed up with a Borgia ring and kept getting changed into a dog all the time. But he kept flashing back. It was kind of a strange little book. It was completely impossible to read. At that time we had the Mouseketeers on hand, so Walt said, "See if you can do something with this book. Get some idea..."

I did a story using Tommy Kirk, and Walt originally tried to sell that as a TV show, but there were some wise new guys at ABC who said no, it wouldn't make a TV show. Walt said, "Well, the hell with these guys, we'll make a picture out of it and make a lot more money than it ever would make on TV." I thought, "Well, that's Walt talking," or something. But we made the picture and it did make quite a lot of money. So he was right. How he was right I don't know, but it made a lot of dough. It was a cheap little movie to make.

The Absent-Minded Professor came from a little story that he bought from *Liberty Magazine*, which was before you were born, probably. Picked up these strange little bits. There was a series called "Letters to the President", which were written during the war, and one was about a goofy old professor who invented a form of artificial rubber. He was writing the president that he knew a new way of making rubber for the war. Another one of the stories was that he had an old flivver which he could make fly. And these little things were like hundred-word stories in the form of a little letter. They used it in front of the magazine. Walt bought these things for a couple of hundred bucks apiece and put them on the shelf. Every now and then he'd take these things down and said, "Is there anything we can do with these?" That's the way those things started.

A thing like *Toby Tyler*, which was an old circus story, came in there somewhere.

CF&LR: Now *Mary Poppins* he'd wanted to make for a long time.
BW: Yes, because his little girl had it on her nightstand for quite awhile and that's when Walt was first conscious of it. He spent many years trying to talk Mrs. Travers out of the rights, but Mrs. Travers was a fairly stubborn lady.[1] It took some time to bring her around.

CF&LR: How did he manage it?
BW: Walt just went over and turned on the charm himself one time. He was in London, and I think he went over and had tea with Mrs. Travers, who finally felt the time was right. Everyone had been trying to get it: Goldwyn, Rogers and Hammerstein.

CF&LR: Had he ever thought of doing it in animation?
BW: I would imagine he'd had that in the back of his mind, but this time he was more or less going for the live action. That's the way he apparently talked it to her. Walt was a pretty good salesman. He sold her. And he came back with it.

CF&LR: Now she's listed as what? Consultant on the film?
BW: Yes.

CF&LR: Did you in fact work closely with her?

---
[1] See the interview with Brian Sibley in *Walt's People: Volume 4*.

BW: Not very.

CF&LR: Did she come over at all?

BW: She came over once for about a month or so. I don't think she was too pleased with us, to tell you the truth, because she kept saying things like, "Well now the rustle of Mary Poppins' skirt: there's a certain kind of sound it makes and there's a draper's shop around the corner and we *must* have that fabric." Walt was fairly pragmatic and he'd say, "God, let's get the picture done, let's cut through. We're not going to spend all that time looking up draper's shops off the Kensington Road." She would say, "Well now the letter box: there's a certain shade of red that it must be." She was getting hung up on these details all the time. Meantime, what we're trying to do is get a workable storyline. The original *Poppins* was just a series of little fragments with no story whatsoever. It was a character, a sensational character and funny little bits of episodes. But we needed a story to tie the whole thing together. And she didn't like the idea of putting songs in it. That was another hang-up. When she did accept the idea of songs, she wanted something like "TraLa BoomDeeAy" or "Greensleeves". So there were little bumpings of noses going on all the way along the line, until we finally got the whole thing done.

I think she finally accepted it as a *fait accompli* when the time came, and I presume she's satisfied that we didn't destroy her character. Books sold about four times as many as they used to. It used to be kind of a cult, particularly in this country. Oddly enough, the people who came from England didn't know what we were talking about when we talked about *Mary Poppins*.

CF&LR: I know, I was brought up in England and I didn't know *Mary Poppins*.

BW: That was very strange. Now, of course, everybody in the empire's got it. The good part that happened, as I was trying to explain to her once… I said, "Okay, we're doing our version of it, but what will happen is people will go back to the original *Poppins*, then they'll start buying the books like crazy," which is precisely what happened. I said, "Then it's no longer a strange little cult of people: this is going to be for a lot of kids. You're opening the whole thing up." I think on that basis she finally bought it, because she saw it as a much bigger audience for *Mary Poppins* than it had ever been before. I think we parted friends.

CF&LR: How did you decide on Julie Andrews? Because I gather that all the other studios decided she was just totally un-photogenic, that she was a marvelous stage performer but you couldn't possibly put her on the screen.

BW: Walt saw her in *Camelot* and he liked her in that; there was a kind of funny song in there. He liked the way she whistled. She's a great whistler and he thought that was amusing. So he asked Julie to come out and listen to the songs and talk to us. At that time, Julie found out what had happened with *My Fair Lady*, so she said "the hell with it" and she took a chance with us.[2] Of course it turned out just fine for everybody. She was funny. Once she decided she was going to accept it, she loved it. I remember one time we went to a foreign correspondents' dinner and Jack Warner was there. We introduced Julie and she said, "I want to thank Mr. Warner for giving me my chance." Jack was furious! Later on I think they became friends, but I don't know deep down who is friendly with who. I think Julie would have liked to have done *My Fair Lady*. It was her show, after all. But her life might have been a lot different.

CF&LR: What about Dick Van Dyke? He's the one thing who really worries me about that film. I found him a little hard to take.

BW: We didn't want it to get *too* English. After all, we were making it for a world market. Dick was very hot then with his own show and he wanted to do a picture, but he was very nervous about what he wanted to do. So we just got there and conned him until he decided to do it. I suppose there might have been other people who would have been more apropos, but Dick brought a certain kind of energy to the part and he was enormously popular then. I think it was very helpful to the film.

CF&LR: On that same subject: how come the studio has made such use of English properties and English actors? I mean, it can't be any more to do with the pounds being frozen.

BW: No. I think it was that Walt was basically an Anglophile and a lot of good stories, of course, have been English: *Wind in the Willows*, *Alice*, *Peter Pan*. It just happened that the kind of stories he was interested in were basically all English. He always got on well with the English: He liked to talk to them. That's how he came up with Mr. Finch, Mr. Connery, and Mr. O'Toole. He would give them chances where they couldn't get chances in their own country. Because he was basically an Anglophile and liked to prowl around and walk up and down the streets and absorb the atmosphere. He had a good time over there.

CF&LR: Then in *Mary Poppins* you used David Tomlinson.

---

[2] Julie Andrews had made the role of Eliza from *My Fair Lady* her own on the stage. Jack L. Warner's choice of Audrey Hepburn for the part in the movie was seen as a snub of Andrews, and so it was. Hepburn was chosen by Jack Warner for her greater box-office appeal, and Warner was prepared to offer the role to Elizabeth Taylor if Hepburn turned it down.

BW: It was the first time we used David. We were going nuts looking for somebody to play the father and I saw him in *Up the Creek* on TV. He was the commander of a ship that was in dry dock up a river. Peter Sellers was in it and Lionel Jeffries. It made me laugh, so it made Walt laugh, and he said, "He looks good." Nobody here had ever heard of him. But he's been successful for us. We've done three pictures with him and all made a lot of dough.

CF&LR: Is it a big problem to cast children?

BW: [Whistle] You bet: to keep them natural, believable, to keep them from changing, to keep the parents off their backs. I guess it's about as hard as anything can be in this world.

CF&LR: [The kids in *Mary Poppins*] and the ones in *Bedknobs* are the most natural I've ever seen in the movies.

BW: Yeah, I dug those up myself in London. Got all these Cockney kids, rehearsed them all on the top floor of our building, there on Pall Mall, overlooking St. James' Palace. I must have gone through 400 Cockney kids, all singing *My Old Man*. I thought I'd go nuts. But the kids were good and it was just a question of digging.

CF&LR: When you say to stop them from changing, what do you mean by that?

BW: I mean kids change right in the middle of a picture all the time. That drives you nuts. Because there's an entirely different character you end up with than the one you started with, or their teeth are falling out, or if they're around 11 or 12 and they start shooting up…like Annette! Typical problem. Not a bad problem, but it's a difficult problem. And little boys change so much, their arms shoot out from their costumes and you think they're going to lose their charm if they grow up too fast, which sometimes they do. Too much calcium or something.

CF&LR: The elder of the boys in *Bedknobs* seems as though he's growing up quite quickly.

BW: Yes, he was right on the verge. He was about 15. He was kind of a street kid. They were all basically Cockney kids.

I remember I did a lot of tests on tape and Lynn Redgrave was in there one time. I was thinking of Lynn to play the part of the witch, so I asked her to look at the kids and she said, "We'll get that one, he's really authentic." It was the older boy. See, he's not an actor at all.

CF&LR: The voices were all terrific. I thought they were very natural voices.

BW: If you go for it as honestly as you can, sometimes settle for not so much experience in acting.

CF&LR: You don't have problems with them learning lines or directing them?

BW: Oh yes. But if you try to do it as honestly as you can, you err on that side, which is the best side to err on. If you get the wrong kids, it's murder. Better to get the right kids and try to get some acting out of them later: Try *not* to have them act, that's where it gets to be murder, where they seem to be acting. Then you're in trouble.

© 2007 Christopher Finch & Linda Rosenkrantz

George Bruns (1914–1983)

Interviewed by Richard Hubler on July 23, 1968.

Aside from the Sherman Brothers, or Alan Menken today, Disney composers were seldom interviewed and remain relatively unknown as individuals. George Bruns is no exception. The role he played in Disney's history, however, is no small one. His greatest success came in 1955 when his score and song for *The Legend of Davy Crockett* sold 8 million copies and remained No. 1 on the hit parade for six months. His theme for the popular *Zorro* series sold another million copies.

During his 22-year stint at Disney, Bruns received three Academy Award nominations (*Babes in Toyland*, *Sleeping Beauty*, and *Sword in the Stone*) and wrote themes for such hit films as *The Love Bug*, *The Absent-Minded Professor*, *Son of Flubber*, *One Hundred and One Dalmatians*, *The Jungle Book*, *Robin Hood*, and *The Aristocats*. He also did the music for many of the Disney nature films, one third of all *Wonderful World of Disney* television programs, helped develop Disneyland, and was the original music director of *The Mickey Mouse Club*.

Born in Sandy, Oregon, on July 3, 1914, Bruns studied engineering while he attended Oregon State University. He left OSU a year short of graduation and joined a traveling band and played for a number of swing bands, including Jack Teagarden's.

After World War II, Bruns served as assistant music director at KOIN Radio in Portland and later became musical director at KEX in Portland. Bruns, who mastered 15 instruments along with his favorite, the slide trombone, came to Los Angeles in 1950 where he organized a small combo, made the nightclub rounds, and composed background music for Capitol Records before going with Disney.

After he went to California, Bruns also did the music for some of the Gerald McBoing-Boing cartoons.

In 1953, Walt Disney was working on producing *Sleeping Beauty* when he heard Bruns' cartoon compositions and asked him if he could adapt Tchaikovsky's ballet suite for his film. "I can rewrite it," Bruns replied. "I've been rewriting him for my songs for years."

From 1971 to 1975, when he retired, Bruns commuted from his birthplace of Sandy, Oregon, to Burbank after deciding not to continue living in the Los Angeles area because of the smog. He died on May 23, 1983.

Richard Hubler: How long have you been here, Mr. Bruns?

George Bruns: I started with Walt in 1953 on *Sleeping Beauty*. The first year I did all the TV stuff, and I was still working on *Sleeping Beauty*. I also did *Absent-Minded Professor* and *Son of Flubber* and all the cartoon pictures.

Walt had a very commercial ear. He had a knack for knowing what people like. He figured if he liked it the average person would like it. He did not have a trained musical ear, but he did not like anything high-pitched and he didn't like loud music. He liked soft music, and he liked music through everything. He liked very melodic music. But we had to stay away from piccolos or anything high. He couldn't stand high-pitched music. With all our pictures the music is dubbed down quite a bit. He liked Tchaikovsky very much, and Beethoven was one of his favorites. I think he liked just about anything that was melodic. He didn't like the real modern music like Schonberg, or anything like that.

Another thing about Walt: he was always looking for something new. Once I did a cartoon called *Jack and Old Mac*. It was jazz with the modern voiced harmony, which was straight tone and close harmony. We didn't have anything to do then and I just did this thing, and we finally made a short out of it. He asked what kind of harmony that was and I said it was the modern thing. He said he didn't understand it, but, "If that's what they're buying now, let's try it." He was always willing to go along with something like that. All in all, he had a very commercial approach to music. And he liked music.

Walt was really in on the music, and the producer of the picture had nothing to say about it. It was all him. You dealt with him and that was it. After we got bigger and bigger, he kind of left it up to us because he just didn't have time to get in on these things, with Disneyland and all that.

When I first came here, I worked with Bill Peet on a sequence for *Sleeping Beauty*. I'd never met Walt, but he'd given an okay for me to work on the picture. They had somebody else on the picture earlier, but he and Walt didn't see eye to eye…so that's when I came in on it. I did a sequence with a flute, with some of Tchaikovsky's music, for the birds. We had a meeting and Walt was there and he said, "Yeah, I think that's kind of the idea of what we want to get," because they hadn't really accomplished anything musically yet. He said, "Yeh, I think that's going to work fine." We got through and Bill Peet brought me up. I'm a pretty big guy. He says, "Walt, I want you to meet George Bruns." Walt looked up to me and he said, "God, I'm glad I didn't say anything bad about the music."

RH: Tchaikovsky was the theme in *Sleeping Beauty* all the way through?

GB: Yes, we used it all the way through. I'll say that I had to write…about a third of it is original. I had to match Tchaikovsky, which was a heck of a job to do. But in certain places we just couldn't find anything in the score that would work, so I tried to match his writing and make it work.

The biggest success I had, of course, was *Davy Crockett*. When we were shooting *Davy Crockett*, Walt called me in one day. They were narrating the *Davy Crockett* story throughout the movie. And Walt said, "George, can you get kind of a little throw-away melody under this narration some way? We wouldn't just narrate, we'd have a little ditty or song or something." So I knocked out the song *Davy Crockett*. I took what Tom Blackburn had written, a line from here and there, and made a form song. I had it done when the director of the picture stopped by one morning and I played it for him. He said, "Nah, that's not what we want at all." Walt would always come in at about 7:30 or 8:00 and I always used to come to work quite early. So the next morning, Walt stopped by and he came into my office and said, "You got anything on that?" I said, "Yeah, I played it for…" He said, "Oh, make a demonstration of it and we'll cut it in the picture and see how it works." We did that and he said, "I kind of like that." Pretty soon he'd keep adding it here and soon it was in five or six times in every show. When that hit the air we didn't expect anything. But it just broke! It was on the hit parade for thirteen weeks, as number one, and sold like eight million records on the first score. If it hadn't been for Walt, it would never have been in the picture.

RH: Did you do anything for Disneyland?

GB: As big as that park was, Walt's mind was so much on detail. He even wanted to know the type of every orchestra, how many people were in the orchestra: little details like this. The average guy would never think about it. Walt'd come around and ask, "What do you think we should have in the marching band and in the barber shop?"

I did the music for one of the things down there: the Mine Ride. Walt would come to you and he'd say something like this, "Now, I want the music to sound like it's coming from everywhere; where the waterfalls are. Like something here, something coming out of here, and it'll all blend together." He'd come up with things that had never been done before.

There is the problem to figure out: how in the heck to do that? Actually, it involved a lot of research. This was something I had to devise: a way to record tracks separately on a click track. At that time, back in 1956, they had these four-track machines. I would record the voices separately, then record vibraphones and bubbling clarinets, then a theremin separately, then a harp. These are all recorded separately so we could transfer them to separate tracks, so out of each track there would be true stereophonic sound. We'd record them originally to a click track, which is exact and all of them would blend.

© 2007 Jane Hubler

Buddy Baker (1918–2002)

Interviewed by Jon Burlingame on May 10, 2001.

Norman D. Baker was the last surviving composer of the Golden Age of Disney music—that is, the team of experienced film composers who worked directly with Walt Disney on the scoring of his motion pictures and television programs. "Buddy", as he was known to family and colleagues alike, was honored by the studio as a Disney Legend in 1998.

Baker was Oscar-nominated for his score for the 1972 Disney live-action film *Napoleon and Samantha*, but was equally known for his music for such Disney classics as *Toby Tyler* (1960), *The Fox and the Hound* (1981), and his work on the Oscar-winning *Winnie the Pooh and the Blustery Day* (1968), which incorporated songs by Richard and Robert Sherman. Many of Disney's classic television nature documentaries, including *One Day at Teton Marsh*, were scored by Baker; and the original arrangement of the Sherman Brothers' "Wonderful World of Color" song for TV was done by him. Baby boomers may not realize it, but much of the music they heard on Disney's 1950s daytime-TV staple *The Mickey Mouse Club* was also composed, arranged, or conducted by Buddy Baker.

Baker worked at Disney for nearly three decades, starting in 1954 and "retiring" in 1983, although he continued to write and conduct music for Disney's theme parks around the world on a regular basis. In 1985, he began teaching at the University of Southern California and in 1988 he became head of "scoring" for the Motion Pictures and Television program at USC, which he headed until his death on July 26, 2002. He was 84.

This interview was conducted at USC and was first published in *The Cue Sheet: The Journal of the Film Music Society* in Volume 18, Number 3/4, from July–October 2002.

Jon Burlingame: How much did Walt get involved in music at Disney?

Buddy Baker: He got involved to the point of just making a comment about the type of music he thought [a film needed]. He never, ever, in all the years I was there, was on the stage when we recorded. He knew everybody tightened up when he came around. But it was uncanny how he knew what was right for a scene, what type of music.

JB: What do you mean by that?

BB: Well, he would know. He would say, "Buddy, don't you just feel like a big symphonic sound through here?" Or he might say, "This is kind of cute and light, isn't it?" He would never tell you what to write. Most of the time, he would put it in the form of a question.

JB: Would you spot shows with Walt or is that more detail than he would get into?

BB: No, I wouldn't sit and have a true spotting session with him.

JB: In other words, cue by cue, second by second, he wouldn't do that.

BB: But what we would do with him—you would only have to do this on his own pictures—is that you would run the whole film without stopping for anything and just have a music editor with you. [He would] pick up where [Walt] said, "Do you think there should be a certain kind of music here?"

JB: So the music editor was taking notes.

BB: I remember one time there was a scene going along, I've forgotten what it was about, but Walt said, "I think you should score this." In other words, he wasn't sure whether it was really needed, but go ahead and score it because he'd rather have it than be sorry [by not having music if it was later deemed necessary]. But that was about the only direction you would get from him.

JB: Did you have the impression that he cared about the role of music in film?

BB: There was only one thing that was more important to him in a film and that was the story. He had an appreciation of what music did for film more than any person I've ever worked with.

JB: I want to talk about some of your colleagues at Disney. Can I first ask you about Paul Smith? What was Paul like?

BB: Paul was a very soft-spoken, very quiet type of guy. He was a super musician. I remember on *Swiss Family Robinson* that he called me in one day and he said, "I need a polka here. I don't know how to write a polka." So I wrote that little Swiss polka that's been running for umpteen years in the treehouse down at Disneyland. I probably made more money off of that little polka than he did with the whole score.

JB: You were impressed with Paul's musicianship. Why was that? What was it about Paul that made him such a good composer?

BB: I would look at his scores and you knew how great it was going to sound by just looking at it. I looked at his score and it was like Ravel wrote it, for goodness sake, you know? He was that concise with everything he put down. He was just marvelous.

JB: Was there any one area that Paul was especially competent at scoring?

BB: I think he was probably the best of all of them doing the nature films like *The Living Desert*, *Water Birds*, or *Beaver Valley*. He was marvelous with those because he would be very subtle with the music, but if you listened to it carefully, you would realize that the music's in sync with the action of those animals.

JB: Since Disney employed an entire musical team, who decided which composer would be assigned to a project? During your period of time there, your colleagues included Oliver Wallace, George Bruns, Paul Smith, Joe Dubin...

BB: Walt handpicked. So no [filmmaker] would object to which one of us was assigned because they wouldn't dare say, "Well, I don't want George," because of some reason or other, because they knew that Walt liked George. He did get us pigeonholed. He knew that George and I were more prepared to handle the television pop-score-type things than Paul or Ollie. I never heard any pop thing that Paul did except maybe a vocal background on a song, which was always good, but that wasn't his cup of tea.

JB: Talk about Oliver Wallace. He had been around longer than anybody, right?

BB: I think so, yeah. Ollie was a real character, a natural character. He would do funny things and he liked to play jokes on people. He had a great sense of humor. I remember one time I could hear him working, playing something over and over on the piano. I just copied it down and kept it for a couple of weeks. Ollie said to me one day, "You know, kid, if you get any ideas, let me hear them because I'm running out of ideas." So I waited until he said that to me the next time and I took this thing in and put it out there. I said, "Ollie, I came up with this. I thought it was okay." Then he played me some of the music. He got into it about six bars, then he turned around to me and said, "You son of a bitch!" [Laughter]

JB: How would you assess his abilities as a composer?

BB: I think he was qualified to do an exceptional job on most of the nature things, but big heavy dramatic things? I don't remember much that he wrote in that line, or pop things. But he did come up with... What was that funny tune he wrote in the Hitler movie?

JB: *Der Fuehrer's Face*.

BB: Yeah, so he had a sense of humor, but he couldn't conduct. He got to be an absolute master of click tracks by writing quarter-note triplets across a bar line and all kinds of things like that that were very playable.

He would write like little fermatas, he would write it right in tempo, and I would defy anyone to tell that every note that you hear in any of Ollie's pictures would be on a click track.[1] He had a great sense of humor about that. Al Anderson was a great trombone player. One day they were recording long and the orchestra kind of fell apart on Ollie, and Al said, "Ollie, do we follow you or the clicks?"

JB: Let's talk about George Bruns. George had been a student of yours in the early 1950s?

BB: Yeah, early '50s. I first met him when he was playing bass with a little band down at a ballroom in downtown L.A. George asked me if I gave any private lessons, and I told him that I would. So he studied with me for quite awhile until he got a handle on how to do animation and all that kind of stuff. And of course, we did it a lot more precisely than they do it today. We worked with footage. Everything was by frames and music editors didn't lay it out for us. We made our own timing sheets and gave them to the music editor and said, "This is what we want," which seems to me makes sense.

Anyway, George had been studying with me probably about a year, and then he went to work at a little animation studio called UPA. Working there, George eventually met an animator named Ward Kimball. Ward met George, and he liked the way George played. George was a great tuba player as well as the string bass. George was playing with the Firehouse Five for a while and that's when Ward found out that he'd been working over at UPA doing some little shorts over there. I don't know what transpired after that, but at any rate, George ended up at Disney through Ward Kimball. He had been there, I think, less than six months when he called me to come in to help him on *Davy Crockett*.

He had been assigned the early television stuff on the show called *Disneyland*, which was a Wednesday night show. I guess he had done a couple of those shows, and then a feature came up that George had an opportunity to do. But he had also been assigned to do *The Mickey Mouse Club* and he said, "I can't do it," and that's when they asked me to take *The Mickey Mouse Club*. That was after I had been there two weeks helping George on *Davy Crockett*, something like that. So that's how I inherited *The Mickey Mouse Club* because George just didn't have time to do it.

---

[1] A click track is a series of audio cues used to synchronize sound recordings to a moving image. The click track originated in early sound movies, where marks were made on the film itself to indicate exact timings for musicians to accompany the film. It can be thought of as a recording of a metronome in that it serves a similar purpose.

JB: What was George like?

BB: Great. George was a huge man, around 6'2" or 3" I guess. He must have weighed 250–275. Big, and he had a strange sense of humor. He would see something funny or he would write some music and see it back with the picture, and it turned out to be as funny as he thought it would be and maybe more so, because he would sit there and laugh at his own music like he was the audience. He was also a master cabinetmaker. He was from Oregon, and I know that he bought a house out in Woodland Hills and rebuilt all the cabinets in the kitchen. Gorgeous, you know.

JB: What would you say were his strengths as a composer?

BB: Great sense of humor. He wrote funny music in the same way that Billy May writes funny music. He also had what I thought was a terrific dramatic sense. There was one picture that I was doing and I just didn't have time to finish the thing by the release date, and I asked George if he would do the last reel for me. He listened to some of the stuff I had, grabbed that last reel, and just did it perfectly.

JB: Tell me about Joe Dubin.

BB: Joe Dubin was well educated, spoke fluent Spanish. I think both his mother and father were doctors. His brother was Al Dubin, the songwriter ["Lullaby of Broadway"].[2] Joe was the most glorious slob I ever knew.

JB: What do you mean?

BB: Well, he had a big pot belly and he loved to eat. But he'd go on these diets and he would go in the commissary and have something fat free and all that kind of stuff and then top it off with one or two pieces of cream pie. One time Ward Kimball made a cartoon—I wish I had a copy of it—of Joe Dubin at lunch, and it showed all kinds of stuff falling down his shirt and some flies. It was funny.

JB: What kinds of things would Joe do? Like most of you, would he do some cartoons and some live action?

BB: Yeah, and he worked with us a little bit on some of those 15-minute segments of *The Mickey Mouse Club*. Paul did some of those, too. He did *Corky and White Shadow*. Joe, in spite of the cartoon that Ward made of him, wrote the neatest score I have ever seen. I mean it was very careful. It was perfect.

JB: How many of you had the time or opportunity to orchestrate

---

[2] Al Dubin and Harry Warren were a songwriting team at Warner Bros. in the 1930s and together wrote a lot of classic songs including "The Shadow Waltz", "We're in the Money", "I Only Have Eyes for You", and quite a number of others.

your own music? Did you also have a staff of orchestrators and copyists, an entire music department at Disney like there was at Fox?

BB: Yes. I had Walter Sheets with me [as orchestrator] for 25 years. Cliff Vaughan used to orchestrate for Ollie. I think he orchestrated for Paul, too. None of us had time enough to do our own orchestrations.

JB: Everything in television was scored. Nothing was tracked [utilizing music written for earlier shows], right?

BB: Yeah, even the opening signature for one of those little shows or something, instead of having a music editor try to make it fit, we would just rewrite it and re-record it to fit.

JB: Let's say when *Toby Tyler* came to television a couple of years after the theatrical release, would you have to do anything new?

BB: No. What we always planned there was an adjust-in-case type of thing. I always had a reel of about 900 feet of film and we knew where the commercial breaks would come if they made a television show out of it. I used to plan it. I think George did, too. I would tailor the music so that it could tail off, and they could pop in a commercial, and then pick up on the other side of the commercial. The way I wrote the cue they could break it.

JB: I'm sure Walt must have appreciated that.

BB: Like *Winnie the Pooh*. We designed three episodes of *Winnie the Pooh* so that they could be tied together as a feature. We would have one main title, but each of the separate episodes had its own main title. I would design it so I could get out of one and continue on into the next one, deleting the end title and the main title, so that the cue preceding that would go right into the first cue of the next episode. So we didn't have to re-record anything.

JB: Were composers at Disney respected as part of the overall filmmaking team? Today, it seems as if composers are often thought of as some necessary evil of post-production.

BB: No, we were part of the original team. Even on the animated stuff, I was in on the storyboard sessions before they had even a frame of it done. I knew what was expected. I also knew that there would be changes in it, but I knew what they were aiming for.

JB: Did everybody on the composing team write for both animation and live action?

BB: Yes. We had Franklyn Marks come in later. Actually, I think he came in to orchestrate some things first, and then he did some shorts. I called him in to help on *The Mickey Mouse Club*. He was a fine pianist. Then Bobby Brunner came on. Bobby Brunner was actually a guest playing a theremin on *The*

Mickey Mouse Club. He was on Guest Star Day. He also played good bass and he was a fine piano player. A real talented guy and he wrote very well.

JB: Why is it that the Disney composers seem to have been so ignored when they did such great work?

BB: Well, because we were too comfortable there. Walt was the only one who got credit out of that studio. "That's Disney music." Everything was "Disney". He made it so comfortable for us with benefits and automatic raises and all that kind of stuff that at the time we just didn't think about it. But you can't name anybody that was a better composer than Paul Smith. And you know, Joe Dubin was a very schooled musician. He knew what he was doing, and so did George and Ollie.

JB: On average, how many weeks would you have to write a score for a one-hour TV show, and then how many weeks would you have to score a full feature film?

BB: Usually about four weeks for an hour TV show and about eight weeks for a feature.

JB: And where did you record most of the time?

BB: Most of it was right there at Studio A on the lot, which no longer exists. They didn't tear it down. They just made it a dubbing studio. It's still there.

JB: How many musicians could Studio A at Disney accommodate?

BB: Fifty-five sounded the best in there. I've had 65 or 70 people in there. It still didn't sound any bigger than 55. It just seemed like it stopped hearing.

JB: How many musicians would you usually use on a television show?

BB: By today's standards it was a lot. I used to use anywhere from 20 to 30 people. Twenty-five at least.

JB: And what about for a cartoon?

BB: Well, I did *The Fox and the Hound* there and I had, I think, 55 or 60 people on it. Cartoons usually don't require a band that big or an orchestra that size, but I think for the shorts I used at least 35 or 40 people.

JB: What was the process like? Let's say you were sitting down to do *One Day at Teton Marsh*, which was for the Disney TV show: one hour show, nature-oriented, probably a lot of music. What would the process be like? Would you sit down and spot that with the director or the producer, and how many weeks would you then have to work?

BB: I think on *Teton Marsh*, I had about five weeks.

JB: How did it begin? Did you sit down with the producer and talk about music?

BB: Yeah. I would mainly be concerned about where there was going to be heavy sound effects and we'd go through that. He would say, "Well, you don't need to worry about music here. This is going to be really loud with sound effects," or something like that. In an hour television show, which is really 50 minutes or less, I would have at least 40–45 minutes of music.

JB: How detailed were your discussions?

BB: Not too, because they all seemed to have confidence in what we did. Walt had a funny thing. Every time I would see him he would never say, "What are you working on?" He would say, "What are you scoring?" That was his word. I never heard him say anything else. "What are you scoring?" And I would say, "Oh, Circle-Vision." He said, "Oh, great," because he was comfortable with that. He knew I knew what to do with it. It was pretty much that way even if it was one of the musicals with the Sherman Brothers' tunes. It was just general discussion. I never ran into anybody there that had any pointed, direct ideas of what they had to say about music. They sort of left it up to us.

JB: So it was really your ideas about what to do musically.

BB: Mine or Paul's or whoever.

JB: Then you got to the scoring stage. How long would it take to record a typical one-hour television show? Would you do it in a day?

BB: Sometimes. It depends. I didn't record *Teton Marsh* in a day because we could only record five minutes an hour. I had at least three sessions on that because the union wouldn't let us go over that.

JB: Right; you could only record half an hour of music in two three-hour sessions. Okay. Did Disney have a contract orchestra like the other studios in the '50s?

BB: All the studios had a contract orchestra until the government broke it up about 1958. And then they were all first-call players: Really the same orchestra.

JB: How close to airdate would you actually record the score?

BB: We were always about two weeks ahead.

JB: How often would the composers be invited to dubbing? Or wouldn't you have time to go because you were already scoring something else?

BB: I went to every dubbing. They go through and get everything down, and I would say to whoever was in charge, "The music's too low here," and they might say, "Well, we have dialogue you know." I'd say, "Let's get the director down here and let him hear it." The director would get down there and I'd say, "I think we need to take the music out or bring it up to where you can hear it," and 100 percent of the time they agreed to bring it up.

JB: So then when I was listening to a Disney show at home, the chances are most of the time I was hearing the cue as it was intended to be heard.

BB: Yes.

JB: I don't think a lot of people could say that at other studios.

BB: No, no.

JB: You spent 29 years at Disney: from '54 to '83. Can you say what your two or three favorite experiences were?

BB: First was getting a good handle on what to do with animation because I don't think—and there is no ego involved in this—anybody in the business even today can time things better than I can. I would tackle any of them on that. Second thing, I had an experience of figuring out how to do Circle-Vision, which is a whole different technique. I had an opportunity to learn how to combine audio-animatronics with film for the park things. There were about three or four different systems that you have to use for park music. Everything was like a learning process, really. And that's all besides doing hourly television shows or feature pictures, which everybody would do more or less the same way, only we had a little more of a handle on what we did than certainly anything they do today. But we also were working for people who knew a great deal, and that's not there so much today.

JB: So if you look back on your career, you not only got to do feature pictures, but you also got to do animation and weekly television and unique things in theme parks that nobody else really had a chance to do.

BB: And then besides that, we always had these Disney shows at the Hollywood Bowl. I did one whole evening at Radio City Music Hall in New York. Another thing I started doing: I was one of the first to take my music into the concert hall and synchronize it with a live orchestra so that people in the audience could see how we put music to pictures. I did that one time in Anaheim, one time back in Missouri. But those were all experiences that Disney offered that you didn't get any other place.

© 2007 Jon Burlingame

Buddy Baker (1918–2002)

Interviewed by Jérémie Noyer on July 19, 2001 and January 26, 2002.

Having discussed his collaboration on Disney TV series and movies with Jon Burlingame, Buddy Baker focuses on his contributions to the parks in this conversation with Jérémie Noyer.

Jérémie Noyer: First of all, can you tell me about your background?

Buddy Baker: I studied music at Southwest Baptist University in Missouri. Even though it was a religious school, they had a wonderful music department, so I studied there. That was back in the thirties. Then, after that, back in the late thirties, early forties, I worked as an arranger for a band. I came out to California in 1948, where I've been ever since. I used to write for the big bands that came through Los Angeles that played in places like Ocean Park or in night clubs. The first serious work that I did here was for the radio. And after several years on radio, I got into picture work. I started at Disney in 1954 and stayed there maybe 29 years. And after all that time, I became director of the film music program at USC. But I'm still doing some Disney things such as for the Tokyo DisneySea park.

JN: How did you come to Disney?

BB: That's sort of strange. I had a few students before I came to Disney and one of them got a job there. He had been there maybe for six months or less when he called me and said, "You know, we're getting very busy over here. Could you come out and help us out for about two weeks?" I said, "Sure, I have time to do that." That was the time of *Davy Crockett* and they started *The Mickey Mouse Club* and all that. So I went over for two weeks and stayed there for 29 years! And everything just started to evolve from there. I became music director of the original *Mickey Mouse Club* with Annette, Bobby Burgess, Sharon, and all the kids that were around in that first *Mickey Mouse Club*. I did that for two years.

JN: How did you meet Walt Disney and what kind of memories do you have of him?

BB: That was the third day I was there, in an elevator, in fact. I stepped on and Walt Disney came in. The two of us were in this elevator and

I introduced myself and he said, "Yes, I know." I called him "Mr. Disney" and he told me, "Why don't you call me Walt? All the secretaries do!" That's how he was!

JN: Can you tell me about your job at that time?

BB: We had two rehearsal pianists that were working with the kids, outlining the routines. During these days, Disney was a madhouse because we were on the air five days a week. My job was to get all that coordinated. The first year, I was on the air with the band and I made some of the arrangements. I also had an arranger working with me full-time. My job was to coordinate that music with the live camera work and the routines of the children on stage. It was just like any show that was with live music. The second year, I managed to convince them to pre-score all these songs and dance routines so we could record the music beforehand and then play it back to the Mouseketeers on stage. We worked that way for the next two years.

JN: How was it to work with the Mouseketeers?

BB: Oh, they were wonderful. They were all like 12 to 15 years of age. This was really a nice group of young people, all very nice and very talented, too. They really did a marvelous search for talent for that show. We had fine singers and fine dancers and everything in that group.

JN: Do you have special memories about some of them?

BB: I really loved Jimmie Dodd. He was just great! I used to call him "ten-beat". It wouldn't mean anything except to someone who understands tempos in films. A "ten-beat" is like a "ten-frame tempo" and I used to call him that because it seemed like every tune that he wrote was at the same tempo! He was a marvelous person. He and his wife, Ruth, wrote all those songs that the children did. And Annette, she was just a beautiful child and a nice young girl. It's hard to realize that all those kids in the fifties are almost sixty years old now.

JN: You also worked on the *Disneyland* TV program and composed for series like *The Swamp Fox*, *Texas John Slaughter*, and, of course, *Zorro*.

BB: My primary place there was as a music director. I was underscoring—writing background scores. If we needed a song, I would get with a lyricist and we would make it. I did that with a couple of writers on those shows, but my job at Disney all those years ago was primarily background music scores and dramatic music.

JN: In 1960, you went from TV to theater with *Toby Tyler, or Ten Weeks with a Circus*. How's that?

BB: Actually, at Disney at that time, we were so busy, and television and cinema were hand-in-hand. I did my first feature picture immediately after I had finished *The Mickey Mouse Club*. I hadn't done any television feature before! After that, there were times when I would be working on a television feature—that meant sometimes a one-hour show or a two-hour show in two episodes—and a feature picture at the same time. It's a matter of turning the switch to working with one thing and going to the other. That happened quite a lot! In all those years, I did about 58–59 feature films and about 125 television features, besides all the work I was doing for the park (at that time there was just Disneyland). Incidentally, Disneyland opened in 1955—46 years ago, and we've just had the celebration of July 17—and during those first years at Disneyland, George Bruns (who was that student that brought me into Disney), and I, just the two of us, did all the music for Disneyland. George left after a few years but I stayed on, up until we got into Walt Disney World and finally into Epcot. I was doing most of the writing for Disneyland and Walt Disney World. It was a necessity. At that time at Disney, there were five composers working and we were doing everything that came out at the studio. That was Paul Smith, Ollie Wallace, Jo Dubin, George Bruns, and me. So we did all the work there, and as soon as something came up, whoever was available would take the assignment. That's why we worked on feature films and television shows at the same time.

JN: From 1963 to 1968, you collaborated very closely with the Sherman Brothers.

BB: The strange part of it is that I'm still working with them from time to time. They're both around. Dick Sherman is in good shape. Bob, his brother, has had some health problems, but they're both still around and doing some work. Back in 1963, I was doing a feature picture called *Summer Magic*. That was the first thing I worked on with them. They had six or seven tunes in that picture. The next big film I did with them was the first of the three *Winnie the Pooh* featurettes. We got along great. That's always helpful when you become part of a team and everybody gets along fine. So I'd figure that the Sherman Brothers were just marvelous young guys. They were easy to work with and we understood each other. We never had a cross word, ever.

JN: A great part of your production for the cinema was made during the '70s. Was that a difficult period for the studio without Walt?

BB: In fact, there still was a great need for music. Maybe the films were a little different and required more dramatic music. But my work didn't change very much. There were some changes in some other studios. It was the start of singing groups and music of the day. It was also the time when some music scores had nothing to do with the picture, but they sold records. That wasn't the case in my work.

JN: With Tom Wilhite as the new vice-president in charge of development for feature films and television, the studio began a new era, with new kinds of productions, rather aimed at teenagers. Not exactly the traditional Disney family-oriented films?

BB: During that period, I did films like *The Devil and Max Devlin*—all in London. I also recorded it over there. I think it was during a strike period in the United States, so I went to London for a couple of months to work on that picture. I had an office at the Disney office with a piano. The film was a little different in the subject matter. It was away from the traditional family-type Disney entertainment, but as far as my treatment of it, I think I made the decision to treat all those things just like I would have had with other pictures.

JN: Animation was also a great part of your work.

BB: In fact, the first thing I worked on after I finished *The Mickey Mouse Club* was a little animated short called *The Camel*. It was a sort of an educational film, twenty-five or thirty minutes long. I did two or three of those shorts, like *Donald in Mathmagic Land* that received the Best Featurette of the Year award in Cannes [France], before I started on *Toby Tyler*. After that feature picture, I made two or three television shows and maybe two or three shorts again, like *Aquamania*. Then, at that time, the Sherman Brothers were at the studio and I started working with them.

JN: To you, what makes cartoon music special?

BB: All cartoon shorts are supported almost 100% with music. Some of them are designed to work with a song all the way through and use different treatments of that song. Some just play the action all the way through. In that case, there is no song involved; you just play what you see. That's the main difference between cartoon music and animated features. In animated features you can treat music almost like you would for a live-action feature. Whereas with the cartoon, you can get a little slapstick with it, do funny things and catch silly things.

JN: How did you come to the *Winnie the Pooh* films?

BB: I had worked with the Sherman Brothers on a couple of things and after *Summer Magic*, they wanted me to work on *Winnie the Pooh* with them. So that's how it came about. I had also worked quite a lot with the director. So I got a call at the studio one day, "Buddy, won't you come up and take a look at this *Pooh* film?" And I was assigned to doing it after that phone call.

JN: How would you describe this music?

BB: That's a good example of using the songwriters' music, and it was my decision to pick the instrumentation and make it work with the picture.

Sometimes I'd use maybe the bassoon to accompany a certain section of the film, and then, using the same melody, I'd use the strings section in a different sequence. I played all the scenes with thematic music where the song wouldn't work. For example, in the storm scene of the *Blustery Day*, I wrote pretty straightforward dramatic music for that because a song wouldn't work. And then this music could lead to the next song.

JN: As a score composer and a song arranger, how did you figure the relationship between the songs and the underscore?

BB: Take for example a song by the Sherman Brothers for a film. First, I would make an arrangement with the vocal. We would prescore the vocal (sometimes with a small group). Having done that, and knowing how it was going to work within the picture, I would just design my composition to lead into the song and then lead out of it. I would also put the whole orchestra behind the vocals and take the small group (the scratch track as we called it) out so that here would be an orchestral sound behind it which would seem theoretically coming right out from the underscoring into the vocal background. When it was all put together, it seemed like one thing. That's how we worked in those days. All the vocals were pre-scored. And then, anywhere I could use the melody of the song as part of the underscore, it enhanced it overall because it really made the songs and the underscore be part of the picture. What I had in mind, not only with the Sherman Brothers' songs but also with all the songwriters I worked with, was making the song work as part of the underscore.

JN: Do you remember something personal about these famous featurettes?

BB: That was one of my favorite things to work on. When we started out, there was just the *Winnie the Pooh and the Honey Tree*, just one featurette, and then Walt Disney decided we'd make the three of them and put them together as a feature picture. But we did one after the other.

JN: Was Walt involved in your composition process?

BB: Yes. I loved working with Walt because he had great taste in music. He knew exactly what would work. He would never tell you what to write. He gave us suggestions about what he felt. I remember sitting with him, viewing a film. He would turn around and say, "You know, this suggests a big symphonic sound through here." He had this taste for what type of music would work.

JN: What did Walt like about *Winnie the Pooh*?

BB: It turned out that this film was for him like the classic films, *Snow White* and *Cinderella* and all the rest. At that time, that's what Disney was known for: doing things that were made as children's films, but that were good for adults, too.

JN: One of your greatest achievements in animation is *The Fox and the Hound*.

BB: With Art Stevens, the director of that film, we almost took the idea of the treatment that was used for *Bambi* to make kind of a real, heart-warming film all the way through, with not too much of the bloodthirsty fighting we could see on-screen at that time. It was sort of a mixture of a very sentimental live-action picture with a feeling of tenderness to it, which went along okay.

JN: In this film, your music brings a discourse which is really complementary to the picture, creating a very elaborate discourse. For example, when Copper comes back home after the hunting season, he appears on-screen as an animal killer, with all the skins in Amos Slade's car, whereas your music keeps him loveable, since it recalls the dog he was at the beginning of the film. So, to you, music seems not only to be an accompaniment, but really a discourse of its own. Is that correct?

BB: That's right. There I was trying to capture the fact that they have grown apart, but some way, there is still a connection. Even though it wasn't treated visually and they didn't show that up front, I wanted to suggest that they didn't hate each other. With all the days they had been together, I didn't see how they could go on without that connection, even if it's very remote.

JN: In your music, silence can also be very evocative, the contrast to a lack of imagination. This way, it enhances our expectations at the very beginning of the film, or it can be part of the emotion when feelings are too strong. Silence seems to be truly part of your storytelling in music, doesn't it?

BB: If you keep music going on and on and on, it loses its value. So I think we got three or four minutes on that main title of *Fox and the Hound* before we hear anything. It was only starting out with very soft sound effects, birds and outdoor sounds. And then I did a kind of a sneak-up ahead of where you see the man with the gun, and that gave me a chance to work into that in a subtle way, and create a shock when you do see him: this is trouble! That was my concept on it.

JN: Some time ago, John Debney told me that animation is what differentiates boys from men in matters of film music. Do you agree with that?

BB: You bet! He's absolutely right on that because if you did it properly, you can be exactly on the frame you want to be if you know what you're doing. That traditional approach does separate the men from the boys! But they're not doing that so much today.

JN: During Walt's time, there were staff composers who composed exclusively for Disney, and from the '70s it has changed now that composers are independent. What do you think of both systems?

BB: Well, I was part of the first system, when we had in-house composers. In fact, I was the last composer on the staff of any studio. It's a different process now because they seem to be calling the name values of people and sometime the music doesn't work very well with the picture. I'm a strong believer that big, big names don't sell so many tickets. I prefer it when music fits the picture. But it's a whole different concept. That's why I don't do any more pictures: I don't want to be part of it.

JN: Film music is now evolving pretty fast. How do you see its future?

BB: I heard what Alan Menken did when he came to Disney, and I think he wrote some pretty good songs. For the rest, it seems that we've gotten into highly synthesized scores at some point. But in the past two or three years, it sort of turned around and they're using large orchestras again. Television is still using synthesizers, adding sometimes two or three instruments. But I don't think there's any substitute for the big orchestra. It speaks well for everything any time it's used. I know that Jerry Goldsmith, who is a dear friend of mine, and John Williams always use that kind of orchestra. The same with Elmer Bernstein, who is with me at USC, depending on pictures, James Horner, Alan Silvestri... It doesn't matter whether they record them here or in Europe. The fact is that we're coming back around to the big orchestras. I'm not sure if it will continue that way, but I hope so. I would like to see television using a large group of musicians. Here, we have too many talk shows and none of those types of series that need music scores like *Dallas*. For this series, they needed a new score every week! So I'd like to see some of those come back.

JN: Besides your work for the studio, you were one of the first composers to write music for a Disney park. That was for Disneyland in California. Can you tell me about the music you did then?

BB: George Bruns and I were the only composers there for the first ten years of the park. I think the first attraction that I did for the original Disneyland, back in 1955, was Snow White's Wishing Well. Do you remember the Disney song "I'm Wishing"? I redid that song; that was my very first job. I recorded it with a girl singing and there were little bell sounds with it. And that was actually placed down in the ground, where the water would have been in the well, so that sound came from there. I also did some music for the monorail, for Rocket to the Moon, for an attraction called Autopia, and for Submarine Lagoon. Small World came a lot later. Another thing that I did for the park at that time was all the area music for Main Street. That was a big project. Main Street was using early American folk kinds of songs. Ollie Wallace had a song he called "Meet Me Down on Main Street", a nice tune that was also used in that area.

During the same period, George wrote the music for attractions such as Enchanted Tiki Room, which was very complicated. In that show, there were the famous Sherman Brothers' songs, along with old standard songs, all sung by audio-animatronic birds. George and I wrote almost everything for the beginning of the park. After that, George left the studio (he moved back up to Oregon in the early seventies), just after *Robin Hood*, so he didn't do anything for Walt Disney World, which opened in 1972.

JN: One of your most famous achievements is The Haunted Mansion, isn't it?

BB: Actually, when they were building all the sets, they wanted a song to go all the way through the attraction. So I got together with one of the writers of the show, who was also a great animator, X. Atencio, and who wrote lyrics for that, called "Grim Grinning Ghosts". The song is very "tongue-in-cheek"; it sounds horrible, but it's kind of funny at the same time. In other words, the Haunted Mansion is not a sad, eerie thing. It makes you feel good and it's funny. That's why I kept this light treatment so it wouldn't get too heavy.

JN: It's not just about song: there's a great amount of music within this attraction?

BB: First we came up with the song. X called me and he said, "You know, they want a song and I got this idea of doing one about grim grinning ghosts." And I answered him, "Alright, go ahead and write your lyric ideas." Then I added the melody after we had decided the lyrics worked fine. Then, when we got into the different scenes in there, I made all the scenes with that music in sync. One time, I had 142 tracks in sync. And then it was reduced down to the main control tracks—to probably around 40 or so: all in sync. I used that main theme all the way through the attraction, even in the elevator section where you're "ascending down" for the first part of the ride. In fact, sometimes you can hear a wind sound, but the wind is actually playing the melody of the tune. I worked with the sound-effects department at Disney, where we could do it. It's very subtle; you don't realize that at first. And it's the same at Disneyland, Walt Disney World, and Tokyo Disneyland.

The most difficult thing in doing all that was coming up with new concepts. How to put music and animation and audio-animatronics all in sync! That had never been done before, and we had to figure out a system to do it for rides like Small World and Haunted Mansion. Do you remember the Hall of Presidents at Walt Disney World? That was a top project to work on because of all the speaking lines of Lincoln, when he's talking with all the former presidents around him. That music had to be in sync with all that. I also made extra music so that every time there's a new president added to it, the music is already written. They can expand the show without having to redo the whole thing again.

JN: Did you work with Marc Davis?

BB: Yes, I did. I worked with him for many years on films and then on the park things a great number of times, for example on the Country Bear Jamboree attraction. He was a dear friend of mine. What a big loss!

JN: Have you heard the Disneyland Paris version of the music, arranged by John Debney? In France, it became Phantom Manor.

BB: John Debney is a good friend of mine, and he's a good writer. But I'm not sure the show needed something that heavy, that big. I think lightness is better. Nevertheless, John Debney used the GGG theme and I think it works well. All his music was formed after the statue singing and he did a marvelous job. It's just a different concept.

JN: In 1982, you wrote the score for *Impressions de France*, in the France pavilion at Epcot.

BB: We recorded that in London. It's all French classical music, except certain scenes for which I figured it would be inappropriate to use French classical composers. For example, for the beach scene at Cannes, I was afraid that if I had used any serious composer to put music to that, it would have been funny. So I wrote original music for those sections. But I think *Impressions de France* is still the nicest music done in Epcot.

JN: Speaking of classical music, to you, what is the relation between concert music and film music?

BB: I think, basically, film music—at least during my time—was from the French school. Big motion-picture scores were based on the French concepts of music and composition. I know that my own background has been influenced greatly by the French composers.

JN: So who are you favorite composers?

BB: Debussy, Ravel, Ibert, Prokofiev, and Stravinsky, just to name a few. I think Respighi was great, too.

JN: Have you ever composed concert music?

BB: I've never done it commercially. I tend to be leaning more toward dramatic music rather than writing things for performance sake. I'm not that interested in writing music for the concert hall because I've been working with pictures so long that I think I need a picture to give me the inspiration to come up with something.

JN: Then you left Disney.

BB: That was in 1983, and then in 1985 I started at USC teaching animation music over there. I did that for years, and since 1988 I've been director of the entire film music program.

JN: Yet at the beginning of this interview, you told me you were occasionally still working for Disney. Can you give me a glimpse of your latest creations for the Mouse?

BB: My most recent productions were Journey to the Center of the Earth and Sinbad's Seven Voyages for Tokyo DisneySea. In conjunction with that, there is a new show at Walt Disney World on Winnie the Pooh. It's based on the same music that we used in the picture. I haven't seen it down there, but through the model the scene looks exactly like the picture. I did that one, and they did another version of that, some kind of a contemporary score that they used in Tokyo. They sort of updated the characters and all that. I understand they took some of the music from Florida and used it in Tokyo. But the way the show is designed, it is not the concept you saw in Florida. I don't think the Florida music would work all the way through, because it was designed for something else. As for the Florida show, it was almost like doing a picture over again. Then, at Disneyland, there's a new show called Innoventions, and I did that, too.

JN: It's very satisfying to hear that the Disney legends are still involved in the Disney parks!

BB: I'm glad to do that! There's not too many of us left that could do it!

JN: How did you come to work on the Tokyo DisneySea project?

BB: I haven't been to Japan since 1983. The strange thing about the Journey to the Center of the Earth attraction was that someone else had started to do the music, and they called me in because they didn't like it or whatever. That happens over there from time to time. Usually, people call me when they want something that is very traditional Disney. Because with *Winnie the Pooh* and all the things that I did back in those days when I was at the studio, we more or less created our own Disney sound. You can tell a Disney score without even seeing the picture, just by the way the music sounds. That's why they called me. I never saw a mock-up or anything. I just had a notebook with pictures of the storyboard. I never had to go through a model of the show or anything. That made it a little difficult to write music to scenes that you had no idea of the cost, of the action or anything except those pictures. But finally, it turned out all right. They said that Journey to the Center of the Earth is now one of the most popular rides in the new park.

JN: With so little material, how did you set the timing of your score?

BB: I was helped by Tom Fitzgerald at Imagineering, but I was more or less working blind on that. I wasn't absolutely sure. At the end, we made some minor alterations, but it all turned out very well, timing-wise.

JN: How did you come to work with Tom?

BB: I've known him for all these years. I was at Disney for many years before he even came on board. He had called me up to write a new theme for Journey to the Center of the Earth. He didn't really have any input on what we were doing at that time, but he attended our recording sessions. He was the only one I worked with because I really don't know who the art director was on the show and I wasn't in any meetings.

JN: What about the recording?

BB: We recorded in London. I specified the orchestra I needed to the contractor, George Ajmier: a 55-piece orchestra. At the time we were in London, Richard Bellis was over there, too, recording 20,000 Leagues Under the Sea. George Wilkins was also over there doing some background music, which had an Italian flavor to it. So we were all over in London at the same time. We recorded at EMI, Abbey Road. I conducted. The recording of the different scenes of the ride turned out really fine. I still have 22 minutes to record that we haven't done yet. I don't know if we'll ever do it. It was for a holding area where people can wait for the show to start. This was kind of a mood-type thing with almost a classical touch to it. I wanted to record that back here at Paramount and not have to go back to England to redo it. And some way, they got all messed up with the budget, that was placed on hold and I don't know if it will ever be recorded. But it's all written and copied and everything.

JN: How would you describe your music for the different scenes of the ride?

BB: The first scene that you come into is called Crystal Chamber. It's kind of an ethereal area that's shimmery and a little bit eerie in a way. Then you come into an area called Bio-Luminescent Tunnel. From the picture I have, it just seems like a tunnel! But I did have a timing on it and I used quite a bright tempo. It moves along pretty well. Then we go into the Mushroom Forest. This is an area where I used the orchestra with a lot of pizzicato strings and light woodwind things. Along with that, we had little crickets, frogs in there and insect noises and anything that could be associated with a humid mushroom place. And I had just a girl doing a legato form of the theme itself.

JN: How does all that work?

BB: Some of these things are timed into short pieces, as loops, that run continuously, like the Crystal Chamber or the Mushroom Forest—that's all made out of loops. Then there's an area called the Lair that doesn't have this kind of music because it's an action cue. It's a very discordant and eerie-type thing that is triggered by the cars as they come by. It's only a fifteen-and-a-half-second length cue, and then that goes into another longer cue which is on a loop and that's called Subterranean Sea. It's a low, mysterious, slow version of the main theme, and it sounds like a very underwater-type thing.

JN: Can you tell me about the main theme of the attraction?

BB: All the themes have a bar or two, or something from that main theme. It's sort of a stately, outdoorish sound that could be played almost like a classical piano-concerto-type thing. It's a theme that makes a statement, that's what it does. It's very legato, with a broad sounding, and a bridge, a central part that lightens up a little bit, and then back to the more stately-type thing.

JN: It's a wonderful bridge, played by the flute.

BB: Thank you. You know, we used up to four flutes in this piece. It's a beautiful and eerie sound.

JN: How did you think of the idea of a piano concerto for this attraction?

BB: Like I said, I've never had a chance to go through anything. So I was sort of guessing and this theme came out. And then I told myself that a piano should play somewhere. I just thought it would fit. If it didn't work, they'd just take it out. But they told me it was working beautifully in the ride.

JN: The attraction is inspired by the famous novel by Jules Verne. The same way, were you inspired by French music for this score?

BB: I've always been influenced by French classical music; that's more or less how I think, musically, all the time. So, in a sense, yes, but I wasn't thinking of French classical music in the same terms that I did when I did *Impressions de France*. That show is one of my great pleasures! They get more requests about its music than any other show there.

JN: There seems to be a touch of Debussy in your music for Journey to the Center of the Earth.

BB: Yes, I believe that's right.

JN: What relationship do you personally establish between attraction music and film music?

BB: The only relationship I could see is applying the same technique for a scene. Take, for example, the Crystal Chamber: I would write the same type of music for that that I would if it were for a motion picture. Other than that, none of this music would be exactly like anything in a picture because a lot of this is exciting music for a ride, and it's not anything that would be exactly useful in a picture unless you have an exciting ride scene in the picture. For example, in a motion picture, if you have a scene with a thrill ride of some type, some of this music could have been used for that as well.

JN: Did you appeal more to ambiance music or to Mickey Mousing technique?

BB: The main thing I need to know for an attraction score is if a thing is continuous and can run on a loop. If it's triggered, I need to know, from point A to point B, how much music we need before this bit of action happens in the ride. We have one place in there where the car comes by and it triggers this track and the orchestra goes over. That's a big motion as the car goes up, as if it were on the side of a volcano or something, and stops. And the music stops with it. So, those kinds of things, you almost have to envision them. If you had the same thing in a motion picture, it would be easier to time, because you would know exactly what to do. This thing is a little bit free-wheeling.

JN: Can you tell me now about your music for Sinbad's Seven Voyages?

BB: That's another one that we may have to redo, because after Tom made the final decision, he realized that that ride needed a more or less Small World-type treatment, with a song involved in it. Yet the director of the attraction wanted me to do a heavy Bernard-Herrmann-type treatment, which I did. The music I composed turned out, I think, really well, and they were very happy with that. Yet Tom thought it may be overwhelming the ride itself a little bit. And another thing: there is not enough sound isolation between the scenes. You can hear all of the seven music segments before you get to each scene. The last I heard is that I may be redoing that whole show with a different treatment. And if I don't do it, someone else will do it *à la* Small World. I'm sort of a pioneer in both techniques.

That is difficult sometimes when you work with a director and he wants a certain thing. And then, there's one fellow down at the end who doesn't like it. I've never understood why they just don't go to him in the first place and say, "This is what we're doing." But you know how it works in the motion-picture business. These things happen! I can just tell you that the music in Sinbad is good all the way through.

Take the last scene. It was kind of interesting because they wanted a bright-spirited Indian scene. And they had some audio-animatronic musicians playing some Mideastern instruments. The thing is that, mechanically, they couldn't make those figures operate as fast as the tempo was going. So I devised a way to have musicians playing in one tempo against this fast tempo, this festive-type thing that's going on throughout the rest of the scene there. And thanks to the stereo, you can hear these musicians playing their own thing against this fast-moving melody, and it all works together, with the same amount of frames per bar at the slower tempo or the fast tempo.

JN: Did you think of using ethnic instruments?

BB: Yes. I did a lot of research and I used as many ethnic sounds as I could find, and I found people here to play them. We have great, great musicians here in Hollywood, and I found guitar players who could figure out how to play ethnic instruments.

JN: When one considers the most recent theme park music, it seems that it has become less sing-able than during Walt's time.

BB: You know, that's exactly what Tom Fitzgerald was thinking about. That's true: when you ride Sinbad, you can't sing that. That's a dramatic score, like a motion picture. Younger directors seem to be getting away from the song time. And I really think that's what Tom was thinking for Sinbad: just getting back to that same technique as for Small World. Personally, I think that's a good idea. But if you're working for a director, you do what he wants done. If he wants the wrong format, I can't be responsible for that. I see the advantage of having a theme that goes all the way through that's sing-able. Maybe it's less dramatic, and rather makes things happy. It's a matter of choice, and if they want to keep the same feeling that we started with at Disneyland, Walt Disney World, and even Epcot, it's melody that matters.

JN: From your first collaboration with Walt Disney on Disneyland to the present days with Tokyo DisneySea, how do you see the evolution of Disney theme-park music?

BB: During all those years, since we started Disneyland, we had to come up with new formats on how to match music and mechanics and hydraulics so, during that time, we more or less pioneered ways to apply music to these various formats. George and I had to figure out everything we did, how to make things work together. I think the techniques are now the same that we developed. The technique used in Sinbad is more or less the same that we used in Haunted Mansion or Small World because it's a ride-through. Of course, each attraction has its own unique way of doing that, but in the meantime, back to the opening of Walt Disney World, we already had shows with music running on loops and others that were triggered by the cars. We did the same for the World's Fair in New York and the Expo 67 in Canada. In New York, there were supposed to be shooting stars on the dome of the General Electric pavilion. I knew the timing of the projectors that they were using and I applied motion-picture techniques to the music to make it happen right with the music, at the right time. So it was all a matter of mathematics.

JN: It really was a pleasure and an honor to talk with you as a Disney legend and sharing such experiences with you!

BB: There are not too many of us left around who really worked with Walt. I feel very privileged to have been part of that group. Those were very special years!

© 2007 Jérémie Noyer

Fess Parker (1924–2010)

Interviewed by Michael Barrier in 2003 and 2004.

On December 15, 1954, during its first season, the *Disneyland* TV show aired an episode called *Davy Crockett, Indian Fighter*. It was the first of three episodes about the legendary frontiersman. Fess Parker, who was then 30 years old, had been chosen by Walt Disney himself to play Crockett. Disney had spotted Parker in a two-and-a-half-minute bit part in a science-fiction thriller called *Them!*, about huge mutated ants that were threatening the American Southwest.

Public enthusiasm for the Crockett shows was remarkably strong. Huge crowds greeted Parker on a 22-city publicity tour in 1955, and sales of coonskin caps and hundreds of other Crockett-labeled items rose into the many millions of dollars. Writing about the Crockett craze more than thirty years later, the newspaper columnist Bob Greene was undoubtedly correct when he pointed to Parker himself as the critical element in the TV shows' success:

> In his portrayal of Crockett, Parker brought to the small screen a presence that was palpable; people looked at him, and they listened to him, and they tingled. The face and the voice combined to represent everything that was ideally male in the United States.

Although he had leapt to celebrity in a TV show, Parker's impact was that of a bona-fide movie star. He was tall (six-foot-five) and handsome, but so were many other young leading men in the fifties. Parker brought to the screen two priceless assets in addition to his good looks. For one thing, he was relaxed in front of the camera as few actors are, especially in TV, where the demands for speed and efficiency have always encouraged actors to be tight and guarded. For another, he could deliver dialogue with complete conviction (a perfect example: his speech to Congress about the Indian bill in the second *Crockett* episode). He seemed emotionally open, as good actors must, but the emotions were those of a strong and even stoic man—one with a sly sense of humor, suited to "grinnin' down a bear". Above all, Parker conveyed sincerity, the quality Walt Disney so valued in his animators.

It's a lingering mystery as to why Disney didn't recognize Parker's worth, but instead cast him in a series of misconceived or secondary roles—in support of Mouseketeers in one weak film, as an unsympathetic hero overshadowed by antique trains in another, and so on. There may be a clue in the casting of Jeff York as Mike Fink in two follow-up *Crockett* episodes in Disneyland's second season.

Television was still young then, but York fit a rapidly hardening mold, that of the aggressive, one-note comedian who relies on sheer brass to snag the attention of viewers who are watching the set with only half an eye. Through this casting of a much louder, cruder actor opposite Parker, Disney and his director, Norman Foster—a veteran of TV and low-budget movies—invited their viewers to regard Parker not as strong and quiet, but as passive. Perhaps that's what they thought of him themselves, even though his performances in the first season's shows should have told them otherwise.

Parker never worked with a director of real talent, and he never had the movie career that might have been his, but he has enjoyed great success otherwise. He starred for six years (1964–70) in the *Daniel Boone* TV show before leaving show business to pursue a career as a real estate developer and hotel owner in Santa Barbara. For the last fifteen years or so, he has also been the proprietor of a winery that has made "Fess Parker" a highly regarded label among oenophiles.

The loss is not his, but ours. To cite a role that Walt Disney barred Parker from pursuing, consider the Don Murray character in *Bus Stop*. Murray's fine performance is actually a little scary—it's as if his character were bipolar, on an extended manic high. It's easy to imagine that Parker would have been better in the part—warmer, and far more naïve than crazy. And if Parker had not been foreclosed from trying to claim a place in the John Ford stock company, well...how much better some of the last Ford movies would be if Ford had been able to rely not just on older stars like John Wayne and James Stewart, but on a younger actor of the same stripe.

Michael Barrier first met Fess Parker in 1988, when he interviewed him for a business magazine. Their most recent interviews—part of the research for Michael's biography of Walt Disney—began on September 26, 2003, on the patio of Fess Parker's Wine Country Inn at Los Olivos, and continued by telephone on January 6 and February 3, 2004. Parker reviewed and approved this composite transcript.

Michael Barrier: You were, as I recall, the first adult actor that Walt Disney signed to a long-term contract, so you have a particular significance in his work in live action. I want to get some sense from you of what it was like to work for Walt Disney in his role as a live-action filmmaker. One thing that really intrigued me was what you mentioned in a *Los Angeles Times* interview in 2002, that you left Disney because he turned down the opportunity for you to

be lent out to John Ford for *The Searchers* [1956], with John Wayne. I was kind of shocked by that, because I thought it would have been a perfect matchup. Why did he turn down that loan?

Fess Parker: Actually, it was what happened after that [that led to Parker's leaving Disney]. I was signed for 350 dollars a week, and by the time I was in my second year I may have been [up to] 500 dollars, I don't know. But I was still modestly paid. They had sent me all over the world and exploited me in every way possible, and I'd done everything I could for the opportunity. I wasn't consulted about *The Searchers*. I was en route with Jeffrey Hunter, who played the role [of Martin Pawley in *The Searchers*], and Walt Disney, on the way to Clayton, Georgia, for our locations for *The Great Locomotive Chase* [1956]. The conversation turned to Jeff's greatest experience of his life, which he described as [working in] *The Searchers*. Walt Disney turned to me—we were sitting in the back seat—and he said, "They wanted you for that." I was a newcomer, but I realized even then that you don't get too many shots, and I'd already been heavily exposed in one dimension. Then the movie that I was cast in, *The Great Locomotive Chase*—there was more tender loving care of the locomotives than of their live asset.

To put it simply, Walt Disney was unconcerned; he had so many things on his plate. I have no complaints. He always gave me opportunities to talk to him. But that one went by the board, and then the next one that came up was *Bus Stop* [1956]. I have a book that I went out and bought: the play *Bus Stop*. I took it to his office and I said, "I'd like to work in this picture." In the book I have his inter-office memo, with brown, crumbling edges—Walt Disney Productions, Inter-Office Communications, February 23, 1956. To Fess Parker from Walt Disney. "I am returning your copy of *Bus Stop*. Personally, I do not think that this is a good part for you, and what with present commitments that will carry you into September, I do not believe you ought to consider any outside things until after that time." And Don Murray, a friend of mine who lives out here in Santa Barbara—the idea that it was not a good opportunity is really kind of weird, because Don was able to do it so well [playing opposite Marilyn Monroe] that he got an Academy Award nomination. I don't know if I would have been able to have an equal amount of success, but I sure would have liked to try it.

MB: Were you under contract to Walt personally in the beginning? I know there were such arrangements back in those days.

FP: Yes, the first two years of the contract I was under personal contract to him. Then I changed agents, and my agent negotiated a new contract for me, and Walt didn't want to pay it. So he put me with the studio, a new seven-year contract. Two years into that contract, I'm being cast as sort of an auxiliary character, second billed. In *Old Yeller* [1957], I'm at the beginning and the end. The next thing, they introduced [James MacArthur, in *The Light in the Forest*, 1958], so I'm still in doldrums there. Basically, I just don't think they understood that if they wanted to extract the maximum value out of me, they had to do a little thinking about it, and they weren't thinking.

Then they cast me in a picture called *Tonka* [1958]. I've never [even] seen it advertised. Sal Mineo was in it. I said, "Who's Sal Mineo?" "Well, he's a young actor." "OK, let me see the script." I still remember this, I was so shocked. "My name is Captain James Keogh, and this is the story of my horse Tonka." Over the titles. On the back end, page 95, five pages, I'm killed. I went to Walt and I said, "Are you going to star me in this picture?" "Oh, yes." I said, "I think that's dishonest. I haven't got anything to work with. So I disagree."

If I'd been the only thing on his mind, or if he'd paid more attention to the circumstance—but by this time, he had people doing work that he didn't want to do. So we disagreed. I said, "I'm not going to do this picture," so they put me on suspension. There was more talk between my agent and the studio, and I believed, when I went back, that I was not going to be required to do that picture. But nothing had changed. So I said, "I'm sorry, I'm not going to do the picture." Any other studio, if it mattered, they would just put you on suspension until they were ready to use you again. But in this case, I never said to the studio, "I have no interest in the five years left on my contract." It was just sort of understood, and I left, and that was the end of it.

MB: Do you think they had run out of ideas for how they wanted to use you, and they were content to let you go? Of course, you wanted to leave—

FP: No, I wasn't intent on leaving at all. I had five years to go on a contract. I'm sure, from their side, they thought they were paying me a lot of money, but considering the work I'd done for them in the beginning—not just the film opportunities they gave me, because that was my obligation, but I went all over the world for that company and worked like a dog because I thought I had a vested interest in the merchandise and it was worth working for.

MB: So when you turned down *Tonka* and went on suspension and then came back, you expected that they would offer you another role, and you wanted them to.

FP: Yes, and I can't understand it, even to this day. I talked to someone who'd seen *Tonka*—I've never seen it—and I [would have] had a brief message over the title and four or five pages [of the script].

MB: It's not a big part [Keogh is played in the film by Philip Carey]. You would have been in support of Sal Mineo. But this is what I want

to get clear: it sounds as if it was more Disney's preference than yours that you leave the studio.

FP: I had an agent who was representing me, and I don't really know what the conversation was. It kind of got down to not a suspension, but "do it or else". I felt that I was right and that I had to do what I thought was right. I didn't want to go back to where I'd been.

MB: Walt treasured his great animators, who were in effect the actors in his animated films. It's baffling to me that he wouldn't have had some of the same feeling about the most important actors in his live-action films, particularly people who had shown they could deliver for him the way you had. I don't get it.

FP: I don't, either. I didn't understand it. I'd only been in films for three years, so I wasn't a past master of understanding where I was, but I did understand that without the part, you've got no place to go.

After Disney, I went directly to Paramount, and I was there for four years, from '58 to '62. Then, in '63, I did thirty episodes of *Mr. Smith Goes to Washington*. The Daniel Boone show took me to '70. I turned down a television series at Universal [*McCloud*] that Dennis Weaver did a great job with; I would never have pulled it off like he did. I still had ideas that maybe somewhere I'd get another shot [at feature films]. Plus, my family was growing up—[doing another TV series] just wasn't attractive to me.

I went to Warner Bros. the last three years that I received a paycheck from the industry. I did a pilot film; that was the only thing I did in three years. It wasn't because I was turning things down; it was just that nothing happened. I don't even know why they had me there. I had a big dressing room, a secretary, a limo any time I wanted it. I lived in Santa Barbara, so when I had business in L.A. it was nice to have the limo meet me at the airport. But it didn't make any sense.

MB: This *Searchers* thing is so intriguing—I think of you playing against John Wayne, and I think of the two of you being generally the same sort of actor. You use aspects of your own personalities to make the characters you're playing more real.

FP: Absolutely. I'm also the first to say that accolades for the finest actors in films are all the same. Some guys change their clothes, but it's still Marlon Brando. Paul Newman is Paul Newman. The force of these individual personalities is what the business is about. How many great actors are there, in film? You may laugh when I say this, but I think Gary Cooper was one of the greatest actors ever in films. Look at the range of things that he did.

MB: I was going through the directors' credits on the films you appeared in at Disney, like Norman Foster on the *Davy Crockett* series and the various people who directed the feature films—

FP: I want to tell you, there was not one of them on an A list.

Norman Foster, frankly, tried to get rid of me [during the filming of the first *Davy Crockett* show]. We didn't have any dailies to look at, and I wasn't privy to that, anyway. They simply couldn't get them back from Hollywood to where we were. Finally, they did. Foster invited the whole company to look at them, and on the way out of the theater, he said, "You're coming along." I said, "Well, thank you, Norman." Then it was a little better. But he had been placed in an awkward position. He went off to Mexico to cast for *Zorro* and to find locations, only to come back and find, oh no, we're not doing *Zorro*, we're doing *Davy Crockett*, and here's your boy. He felt a little out of the loop.

MB: Why do you think Walt never hired strong directors?

FP: He wanted the last word. He didn't want anybody to challenge him. When we did *Great Locomotive Chase*, he put a producer in place who had never produced, Larry Watkin [a screenwriter for such Disney features as *Treasure Island* and *The Story of Robin Hood*]. The director was a man who had been an Academy Award[-winning] film editor, [Francis D.] Lyon was his name. He had put together *The Cult of the Cobra* [1955] at Universal and pasted together the newsreels of Bob Mathias to make *The Bob Mathias Story* [1954], and those were his credits coming into making this picture at a distant location, with some extremely difficult logistics, and with a screenplay—when I had a chance, I said to Walt, "This screenplay just doesn't feel quite right." Historically, the character [the Union spy James J. Andrews, played by Parker] was significant, but from a storytelling point, everybody had to root for Jeff Hunter [who played a Confederate railroad conductor pursuing his stolen train] to catch us, because there wasn't any story otherwise. So, every move turned out to be somewhat less than it might have. The industry was waiting to see if I could produce another reasonably successful picture, and I didn't do much.

MB: Of course, there are cases where producers like Walt were exercising the kind of control that really made the films their own, but at the time you were working in the feature films, he was wrapped up in Disneyland and the TV show. He couldn't have been giving detailed attention to the films.

FP: No, he was just satisfied with what he was seeing.

MB: How much do you remember of Walt being present? You mentioned his going down to Georgia for *The Great Locomotive Chase*.

FP: He wasn't there very long. He wasn't a guy to hang around the set. He'd come and sit down if we were in the studio, for a little while.

MB: Of course, the last episode of *Davy Crockett* was shot at the studio, on the sound stage, instead of on location.

FP: I don't remember him on the set at all for that. I'm sure he was, but I just don't remember it.

MB: Even though he was keeping the final word and he was working through these directors who weren't on the A list, still, he wasn't really shaping the films. That seems so sad. I keep thinking, if he'd been willing to hire a John Ford...

FP: More than that. Several studios wanted to buy into my contract, so he could have farmed me out, where possibly I would have gotten some different things to do. I have no idea how they would have come out; when you're under contract, you're under contract. At least there would have been some variety.

MB: Do you think he was concerned, as with *Bus Stop*, that you might appear in a film—

FP: He seemed to care, but I don't think he really understood it: Just the human factor, [the way] an actor [feels toward] someone holding your contract. That was shared, I think, not only by Walt but by Bill Anderson. He'd been a businessman before he came to be an administrator [at the Disney Studio]. Card Walker, who rose to heights there—they weren't picture people. It all seemed to be meat and potatoes.

MB: You were just an employee.

FP: Yes.

MB: I saw [Harrison] "Buzz" Price the other day, and he said he was always aware that the people who worked for Walt seemed to be scared to death of him. He never understood why, but there was one time when he felt that Walt treated him like an employee and basically reamed him out in front of half a dozen important people. Was there ever a situation when you felt Walt treated you that way?

FP: No.

MB: He never put you down in front of other people.

FP: No. His secretary [Lucille Martin] is still at the studio. I used to stop by her desk and say, "I'd like to say hello to Mr. Disney, is this an opportune time?" I'd go in, and Walt might be talking to some people, [but he would say], "Have a seat, and when I get through here we'll talk." I don't remember his ever not being able to see me. Same way with Roy Disney and the chief legal counsel, Gunther Lessing. Those guys were smoking cigars, and Gunther was rolling his. We'd just sit and shoot the bull. I enjoyed being at the studio. It was very open, very pleasant, other than what I've told you here.

MB: It seems so strange that they would be so open, and yet so insensitive.

FP: I don't know why I would engender that. [But considering the demands on Walt's time,] any attention was remarkable under the circumstances, even if it was flawed.

MB: I keep reading about the methods Disney used to control films, the detailed storyboarding, which evidently the director wasn't really in charge of. It was done at an earlier stage, so the director would be confronted with these detailed storyboards that dictated the staging and cutting of the film.

FP: I knew they were doing that. I don't know that they did it on each and every [film that Parker appeared in]. When we did a picture called *Westward Ho the Wagons!* [1956], we had a veteran director who wore an eyeshade and carried the script around in his hip pocket.

MB: That was Beaudine?

FP: Yes, Bill Beaudine, wonderful old guy. He was terrific. But he was used to shooting Leo Gorcey and those guys over at Monogram.[1] This was just a thing over at Disney. I don't know if he did any more pictures after that. And where they got him, who thought this was a great idea to follow up the Crockett things—it sure wasn't Bill Walsh, because Bill was a man of good taste. He knew the business.

MB: But he didn't have as much say over things?

FP: *Davy Crockett* and *Mickey Mouse Club* were his first great successes, so he was feeling his way there. But you saw his choices later on, the tremendously successful things that he wrote and produced.

MB: Robert Stevenson, I guess, was one director who stood out more than the others.

FP: Bob was very nice. In my little scene in *Old Yeller*, I said, "You know, Bob, where I come from, a lot of times when men of the area want to talk, they kind of hunker down. I kind of see doing that in this scene." He said OK, so he put the camera there, and Tommy Kirk hunkered down and we had a little talk. And that was it.

MB: You must not have worked many days on that picture.

FP: No, I didn't. Very few.

MB: Were there long stretches when you simply didn't have anything to do when you were under contract with Disney?

---

[1] JB Kaufman notes: "This is a reference to Beaudine's work on the *Bowery Boys* series. Beaudine had an outstanding career behind him by that time. He had been a top director in the 1920s and had made some distinguished films, including some Mary Pickford features."

FP: Oh, yes.

MB: That must have been frustrating.

FP: Well, you know what? I'm a happy spirit. I had a sailboat and I went down and got on it. I didn't miss a day.

MB: You took advantage of the situation.

FP: I did.

MB: I've heard that Buddy Ebsen was being seriously considered for the role of Davy Crockett before they discovered you. Did Buddy himself ever say anything about that to you? Had the Disney people ever talked to him about playing Davy Crockett?

FP: Buddy was in costume when I met him. Walt Disney introduced me to him in the hallway of the studio's administration building. I actually saw a list of practically every male actor in Hollywood that they had considered, looked at, some of them rejected them out of hand, I don't know. But it was a single-spaced page, two columns of names that they had sort of run through the hoops. My inclination is that, yes, he was seriously considered for it.

MB: But he never thought he had it and then it was taken away from him.

FP: No, he would have said something, because we became lifelong friends. He would have said something like, "You know, Parker, you did something to me."

MB: You've mentioned your admiration for Gary Cooper, which I share, and you've been compared to him. You were onscreen with him in *Springfield Rifle* for a minute or so. What do you remember about that experience, about working with Gary Cooper? Did you carry something away from that that you were able to use later?

FP: I had a chance to do that scene with him, and then I hope I didn't make a pest of myself, but I hung around wherever he was relaxing or in conversation—I wasn't trying to eavesdrop or anything. He was probably my favorite actor, among all the wonderful Fondas and Stewarts and so on. I think the thing that separated Cooper from most of the other actors, with the exception of Fonda, was a sort of physical grace that he possessed. He broke his hip many years earlier in a horse accident, and so it was hard for him to ride. He required a horse that was pretty narrow. I don't know if he was in pain, but whatever it was, he took care of it and handled that horse work beautifully. I still have pictures of him in my mind. He had a graceful way of spinning on his boot heels, and the man had probably the most expressive hands of any actor. You might think it's kind of peculiar to isolate items like those, but the other part of Cooper, the intellectual, the actor, however you want to describe him in his profession—it was all there, he could do comedy, drama, action. When he was Sergeant York that was one thing, *High Noon* was another, and he just pulled it off. He's probably the most underrated actor in my lifetime. I think the others were probably recognized—certainly Jimmy Stewart was, and Fonda, for his versatility.

Fonda had the same kind of grace; it was a more shambling kind of grace, if I can put it that way. I had the pleasure of spending a number of weeks onstage with him. It was my first job, and I stood in the wings of *Mister Roberts* and watched him night after night do a scene that was tough to pull off on stage. It was a recognition of what the crew had done on his behalf, and his technique, and his reaching the emotional moment—I know that it could not always be the same, but it appeared to be the same and had the same effect. That was a great experience.

MB: I hadn't realized that you had done stage work.

FP: I was in *Mister Roberts* the summer of 1951, from June until September. We played the Geary or the Curran, I can never remember which theater, in San Francisco, and the Biltmore Theater in downtown L.A.; it's now a parking lot.

MB: I've always thought of screen acting as being in many ways more difficult than stage acting because you're shooting things out of sequence. You may be shooting on location and you step through a door, and a month later you're through the door and inside, on a sound stage. I would think it would be very difficult for an actor to perform in the sort of emotional arc I think you're describing in Fonda's performance, where you rise to a climax and your own feelings are built into the way this character is developing. As someone who was mostly a screen actor but had some stage experience, how did you compensate for the characteristics that screen acting necessarily has?

FP: It's sort of like this: if you don't know anything about what you're doing, and they tell you to pick up the anvil—if you really want to be there, you'll pick that anvil up, one way or another. I didn't realize until later on how difficult it was. An example is my first experience onscreen to speak a line. This was my line: "You didn't say nothin' about there bein' no way to get to it from here." That sounds simple, and I probably can't repeat it again, but I waited for weeks to say that line. In fact, the director turned to the first assistant and said, "Does he speak?"

From that point on, I got jobs, and had more lines in *No Room for the Groom*, and finally the very popular director Douglas Sirk was doing a picture for Universal. I had a scene to do, some very brief but key lines.

It was in a saloon with a whole bunch of extras and it involved a bit of tricky camera work, saying a line and holding a newspaper in the precise location it needed to be. Unfortunately, I probably held up the company for fifteen or twenty minutes, which did not make me a more popular candidate for future Universal Studios films. But that's the way it goes. When you see an actor come in and deliver a short line, these guys are working sometimes without knowledge of the script. They're just kind of briefed, and they come in and deliver. It's amazing.

MB: We were talking about John Wayne and about actors' using aspects of their own personalities to make a character seem more real, and I would guess that's particularly important in screen acting. If you're doing a scene, and to a large extent you can play yourself—assuming you know who you are—that would give you a big head start.

FP: I can tell you, a lot of times, actors that I've known and I've worked with, they get into a character and they basically try to stay in it till the job is over. It is a sort of mental discipline and a concept that goes back to the days when you were playing in the back yard. One day you wanted to be Clyde Beatty, and the next day it was Buck Jones. You played them both equally well.

I watched *The Searchers* recently, and I thought John Wayne was really outstanding in a lot of scenes. But *The Shootist* [1976], his last picture, was life imitating art, because he played a dying man, and he was in fact dying himself. Ron Howard, Hugh O'Brian, Lauren Bacall—all the people in that movie were just splendid.

MB: Speaking of *The Searchers*, I was thinking about how you would have fit into that Martin Pawley role that Jeffrey Hunter played.

FP: You know, my impression was, not nearly as well as Jeff did.

MB: My feeling was that they would have had to rewrite that role, because you're a stronger screen presence than he was. You said that Jeff Hunter told you that working on that film was the greatest experience of his life, working with John Ford, and I'm wondering if you remember anything of what he said about what made it so special.

FP: His first words, of what made it so special, were "working with John Ford". For most young actors in those days, to have John Ford's interest was a fantastic thing. John Ford was such a dominant man in his arena, and at a time when the films were most popular that he was making, his company of actors were really family. If there was ever anything specific or even general that he could do for those people, he did it. So Jeff was admitted to the great circle. I don't think that he ever had another chance to work with Ford, but he had done it in a very important picture. [Hunter actually had important roles in two more Ford films, *The Last Hurrah* (1958) and *Sergeant Rutledge* (1960).]

MB: Of course, Ford was an icon among directors then, but what was it, for an actor, that made working with Ford so special? What did he bring to an actor, or ask of an actor, that was beyond what an actor would get from an ordinary director?

FP: I can't remember anything that Jeff said specifically, but my hunch is that it was sort of like going to school and somebody says, "You better not get in his or her class." If you're in there, you're going to have to work extremely hard, and there's no slack. Either you cut it or you don't. Ford was so strong a person and so much of an enigma—first of all, he was hiding behind those glasses, and [one lens was opaque]. His handkerchief habit, of chewing on the handkerchief. And he wasn't social by any means. I think the fact that you were going to work for him meant that you were at your highest level of attention. Whatever he told you to do, you'd better do it right, or you would suffer humiliation until you got it right. He was unmerciful with John Wayne, Ward Bond, you name it. It was a badge of honor to have worked with the old man. He was several people in his lifetime, really. Can you imagine him as a linebacker? His nickname in high school was "Bull". At the stage that I began to observe him, he wasn't a physical man, but he had been.

MB: So you actually had some personal contact with Ford?

FP: Oh, yes. Before *The Searchers* was made, I went one evening to the apartment of Olive Carey, the widow of Harry Carey and Dobe Carey's [Harry Carey, Jr.] mother. This was an evening that was primarily Ford family people. It was an open house and a buffet, and there were musicians playing in the kitchen and guitars and western music and so forth. I listened to the music for a while, and my girlfriend, Marcella, was in the front, with Olive in the living room, with the ladies, so finally I decided to help myself to some of the beans and chili and whatever was on the table. As I turned away from the table, Ford was standing right beside me. He took my plate, took my fork, stuffed it into the food, popped it into his mouth a couple of times, stuck the fork back in, and turned around and walked off. I don't know how far down my chin can go, but it must have been at its optimum position. Then I went into the kitchen, and I was just listening to the music, leaning up against the cabinet, and he came in and stood beside me. That made me nervous. Then he took his elbow and jabbed it into my ribs. I turned and looked at him—I don't know what expression was on my face, but I couldn't believe it. I decided to just ignore it, and he did it again. I just kind of walked away from him and went back in the other room. What in the world can you imagine that he was after? It's still one of my funniest experiences in the film business.

MB: When did this happen?

FP: I had just finished *Westward Ho the Wagons!*, which was the first picture Disney plopped me into. That was a picture they couldn't decide if it was for television or a movie theater. It had *Mickey Mouse Club* members in it.

MB: And this was before Ford offered you the role in *The Searchers*.

FP: Yes. I didn't know much about him. I certainly had seen his movies. Liz Whitney, the wife of the producer, had come out on the set, and I had met her. Apparently, the Whitneys requested me, or approved me, or something, but I didn't realize the significance of that visit until a long time later.

MB: I wonder why Ford would not have pursued you for roles later.

FP: My feeling is that if he thought that you didn't want to work with him, had any inkling of that, he wasn't the kind of guy to give you much. I went to him when they were going to make *Horse Soldiers* [1959]; I called on him. He was officing at Batjac [John Wayne's production company], and I went over and said, "I'd like to speak to Mr. Ford if he has a moment." I was shown in, and we chatted a few minutes, and I said, "Well, Mr. Ford, I know you're busy, but I was just wondering if there's anything in the film I could do for you." He said, "Well, you know, doggone it, I just hired a guy, his name is...oh, uh..." He went through a bunch of sounds that finally led me to say, "Are you thinking of William Holden?" He said, "It's William Holden." He had more fun than anybody. So there was nothing for me in the picture; Bill Holden had beaten me to the part.

MB: Looking back to *Them!* [1954], you're very good in your little part in that picture, but you're not Davy Crockett, and I wonder if you knew what it was about your performance in that picture that led Walt or whoever it was to say, "This is the guy we want."

FP: I don't know. Maybe the accent, the unsophisticated sort of appearance. It was determined by one of the casting directors who called me. I was on location, making a film for the Navy medical department on battle fatigue, in southern California at Camp Pendleton or someplace, and the casting man called me. He said, "You're a featured player, and I know that you don't want to do day work, but I have a part that I think would be good for you." I said, "If you think it would be good for me, I'll do it." I didn't know what it was. And sure enough, I had no idea how good it would be. If Walt had taken a phone call or lit a cigarette or sneezed, I wouldn't be talking to you today.

MB: And Walt himself was the one who saw you and singled you out.

FP: Yes, he said, "Who's that?" It wasn't as if he was screening the film to find anybody. I think he was looking at Jim Arness as a possibility, but I think he got interested in the little story, and just happened to stay long enough to see that.

MB: You've mentioned Bill Walsh very favorably, and I was wondering what you could tell me about him, as somebody you worked with and whose work you admired.

FP: Bill was an orphan and was raised in Cincinnati, in an orphanage. Then he got a chance to go to a junior college or something there. Barbara Stanwyck and Frank Fay came through town with a theatrical company, and he was interested in that, and went down and offered to help on the setup and so forth. By the time they finished their engagement in Cincinnati, they were interested in Bill and invited him to come along with them. That's how he got out into show business. He did a lot of things before he became a producer; he worked as a publicist for a firm called Maggie Ettinger, one of the top Hollywood firms. Then, his sense of humor and his ability to write led him to be one of the writers for the Edgar Bergen show. The years went by and somehow or other he got connected with Disney. Anyway, Walt Disney told him he wanted him to produce a movie—I think it was *The Littlest Outlaw*. He told Walt, "I don't know if I can do this," and Walt said, "Well, there's no time like now to find out." Bill did a nice job on it, and when *Davy Crockett* came along, shortly thereafter, he made him the producer.

He was the all-time dollar producer, until *Star Wars*, in motion-picture history. His pictures were the mainframe, or the guts, or anything you want to say about the Walt Disney film successes from the middle fifties [until the late sixties]. He was my best man at my wedding, and his wife stood up with my wife. Bill was a very complex man, and everybody that knew him felt attached to him. There's not that many of us any more, but when there were more, whenever we'd be together a lot of our conversation would be about Bill Walsh, because he was still fascinating to all of us.

MB: Of course, he died prematurely, and I've heard references to how much stress he was under, in the position he was in, being in many respects Walt's right-hand man in that period. It was a hard life for him. Is that what you observed?

FP: When Bill was really frustrated, this was the way he expressed it: "Hoo, boy!" [in an exasperated tone] That was about it.

MB: That was brought on by Walt?

FP: I used to hear Bill say, "Walt came in in his bear suit today." They were quite a team, and they worked extremely well together. There were other Disney producers, but none of them approached Bill's success, picture after picture.

MB: I was doing some time comparisons, and I realized that the first *Davy Crockett* show, which had such a tremendous impact, aired on December 15, 1954, exactly a week before *20,000 Leagues Under the Sea* opened. That was Walt's first big live-action picture, with real movie stars in it and a very large budget for the time, and it was a successful picture. But evidently Kirk Douglas was not the easiest person to get along with—

FP: I believe that's an understatement.

MB: Douglas himself wrote in his autobiography that he wound up suing Walt because he didn't like Walt's using some footage of him and his sons on Walt's train in his backyard on the Disney TV show. Clearly, the impact of the *Crockett* show was your impact—people were responding to you in that title role, more than anything else about the program—and, as I've said, it has puzzled me that Walt didn't take advantage of your movie-star qualities in a way that would have made sense for both him and you. I wondered if some of his experiences in dealing with Kirk Douglas and *20,000 Leagues* had some backlash on you. Did you ever have any hints of that?

FP: No, I didn't. Your question about why they didn't give me strong material—frankly, I think attention was split between the development of Disneyland, which was still in its infancy [,and TV and movies]. Walt hadn't expected television to have the impact that it did. I don't know why he didn't, but none of us did, as far as I know. Then they decided that if their merchandising program was a log fire, they were just going to throw another log on, and that was me. They sent me all over the country.

The merchandise thing didn't quite work out as advertised. Walt had given me 10 percent of Walt Disney Davy Crockett merchandise, but then they had run into legal problems because they didn't have the [exclusive] rights to [the Davy Crockett name]. The rest of the world decided, forget the rights, we're going to make it, sue me. There were hundreds of products. So the follow-up was very weak.

Westward Ho the Wagons! was not a good presentation. I was very grateful for the paycheck and the opportunity, but—I hate to say this—I was not sufficiently understanding [of] the business I was in. If you grab the brass ring once in a career, that's wonderful. If you grab that brass ring and do some follow-up and some growth in the industry, that's really what everybody hopes for. I guess when I saw that I was just going to sort of do the same thing all the time, I bought a sailboat and went sailing. When it was time to work, I'd come back and do that.

MB: At the time they put you into *Westward Ho the Wagons!*, was it up in the air as to whether it would be for theaters or TV, or did they start with the idea that it would be for TV?

FP: They couldn't make up their minds exactly what they wanted to do with it. Bill Beaudine was a fine old gentleman, but, basically, he wasn't much help. He just set the scenes up and we shot them, and that was that. Walt never had strong people; he didn't want any strong people.

MB: I get the impression that a lot of the directors at Disney were basically mechanical directors whose real skill was in setting things up so that scenes worked on the screen and the actors didn't get in each other's way.

FP: I think Walt was a counter-puncher. My impression is that he wanted to reserve the right to counter-punch with any effort that showed up in the screening room. He obviously had a great sense of story, in things he was interested in, and was quite a fine actor, if you listen to the people who worked closely with him. But I saw people come to the studio, people he'd hired to do huge, difficult projects, who had never done a simple project. Larry Watkin, the producer of *The Great Locomotive Chase*, [is a good example]. There were two companies shooting at the same time on a distant location. Peter Ellenshaw,[2] the artist, was directing a second-unit company. He had certain things that he had to do from a matte standpoint, so he was out there with a second unit.

MB: Making sure that they were shooting things so that he would be able to put the mattes in.

FP: Yes. This was a huge undertaking. A narrow-gauge railroad—and let's just say that when you run a horse through a scene, it's pretty easy to turn around and do it again. But when you've got a train, it's a little more complicated. It was a pretty dull picture. As a matter of fact, it was my Waterloo, I think. If I thought of myself as an arrow, I'd stopped heading up and started heading down with that picture. I was put in a role of being pursued and caught and hung.

MB: It flabbergasted me when I thought about that. Here's their new star, and they have him hung at the end. I can't imagine what the thinking was that led to your being cast in that part in the first place.

FP: I had a friend, now deceased, whose name was Burt Kennedy. Burt was a writer and director and a close friend of mine at the time. I showed him the script, and he said, "Oh, my God! This has got a lot of problems." He spoke of some of the things that we've alluded to here, relative to the film. I didn't speak to Mr. Disney about it until we were on location, or on the way to location, somewhere before we actually started to shoot, and

---

[2] See *Walt's People: Volume 4*.

I mentioned something about the script, and he said, "No, this is what we're going to do." No discussion. And it was too late; he was right about that.

When I did *Davy Crockett*, I had an opportunity that I didn't understand. And that was [predictable], because things got a little unique. Burt Kennedy came to me and said, "Fess, you need me to be your manager. And I'm willing to do that." I thought about it, and I didn't know what he meant, really. I didn't quite understand the role that he foresaw. It's interesting, the last conversation I had with him before he died [in 2001], I went down to his birthday party, at his house in the valley, and he said to me something like, "We should have made a picture." I said, "Well, Burt, I agree, but we'll probably have to put it off until we're on a bigger stage." But he knew what my strengths and weaknesses were, because we had been friends from the day I first worked in films. I'd met him in the fall of 1950, when I was going to school at USC, and his girlfriend had a little sister that I became acquainted with. That's how I met Burt. Later, I moved to an area that was very close to where he lived, and we used to spend the mornings drinking coffee and reading the *Daily Variety* and talking about pictures and directors and so forth. He was very astute. He was born in a trunk; his family was in vaudeville.

MB: You've mentioned that you were under personal contract to Walt. Was that a typical arrangement?

FP: As far as I know, I was the only person he ever put under [personal] contract.

MB: Why did he do that, as opposed to putting you under contract to the studio?

FP: I really don't know. And when I asked for 10% of the Walt Disney's *Davy Crockett* merchandise, he gave it to me.

MB: But that didn't translate into much money.

FP: No, it did not. When I asked for more money, the late Ray Stark was my agent. So there was the contract I had with Walt, and then a new contract. Things were changed and deals were struck in my behalf that I think basically eliminated their requirement to pay me that 10%. I really wasn't aware of it at the time, or if I was, I can't remember it. My background in the film business was very shallow. I was playing very small parts; they were getting better, but they were small parts. I wasn't immersed in the culture.

MB: So you simply didn't have the background to be fully aware of all the subtleties that were involved in such negotiations.

FP: No, but it's not a big deal. I was out on my sailboat, and I wasn't thinking about it too much. I can't buy back that time; I enjoyed it.

MB: You worked with Michael Curtiz on *The Hangman* [1959] after you left Disney, and I guess the other two major films you made at Paramount were *The Jayhawkers* [1959] and *Hell Is for Heroes* [1962]. *The Jayhawkers* is historically kind of crazy, but you're awfully good in it.

FP: It was hard to understand that picture. Mel Frank was basically a writer-producer, and he finally decided he wanted to direct the film. We had a man on the set, constantly, who was his mentor and really was directing behind the scenes. I'm trying to think of his name. He should be listed somewhere [in the screen credits] as an advisor, or something.

MB: You were working not only with stronger directors than you had at Disney, but also with stronger actors opposite you. People like Jeff Chandler and Steve McQueen. When you were making those later features, what stands out in your mind as being most different from your work at Disney?

FP: It was similar to Disney in that Y. Frank Freeman owned Paramount, and he used to invite me in, and we'd sit and talk. The old gentleman who was about 90 years old, Adolph Zukor, would be sitting around during these conversations. Clearly, they saw me as in sort of the Dean Martin role, playing the second man. Which was OK; that was fine for me. I enjoyed Robert Taylor and Jeff, and I found that working with Steve McQueen was the most interesting. I didn't have a lot [of scenes] with him, but I was very comfortable. He seemed to always work within himself, but in my brief scenes with him I felt that we [worked well together]. With Jeff Chandler, bless his heart, we went six, seven, eight takes every scene that we were together. During the fight that we did in the bar, he nailed me with a punch and I had to go get a couple of stitches over my eye. I didn't realize what great pain he was in. Shortly after that, he had this operation; his back, evidently, was really bad. [Chandler died after back surgery in 1961.]

I tend to be fairly steady with dialogue. Finally, we came to a Friday night, everybody was trying to leave for Palm Springs or wherever they go, and we were doing this scene, and all of a sudden I had a problem. We probably did twelve or thirteen takes, and the tension gets greater and greater when you get into that circumstance. Jeff was gleeful: "You son of a bitch! You finally blew it!" We had a good time. Norman Panama [Melvin Frank's co-producer] had us to his home for dinner, and Jeff was there with Esther Williams, and she made quite an impression.

MB: You didn't make that many films with Paramount…

FP: No, that was it, in four years.

MB: It seems strange, again, that they didn't put you in more things.

Was it because westerns were petering out at that point, and you seemed like a natural western star?

FP: I think something was happening in the ownership. I always suspected that Y. Frank Freeman's son was the person who urged his dad to buy his company. I got the feeling that the movie side of the business kind of went on—Mr. Freeman approved things, obviously, but by the time I got there, he was not a young man. I think they were just kind of running it as a business, which is sort of unusual. With *Hell Is for Heroes*, all of a sudden there was an edict that there would be one or two more days, and that's it. So we didn't finish the script. My scenes that made sense for me to be in the movie were never shot. All of my gut-impact material was at the end of the picture, with incoming troops relieving our group. There was a nice tie-up.

MB: The film does end abruptly. I hadn't really thought about that, but it does come to a stop quicker than you expect it to.

FP: That was the business side of it: no more money in this film.

MB: Talking about the directors, though, like Siegel and Curtiz—on the evidence of their films, they were much stronger directors than the people you worked with at Disney. What difference did you feel, as an actor, in working with directors like these?

FP: There wasn't any real difference except in the case of Mel Frank, with the man who was constantly observing the scenes. Curtiz was surprisingly easy to get along with. He had such a reputation as a character, but there were no problems. Tina Louise was with Robert Taylor, and Robert Taylor was a very pleasant man. He had a reserve about him, but he wasn't unfriendly, he was just sort of a man who was smoking himself to death.

MB: What about Don Siegel? I read somewhere recently about *Hell Is for Heroes* that some of the actors had trouble taking it seriously.

FP: Don Siegel seemed to me to have the old Hollywood mantra down: stick with the money [that is, give the most attention to the highest-paid stars]. He was competent, but as far as his giving me any sort of directions or instructions or help as a director, none. And that's usually the case. There are some people who do try to lead or suggest or something, but most of the time, if the scene works, the good people let you bring what you bring. And if it's obviously wrong, they'll tell you.

MB: So you never really had the chance to work with a director—

FP: I'll be honest with you. I don't think I was ever challenged. I just kind of walked through everything.

MB: It has always seemed to me that there was a lot more you could have done if somebody had been smart enough to ask you to do it.

FP: I wanted to do something that would move me along and mature me in the business, but at a certain point—when I went into *Daniel Boone*, I felt that the opportunities that lay out there in the future [would grow out of] that show, that there was little that I could expect [from continuing to work in feature films], so I just decided to leave.

MB: Did you have any contact with Walt after leaving the Disney Studio?

FP: I saw Walt Disney pretty much as a father figure, and I hated parting on the basis that I did. When I ended up doing *Daniel Boone*, there was an NBC affiliates' meeting at the Hilton Hotel in Beverly Hills, and there was a cocktail party prior to the dinner. NBC wanted *The Further Adventures of Davy Crockett*, which I thought I had to consider, because I had a family by that time. Walt had the number-one show on NBC, and he said, "No, I own five one-hour films of Davy Crockett, with Fess in them, and I don't want to see that." NBC had that frontier mode in mind, so they said they'd like to have me consider *Daniel Boone*. Maybe I'm the first guy in the actors' witness protection program. I put on the cap, and I said, "My name is Daniel Boone, and this is my wife, and my children. I live in Boonesborough, a far piece from here." Well, thankfully, the American public sees entertainment for what it is, it's entertainment, it's not life, so we were able to spend six years on it.

MB: On the Disney TV show around 1960, there was a Daniel Boone series with Dewey Martin—

FP: A good friend of mine.

MB: I remember looking at this and thinking that it was something that should have had Fess Parker cast in the role. I didn't think Dewey Martin was convincing as a frontiersman. Was that something that was being talked about before you left?

FP: No, no.

MB: So did you have an encounter with Walt at this affiliates' meeting after you had undertaken to do *Daniel Boone*?

FP: Yes, the pilot had been picked up, I was going to go on the air with *Daniel Boone* and there was a cocktail party. I didn't know he was in the room. I was standing talking to someone, and I felt someone tap me on the shoulder. I turned around, and it was Walt. He said, "I just wanted to wish you well on your new series. Say hello to Marcella." I said, "Is Mrs. Disney with you?" He said, "Yes, she's right over there." I said, "I'd like to go over and say hello to her." And I did. To me, that was like reconciling with my father, in a way.

MB: Was that the first time you'd seen him since you left the studio?

FP: Yes.

MB: Did you ever see him again, or was that the only time you saw him?

FP: That was the only time I ever saw him.

MB: Did you ever have any contact with him by letter or phone?

FP: I don't think so. I don't recall if I did. I don't know on what basis I would have had a [telephone] conversation with him.

MB: Speaking of Walt's not wanting you to be Davy Crockett on that NBC show, there was this Bob Hope movie called *Alias Jesse James* [1959] in which you appear uncredited in one scene. You're not identified as Davy Crockett, but you're clearly supposed to be Davy.

FP: That was when I was over at Paramount. Bob Hope gave me a diesel engine for that moment. I guess he thought it would be good for my sailboat, or something. My agent had purchased the *African Queen* [the boat used in that movie] and made it into a little yacht. I never realized, until maybe right now, that the fact that I got a diesel engine was kind of suggested by my agent, who probably knew that I didn't have any place to put that engine. So it ended up in the *African Queen*.

© 2007 Michael Barrier

Walt Stanchfield (1919–2000)

Interviewed by Christian Renaut in 1987.

Walt Stanchfield is famous today in the animation community for his exceptional animation-art-class handouts which can be downloaded on quite a few specialized sites around the Web.

Walt started in the animation industry at Mintz in 1937. He also worked for two years at Lantz. In 1948, he went to work for Disney and, with the exception of four short retirements, had worked there ever since. Walt worked on every full-length cartoon feature, from *The Adventures of Ichabod Crane and Mr. Toad* (1949) to *The Great Mouse Detective* (1986).

According to Don Hahn:

> Throughout those years, Walt developed an insatiable enthusiasm for teaching the craft. He supported his numerous drawing classes with weekly handouts that taught not only animation and drawing principles, but philosophy, attitude, and life lessons.
>
> Walt's personal work was full of vitality. He was a tireless sketcher, a painter of landscapes, seascapes, still lifes and people. He was an avid writer, penning hundreds of pages of notes about the art of animation as well as poetry and stories. He also loved music and spent an inordinate amount of time at the piano—that is, between caring for his vegetable garden and playing his most beloved game: tennis.

Walt Stanchfield passed away in September 2000.

Christian Renaut met Walt Stanchfield in Glendale when the studio had moved there for a while as artists were tackling *The Little Mermaid* in 1987. Walt was still working there as a sort of consultant, the way Eric Larson had done in the early '80s.

Christian Renaut: When did you start in this business?

Walt Stanchfield: I started in 1937. I worked with Charles Mintz for two years first.

CR: Which feature did you work on at Disney?

WS: I can't even remember the first feature I worked on. I think it was *Cinderella*. As far as animation is concerned, I did my first animation on *Sleeping Beauty*, I believe, and then a little bit of animation on all of them.

CR: On *Cinderella* you were an assistant?

WS: Yes.

CR: Who did you work with?

WS: I was sort of freelance at that time. Very soon after I came here, I worked with Lounsbery; then under him I went into animation. I worked for him for ten years and then I went to work with Ollie Johnston, and worked with Ollie for ten years also.

CR: I met Ollie the other day and when I told him that I'd see you, he said he would never forget what you did for him, especially when he was ill and you both worked together on *One Hundred and One Dalmatians*.

WS: We got along fine. There was a lot of chemistry going on there. My style of drawing suited his needs, so we worked well together.

CR: I suppose you worked on the fairies then, if you worked with Ollie?

WS: God, I wish I had a better memory. I think it was during *Sleeping Beauty* that I switched from Lounsbery to Ollie. I did work on the fairies, yes.

CR: Could you tell me what it was like working with some of the Nine Old Men?

WS: Everybody knew that Milt Kahl was one of the best artists and we all went to him for drawings and help, even Ollie, Frank, and Lounsbery. They'd come back with his beautiful drawings and say, "That's beautiful, but I can't use it." It was a slightly different style. One time, a scene came back from camera because at the time we used a Moviola; now we use a tape machine. A scene came back that Milt Kahl had animated and Stan Green said, "Milt, this scene is back, do you want to see it?" "I animated it. I know what it looks like." It proves two things: it proves Milt was an egoist, but also he knew how good he was, and he was that good!

I also remember another story: Woolie Reitherman wanted to change something Milt Kahl had done, so he had me change his animation. I had to keep something handy, ready to cover his scene in case he came in the room. That was a real thrill, you know, changing his animation!

CR: After *Sleeping Beauty*, you worked on *One Hundred and One Dalmatians*.

WS: I did mostly clean-up on *Dalmatians*: thousands, and thousands and thousands of spots! But it was an enjoyable picture. Was it on *Dalmatians* that they started using "touch-up"?

CR: What do you call "touch up"?

WS: When you do clean-up, you take a rough drawing and then put a clean sheet of paper over it and you draw clean on it; while touch-up is when you just take the rough and you erase the extraneous lines and connect lines that are not connected. You'd better check on that, but I think it's when we were doing *Dalmatians* [that we started doing it]. There was a marriage of background and drawings, and they tried to make it all look like a drawing. They just made swatches of colours and the drawings were like lines over them. I enjoyed this Xerox technique.

CR: You also worked on *Sword in the Stone*.

WS: I did some animation on *The Sword in the Stone*, but most of the time, I did clean-up.

CR: Milt Kahl did all the model sheets, didn't he?

WS: Yeah. He would animate some scenes, and then they would take some drawings out of his animation and use those as the model sheets. Sometimes it could be Frank, Ollie, or Marc Davis, but Milt was pretty much in charge of establishing characters.

I remember I was working on God-knows-what character, but I needed a model, so I went to Milt and he took a sheet of paper and it was just like he had it all in his mind. He was just tracing it, and there it is: no rough, no test, he just drew. Amazing! It took him five minutes.

CR: Surprisingly enough, although he worked on many beautiful characters with strong personalities, Milt Kahl always said his favorites were Kay and Ector in *The Sword in the Stone*, which are rather forgettable characters.

WS: He loved these characters. I don't know why. I guess they gave him an opportunity to do some of the things he liked to do.

CR: Broader things, perhaps?

WS: Yeah, but also some of the baddies.

CR: I also saw your name in the draft more often on *The Jungle Book*.

WS: In *Jungle Book* I did some monkeys, some of the scenes with Mowgli, a couple of scenes with the little girl, and some of the panther.

CR: The panther is incredibly well rendered, although such animals are very delicate, with smooth moves. Did you use any live-action references on that?

WS: No, we didn't use live action on the panther.

CR: *The Fox and the Hound* was a troublesome picture to achieve, right?

WS: We had reached a point of transition of directors on *Fox and the Hound*. Woolie Reitherman started on that picture and Art Stevens was there to sort of coordinate things. When we started out on that picture, we had lost lots of the older animators. There was a point when they retired, and so we had a whole new crew. We had a lot of inexperienced people, so the drawings weren't that good. They couldn't be just touched up. They had to be redrawn and cleaned up. But at the beginning Woolie wanted a touch-up, as he was used to having it because he had Milt Kahl and Ollie Johnston and you could touch-up their stuff. So I did a first scene and brought it to Woolie and he said, "Well, you just connect the lines," and I said, "There's just no way you can do that!" Art Stevens agreed with me. Finally, there was a rift. Art Stevens won the battle and he became the sole director. When Woolie left, he said to me and Art, "You'll never do it on time," and that was a challenge. So we worked like dogs, twelve hours a day. I really put my heart and soul in it.

CR: I met Art Stevens; he told me it was his favorite movie.

WS: Yeah, I would think so, probably because he was so involved in it.

CR: Did you use the same technique in *The Black Cauldron*?

WS: That one was a combination clean-up and touch-up. For people like Andreas Deja, you could just touch-up; he did such marvelous drawings.

CR: What kind of a director was Woolie?

WS: When Woolie Reitherman became the director, he used a lot of re-uses, reverse the things. He would even use actions with different characters and have them re-used with the characters redrawn.

CR: To cut expenses, I suppose.

WS: Partially so and partially, I think, because Woolie... I don't want to say that he didn't see things, but he had to have something visual to start with. When we start a film, they shoot all the story sketches and they get reels of that. But he had a hard time envisioning what he wanted by just looking at a story sketch. It would be better for him to have a scene cut in there. If it was a different character, but something that came close to the action that he wanted, he could work from that and develop it. So we had reels that had different selections of things.

CR: Was there any jealousy about Woolie being a director?

WS: I think there were others who could have taken the job and others who wouldn't want to.

CR: Could you tell me more about one of the least known of the Nine Old Men, John Lounsbery?

WS: John was a very likeable guy. Everybody liked him. He was a real cartoonist, as opposed to the artist that Milt Kahl was. His animation was more cartoony, humorous, broad. He was meek, but it didn't mean he didn't have a lot of fire inside of him. He had a technique... Well, I will give you an idea of the different techniques: he picked up a scene from the director, and then he would get as much information as he could from the director, the story, etc. He would then light up a cigarette, walk around, have a cup of coffee, and talk, small talk. But this stuff is going around in his mind and you could tell when it gelled. You could almost see the look on his face. He'd get up, he'd go in his room, then he'd take a sheet a paper and it's all planned out for him up here, and it blew out of his mind, and it would all be done in no time at all. To give you a contrast, Cliff Nordberg would pick up his scene from the director, and he would start making drawings and writing things down. He'd make experimental drawings and work the things out.

CR: Lounsbery did the excellent Italians in *Lady and the Tramp*.

WS: Oh [laughing], one story: He happened to draw some gestures that turned out to be an obscene Italian gesture, and he had to change it. Clyde Geronimi spotted it and had him change it.

CR: Did you retire at the time of *The Rescuers*?

WS: *The Rescuers* is a picture I did very little work on. In fact, I had retired, and later I got a call from Ed Hansen, who said, "That's a picture we can't get finished." So I said, "All right," but I said only if I can work here, where I had retired. I came down and I picked up enough work for a week or two, to do clean-up. I worked isolated.

CR: Still, you also worked on *The Fox and the Hound*.

WS: More or less. At that time they needed some quality-control person, and I became that person; I did all the model sheets and I checked the work of the youngsters.

© 2007 Christian Renaut

Marc Davis (1913–2000)

Interviewed by Richard Hubler on May 21, 1968.

We've already met Marc Davis twice in *Walt's People: Volumes 1 and 4*. In this interview he shares with Richard Hubler a few of his memories of Walt.

Marc Davis: There was an early time when Walt's social life was with the men that he employed and a certain echelon of people that are dead now: Freddy Moore, Norm Ferguson, Ham Luske, etc. These men played badminton with Walt. They went up to his house when he lived in Los Feliz and so on. Then, when this studio began to become really something, a few of these men weren't growing in the same degree that he was. So pretty soon his associations became more-important people away from the studio and his life became divorced from the studio. Many of these men never could understand that Walt had outgrown them and had changed.

I was never ever a part of his social life. And I'm very pleased. I think that's the way it should be. But I have been many places with him and worked very closely with him.

He had a terrific memory. He learned very quickly. As a result, he became very impatient with someone who had to have something explained to him two or three times. This man had a memory. He could remember a statement I had made three years ago and call me on it.

One evening, probably ten years ago… Walt liked the Tam O'Shanter restaurant. He had very plain tastes in food. My wife, Alice, and I were there and I had about ten dollars in my pocket. Here's Walt sitting all alone and he was obviously lonely. So he came over. This was the first time Alice had ever met him. We'd only been married about six months or so. Walt was obviously lonely, and so we invited him to go with us, up the street to see some movie. And he drew the curtain just like that and said, "No, I'm going to stay at the studio… No." He was apologetic. But I had the opportunity of buying him a drink. He was a hard man to do anything for. After we got out of there, I said to Alice, "My god, I damned near didn't have enough money to take care of this," which would have been embarrassing.

He and my wife got into a real hot argument over some damn thing. Alice is a very strong gal. Walt was very fond of her. He liked strong people. Yet on the other hand you had to know when to talk and when to shut up.

Richard Hubler: What was the first intimation you had before his death that he was sick?

MD: The only information that most of us had is that he constantly complained of this bad hip. And he coughed all the time. But, frankly, most of us thought that he did that simply to warn us he was coming down the hall and shape up. Walt hated to walk in on any kind of embarrassing situation where guys were maybe throwing push pins at targets. He didn't like to walk in on this. So you'd hear the cough a couple of times and you knew it was his cough. We felt that this was really kind of a warning. So you looked halfway decent when he came in. He knew everybody pulled gags. He knew everybody did stupid things. But he didn't want to be a part of it. When he came in he was friendly and all that, but he wanted right now to get to work. It's pretty easy to understand why when you consider the amount of ground this man covered every day.

[About Walt's relation to educational projects.]

During the war we had professors in almost every field to work on our films. And Walt got sick of these people because they were saying what you could do and what you couldn't. Right at the end of the war I read A Trip to the Moon in LIFE Magazine. And I thought, "What a great film we could make out of this article." This was four or five years before anybody had done anything along these lines. I told Walt we ought to do this. It was bad judgment and a horrible presentation on my part, because I didn't show him anything, and he said, "Goddamit, Marc, I don't want to do any more goddam educational films. I'm tired of these goddam professors and these people." I understood what he meant, but he didn't understand what I meant. This would have been a marvelous time for us to have done this in animation. I had thought of hiring Chesley Bonestell to do all the backgrounds and all this stuff.

[About Walt.]

I went to the GE show [Carousel of Progress] with him and I sweated for a couple of days being sure everything was good. As I went to walk in with him, I said, "Now look, don't be too disappointed: this ride has gone downhill." He asked what I meant and I said, "Well, you know, tired machinery, etc." We got in and sat in the back row. We go thru Act 1 and I get this nudge in my ribs and he said, "Hell, this doesn't look too bad." If I had said, "Boy, does this ever look great!" he would have said, "My God..." you know. This was very typical of him. I had downgraded it, so he upgraded it.

© 2007 Jane Hubler

Alice Davis (b, 1929)

Interviewed by David Oneal on August 22, 2004.

Disney Legend and widow of one of the Nine Old Men, former Imagineer, Alice Davis was among those few people who knew how to face Walt without offending him and was a splendid artist in her own right. The fugures of two of the most classic attractions of the Disney parks, It's a Small World and Pirates of the Caribbean, would literally have been naked without her.

A native of Escalon, California, Alice Estes Davis grew up in Long Beach and Los Angeles. Upon her high school graduation from Long Beach Polytechnic, she received a scholarship in 1947 to attend the prestigious Chouinard Art Institute, training ground for many Disney artists and where her future husband, Marc, taught for over 17 years.

She began her professional career designing women's lingerie and undergarments for the Beverly Vogue & Lingerie House, becoming head designer after only two years. This was followed by designing two lines of fashion lingerie as head designer for the Davis Pleating Company. An expert pattern-maker and authority on the uses of fabrics then led to her being named head designer at the Textile Corporation of America.

One day she received a call from her former art instructor and future husband, Marc. He needed a costume designed and created for Helene Stanley to wear for some live-action reference footage being filmed to inspire his animation of Briar Rose in *Sleeping Beauty*.

Alice's early Disney studio work also includes designing costumes for the Disney circus film *Toby Tyler*.

When Walt Disney began to create audio-animatronics for the 1964 World's Fair in New York, he called upon Alice's expertise to be the first costumer to work with the Disney artists and engineers on designing and dressing the animated figures, formulating costuming procedures, setting up a manufacturing base, and introducing refurbishing techniques to ensure quality control. Her methods are still in use today. Her pioneering and innovative work led to her personally designing over 150 costumes for the renowned classic It's a Small World. She also designed, fabricated, and dressed all the original costumes for Pirates of the Caribbean. Her additional costuming credits with Disney include the GE Disneyland show Carousel of Progress and Disneyland's Flight to the Moon.

David Oneal: How did Marc get started with Disney?

Alice Davis: Marc was up in northern California. His father was a very fine jeweler, but he also was a rainbow chaser. Marc went to 23 schools before he was out of high school. He lived all over the United States. In the south he had a wonderful southern accent. When he went to the north he had a northern accent.

Having to go to all these different schools, the boys would "ring" him when recess came and try to beat him up. He found that if he drew pictures, they all wanted a picture and didn't beat him up. He started drawing, and drawing was his entertainment. He was an only child and I think there was only one school he was in for over a year. So he was constantly changing friends and seeing all kinds of things. He saw the Ku Klux Klan burning crosses in people's yards. They were taking one man up to an oil derrick to hang him for speaking to a white woman. And when they would go to the north, even the history in school was different.

He was trying to help his family in the Depression. His father was making money, but it was hard times. He had his grandfather, a woodsman up in Eureka, who left him a great deal of acreage of redwood trees and sugar pine and so on. They had to sell it for something like 50 cents an acre. To buy one redwood tree for lumber now is thousands of dollars, just for the wood.

Anyway, they "ate" all of Marc's inheritance. So he got a job painting signs up in a town I can't remember the name of right now. One of his friends said, "You should go to Los Angeles and go to work for Disney." His father was telling him about this wonderful film he saw named *Who Killed Cock Robin?* and also *Three Little Pigs*. So he did go and see that with his father.

His father died of a heart attack very shortly after that. He was only 48. That left Marc with only his mother to support and himself, of course. He came down to Los Angeles to find a job. He went to some newspapers to see about doing some drawings, and somebody sent him to the main rabbi at the temple on Wilshire Boulevard. He suggested that Marc go to see Walt Disney and find out if he could get a job there. Marc went and showed his portfolio and was hired right on the spot.

Usually you started at $15 per week, but since Marc was such a good draftsman, especially with animals, they started him at $20 or $23, somewhere around there. The first animation he did was on *Snow White*. They were working on *Snow White* when he came. His first animation that he was so proud of was Snow White dancing with the two dwarfs, one standing on the shoulder of the other. He was very thrilled that he got to do that.[1]

---

[1] JB Kaufman notes: "Davis worked on *Snow White* principally as an assistant to

Marc and I met in a rather interesting way. It starts with Chouinard Art Institute. When I was in grammar school, we lived just two blocks from Chouinard Art Institute. I was determined I was going to go there some day. I would walk out of my way coming home from school so I could go into the gallery and look at all the paintings at the school.

When I graduated from grammar school I won a scholarship to go to Chouinard. I was most excited except my parents had bought a house in Long Beach. We moved to Long Beach and I didn't get to go. It was a miserable summer had by all because all I did was cry and mope at the fact that I couldn't go to Chouinard.

When I graduated from high school, the Long Beach Art Association always gave an art scholarship to one of the high school students if you presented a portfolio. They would take all the portfolios and look at them and they would give the scholarship. So I put my portfolio together and was all ready to take it in and deposit it with all the others for trying out for the scholarship. Then I thought, *Oh, I'm never going to get this.* So I didn't bother taking it. My mother came home from work and she said, "Did you turn in your portfolio today?" I said, "No, I haven't got a chance." And she said, "You, young lady, you get up those stairs right now and you get that portfolio and you get out to the car." I got in the car and she drove like Barney Oldfield all the way down to the Board of Education building.

The truck was a "stake-back" truck. All the portfolios were in it and it was just pulling out from the curb as my mother pulled up. She said "Child, you'd better get out of the car and run after that and throw that into the truck because you're not coming home until it gets into that truck." I literally ran down the street and threw the portfolio into the truck.

We went home and it was a rather quiet evening. A couple days later it was graduation. They held the graduation ceremonies down at the Civic Auditorium because it was right after the war and there were so many students. We could only have our parents come. It filled the auditorium.

My parents couldn't come because my father wouldn't get home from work in time and my mother didn't get off work until 9:30pm or 10 o'clock. She was waiting for me to take me home, because I wasn't going to go out for sure, as far as she was concerned.

My name wasn't mentioned on the scholarship, so I thought, *Well, I didn't get it.* I knew I wouldn't get it. The next morning when I went to school, the last day of school, Miss Warner, the art teacher, came running across the quadrangle waving this paper in the air. "Alice! Alice!" I had won the scholarship.

Grim Natwick. The action Alice describes here (Snow White dancing) was a rare instance of Natwick turning a scene over to Davis to animate by himself. That's surely why it stuck in his memory."

The summer went by slowly because I was waiting for September to come so I could start Chouinard. I went up a week before school began to start to enroll. Fortunately for me, Mrs. Chouinard was helping the registrar register students. I showed her the scholarship paper that I had gotten. She said, "I'm sorry my dear, but you can't start for two years yet." I said, "What?" She said, "We have such a backlog of the GI Bill vets coming to school, we don't have room for any openings for two years."

I started crying because here again I won the scholarship and I wouldn't be able to go. Also, I didn't have the money to be able to go. That was the "dashed against the wall", so to speak.

Mrs. Chouinard looked at me and said, "You really want to go to this school that badly?" I said, "Yes." I told her that I had had a scholarship before that I wasn't able to take. She said, "Just a minute." She left and came back a few minutes later with this woman with a smock on. They looked me up and down and they left.

Then Mrs. Chouinard came back. She said "Well, you are starting school next week and you are going to be a costume-design major whether you want to be or not because that's the only opening in the school." That is how I became a costume designer.

When I started school, I had some duties I had to do for the scholarship. One of the duties was to take two perfect pieces of chalk to "Our Mr. Davis" for his lectures on Tuesday evenings. That's when he had his class. That is how I met Marc, taking the chalk to him every Tuesday evening before his class started. Then I called the roll in the class later on in the evening.

I wanted to be an animator or an illustrator. Mrs. Chouinard talked to me and said, "I'll give you two extra classes… That's if you can handle it. You can take the illustration class and you can also take Mr. Davis' animation drawing class." So I became a student of his.

Everybody later thought that because we were married there was something going on at the time I was a student. That is not so. Not only that, but everybody admired Mr. Davis so much. Everybody called him Mr. Davis and he kept saying, "Just call me Marc. Everybody at the studio calls me Marc. Just call me Marc." Oh no, Mr. Davis, you're the genius.

After I graduated I went to work. I didn't see him for a while and the fiancée of a friend of mine was going to Mexico to study sculpture. She said, "He wouldn't come to the party that I want to give him, unless Mr. Davis comes." Mr. Davis was his prized teacher. He wanted to see Marc again before he left for Mexico. She said, "I know you know Mr. Davis because you were in his class and you used to call the roll." I said, "Yes." She said, "Would you call him and ask him to come to the party?" And I said, "Yes." So I did. I said, "We'd like to have you come and bring a date."

Marc came to the party, but he didn't bring anybody with him. Then the next evening he called me on the phone to thank me for asking him to the party and that he had a very nice time, and that he would like to take me to dinner because of my inviting him to the party. I said, "Well, if you want to take me to dinner because I invited you to the party, forget it. But if you want to take me to dinner because I'm Alice Mae Estes, I would be delighted." He said, "I will pick you up at 7:30 p.m. tomorrow evening." That's how it all started.

Marc's work at Disney was quite different from most. He worked on very few shorts, whereas all the other Nine Old Men worked on the shorts. Walt liked Marc's storyboards. He also liked his writing. When Marc would finish a feature film, Walt would put him to work developing and designing characters and doing story. Then he would go back to animation. The other guys were working on shorts while Marc was doing this. But he never got credit for it. That was the part that was not so good. Like in *Victory Through Airpower*: he worked on that for a long time and they didn't even put his name on the credits. He complained about it and they said it was too late. The credits were already on the film.

Then when he finished *One Hundred and One Dalmatians*, Walt wasn't pleased with that there wasn't anything humorous in Disneyland. He wanted some humor put in it. So he said to Marc, "You know, instead of starting on another film right now, I'd like to have you go down to the park. Walk through the park and see where you can put some humor in." Marc went down. He took his sketchbook along and made notes. I guess he did it for about a week or so. He did some drawings that he thought would add to the park. He showed them to Walt. Some of them were changes in The Mine Ride Through Nature's Wonderland. He had a lot of drawings he showed Walt. Walt said, "Oh for God's sake, I just spent $50,000 redoing that and now you're going to cost me money because what you've done is much better."

The thing that Marc disliked most about it was when you got into the train to go for the ride, instead of looking at the ride, you were facing a total stranger. It was not comfortable looking at a stranger. You had to strain, to twist your body to see what was coming at you. So they changed the seating in the train, which was much better.

The other thing Marc was very set against was using animal fur. He said that it doesn't last and Disney does not kill animals to have a skin. So he started putting on synthetic fur, using fur cloth, which is the only thing they use now. It also solved one of the bird problems. The birds were coming and pulling the fur hair out to make their nests. Pretty soon you had a deer that didn't have much fur on him. It looked rather mangy.

When he started working on the New York World's Fair, the attraction Great Moments with Mr. Lincoln was a very difficult one to do because they were just learning about audio-animatronics and you had to do the whole track perfectly. If any little jerk or anything else happened, you'd have to start all over again.

Everybody was very nervous and uptight about it. But I think they were about two weeks late. When it did open it was quite a success, except that the Japanese Pavilion was next door. They were giving out free ball bearings to people. People would go there and get the ball bearings and then would go see Great Moments with Mr. Lincoln and throw the ball bearings at him to see if he would scream out. They thought he was a real person looking like an audio-animatronic figure.

To go out to work on the figure it would be worth your life, because you were walking on all these little ball bearings. You couldn't keep your balance. You were sliding all over. They finally went over and asked them to stop giving them away because it was causing a number of injuries.

The Magic Skyway has a funny story to it. Walt told Marc that he wanted him to go with him to walk through the New York World's Fair and see what was happening. He also took along one of the head men that was taking care of the Disney shows at the Fair. Walt always insisted on standing in line. He wouldn't go in the back door. He did the same thing at Disneyland. He said, "If people have to stand in line, so do I." Very seldom did he go in the back door: only when he didn't have enough time to stand in line.

So they got to the line for the Ford show. They were standing in line and there was this woman and her husband. Her husband said, "That's Walt Disney." She said. "It is NOT." And they started this terrible argument. Fighting, you know. They were maybe about 15 or 20 couples ahead of Marc, Walt, and the other gentleman. When Walt got into the car to go through the ride everybody started applauding. Marc looked back. The husband was standing there with the biggest grin. Humm.... I was right! But he didn't dare say it because she would start another fight.

The Small World ride was a difficult one because we had exactly one year to design it, make the costumes, the figures, chose the color patterns, do the sets, then put it all together on the number-one sound stage at the studio, tear it all down, ship it to New York, get to New York, and put it all together: in one year! We did it, but it wasn't easy.

DO: After the World's Fair you go back to Disneyland. Things were installed there. You've got Small World. You've got Lincoln. Pirates is coming up. We can maybe discuss that because it's pretty much all Marc. Let's go ahead and talk about Pirates a little bit.

AD: Marc did a few pirate drawings before things were brought back from New York. Walt wouldn't look at them because he didn't want to get carried away with it at the time.

When everything was back in working order, then he started with Pirates. Walt loved it. He could hardly stand it that he couldn't see it. They did a mock-up of Pirates at the back of the shop at WED, which is now Imagineering. We set up the auctioneer. We had him all dressed and ready to go. That's the only figure Walt saw completely dressed and working. He passed away shortly afterward. It was marvelous to watch him when he saw it.

Walt loved Marc's drawings of Pirates so much that he had an open house at WED. He had a whole wall there of Marc's paintings of Pirates.

We went to the open house and I was standing with Marc and Mary Blair and a few others. Walt came over and said, "Marc, excuse me. I want to take Alice and show her something." He took me by the arm and stood me in front of Marc's paintings. He said, "Alice, I want you to look at these." And I said, "Walt, I look at them every day. I'm doing the costumes for the show." He said, "I don't mean it that way!" He said, "I want you to look at the work of genius." He said, "Marc is a genius. He has been able to do all these things for me. I haven't used him the way I should." He said, "We are going to do some great things together." He said, "This Pirate ride is going to be a smash. It is really going to be a good show."

I thanked him very much. Then I realized Walt was never able to say to you directly that he liked what you did. But he knew who your closest friend was, who would come and tell you real quick. So he would go tell them, "Boy, you should see what Marc's doing. He is doing some wonderful things. I really like it." He immediately knew I would run and tell Marc, "Boy, Walt sure likes your paintings."

I remember Marc took off some weight and Walt came to me and said "Marc's really done a good job of getting that weight off. You ought to tell him I'm glad that he's taken it off." I said, "You don't have to do that. You can tell him yourself." He frowned at me. That's when I learned that you go tell him because Walt doesn't want to do it. He could never tell you himself. Unless it was something really fantastic, and if that happened you wouldn't recover for a week.

Whenever Marc worked on a ride he did a tremendous amount of research and drawings. He did one drawing after another after another. Say there is one idea: he would do five different ideas of that certain section. He would say that Walt would always like to have a number of things to look at to able to choose from it what he wanted.

Marc told me once that a young man came in and he was drawing some ideas for Walt on something, and he did one drawing and he brought it to Walt. He said, "Walt, what do you think of this?" Walt looked at it and kind of frowned, and then he turned back to the young man and smiled and he said, "It is very difficult to choose between one." From that time on, the young man knew he should do more than one drawing.

When I started working on the Pirates ride, doing the costumes, it was a bit of a shock to the system, because to dress the figures, the feet were bolted to the floor. If they were sitting on a chair, they were bolted on the chair. Like the pirate that's on the cannon: his whole body is bolted to the cannon. His hands are bolted together holding the gun. The elbows are bolted to the cannon. His knees are bolted to the cannon. His ankles are bolted together. To try and figure out how to dress them and get the clothes on is something else.

I started thinking they should have more than one costume. They should have two costumes for each figure. If something happens, there are hydraulic cords that go through. If one of those cords gets twisted and snaps, you have this terrible red oil that comes out. You can't get it out of the fabric. It's lost.

I told them I thought we should have two costumes. They said, "We don't have the time. We have to have just one costume as quickly as can be." You can cut two out in the same time you cut one. I just decided I was going to make two costumes. When I went to the bookkeeper to say how much material I needed for shirts and pants and all this, I would give him twice the amount I needed. He didn't know. So I made two costumes and I hid one set. On hats and things, if they got damaged, it would take a week or more to make a new one to replace them. You can't keep the whole thing shut down because of hats missing. I made two hats for figures where it would be a problem.

Sure enough, when the ride opened everything was fine, except that a month and a half later they had a fire. The sprinklers went on and it destroyed some of the hats. The costumes were burned on three of the figures. They came running to me, "What are we going to do? We have to keep the ride closed until we get more costumes. How long will it take you?" I said, "Well, if you bring me the fishing pole to put hats on, I will have everything ready for you in half an hour." I showed them that I had made two sets. They didn't know whether to hit me or kiss me. The show was only closed for one day.

Marc first started designing the Country Bears for Mineral King. It was where Walt was going to have a ski resort. Walt felt that they had to have something more than just skiing, something to entertain people. Not only to entertain but to go up and stay overnight, and have two days of skiing and food and so forth. So Marc started designing different kinds of bears. He had a bear band, he had a one-man band—a one-bear band, I should say. He had a jazz band. He had a circus band. He had all these different characters, very funny bears. But finally they decided to hold off for a while because Mineral King wasn't doing so well with different factions not wanting to have the natural forest destroyed with commercial items.

Later on, Walt decided it would be kind of fun to do the bears in the park. Walt had been ill. He came back to WED to see Marc and some of the others. He walked to Marc's room and sat down. A number of people came and Walt reached out with his hand and patted a couple of them on the tummy and said, "I just want to see Marc for a while here. I came to see Marc."

Marc said he looked terribly thin and drawn and wasn't too well at all. He asked Marc what he had been doing with the bears. So Marc got all the different bears out. Walt started looking at the different bear bands and started laughing. Marc said when you had a lot of things to show Walt and Walt was enjoying it, it was like giving presents to little kids to open at Christmas.

DO: America Sings. Marc finished Country Bears. He had finished Pirates. And all of a sudden he came home one day and probably told you something about America Sings. It had to get done pretty fast, as I remember it.

AD: Yes, because General Electric had yanked their show [Carousel of Progress] from Disneyland because they said that 80% of the people that came to Disneyland were Californians. They would see the same show over and over again. GE wouldn't get the advertising that they wanted. They were keeping the one in Florida because they had people from all over the world going there and they would have the advertising. So there was this empty building and they needed a show for it.

This was the first time that Marc did a show all the way through without Walt. Walt had seen the bears, but Marc had designed the stage and such for the bear jamboree. He finished it without Walt. Walt was in the beginning of it, so America Sings was the first show that was all Marc. I think he did a very good job on it.

There was a girl whom I had been training to work with the audio-animatronic figures. Her name was Alice, too, Alice Morgan. She did the costumes for the bears and for America Sings.

DO: Going back to the beginning of America Signs. Marc came home and said, "Guess what, GE is out. I've got to do something all by myself, and they want it to be about music because the bicentennial is coming up."

AD: I think the music part was his idea. Nobody had done the history of music from starting in the United States up to the present time. He thought it would be fun to have all the different styles: the jazz, the blues, rock and roll. I loved the finale with the birds on the motorcycles. The year that the show opened, somebody did a float for the Rose Parade and it was the two chickens on the motorcycles: copied exactly. Disney never did anything about it. I thought that was kind of keen.

Marc chose all the music for the show. He very much liked working with Burl Ives to do the narration and such on it. Burl Ives enjoyed it. Chill Wills would not go on the ride. Chill Wills did the voice for the turkey. He wouldn't go into any building that moved. He was sure he would be killed. He was very strange. He wouldn't go anywhere near it. He didn't stay for all the functions of the opening because he wasn't going to have anything to do with a building that moved like that.

DO: Did Marc pick Burl Ives as a personal choice for Sammy Eagle?

AD: Yes, Marc more or less chose the different ones. There also was "Who Shot That Hole in My Sombrero?" They did it with a Mexican accent. Boy, they were up in arms over it. They had to change it. If you noticed, a short while later it was with a Texas accent.

DO: This attraction seemed to have a lot of caricatures of different people if I'm reading it right. You could kind of see the show on two levels. If you were a kid, it looked like some happy birds and things like that. If you were an adult, you could kind of see parodies of certain personality types.

AD: Yes. It also had to do with the history of music and what times were like at the time when cowboy music was popular. That was in the '30s. That was when the Grand Ole Opry started on radio. I thought it was kind of fun and it didn't age. It was one of my very favorite shows. I was terribly upset when they closed it. I think Marc enjoyed the birds on the motorcycles. He liked the finale with the alligator: the "A-Tisket A-Tasket" bit and all of those other things.

I like the cowboys singing, and all the snakes and birds and when everything started coming up and appearing.

DO: Did Marc come up with the weasel as well? The little "pop goes the weasel"?

AD: Yes.

DO: Al Bertino and he worked really closely on this. Did they always come in and agree on everything?

AD: Big Al worked mostly on lyrics. The overall show, the different animals and that were all Marc's, the gags, too. The day they were having the big opening, Al was with Marc on stage and they had all the press out in front. They started to interview them. I don't know whether he walked backward or he just forgot the hole was there or what. He walked forward… shewwmmmp! He went down the hole. So instead of having the show get the publicity they were hoping for, they got Big Al being carried out on a stretcher to the ambulance. Marc said, "He didn't fall down the white rabbit's hole, he fell down the "gray" rabbit's hole." [Alice laughs]

DO: It is up to you if you want to talk about this or not. I was going to mention that the characters from America Sings were stuck into Splash Mountain. Is there any truth to the rumor that they were kind of minor characters from *Song of the South* and found themselves in some of Marc's sketches when he worked on *Song of the South*?

AD: No. The characters that he did for America Sings went along with the music of that time and the characters of the singing "Going to Lay My Burden Down", "Down by the Riverside"... that was the blacks singing. It was their song. Unfortunately, when they closed the ride they took the pieces and put them in [Splash Mountain]. Marc was still alive. He was very upset about it. He didn't go on Splash Mountain and neither did I. Everybody said it was America Sings up there because of all the different characters. Then to rub salt in the wound, they took a couple of the characters and made them more sophisticated. With hand movements and such. They showed to Marc how they improved things. They did it in a very nasty way. It was very hurtful, but he never said a word. He was too much of a gentleman.

DO: Not to mention the two geese they stuck in Star Tours. They just threw the whole feathers off the audio-animatronic. All that is left is the duck beak. Yes, when you go up Star Tours there are two little droids. And those are two of his geese. They just ripped the body off and put a different head on it. If you look, there are duck or geese feet.

AD: For the haunted house: did you see the tombstones that they have for all the different [people] up on the hillside?

DO: Yes.

AD: They took some of those out. They took Marc's out and brought it in and put it in his room. And he was sitting there working, and he said he kept turning and kept seeing his tombstone. He called someone the next day and said, "Would you please come and get this out of my room? It does not make for a happy day." They put it back out there, I guess, because I saw it not too long ago. It was pretty well grown over with ivy.

He did a lot of fun things like duels from the chandelier, the two people paintings—the drunk on the chandelier, it was—the black cats warming themselves at the fireplace, the drunk under the table, the drunken ghost under the table looking up. There were so many little things to look at. That says something else that Walt liked, because he said when you go through at a certain pace, there is always something more to see that you didn't see the first time.

DO: There was always funny stuff. That humor. Did he always have it?

AD: Always, yes. He had what I call a chortle. When he was drawing and it was going to be something funny, he would chortle while he was drawing this. It was marvelous. When he was watching it he would chortle. It's a little funny giggle from the throat that you can barely hear, but it was there. He always said it takes a serious person to be funny. He always had a wonderful sense of humor. Everything that he did was marked with some humor to it.

The ride that Marc designed that he was most disappointed that they didn't put in was the Western River ride. They had built the whole scale model, and in fact had all the figures of the people finished. I think there were 26 figures that O'Brien modeled. And somebody in the middle of the night came in and took every one of those figures: swiped them. O'Brien was going to find who did it and kill him! [Alice laughs] He had to remodel all the figures again. They weren't as good as the first batch. I think it was because he was so angry about it.

When it was all set and ready to go in the park, they turned it down because there was another ride that was cheaper. It didn't cost as much money. They put it in instead. Marc was very disturbed about it.

It would have been a fun ride. It was a river ride, so you went in a boat. It started out with cactuses singing, buffalo singing with prairie dogs, and a cowboy with his banjo playing. The longhorn cows are singing with him as a chorus.

Then you get to the town and to the town drunks. One is so drunk that he has his horse on the roof of the saloon. There is a group that tries to come in and rob the bank. There is a guy that is in jail and the sheriff is sitting on his horse outside the jail. You can see this burrow of dirt going underneath the horse, so the guy is escaping out from the jail. Then there are the women walking their children by the saloon, and they have got their hands over their eyes and fingers in the ears so they can't hear or see what is going on in the saloon, the medicine man with the little kids watching to see what the medicine man is talking about, the dogs having a fight over on the other side, a pig coming by with her litter: all kinds of fun things all the way through. There was a stagecoach robbery. The horses had bandanas on along with the robbers.

There were also some Indians doing a rain dance so they could get rain. They were up on a plateau and it is raining on the plateau where they were dancing, but it was not raining anywhere else. There were grooves of water coming down from the top of the plateau, like little waterfalls. There were Indians that were very disturbed by the drunks, and the drunks were firing off guns, and the Indians were sitting there with their fingers in their ears with very pained expressions on their faces. There was one that was politically incorrect. That couldn't be used now. It was a drunken Indian tipping his hat to a tobacco-store Indian out in front. It was the Wild West and what it was like.

[Then there was an attraction that was] a variation of Nature's Wonderland. It would be a building that would have four large rooms. One would be spring, one would be summer, one would be fall, and one winter. The temperatures in the rooms would be that time of year. There would be spring where the flowers were starting to bloom. That would be a crisp but rather pleasant temperature. You would go into summer with the new babies and so on. Then go into fall with the changing of the color of the leaves and so forth, then the winter with the snow. I think it would have been a nice attraction, especially in the summer time because you come out from the snow and enjoy.

He also did an attraction that was called the Snow Palace. It was all in whites and blues. It had white doves...

DO: Was there any Snow Queen designed?

AD: There was a Snow Queen and it was very funny. Marc had penguins doing funny things. He had a polar bear and a mouse on a sled coming down the mountain in the snow. The polar bear was absolutely terrified. You know, this horrible look on his face, and the mouse was just loving it. He had gnomes coming down and rabbits. It was great fun. He also had these beautiful women in white and sparkling...

This was an attraction that would be the Snow Palace, a very elegant way of enjoying the snow with some beautiful women and a ballerina. He also had animals and the animals having fun in the snow. The penguins jumping into the ice water. The different ways they would do it would be very funny. It would have been a marvelous show, especially in California when it is hot. Even in Florida when it is hot. To have a place to go in and cool off. But that was put to the side.

Then he designed another show which was riding on a waterway. You would ride in different levels in the water. It would have fountains, different fountains. Each fountain would have its own story to it. It would be quite beautiful and elegant. That was put to the side because it was too expensive. Everything was too expensive. So Marc just finally said, "I don't retire. I quit."

Marc said that Walt Disney was the best art school he ever went to. Walt would always bring in all kinds of important people to give lectures to the artists. I think it was Wednesday nights he rented a theatre in Hollywood. He would have them come and Walt would find films, European films. He would find all kinds of films for them to see. And then after they watched the film, he would go over the film with them and say, "How did you like the staging on this, and what staging would this be?"

There was also a fine artist who was in the Mexican movement in the '30s and '40s. His mother was a Mexican lady and his father was a Frenchman. His name was Jean Charlot. He was a master at staging things. Walt had him come and he taught something like 26 classes on this. Marc still has all the lectures, every one of them. He was terribly impressed with them. He said he learned a great deal from Charlot. Jean Charlot was finally put in as the artist for a Hawaiian university.

Walt constantly had them looking at different things. Marc would eat in his room every once in a while. He would go the library and get a book out on different artists. This one day he picked out a book on Salvador Dali. He was sitting reading it and Walt walked into his room and said, "What are you reading?" Marc said, "I'm reading about Salvador Dali." Walt said, "Can I look?" Marc said, "Sure," and handed him the book. Walt looked at it for a while and handed it back to Marc.

About an hour later, Walt's secretary called Marc on the phone and said, "Walt wants to know if he can borrow your book on Salvador Dali?" Marc said, "I can't see why not. It is his book. I got it from the library." So he sent the book up to Walt. Walt came back a few days later. He said, "You know, I'm interested in you spending your lunch hour looking at different artists. I think it would be good if a lot of these guys started doing this. I can't afford too much, but I'm going to give you some money. You buy some of these types of books of the old masters for the people to study. I think we should have it in the library for everybody." Marc had a field day. He got to go buy all the books he wanted to buy and he could sit and read them. He said it was the best school he ever went to.

© 2007 David Oneal

T. Hee (1911–1988)

Interviewed by Richard Hubler on July 2, 1968.

T. (Thornton) Hee will always be remembered for his delightful caricatures of fellow Disney artists, but he was also one of the great directors and storymen of the studio. His talent influenced many of the best Disney projects from the late '30s, '40s, and '50s.

Born in Oklahoma City, Oklahoma, T. Hee began his career with the Hal Roach Studios at MGM, where he created caricatures of contract stars and studio personnel for the publicity department. In 1936, he moved to Warner Bros., where he designed a model of the famous Hollywood stars for Warner Bros'. *The Coo Coo Nut Grove*.

In 1938, he joined the Walt Disney Studios and provided caricatures of such well-known celebrities as Katharine Hepburn, Spencer Tracy, Clark Gable, and W. C. Fields for the Oscar-nominated short *Mother Goose Goes Hollywood*. He then became a sequence director on *Pinocchio* (on the Honest John & Gideon sequence), "The Dance of the Hours" sequence from *Fantasia* (which he co-directed with Norman Ferguson), *The Reluctant Dragon* (1941, titles), *Victory Through Airpower* (1943, story adaptation), *Make Mine Music* (1946, story), *Noah's Ark* (1958, styling), and *The Shaggy Dog* (1959, titles).

He left Disney in 1946 to work as a writer/designer at UPA on many films including several Gerald McBoing Boing and Christopher Crumpet shorts. After working with director Frank Capra on *Hemo the Magnificent* and *The Case of the Cosmic Rays*, he returned to Disney in 1958 to write and design the studio's first stop-motion animated film, *Noah's Ark*.

He retired from Disney in 1961, but was re-engaged by Walt Disney in 1964 to work at WED Enterprises (now known as Walt Disney Imagineering) on various projects for Disneyland, Walt Disney World, and the New York World's Fair.

T. Hee taught at Chouinard Art Institute beginning in 1948 and served for a brief period as a department chairman. He later taught at CalArts. He also headed the short films branch of the Academy of Motion Pictures Arts & Sciences, and was chairman of their student film awards committee. Finally, he also served on the board of directors for the Academy Awards from 1971 to 1982.

T. Hee passed away on October 30, 1988.

RH: When did you first meet Walt?

TH: I met him for the first time when I came to the Hyperion studio after Frenchy de Trémaudan had presented my drawings to him.

RH: When was that?

TH: That was 1936, on George Washington's birthday. I was 24 and that makes Walt eleven years older than I was. I think I was about the youngest fellow in the studio at that time—I'm pretty sure I was.

RH: What had you been doing previous to that?

TH: I had been writing cartoon stories for Warner Brothers—Merrie Melodies—and had been designing their characters and drawing their backgrounds.

RH: Why did you come to Walt?

TH: Well, I wanted to come to Walt before I ever came here. I even submitted samples, but I wasn't good enough. Working for Walt Disney had been my desire since I had seen some of the animated films.

RH: Did he interview personnel?

TH: No, he didn't. They had a fellow here named George Drake. George Drake interviewed me, and Don Graham was with him at the time. When I was waiting out in the reception room a young fellow came out and he said, "ARE YOU TEE HEE?" I said, "YES." I thought perhaps he was hard of hearing, and so he said, "FOLLOW ME," and I said, "Certainly". So we started walking along and he said, "You're not really deaf, are you?" I said, "No, I'm not." He says, "Damn that George, he told me you were hard of hearing and I'd have to shout." So, I said, "Thank you very much." We went into George's office and George was sitting there with his feet up on the desk and Don Graham was sitting there running his fingers through his hair—my first introduction to both of these gentlemen—and George got up and said, "Tee Hee?" and I said, "HUH?" and he said, "YOU'RE TEE HEE?" and I said, "Yes, but you don't have to shout." Don Graham practically fell through the floor because he had been in on this and George turned about fifteen different colors and the young boy was still standing there at the doorway. I looked around at him and he was grinning and chuckling because this had turned on George.[1]

---

[1] JB Kaufman notes: "The time frame of this story isn't entirely clear from the way T. Hee tells it, but it seems to be taking place early in 1936. For what it's worth, in the film *Love Before Breakfast*, there's a scene in which Carole Lombard introduces two strangers at a party. As a practical joke, she tells each one privately that the other is hard of hearing. This leads to a scene on the dance floor, with the

I presented my samples then and they said there wasn't anything at that moment and he'd take my name and to check back in now and then. But I couldn't wait, so I went out to MGM and Hal Roach and started doing caricatures of movie stars, and I subsisted that way for a couple of years. And then about the third year I went to work for Warner Brothers.

RH: When did you come to Walt and how? How did you get in?

TH: This was through these caricatures again. Thank goodness they were the entrée because my drawings were not good enough and Walt liked the caricatures. He thought they were great and he said, "I think we can use him on *Mother Goose Goes Hollywood*," the film that they had not been progressing very far with.

RH: How had he seen the caricatures?

TH: An animator named Gilles de Trémaudan had a sister who lived in an apartment house where we lived, and she saw them and said, "Boy, these are great! I'll bet Walt would like to see those." She said, "I'll get my brother Frenchy to take them over there if you like." I said, "Would I like? That's great." So he took my armful of caricatures of the stars to the studio and showed them to Walt, and Walt was the one who hired me.

RH: Do you remember the first conference that you had with Walt?

TH: Yes, I do. I must preface this by saying that in those days I was a rather nifty dresser because I was rather poor and I wore burlap pants which my wife had made me, and burlap shirts, but I wore very fancy Mexican huaraches and brilliantly colored neckerchiefs.

RH: You were a hippie before there were any hippies.

TH: I apparently was one of the early hippies. I had long black hair, and I weighed about 240 pounds at the time. I finally got to 260, which amused Walt.

Anyway, here I was with this burlap and I looked like a big sack of potatoes I imagine, and wrinkled. Walt knew that I was there and he knew I was working on this story. I was working with a fellow named Ed Penner, who also was somewhat of a character, in that he would wear mustard-colored pants and he wore Indian moccasins. Not the American Indian, but the East Indian moccasins—the pointed toes that curved up—and he wore strange-colored shirts and so forth. I guess we were matched pretty well.

---

couple shouting at each other at the top of their lungs, to the amusement of the other dancers. *Love Before Breakfast* was released early in 1936, and it's tempting to think that Drake had gone to the movies the night before and had seen that scene, and decided to pull the same gag on the new applicant."

And I was very calm and he was very nervous. We worked together on this storyboard, and when we heard that we were going to have this story meeting I was particularly clean that day. I was not dirty, ever, but I had my wife press the burlap pants, and when Walt came in he said, "Well, good morning, fellas." He looked around and he said, "You Tee?" and I said, "Yes, I am," and he shook hands and said, "Well, let's see what we've got here."

When we started going through it, I had enough ham in me that when it came to the parts of the characters, I would enact them, standing up in front of the people—there were about twelve or thirteen people there, including Walt. I did Katharine Hepburn saying, "I've lost my sheep, really I have," Edward G. Robinson...

RH: At 250 pounds.

TH: Yeah. I was doing my flitting around, you know, like they would do. And I think Walt was entranced. He laughed, and all the other guys laughed, too.

RH: A second later...

TH: ...a second later. And there were quite a few people who weren't sure that this was going to be accepted at all. But Ed Penner and I, we had the conviction that Walt would like it, and while I'd never met him, I just felt this was what he would like. So when it was all over with he said, "Well, I think it's great. What do you guys think?" And they all said it was great. So I knew I had a friend.

RH: I love these instinctive modern executives who kowtow to the top man.

TH: That's just exactly right. Now there were a few fellows who were on our side, but there were some others who were very reticent about saying we had what he wanted, because even at that time in 1936 there were those who felt that certain things should be done and certain things should not be done. Walt was not one of those. Walt believed in progressing and doing things differently. I think about that time they were trying to get him to do another *Three Little Pigs* and he said, "No"—he was already off into *Snow White* when I came there.[2]

RH: What was your starting salary?

TH: I was making $50.00 a week, which was a lot of money for me. I had been making $22.50 at the other studio. I started at $16.00, worked up to $18.00, finally up to $22.50, and that was over a period of about a year and a half, so $50.00 looked like a lot of money. And I went out immediately after I had a

---

[2] In reality, at that time the studio was finishing up its *second* Pig sequel, *Three Little Wolves*.

few checks and bought a little red sports car. It was only one of four in the United States, called a British Nippy. And this big me in that little car—I could just sit down like this and strike a match—and Walt was intrigued by this, too. He just couldn't get over it. When *March of Time* came out to do a film on Disney's, he said, "Be sure and get Tee getting in and out of that car." So they shot some film on that. I have it somewhere. It's a 35mm clip.

RH: Well, at this point, my sympathy goes out to your wife. Is she an artist, too?

TH: No, she's not. She was an artist of a different kind. She had been a singer with bands—orchestras—and she wanted to get away from that, so she was happy then. She liked me. She thought I was kind of amusing: cute, heavy. Forgive me, but she would embarrass me by saying, "Isn't he pretty?" But I knew I wasn't.

RH: What was your next encounter with Walt?

TH: Well, the next encounter was that after this film had gone into animation, he said, "I want you to go with [Wilfred] Jackson"—who was the director on that picture—"I want you to be up there with Jackson when he's planning all these characters, so that they look like what you have here."

RH: Did you have some difficulty working there?

TH: Not with Jackson, with a couple of animators who wanted to redraw them. Jackson was 100% for follow-through and with Walt's directive. It turned out the way that Walt wanted it, which I was very happy about. But while I was doing that, Walt started on *Pinocchio* and he said he wanted Ed Penner and me to take some sequences on *Pinocchio*. He said, "Read the book and find what you'd like to do." We both liked Honest John Foulfellow and Gideon, his cohort, so we asked if we could have those sequences. He said, "Sure, that's fine." So we started working on that together and apparently, because again Walt was very pleased, within a year he made me a director of sequences on *Pinocchio*.

RH: As soon as those characters come on the screen it lights up.

TH: The two of us concocted the original version of the song which later was written by Ray Gilbert: "An Actor's Life for Me".[3] We had a rough lyric on it which when the boys came in they changed slightly.

RH: What did Walt say when he saw the sequences?

TH: He loved them again. He raised my salary to $150 a week, which was phenomenal, and after I worked with him, he came in and he worked

---

[3] "Hi-Diddle-Dee-Dee", like the rest of the songs in *Pinocchio*, is credited to Leigh Harline (music) and Ned Washington (lyrics).

closely with us. He loved those characters, and he would get up and go through the routine of the fox and so forth. We had one gag in there that just broke him up, where the fox was talking to the coachman in a kind of an eerie little inn and they were whispering and the cat couldn't hear, so he took his finger and stuck it in the fox's ear and wrung it out and then he put his ear up against there. Walt says, "That's the nuttiest thing I ever saw." We had a good rapport, a really fine rapport. We had lots of laughs together. He would build things, and Ed and I would look at each other and say, "Why in the hell didn't we think of that?" But he always gave us credit for being a good team and kept us together for quite a number of years.

RH: How long did this particular stand last?

TH: Well, 1936, '37, '38, and then I think we moved out here, wasn't it '38?—late '38 or '39. And at that time he wanted me to work on "Dance of the Hours" in *Fantasia*, and I had been working very closely with Norm Ferguson, who was a wonderful animator—he really was a genius at timing animation, and Walt said, "Take Norm with you and you'll work together on *Fantasia*. I've got plans for Penner." So he broke our team up at that point.

RH: Why did he break it up?

TH: I think simply from the standpoint that he was a great casting director. He wanted to get more dimensions from each of us. There was nothing personal in it at all.

RH: How did you work with Ferguson?

TH: Very well. Walt gave me a free hand on "Dance of the Hours". When I told him I would like to photograph some ballet dancers, he said, "Go ahead." He said, "What are you going to do about the hippo?" I said, "Well, I've got a Negro woman, her name is Hattie Noel, she's a perfect size and shape." He said, "Is she a dancer?" I said, "No, but we could get her to pose, have her go through it." We had her shot and used her as a prototype. We had another girl, I don't recall her name, and she did the ostrich with great élan.

RH: Were you as satisfied with that sequence as you were with *Pinocchio*?

TH: Yes, in a different way. I thought it was very successful, because when we went to see it at the premiere, people were ready to laugh and wanted to laugh in *Fantasia*. And when this came on they really laughed…you know, *Fantasia* being such a different kind of expression for Disney that they just didn't know quite what to expect.

RH: What was your next assignment after *Fantasia*?

TH: I think about that time it was *Make Mine Music*. I'm a little bit confused about actual dates. I don't pay any attention to dates or addresses—I just go by poles and trees and things like that—but I think it was *Make Mine Music*, and then I was working on story after that. In the meantime, I had been to New York at the invitation of Fred Allen to talk about *Pinocchio*. He was intrigued by the name Tee Hee and Disney having an artist named Tee Hee and wanted to know if I came out of an inkwell and the usual thing that he would have. When I got back, Walt called me in and he kind of frowned and he said, "Now goddamn it, Tee, you don't do everything around here", and I said "Well, I didn't say I did. I gave you credit, and I gave everybody else credit that I could think of." But unfortunately, I had left out a couple of people. So I was back in story then, I wasn't directing. I said, "Well, Walt, if directing entails having to be chided by you for not mentioning people's names, I'd like to have my baggy pants back and go back to the story department."

RH: What'd he say?

TH: He said okay.

RH: Did you take any cut in salary?

TH: Nope. No, I didn't.

RH: How long did you work in story?

TH: I made *Make Mine Music*; I don't recall the length of time, and I was on story adaptation on the film that we made during the war called *Victory Through Air Power*—and something else after that. Oh, I worked on *Peter Pan* for a while in story.

RH: *Song of the South*?

TH: No, I didn't work on that at all. I traded some jokes in, gags, with some of the boys because I was interested in that film. I think probably an incident that occurred during the film prevented me from working on it. Walt had had some of us come in and look at a rough cut and I was working on another story at the time and Ed Penner and I had been going to writing school, studying playwriting and screenwriting. We were very serious about the writing end of it and we'd been going nights—three nights a week—we'd been going for a couple of years, and every Saturday night we'd go to the Pasadena Playhouse or some theatre. So we were serious about the content of the films, we knew that we were going to get into this more and more. Walt called a lot of us in to see a rough cut and he was unhappy with what was happening on the screen as far as the story was concerned. He said, "There's something wrong here. What are we going to do here?" He had a couple of writers there that he'd hired for this, and I had already talked to him previous to this and told him that I thought that it was a mistake to hire Hollywood writers, that I thought he had people right here that could do a Disney film. He said, "No. Tee, you stick to your business and I'll stick to mine." I said, "Okay." That got screwed up in the history and some people said I told Walt I didn't like the way he was running the studio, and he said he didn't like the way I was trying to run it. But that wasn't it at all. He just said, "You stick to your business and I'll stick to mine." So I shut up—I didn't say anything—until this meeting. I saw what was wrong. At least I thought I knew what was wrong, and I said, "Well, why don't you…" I was cut off several times by Walt musing aloud which he did, he was lost in thoughts, he would just start talking and something would come out of it, eventually, and he was worrying it around in his mind: So, they became stumped again. I said, "Well, Walt, why don't you do so and so and so and so" which would have given a direction. He didn't pay any attention. He just hit the edge of the chair like he'd do with his hand and went on through and nobody else said anything. There were maybe twenty of us there and they all thought I was crazy to even open my mouth, and I perhaps was. So after a while Walt started talking this very same thing that I had mentioned. And then these other people who were there, including these two writers, they said, "Yeah, Walt, that's a great idea, that's good." Something hit me. Bam! I got a little upset and I said, "Walt, that's what I've been trying to tell you for the last half hour." And he looked at me and gave me the eyebrow. You know, the elevated eyebrow. He didn't say anything, but he sure looked right into me. And after that I was put on a film that I didn't like and I didn't want to do.

RH: What was that?

TH: It was called *Ben and Me*. And the way they wanted to do it was to make Ben Franklin a dope and to make the mouse a smart aleck. I thought it would be better to make the mouse a smart aleck, thinking he knew everything, and Ben Franklin a nice kind of guy that would be willing to give him the credit, but knowing all along that he was the one who thought of all these inventions. I suggested that and I didn't get anywhere. I was upset because they didn't follow that line of thought and I guess I was here for about a year after that—that was about 1946—and I didn't do very much, but Walt still paid me hoping that I would snap out of it. And then finally I got the message that I wasn't contributing enough and so I was let go.

Then I went to Paramount and wrote material there for comedians, Bob Hope, others there, a little over a year. I was kind of disenchanted with the motion-picture business; I wanted to be a farmer. Walt had already been out to my place.

You may have heard the story about the goats. While I was still working here he was intrigued to know what I was doing outside because people started talking about Tee and his goats. When my children were born—when my son was born—curiosity I suppose caused Walt to wonder what I was doing out there on the little farm that I'd got. One day I was out in the back working in the goat corrals and my wife came out and said, "Tee, you have visitors." I said, "Who?" She said, "Come and see." So I went out to the front and here was Walt with Lilly and Diane and Sharon and Lilly's older sister and I was very surprised, but delighted, and he said, "What are you doing?" and I said, "Oh, I'm out here building a pen for the baby goats." And by that time the baby goats were coming out from the back part of the property there to the front and the girls ran down and put their arms around them and hugged them. The little goats were as cute as can be—they're the cleanest things in the world, they were bleating and so forth. Walt had his camera out and was taking pictures of the girls hugging the goats. He said, "Tee, you get down there and I'll take a picture with the goats." And I did. I said, ""Well, how about you?" and he said, "Yeah, okay." He got down and I took a picture of him, and Lilly was in the background. Then he came in and shot a picture of us and came out and he said, "Boy, I envy you", and I said, "WHAT?" and he said, "Yeah, boy, some day I'd like to live on a ranch and have animals myself." And he really gazed off and said, "When I was a kid we lived on a farm and we had all kinds of animals. I'd like to have that again."

The next day was Sunday, and I knew that the family and some of the other employees would come over there, to the studio, and play ping-pong. So I got there—it was about 11:30 I guess—I drove in my station wagon. The cops knew me and they said, "What have you got?" and I said, "I've got a little goat in here," and the goat stuck his head out the window. He said, "What are you going to do with it?" I said, "I'm going to give it to Walt." He said, "Geez."

I got out, the goat followed me down to the cafeteria and I saw they weren't out on the patio at the ping-pong tables. I walked into the cafeteria and I saw they were sitting at the counter and the little goat...the little feet...were "tat-tat-tat-tat-ing" right across the floor and saw the little girls and "Baa, baa," and they got off their stools and ran to that little goat and Walt said, "What are you doing here?" I said, "Well, you said you wanted an animal; I brought you a goat for the girls." He said, "You didn't." I said, "I did, too." He said, "Well, that's terrific." Lilly just looked daggers at me—but he didn't notice that. Walt said, "What do I do—what do I feed it?" I said, "Just feed it some grains and barley and just make a little pen for it. He'll be happy at your place—you're up there on the side of the hill, put it out in the back." The girls were delighted, Walt was delighted.

About three or four weeks later I was coming in to work, and he got out of his car and we met on the street here and he said, "You're just about to break up my family." I said, "Why?" and he said, "Lilly told me it was me or the goat. You've got to take it back." I said, "Well, I can't. I can't take a gift back." He said, "Why can't you?" I said, "If I take a gift back then the gift is wiped out. You'll have to get rid of it. Give it to someone, so then the gift will be continued." He said, "Who the hell am I going to give it to?" I said, "Well, that's your problem." So he saw me a day or so later and said, "I haven't found anybody yet." And I said, "Why don't you give it to Sling, the cop." He said, "Yeah, that's an idea." And he did, he gave it to Sling.[4]

RH: What did you have at the farm?

TH: I had goats.

RH: How many acres?

TH: I just had a commercial acre. I always loved the country, so I went to a section where there wasn't anybody. Goats and chickens and ducks and geese and pigeons, and I had everything—fruit trees and gardens, and this is what he was looking around at. It was like Nature's Half Acre, you know?

RH: Did you come back to the studio after that?

TH: Oh, I was working there when he came out.

RH: When did you go back to the studio?

TH: Let's see... I think it was almost 10 years later since I left there in 1946 and came back around 1956.

RH: What was the occasion of your coming back?

TH: To do the film *Noah's Ark*. Walt had a liking for peculiar word phrasing. You know, like Bibbidy Boo, and all that sort of thing that went into songs. He always liked alliterations for one thing, and this particularly stuck in

---

[4] In the book *Remembering Walt* by Amy Booth Green and Howard E. Green (Hyperion, 1999), Diane Disney Miller, Walt's daughter, remembers the story differently:

"I must have been ten the first time I remember any discord in our family. We used to always go to the studio and have a big picnic with the personnel on the Fourth of July. One of the animators raised goats and had brought a kid to the picnic as a gift to us. It was a female, with a big red ribbon and bell around her neck.

When it came time to go home, Daddy put the goat in the car and Mother said, "We're not taking this goat home." Daddy said, "What do you mean?" "I won't have it," she said. "Of course, you will," he said. "It's a gift for the children."

So he put the goat in the car and we were on the road home, when all of the sudden I heard this sobbing; Mother was sitting in the back seat, crying. It was the first time I had ever seen her cry. These furious tears were just streaming down her cheeks.

Daddy got mad and said, "Okay. We won't keep the goat!" He took us home and headed back to the studio with the goat. He spent half the night in his apartment at the studio."

his mind. When I was called in to do a film for him, X. Atencio and Bill Justice were working together as a team and they wanted to experiment with some three-dimensional work, and Walt had picked out this title as a possibility: *A Rag, A Bone, A Hank of Hair*.[5] He remembered me doing caricatures at the studio when I was there, and he told them, "Look, Tee makes things out of spoons, ice-cream spoons, and screwdrivers and nuts and bolts and everything. Let's get him in." So I came in and talked to Walt, and he mentioned a number of subjects that he was interested in, and I wasn't interested in them. That's always been a kind of peculiarity with Walt and me—it doesn't mean that I wasn't interested in everything he had to say, but there were certain things that I didn't feel I was capable of doing. It wasn't my cup of tea. So I went home and thought, "I'd like to work with Walt again. Now what is it that he really would like to see. What is it that I could present to him that would be Disney-like?"

I recalled that he had made a film at one time, a musical, based on *Noah's Ark*,[6] and he was very fond of it…and he had told us many times that he only had one letter from one person—he never told who it came from—criticizing for having done *Noah's Ark* because it was Biblical.

And I thought, "Now Walt always liked that picture. Perhaps he would be interested in *Noah's Ark* done with this *A Rag, A Bone, A Hank of Hair* technique." We had been talking about using brushes and weenies and things like that for dogs. He liked the idea of doing a dog film. I didn't have any idea on a dog theme. I thought that we could do *Noah's Ark*, so I told Bill and X. [Atencio] this was what I was going to try to sell Walt. And I made some characters—giraffes and elephants, crazy-looking birds, and things like that—out of grapefruit—and had them come out and they shot some color pictures of them. Harry Tytle was there at the time, too. They apparently sold him on the idea that this was possible to do as a three-dimensional experimentation. They had done a little piece of film with cut-outs that had been jointed. Walt was very intrigued about it and some of the people said that this would be a great way to do television commercials. He said no—this was too good for television commercials, that we should do something for ourselves. So they called me and said that they liked the idea.

Now I had to come up with something to please him. I knew he was interested in musicals—always had been—and I concocted a story. Mel

---

[5] The final title was *A Rag, a Bone and a Box of Junk* (1964).

JB Kaufman notes: "The line 'a rag and a bone and a hank of hair' originally came from Rudyard Kipling's poem "The Vampire", which in turn inspired the play and the film *A Fool There Was*. The film, in 1915, was probably Theda Bara's most famous portrayal of a "vamp".

[6] The Silly Symphony *Father Noah's Ark* (1933).

Leven, who works here now as a songwriter, had been working with me at UPA. I asked him to come out and look the story over, and I had songs suggested throughout and would he help on the lyrics, and he did. And I said, "Now, you have to come in with me when I present this and play your ukulele and sell it to Walt. I'll read the narrative and you sing the songs." He's not a singer, but he's a good showman. And when we had it presented, Walt says, "Well, when do we go into animation?" to Bill Justice, and Bill said, "This is one we don't want to go into animation." Walt looked at him and said, "What? What?" Bill says, "We want to do it with that three-dimensional thing. Get Tee here to work with us and make things out of corks and screws and so forth." And Walt says, "Go ahead."

RH: How'd it come out?

TH: It turned out very well. I understand it won some kind of a big award at Cannes, I think it was.

RH: Why didn't you continue?

TH: Walt asked me to continue in another area. He wanted me to do a screenplay treatment of *Hans Christian Andersen* where we could use this technique.

RH: Did it ever work out?

TH: It did not. Walt liked what we were doing with our different presentations of the medium using paper sculpture for *The Emperor's Nightingale*, and cut-outs for *Little Fir Tree* (textured cut-outs) and he, in the meantime, had been trying to find somebody to take the part of Hans Christian Andersen. He'd been checking with somebody in Europe; he checked with the Danish comedian, Victor Borge. He had him out here and he talked about it. Victor Borge said he was no actor, but if he would be a character he could be himself and perhaps it might work as a storyteller. So Walt, I think, had some tests made of a man in Europe and apparently didn't like the tests and decided not to go ahead with it at that time.

RH: Then this whole technique is lying dormant.

TH: Yes, it is. It was used once again in a film that X made which, I believe, was presented at the Academy Awards. I don't recall the name of it, but it was a series of short musical sections [*A Symposium of Popular Songs*, 1962].

[*Noah's Ark*] was the first time that we had tried it and it was rather unique in that Bill and X were very proficient in moving these dimensional figures under a special camera that we had here, and they were able to do it [cheaper] than it would cost to animate it, and Walt saw great possibilities. That's why he thought we could do *Hans Christian Andersen* for a reasonable sum.

RH: How long did you stay with the studio?

TH: I was there three years.

RH: Why did you quit?

TH: I didn't quit. Walt fired me again.

RH: Why?

TH: Well, I'll have to go back to give you a reason. When I left in 1946, I had been gone about a year when I got a call from a man named Meredith Willson, who said that he had my name from Walt Disney, and that he wanted to talk to me about doing a caricature of him for a book that he was writing called *There I Stood with My Piccolo*. I said, "Okay, where'll I meet you?" He said, "Meet me at the Taft Building in Hollywood." I said, "What time?" He told me, so I met him, and when I met him he gave a big sigh of relief. We joked for a minute or two, and I said, "What's that for?" and he said, "Well, Walt told me when I asked him who he had at the studio that could do a caricature and he said, "There's just one guy and he's not with me anymore, and he's so damned independent that if he doesn't want to do it he won't do it." I said, "He did?" He said, "I hope that that opens the door for you to do it for me," and I said, "Well, I don't know why Walt would say that." So I thanked him anyway for the job, 'cause I needed it.

Now, I'll go back to the other thing. When I finished with the treatment on *Hans Christian Andersen*, Walt asked me on the way over the cafeteria one day. He said, "Tee, I'd like for you to start on another project." I said, "What project?" He said, *Baron Munchausen*. I said, "That old-hat thing?" He said "What do you mean, old-hat thing?" and I said, "God, that thing's been around for years and years." I said, "That's not for me." He said, "Why isn't it for you?" I said, "It isn't hip." He said, "You can make it hip." I said, "No, I can't." He said, "Well, what do you want to do?" I said, "Well, I've got an idea I'd like to do about turtles, animals, and things like that. I think it would be very funny as a TV series." He said, "Okay, go ahead and do it." And so I started. He said, "Let me know what it is all about." So I wrote a three-page resume of what it could be and I got back a note from him saying it sounded like a great idea, go ahead. So I did. Then I couldn't get him to come in to look at it.

RH: What was it? What title?

TH: What title? I don't recall now. But it was the southern animals, raccoons, skunks, and all this. And we thought about doing it—X and Bill and I—in dimension again, although it could have been a good animated film. But I couldn't get Walt to come in. I'd say, "Walt, would you come in and take a look and see how we're getting along." No, he wouldn't come in; he was always too busy. Finally, after months, I was going a little nuts sitting there looking at the storyboard and not having any okays. He said, "Okay." We had a meeting in a projection room and I didn't get maybe five or six storyboard drawings explained, and he said, "I don't like it." I said, "You don't like it?" "No," he says, "It's terrible. It's juvenile… it's… it's… I don't like it at all," and he started to get up. I said, "Well, that's all? Anything else?" He said, "No, that's it." I said, "Thank you." So I got up and went to my room and started packing up, putting everything away, my own personal things, and the phone rang. And his secretary said, "Tee, Walt wants to talk to you." He said, "Tee, you've got a hell of a lot of talent, but we just haven't learned how to use it." I said, "Thank you very much."

RH: This was in 1959?

TH: Yeah, '59. I was gone in 1959, '60, '61, '62, '63.[7] I think it was around '64 that I came back.

RH: Why?

TH: Well, he called me up, and he said, "Tee, I'd like to talk to you about CalArts, about Chouinard. Can you have lunch with me?" I said, "Sure." So I came over and he told me about what he was planning to do.

RH: What was he planning to do?

TH: Planning to expand the school. He said he had an idea for a real school.

RH: Did he explain it in any detail?

TH: Not in great detail at that time. He did later. He said "What are you doing?" "Oh," I said, "I'm doing some freelancing and anything that comes up." Then he talked more about the school and my relationship to it. I was teaching there—had been teaching there [at Chouinard] since 1948. A couple of weeks later I got a phone call from Bob Millard in WED, the personnel director there. He said, "Tee, Walt wants you to come over and see about working at WED." I said, "That's fine, that's wonderful, but I can't do it now." He said, "When can you do it?" I said, "Well, I can't get over there until July 12." This was about the 1st of June. He said, "Walt wants you right away." I said, "Boy, I'd like to be over there right away, but I've got an assignment for CBS I'm trying to get done." He said, "Gee, I'm in a terrible spot." I said, "Just tell him that I'm tied up and I'll be over there on July 12. I've got to hand it in on July 11 and I'll be there on July 12." He hung up, saying "Okay, I'll try." Then about every week after that he'd call me and say, "Are you going to be here on July 12?" I'd say, "Yeah, I'm going to be there." So I made it on that July 12—this is the beginning

---

[7] In reality, according to both Bob Kurtz and the Disney Archives, T. Hee left the studio in 1961. He did return in 1964.

of the third year and I feel just like I did when I came in to the old studio. It was really wonderful to be again with Walt. I used to see him on the average of twice a week—three times a week sometimes. He'd drop in to see what I was doing. He always laughed at what was going on. That is practically the story of my life.

RH: What did Walt say when you came back on the 12th?

TH: He told Dick Irvine, "You know Tee Hee?" And Dick had known me because Dick had been there a number of years. Dick said, "Yeah, I know him." And Walt said, "Well, Tee's got a hell of a lot of talent. We want to find a way to use it." So Dick was on the spot. He didn't know what the hell I did, and he didn't know how to use me, so he didn't know whether to put me on doing posters for Disneyland or what. And then Walt said, "There's something coming up with Monsanto. Put him on Monsanto. Give him something important to do." So Dick told me I was to be on Monsanto. I went down to Monsanto to check it out and find out what they had, and I was there about two days. I got back up, and I was sitting in the library (they didn't have an office for me) and I was writing up my impressions of what I should try to present to them and I got a phone call that said, "You're going to New York to the World's Fair." I said, "I am?" They said, "Yes, you and your wife are going with a Disney group to see the World's Fair. It's on a business trip." So we went and spent a week there and I learned more about moving people, attractions and things. We had Dick Nunis there—he was the operations manager at Disneyland—and he was our guide, showed us all around and explained how things worked.

I came back with a whole new idea of show business. I guess I had been back on Monsanto for about a week when I had a call from Dick Irvine, who said, "Walt wants you on the shooting gallery." I said, "What kind of a shooting gallery?" and he said, "He wants an idea for something different." I said, "Well, I've been kicking around an idea for a long time that might work—it's a space thing." He said. "We've tried something on space," and I said, "I'd like to present this." So I did. I said, "These are guys that shoot back. When you shoot at them, they shoot at you." He put me with Yale Gracey, who's a genius—he really is a fantastic guy. He has a real Goldberg facility for making anything work with pieces of string and rubber bands. I just marvel at him. And the two of us then began to come up with conceptions of how these things would look. Walt heard about it, apparently, and said, "That's good. That's a good idea." Then he came over to see this thing that we had. One character that we had, we had an electronic gun that you would shoot at the target—it would make the thing explode and do various things. We had the head blow up and the body fall down and the mouth going up and down and the lights in the top of the head flashing and the eyes revolving and the horn sound "boing, boing, boing". Walt shot at it and said, "Is that all it does?"

I picked up the cue right away. I knew he wanted to do something really fantastic. We did some other things, and finally he said, "Now you're doing it where it's getting along." Yale was going to pull a gag on me. One of these characters we devised, you'd shoot at it and its pants would drop. This is a thing from outer space. You'd shoot at it and its pants would drop down, and you could see it in its under-drawers and its eyes opened up and it looks surprised, and then the thing drops down into the pants and disappears, comes back again ready to be shot at again. And Walt came in ahead of me. Yale thought he would pull the joke on me, but Walt said, "Hey, that's an interesting one, let's see what happens." Bang. He shot and Yale had put a sponge rubber penis on it that popped up like this—and Walt laughed like hell, and Yale said, "Oh, ah, well, we didn't mean to do that for you, that was for Tee." Yale started to take it off and Walt said, "No, no, don't take it off, leave it on there." He brought guests around: General Joe Potter and various people like that from the Florida project to see this thing…

RH: What are you working on now?
TH: I'm working on a couple of things. I'm following through with this Planet Moon shooting gallery for Florida and Disneyland. And I'm working with Marty [Sklar] on a film idea for Florida based on the generation gap that would be for a lessee. The idea is that the old should be revered and the young should be accepted. We want to do it in a comic, humorous fashion. We want to give it a humorous twist.

RH: Do you remember any more encounters with Walt?
TH: I can't tell you the date of this, but Bill Cottrell and I were working as a team. We had worked together on *Victory Through Air Power* and Walt liked what we had accomplished there so he let us team up as writers.

RH: Then you had abandoned caricatures and had gone in wholly for writing?
TH: Yes. But I still had to draw. We drew our storyboards. And Walt gave us carte blanche. He just said, "Come up with something that would be good. However," he said, "I like the idea of doing a Mickey feature. See what you can do with that." So we were kidding around. We said, "Wouldn't it be funny if Disney would do a takeoff on *Jack and the Beanstalk* the way Hollywood would do it?" You know, the part of Jack being too big for one star so they'd have to have three: Donald, Mickey, and the Goof would all be called Jack. Everyone would refer to them as Jack: Jack I, Jack II, Jack III.

So we got off onto this real nutty tangent. We did it as a musical. Musicals were real big then, with this Brazilian girl: Carmen Miranda. We had a number with string beans that sang and stripped... We got ready, we made recordings and we got a starving scene in there of the Duck: he went berserk and he was eating Mickey and the Goof. This was going to be a feature.

Walt came in to find out how we were doing. Bill and I went through this story, and he burst out laughing and when he laughed, he really laughed, tears running down the sides of his face and he was hitting his knee and he was just going on... And he said, "Wait a minute." We hadn't finished yet. He said, "Let's get the guys in here." So he got in Ward Kimball, Milt Kahl, Wilfred Jackson, and a lot of others, like Frank Thomas, Ollie Johnston—a whole group of people—and he says, "Tee and Bill have got a new version on a Mickey feature. See how you like this." He had a very straight face, by this time, he had recovered, wiped his eyes with his handkerchief. We started through it again and he started to laugh again like he did before. And then they started to laugh, and they laughed, and everybody was just rocking with laughter. And we got through the whole thing this time and he was just in tears. I was very happy and so was Bill. We said, "Well, when do we go into production?" And he said, "Well, Tee, we don't." I said, "WHAT?" He said, "No." When he said that, boy, you could have heard a pin drop. Everybody stopped laughing. There wasn't even a chuckle—just a gasp. And certain fellows excused themselves, said they had to do things. We were finally left alone with Walt and I said, "Well, Walt, why? You laughed, you enjoyed it, you had tears running down your face, you wiped your eyes, you were having a great time, you were pounding your knee." "Yes, I know," he says, "it was funny as hell, but you have murdered my characters. You've really killed them," he says. "You have destroyed with this one film, if I made it, what I've been working years to build up. I've got my audience and they expect a certain thing of my characters, and this isn't it." And he was absolutely right. At the moment we were absolutely crestfallen; we had thought we had done something great—we sat there about thirty minutes staring at the board. And I guess it took thirty minutes for it to sink into us that he really was completely right. He had built up a market of his own. It was at that moment, I think, that the seed was planted in my mind that he was the most creative businessman in the United States.

RH: Do you remember any more encounters with Walt?

TH: Yes, I had all kinds of strange ones. This particular one, I guess, stands out in my memory because of the way he reacted. I had fallen off a horse at my farm and I had injured my hip bone. I was walking around with a cane. I got rid of the cane, but I was still limping around. I was coming out of one of the writers' offices down here on the third floor, and Walt was standing in this main hall with Jim Algar, one of his directors. I started to go along because I saw they were in conference, and I said, "Hi, Walt." He said, "Hi, Tee, how's the leg?" I said, "It's a lot better." With that he walked over toward me and looked at me and said, "Feeling alright?" I said, "Yeah, why?" And he stared right at me and he said, "Do you dye your moustache?" And I said "Yes, sir, every morning I put chicken shit on it." And he rolled down the hall saying, "Oh, you S.O.B."—laughing and hysterical. Jim Algar's face turned about 15 different colors, he didn't know whether to laugh or not. And I just went on, limping down and got in the elevator, but Walt was rolling, hitting the wall as he went. And I thought that was a funny reaction. Well, I didn't do it to shock him, really, but somehow or other felt it was none of the damn business of his whether I dyed it or not. Now this may be the reason Walt says I'm so damned independent.

Marty Sklar: You told me another amusing anecdote, and that was the RAF story.

TH: This was prior to 1946, during the war. I was ready to go home and started walking out toward the parking lot. Walt was behind me and caught up with me, and said, "Where are you going?" I said, "I'm going home." He says, "I've got to go out here to see some RAF flyers out in Bel Air and talk about the gremlins. You want to go along?" I said, "Yeah, sounds good, but I'd better call my wife and tell her I'll be late." He said, "Okay." So I called my wife and said, "I'm going out with Walt to Bel Air and will probably eat out there somewhere so don't wait dinner for me." She said, "What time will you be home?" and I said, "I don't know."

So, on the way down he talked all about this gremlin film, about these little guys that came out on the wings, saving the RAF flyers and everything. We got down to this kind of a deep canyon and a big old house and it was colder and foggier than hell down there. The windows were open in every room, with windows from ceiling to floor, the doors were open. The RAF men were all in their uniforms and the British women were in there with their low-cut, sleeveless gowns, and Walt and I had our overcoats on. We hesitated about taking them off because it was so goddamned cold in there, but they had fireplaces going in every room. Finally we took them off, and they served us drinks and these were the typical RAF flyers—like the Terry Thomas guys—with the big mustaches, the whole thing, you know. They were talking in that very British, clipped way—very difficult to understand and the women were even more British. Both of us being Midwesterners, I think that that kind of grated on our ears, but most of the evening, before we had dinner, most of the RAF flyers were in the den, and they were telling off-color stories and Walt was laughing at them because they were funny. But he wasn't there for that, he was there to talk about the gremlins for the film. Every time he'd bring it up, why they'd get off on some other tactic about their experiences. So we had dinner and I could see that Walt wasn't too happy because he couldn't get the conversation back to the gremlins.

We left late, pretty close to midnight, and we got in the car and he was silent and I said something about, "You know what you could do with those gremlins…"

He said, "I'm not going to do the film."

I said, "You're not?" And that was the end of it.

RH: Did Walt really have anything in mind [about CalArts] before he died?

TH: He called me one evening over at WED. It was about six o'clock, and we talked for an hour. He talked to me, I didn't talk to him. I just said, "Yes, sir." And he was wound up and he said, "I want to talk to you about CalArts. I want to have a real film department there. I want people to come out of there that are really able to do things. I don't want a lot of theorists. Hell, I can hire theorists from any school. I want to have a school that turns out people that know all the facets of filmmaking. I want them to be capable of doing anything needed to make a film: photograph it, direct it, design it, animate it, record it, whatever. That's what I want. Hell, I've hired theorists and they don't have any knowledge that I can use. I want to have everyone in that school come out being capable of going right in and doing a job. These dilettantes who come out with pseudo knowledge give me a pain. When I was sixteen, seventeen, I had to work. I was working, making a living; doing what I wanted to do and what I had to do, and I suppose you had the same kind of problem." I said, "Well, I was working…" and he went right over me, and said, "Well, that's what I want people to do when they come out of school. Now this is the kind of school that I want. I want to have a department that if they want to have an actor, they can go and get an actor right out of the school. If they want to make a film test, they use an actor from the acting department; if they want a musician, they go to the music department and they get musicians to compose music for the film.

RH: It moved very slowly, didn't it?

TH: He wanted things worked out completely in his mind.

RH: Was he supporting Chouinard from 1960 on?

TH: He told me (this is not in reference to Mrs. Chouinard) about some of the instructors and students at Chouinard's that were anti-Disney. He said, "Damn it, Tee, Roy and I have been subsidizing that place for years. If it wasn't for the money we put in there, they wouldn't be there teaching and those students wouldn't have a school." Now that's all I know about that.

RH: Did he ever say anything else about CalArts?

TH: He did tell me that he thought CalArts was one of the important things in his life and that he wanted to see it work.

RH: I talked to Dr. John Vincent, who was the director at one time. Why did they break up?

TH: Dr. Vincent is a very fine man, but I think that possibly he didn't know when to be still when Walt was talking. I think there were a lot of people that, also, are very fine and that hadn't learned this. I had to learn it a long time ago.

RH: Was Walt able to draw himself?

TH: I don't know but that I ever saw but one drawing that he did, and that was recently at WED. One day I went to Marvin Davis' office at WED and I saw this great, scraggly, spidery-looking thing on a piece of tissue. Marvin was looking at it. And I said, "Hey, Marvin, that looks like some sort of a cell. It looks like some sort of an amoebic cell that's breaking loose somewhere. It's going to go places." And he said, "That is Walt Disney's version of Florida—the Florida for Disney World." I said, "That's a Walt Disney drawing?" That's the first one I'd ever seen. He said, "He made that—that's his—he laid it out. He had the waterways, indentations of land, and it's still that way."

RH: Any more encounters that you remember with Walt?

TH: Oh, I'll tell you one little incident about Walt that was characteristic. Major de Seversky had one leg. The other had been shot off in the war and he wore a false leg. It had a habit of squeaking as he walked from one part of the set when they were filming scenes—it would squeak. We had a sound man here at that time, named Sam, who had an ear just like an owl.[8] He could hear everything. They would make a take and Walt would say, "That's good." And Sam would say, "No, Walt, there's a squeak there in the background." So they'd shoot it again, and he said this about three times and they were running late, and Walt said, "Well, what the hell's the squeak, Sam?" And de Seversky said, "Well, I think it must be my leg." He swung his leg back and forth and he said, "Well, you know, it's squeaky." Walt said, "Oh, hell, my knee squeaks like that sometimes," in order to make de Seversky feel good. So he said, "Leave the squeak in, Sam, let's go ahead."

I liked the encounters I had with Walt which endeared him to me as a human being. I felt that in later life he became so involved with all of the various interests that he had that he didn't have the same rapport with a lot of his workers. In the early days he did.

© 2007 Jane Hubler

---

[8] JB Kaufman notes: "The 'sound man named Sam' is probably C.O. Slyfield. (I don't know what the 'C.O.' stood for, but he was known as 'Sam' around the studio.)"

Maurice Noble (1910–2001)

Interviewed by Harry McCracken in January, 1991.

Maurice Noble's career in animation began at Disney in the 1930s, but he is undoubtedly best remembered as the designer who made so many of Chuck Jones' Warner Bros. cartoons from 1952 on some of the best-designed animated films of all time. Noble's association with Jones continued into his later work for MGM and Warner's.

Born in Spooner, Minnesota, on May 1, 1910, Noble moved to California and attended Chouinard Art Institute. He began his career in advertising, designing the famous Red Door for Elizabeth Arden, but discovered his true calling at Disney, where he worked on the Silly Symphonies as well as *Snow White*, *Bambi*, *Fantasia*, and *Dumbo*.

During World War II, Noble was a member of Frank Capra's U.S. Army Signal Corps unit, which created animated films for the Armed Forces. During this period he met his future colleagues Ted Geisel (better known as Dr. Seuss) and Chuck Jones.

After the war, Noble and Jones entered into a partnership that continued on and off for nearly 50 years. Among the animated short subjects Noble created during that time are *Duck Dodgers in the 24th-and-a-Half Century*, *Bully for Bugs*, *Duck Amuck*, *What's Opera, Doc*, and *The Dot and the Line*.

His partnership with Jones continued through the 1960s, when they produced numerous animated versions of Dr. Seuss classics, including *The Cat in the Hat*, *Horton Hears a Who*, and *How the Grinch Stole Christmas*.

Following a leave in the 1970s, Noble returned to animation in the 1990s to contribute designs to Chuck Jones Productions and Warner Bros. and to form his own studio, Maurice Noble Productions.

Noble passed away on May 18, 2001.

Harry McCracken conducted this interview in January 1991. It was edited for publication by Noble and him, and originally appeared in *Animato* number 21.

Harry McCracken: I should start by asking you how you got interested in animation in the first place.

Maurice Noble: I was doing design work for one of the largest department stores in Los Angeles, and I had designed a children's department for two

Christmases. One of the scouts from Disney saw the work, and this scout had also known my work when I went to the Chouinard Art Institute. I think I had the first one-man watercolor show at Chouinard. I was asked to come out there and try out as a background painter, and that's how I got into the animation business.

HMC: Had you been interested in animation before that?

MN: No, in fact being something of a highbrow [laughs], I hadn't paid much attention to it, although I guess I had seen and enjoyed *Three Little Pigs*, which was a turning point for the Disney Studio. I had never even thought of animation as a job or career. I had an attitude that it was kid's stuff. The kiddies got down in front and jumped up and down when you put on a cartoon, but the adult approach wouldn't be considered until the making of *Snow White*.

What they needed out there were people who could handle watercolor rendering for their backgrounds. I had been doing a very creative job and designing all sorts of things, from departments to all sorts of windows. I helped design the exterior of the building and all that. I went out there [to Disney] and sat down, and the first job they gave me was painting an apple with a wormhole in it. I thought, "Oh, what did I get myself into?" This was pre-*Snow White*. The big product at that time was the Silly Symphonies. We worked on *The Old Mill* and some of the things that led up to *Snow White*.

HMC: Did you enjoy animation right away, or did it take some getting used to?

MN: I enjoyed the work and was hooked. It was a challenge, because at the time we were painting these backgrounds. Everything was done in transparent wash, and we weren't allowed to use any opaques at all. The Whatman paper was stretched on boards, and a pencil outline was traced. Then we were given a pencil rendering with precise detail of shadows and forms and so forth, and we had to transpose that into a color rendering. There were certain guidelines that were set up, but we would be given a sequence of three or four or five or six backgrounds that tied together. You can imagine the difficulty of matching transparent washes with different backgrounds that would be cut from one to the other.

HMC: Was this a very creative job at this point, or were you mainly doing what somebody else told you to?

MN: It was more or less following what somebody else told me to do, because the pencil renderings were very detailed and specific. We were creating a mood, and we had to exercise our judgment in that, but we were working within a framework. Every picture must have a framework: story, visuals, and music—a total composition.

HMC: You had to work within the Disney style.

MN: That's right. I doubt whether we'd call it a Disney style at that time. *Snow White*'s style was set up for that particular picture. I suppose in a sense it was realism, but realism with an overtone of Arthur Rackham or something like that.

I worked on *Snow White* and *Bambi*. I worked on the Stravinsky "Rite of Spring" sequence in *Fantasia*. I had screen credit on *Dumbo* as color coordinator. I might have painted one or two backgrounds on *Pinocchio*, but not a great deal because I spent almost two years doing sketch work on *Bambi* and that overlapped into *Pinocchio*.

HMC: Was that more interesting work?

MN: Yes, that was completely creative work. I became fascinated by the potential of the medium. I was doing thumbnail sketches for mood and continuity and so forth, searching for a way to present the picture. Originally I worked with Gustaf Tenggren, who was a well-known illustrator. I worked about three months with him, and then I believe he left the studio and went back to New York.

About that time they were constructing their new studio in Burbank, and the *Bambi* unit was shifted over to a small building down in Hollywood on Seward Street. That's where we were isolated for almost two years. All I did on that particular picture was sketchwork; I probably did three or four thousand watercolor sketches for it. As it finally appeared, my influence was probably minimal, because they decided to go with the approach that Tyrus Wong gave it: a certain Oriental flavor, if you recall the film. My view of the story of *Bambi* was more on the grand scale, and Tyrus' rendering and type of background seemed to lend itself to the intimate approach. My contributions were probably more indirect on the film.

HMC: Did you know Walt Disney well personally?

MN: I wouldn't say that at all; did anyone? He was kind of a law unto himself, you know. I sat in the sweatbox with him and discussed color breakdown on characters and so on. When I was working on *Snow White*, I had a room that was sort of catty-corner over from Walt's, and he could look over in my window and I could look in his window. I was working on the final sequence when the Prince awakens Snow White, and I'd be there sometimes to eight, nine, ten, eleven o'clock at night. Walt would say, "You still here, Maurice?" I'd say "Yes, I have a little something to finish up," and he'd say goodnight and leave. I think the whole studio was feverishly caught up in the *Snow White* production. But no intimate lunches or that sort of association with him.

HMC: How did you come to leave the Disney Studio?

MN: I left there by invitation. I was a member of the group that decided that the wage structure of the Disney Studio wasn't fair, and so I went out on strike and consequently lost my job. This was a very traumatic experience: loyalty, opportunities, and finances were involved. Walt Disney set his standards high, and all credit should be given him, even though we went out on strike.

World War II was about to break out, so after Pearl Harbor I enlisted, through the Academy of Motion Picture Arts and Sciences, in the Army Signal Corps. They were asking for technicians.

HMC: Were you glad that you ended up leaving the studio?

MN: That's one of those moot points. I really feel I was able to be far more creative on my own, taking the route that I did. Disney has a tendency to over-refine their product, and in that way they lose a lot of their spontaneity and zip. By that I don't mean flashy zip, but the kind of a joyful quality that I found later in a lot of the really silly things we did at Warner Brothers.

HMC: Did you find that your Disney training gave you a good background for your later work?

MN: Oh, yes. I really think the training was very valuable. I know that many of the young people in the business today work at Disney two or three years, and then they go on into the other studios. They should be commended today for upholding the quality of animation, which is not found in many of the other studios. The Disney Studio still believes in drawing, which is the basis of animation.

HMC: I know that you worked on the *Private Snafu* cartoons during the war, so you were working on Warner cartoons several years before you actually joined the studio.

MN: This was one of my first contacts with Warner Bros. The Signal Corps post was at the Fox studio; we called it Fort Fox. I had been down in Louisiana, and we had the Signal Corps units down there. They were organized and then moved out overseas. I was in a position to take groups of men over to the post theater to see Frank Capra's various films, and after watching them so many times I noticed the men were responding in the same general patterns. I set up a graph and tracked responses of the men all the way through. I thought, "Gee, this is real interesting stuff," so I sent it off to Colonel Capra.

After much waiting, all of a sudden I was transferred to Colonel Capra's organization in Hollywood. My commanding officer was Ted Geisel, who was famous as Dr. Seuss. It was a very creative bunch: we did the Snafu cartoons, we did propaganda booklets and leaflets, we did various warnings about health problems and venereal disease, we did charts that were inserts for Capra's films, when he was showing various battle movements and so forth. It was a very productive small unit—perhaps ten men.

I was working on design and renderings and things of that kind. The story unit did the storyboards and lots of times I would be called to design in black and white for the backgrounds. The story and the background designs were then shuttled off to Chuck Jones over at Warner Bros., and they would produce the cartoons as subcontractors.

HMC: You weren't working directly with Chuck Jones at this time?

MN: I was over there a couple of times, but in a sense I wasn't directly working for him, because his layout men had to adapt our work. What I did, I assume, had some influence on the way the films were styled. As a matter of fact, I can barely recall what the films were about! [Laughs]

HMC: Oh, they're basically propaganda—funny propaganda, but propaganda.

MN: I remember we did one about Japan, and one about German spies, and I don't know what else. They were all done in a comic-serious vein. They all had a message.

HMC: What did you do after the war was over?

MN: I had some domestic difficulties and went back to St. Louis and started to do filmstrips for an organization that was indirectly connected with the Lutheran church. I worked there a number of years. One day I got a call from Johnny Burton back at Warner Bros. asking if I'd like to have a job doing layout for Chuck Jones. I said, "Confirm it with a telegram and I'll be there." So that's how my wife and I came back to California, and subsequently I worked with Chuck for almost twenty years.

HMC: So you came in and out of the animation business a few times over the years.

MN: Well, I was in the filmstrip business, but I was always involved with film. Oh, and I worked at the John Sutherland Studios for a time. Warner Bros. closed its studio at one time [1953]. I, not knowing that the studio was going to close, took a job at Sutherland because I couldn't get a raise. I happened to leave the week before it closed. I didn't know anything about it, and everybody accused me of having inside information.

Sutherland was going to do a very important picture for U.S. Steel, and I was asked to come over there and design it. It was a film to inaugurate the large stainless-steel dome at the Pittsburgh amphitheater. We did the history of steel; I designed it and Eyvind Earle painted it. It was a fine picture. While I was at Sutherland, we made one of the first films on cancer research for the Sloan-Kettering Cancer Institute in New York. We did some films for insurance companies. I remember one time I met John D. Rockefeller, Jr. We must have been doing something for Standard Oil. It was a very interesting, top-drawer type of operation.

HMC: When you started with Chuck Jones, did you know right away that you had a job where you'd be able to experiment and do interesting things?

MN: I guess I just kind of grew in the way I handled things. I'd always had in the back of my mind that super-realism in the backgrounds behind flat animation was not the right approach. So when I got the opportunity, I started to place more emphasis on shapes. I started to leave off the airbrush and create the spaces by shapes instead of a lot of fussy shadows and so forth. I tried to create each frame to support the action and not clutter up anything or interfere with a gag or bit of action. The style just evolved little by little. Chuck was an inventive director, and in retrospect I wonder how the heck we got away with a lot of the things we did. On the other hand, as long as we turned out those Road Runners and Bugs Bunnys and all the various things that were our bread and butter, once in a while we could get in a *What's Opera, Doc?* or *Duck Amuck* or some of the more outstanding pictures.

I am a great believer in the idea that color and visual impact have a lot to do with the response of the audience. I would play for dramatic impact in both design and color, in terms of putting over a story point. No background is any good unless it's appropriate to the given situation or mood of the thing that's being portrayed. I think in terms of *Claws For Alarm*, which is one of my favorite pictures, in which we did that old haunted hotel. A lot of dramatic shots and color were used to enhance the mood in that. *Boyhood Daze* and *From A to Z-Z-Z-Z*, the Little Ralph [Ralph Phillips] pictures, were sophisticated, useful approaches to design, simplified and supporting the young spirit of the films. In *What's Opera, Doc?*, I did the sketches and Chuck built back into them. I quickly did away with the proscenium arch and everything, and let the audience move right in on the picture almost immediately. Then I treated it as super-grand opera and satire. It was kind of a tour de force.

HMC: Did you realize that you were working on a film that would come to be regarded as one of the best, if not the best, Warner Bros. cartoons ever made?

MN: As it went along, I was aware that something was kind of happening. I put in a lot of innovative ideas, and I would get calls from the ink and paint department saying, "Now, you don't mean to say you're going to paint this character all red?" or something like that. I'd say, "Yes, that's the way we want it." And Chuck was backing me up on it. As we sketched and designed and put this thing together, when we finally got it, it was just one of those things that came off. It could have been a pudding.

This is one of those strange things about doing something creative: You take a big chance, and I suppose I could have been put out the front door if it had fallen on its face. But Chuck backed me up on it, and we have *What's Opera, Doc?* today. I still get a boot out of just watching it.

HMC: One of the things I find interesting about a lot of the films you worked on with Chuck Jones, especially during the late 1950s and 1960s, is that the graphic style is radically different from film to film, depending on the subject matter. *What's Opera, Doc?* looks like no other Warner cartoon, and neither does *Robin Hood Daffy*. The Bugs Bunny cartoons that featured Witch Hazel have a look all their own, and so forth. That's not something you see in the works of other directors. Were you consciously changing your style?

MN: Oh yes, this was very deliberate. I was trying to shape the style to fit the cartoon. The zany quality of Witch Hazel immediately suggested a zany approach: cupboards painted on the floor and up the wall, and so forth. She was a marvelous character, and certainly wouldn't be in a normal setup. The same thing would hold true for *Robin Hood Daffy*, which was a slapstick Robin Hood. I hit on this free, fun style to support the free and fun slapstick quality of the film. I think one of the great moments of animation is that line when Daffy is sitting on Porky's lap, and they're laughing and laughing and laughing, and all of a sudden Daffy says, "How jolly can you get?" It's timed beautifully, and I look back on that as one of the great spots in animation.

I call it stepping into the picture. You look around and say, "Gee, what's this all about, and does it feel right for this given picture?" And then you go ahead and design from that standpoint. I'm not particularly aware that this is my style. This is the way it happens as I design and draw a picture. It was a conscious seeking-after-something that I thought would support the mood of a given picture.

HMC: So you were more interested in adapting to what was needed than forcing your style onto a cartoon?

MN: Oh, absolutely, because I don't believe that any cartoon is successful when you force a design onto it. I think that this was one of the problems with UPA: They over-designed. I talked to one gal who worked over there, and I said, "Gee, that was an interesting picture, but what was it all about?" And she just said to me, "Well, I had fun." This is not communicating the spirit of animation to the audience.

HMC: Were you influenced by UPA at all? I think animation fans tend to think that UPA influenced everybody with their stylization in the 1950s. Or were you moving toward being more stylized anyway?

MN: I'll be very frank and say I don't believe I was influenced by UPA at all. I did my own thing. In fact, I refused to go over to UPA. I preferred to stay working with Chuck at Warner Bros. I think UPA outsmarted itself in over-designing and being kind of smart-assed. In a sense they were walking in their hallowed artistic halls.

I think I can honestly say that I've never designed anything that I didn't think was going to communicate to the audience. After all, you have to have an audience. I'm not downplaying some of the good things. I think that Hubley's *Moonbird* is one of the charmers of the animation library. But if you ask me what films do I remember that they did at UPA, I can't really recall one.

HMC: Well, people remember Warner Bros. cartoons a lot better today than they recall UPA's.

MN: Oh, yes. They'll say, "Did you work on *Duck Amuck*?" or "Did you work on *What's Opera, Doc?*"or "Did you work on those Road Runners?" or "What about that thing with all the mice in the hotel?" They remember the strengths and the fun of the Warner Bros. cartoons.

HMC: I can't think of any director other than Chuck Jones when he was working with you whose style changed so much from film to film. That wouldn't have happened at Disney.

MN: I think that in the Disney mechanism, they're tied into the ghost of Walt. It's a fanciful realism. They've created a lot of beautiful pictures, but that's their way of doing it.

HMC: Did you especially enjoy working on some of the more abstract pictures you did during the 1960s, like *High Note*, *Now Hear This*, and then later *The Dot and the Line* over at MGM?

MN: *The Dot and the Line* was built on Norton Juster's book. The adaptation of it tried to stick very close to the dialogue and development, but to put that over into moving graphics was a real challenge. I think we got a good picture out of it. I just consider each picture a challenge. If it calls for abstract, okay, let's go abstract. If it calls for sentimental, let's go sentimental. I think this is what good design is all about.

HMC: Did you feel like you were drawing on artistic traditions other than animation? I think you told me you felt a special kinship with Matisse.

MN: Somebody asked me, "Who is your favorite artist?" and I said Leonardo da Vinci. They were kind of aghast. But when you think about it, here is a man who was inventive, who could draw, who had a sense of color and drama and composition. He was really ahead of his time in terms of so many things.

I can't say that any particular artist directly influenced me. You take in a lot of material, and then your subconscious takes over. I really do believe that the designers and people who have worked with animation have created their own genre of art. I'm not trying to take any credit, but I really think we were innovators. We were designing in terms of length. All these other designers and painters were designing a composition in terms of a static viewpoint, and we were teasing the eye with the way the color and the actions and the accents happened in a continuity on the screen, so in the end we got a total composition. This is something that had never been done in the graphic world before.

There is a very definite relationship between animation and music. One entertains the eye and the other, the ear. Both touch the emotions.

HMC: Was there a character or series that you enjoyed working on most?

MN: I enjoyed working on the Little Ralph pictures, because I thought they were gentle, imaginative, and tender little pictures.

HMC: Was there a reason why there were only two of those?

MN: I don't know about that. Whether that's the sum of what Chuck wanted to do with him or somebody put their foot down, I don't know. In the chain of command, one never knows. Chuck did a couple of things with the Three Bears, and I heard the story that it was previewed up at Hearst's castle. He had a theater up there and a bunch of guests. Somebody announced that, "Now we're going to have a cartoon about the Three Bears," and some dodo gal up there said, "Oh, not another story about the Three Bears." This got to Warner Bros., and they said to never make another Three Bears story.

HMC: Were you at Warner Bros. up until the time that the animation studio closed down?

MN: Oh, yes. I was there after Chuck left. We did *The Incredible Mr. Limpet*, and I was designing and Phil DeGuard was painting backgrounds, and Friz Freleng and Hawley Pratt were doing a lot of the directing on the animation. I remember working with Johnny Burton, Jr. on the wonderful matte shots that he did. Considering the almost primitive equipment that we had at Warner Bros., it's a marvelous job of matting of the live action and the fish.

HMC: That was during the last days of the Warner animation studio. You must have gotten back together with Chuck Jones fairly soon after that, since you worked together at MGM.

MN: I was there with him when he started up with Tower 12, which became the MGM [animation] studios. We did *The Phantom Tollbooth*, *The Bear That Wasn't*, *The Dot and the Line*...

HMC: On some of those films and the later Warner Bros. cartoons, you were credited as Chuck Jones' co-director. Was that because design had become more important, or had your role in production changed?

MN: Lots of times, the credit of co-direction would show up and I wouldn't even know I'd been given it. I would go in and check the animators, maybe sit in on a recording session. I was just all over the place, kind of pulling things together, ironing out a lot of spots while Chuck was going ahead with the next picture. I really don't recall a role as co-director. Someone called me the catalyst.

HMC: I think you told me when we were talking before that you feel the role of the layout artist has changed in animation in recent years.

MN: This is what I've observed, from what little I've been back in the studios. A rough sketch is made of the background, and the layout man in a sense is the animation layout man. He just turns the animation with a rough layout over to the background person, and they paint a background. I suppose it gets some okay somewhere along the line. The person who designed the picture doesn't have control over how it looks, which I think is a great loss.

If you're designing a picture for mood, you have to follow through on the thing. That's what I've always insisted upon when I'm working on a picture: if I'm designing it, I'm going to see that that's the way it gets on the screen. Their present mode of operation is one of such rush. Produce it and get it out, and jump on the next one. How do you do three stories in a week, like some of these studios do? Their pride in a picture is almost lost.

HMC: You were lucky that you didn't have to do that many films a week. You didn't need to do sixty-five episodes a year.

MN: Listen, we did an appalling amount of work. [Laughs] Chuck and I produced eleven short subjects a year, but think of the amount of work that went into that: story, character sketch by Chuck, and my design work, and all the animation and ink & paint and dialogue and music scoring and sound effects. That was done for eleven pictures a year by a small crew: there was Chuck Jones, Mike Maltese, myself, Phil DeGuard, the marvelous background man, and I think we had three animators and three assistants—ten to twelve people producing all these short subjects.

HMC: It must have been a lot easier to keep tight control over the look of a cartoon when you worked with a small crew like that.

MN: Not only was one able to keep more control over it, but there was also the esprit de corps and the spontaneity of the thing that made these Warner Bros. cartoons what they are. They're considered the fun classics.

Our input was important, and we felt responsible and proud of our work on them. It's what I call the interference of the walnut desk with the creative process at the studios today. They want this character or that character because they're going to make a plastic doll out of it. Consequently, this is worked into the story whether you want it or not. Inexperienced people are sitting up there behind that walnut desk making decisions on the pictures, and they're really not the creative personnel.

I've not only experienced it myself; I've gotten this from very talented people, at the Disney organization, and other organizations, too. They've put the cart before the horse, and I think it's resulted in some instances in a very low-grade, semi-animated cartoon. These pictures are going to kill off the industry. There's no in-depth analyzing a character to even develop a personality. It's smash, bang, boom, crash. The cartoons today dote on violence and an almost cruel sense of humor.

I'm kind of on my soapbox regarding this. By cluttering it up with a lot of fast, fast, fast gags, they make people think they've seen something, and they really haven't. There's no time for development.

HMC: Do you think there's room for good work in the kind of limited animation that's done for TV today?

MN: Yes, I do. I think one of the really big successes is the Charlie Brown series done by Bill Melendez. This animation is certainly limited, but look at the charm of the things. I think one of the great moments of animation history is when Linus reads the Christmas story on the Christmas program. I watch it every year, and I get a lump in my throat every time. It's so utterly charming and direct and simple: Simple staging, simple dialogue, the tone of the voice. And this is very simple animation, but it's the way it's done, and it's in character with their voices and what they're doing. Let's just say they have "love". This is one example of limited animation being done in an appropriate way.

I think the Europeans in some of their films succeeded in doing it; I think back to a Yugoslavian thing called *Ersatz*. A great design thing, but in a sense it's almost limited animation. It's the quality of thought that goes into it. It's the quality of approach, and dialogue, and story construction. There's no cartoon unless you have a good storyline.

HMC: And good characters.

MN: Good characters, that's right. If you have a good character and you build a good storyline around it, then you have a cartoon. This is one of the things they did at Warner Bros. I always thought of Daffy and Bugs and Pepe LePew and all of them as people. I didn't think of them as cartoon characters; I thought of them as individuals. I could sit back and laugh at a lot of stuff that would come out of Daffy's mouth. "What's this little smartass up to?"

I can't warm up to these [new characters]: smash, bang, pose, blink-of-the-eyes, then zip off and crash off-screen, and shake everything, then you pick up on them and they're cross-eyed and stars are whizzing around their heads. This type of thing is the cheapest approach. We've had a couple of generations of children that were raised on cruelty and violence. These kids sit and look at it for four hours a day.

You wonder what kind of responses they're developing. I really wonder; I really worry. But when they talk about what they really like—these are the kids that watch all the shoot-up live action and cartoons—it's Bugs Bunny and Daffy Duck and Mickey Mouse and these gentle things. I think we created some classics, kind of like Aesop's fables.

I think *Who Framed Roger Rabbit* is a very cruel picture. And it's an unkind picture. There's nothing funny about laughing at a half-wit.

HMC: Well, there's not a lot of humanity in it.

MN: No humanity at all in it. This is why I worry. My neighbor moved just before Thanksgiving, and I went up to say goodbye. He introduced me to the young moving man, saying I had worked on *Snow White* and all these various things. The guy was duly impressed, and then he turned to me and said, "Did you work on *Roger Rabbit*?", almost hostile. I said, "No, I didn't." He said, "I took my little girl to that, and it was a cruel picture."

HMC: A lot of people would say that the Road Runner pictures were cruel and overly violent. I don't agree, but they do say that.

MN: I've heard the same thing, but what happened to the coyote was that he got his comeuppance for whatever he did; everything backfired on him. It soon became understood that he was indestructible. I'm not defending the violence of the Road Runners, but this was why it was more acceptable.

HMC: The funny thing is, I imagine a lot of the people who work on these new films you're talking about feel that they're influenced by the Warner Bros. films you worked on.

MN: I've had the opportunity to talk a number of times with groups, most recently at the Disney Studios, and there's a real hunger among these young animators and designers to really do some good work. They really want to get in there and do good animation, good stories, good gags, and so forth. But the word comes down across the walnut desk: "We have to have three pictures out this week." So the crew works like crazy and gets their three pictures out, but they don't stop to look back at it, because "Oh well, it's going to be sent over to be done in the Orient, and who knows what we're going to get back, anyway." There's no esprit de corps.

I think there's a lack of personal satisfaction on the part of the people who are trying to do the creating today. They're so remote from the final product. This is one thing that we were fortunate in with our comparatively small crew at Warner Bros: everybody knew that we were depending on everyone else to really deliver the goods. And this resulted in a lot of these gems of cartoons. I didn't know that we were doing that at the time, but in retrospect this is evidently what we did.

HMC: Are you surprised that the interest has continued in your work, and that people are writing books and magazine articles about what you did?

MN: Oh, I'm constantly surprised. I meet a lot of people that know more about what I've done than I do. I was speaking to [Steven] Spielberg—we had met—and I told him it was an honor to meet him, and he said it was an honor to meet me, and we had a nice exchange of conversation. Somehow design came up, and I said, "I always designed stuff to please myself." He got that kind of quizzical look on his face, and I said, "Well, you can't really expect anyone to like something unless you like it yourself."

This is what Chuck and our crew and I were doing: We were turning out cartoons to please ourselves. In that way we got a certain spirit to them that came across to the audience, and they joined in the fun. If you get too darn remote from a given creative project, all of a sudden it becomes sterile. I think this is what has happened in the studios today.

I really do believe that animation is a unique and wonderful art form. I hate to make it an American art form, but I really think that's where it developed. I think it has vast possibilities; I'd like to see a museum where you could go in and sit down and see *What's Opera, Doc?* or *The Dot and the Line* or any of the other short subjects, just as you go into a gallery and see static pictures. I think it would be very popular, and it may happen someday. People would come out of a museum laughing. Wouldn't that be great!

© 2007 Harry McCracken

Al Dempster (1911–2001)

Interviewed by Christopher Finch and Linda Rosenkrantz on May 31, 1972.

If one were to invent a ratio between fame and the quality of art created, the Disney background artists would probably appear lowest on the chart. While their art is key to the feelings animated movies generate—be they reassuring feelings like in *Snow White* or jazzy ones like in *The Jungle Book*—it is also at its best when it's absolutely non-obtrusive. No wonder then that aside from notable exceptions like Maurice Noble, background artists are often forgotten by official histories of animation.

Albert T. Dempster worked as a background artist on virtually all of the Disney animated features from *Pinocchio* to *The Rescuers*, where he was responsible for color styling.[1] Throughout his career at the studio, he also tackled quite a few shorts, including *Canine Casanova* (1945), *Father's Week-end* (1953), *Casey Bats Again* (1954), *A Cowboy Needs a Horse* (1956), *The Truth about Mother Goose* (1957), and *How to Have an Accident at Work* (1959).

Born on July 23, 1911, he joined the Disney Studio on March 6, 1939, in layout and was transferred to the background department on June 27, 1939. From November 1945 to January 1952, Al Dempster left Disney "to work on a ranch doing children's book illustrations", including over a dozen Disney Golden books. He returned to the studio on January 7, 1952, and resumed working as a background artist until his retirement on July 31, 1973.

Al Dempster passed away on June 28, 2001.

---

[1] Steve Hulett remembers that Al Dempster explained his experience on *The Rescuers* this way:

"Woolie was always telling me how to paint backgrounds, what colors to put in the sky, and I couldn't take it anymore. So I left. But when the studio was doing *The Rescuers* and they needed a background artist because Ralph [Hulett] had died, they called and asked me to come back. I said, 'No way.' But they offered me a lot of money and told me Woolie had changed. So I told them, "All right, I'll work for six months."

And two weeks after I was back, Woolie came into my room and wanted me to put more pink in a background and I thought 'Nothing's changed at all!' I did my six months and got out."

The transcripts of the interviews conducted jointly by Christopher Finch and Linda Rosenkrantz do not mention who between Christopher and Linda asked each specific question.

Christopher Finch & Linda Rosenkrantz: What we wanted to talk to you about was who was working here in general and working on backgrounds in particular, and more specifically *Robin Hood*, because we'll be doing a section on the making of *Robin Hood*.

Al Dempster: Well, let's see, as far as the background aspects go, it's no different from other pictures. We have the same set of problems for everyone, in that the characters are always the constant and we can't change the lighting on them in one scene. We try to keep them all the same color and value so that they are consistent. Then the backgrounds have to be consistent in the sequence, especially to follow through in dark and light and color, too, so that there's no sudden drop-off in lighting. But they still have to read in quite a variety of settings, and against a variety of values which makes it a little difficult at times. Because of this, we subordinate what we call the background, and it strictly becomes a background, a supporting thing for the action, to enhance the action and put it in a setting, to make it believable. That's what we do, and we're the last people that handle it before it goes to camera.

CF&LR: The animators work with the layouts?

AD: The animators work with the rough layouts and after the rough layouts are proven with the animation in running black-and-white tests, the animation is cleaned up or whatever is necessary, and the layouts are cleaned up. In *Robin Hood*, as in other pictures that we've done, like *The Aristocats* but not *The Jungle Book*, we use a Xerox line for backgrounds as the characters also do. We receive a cel print (which is called the CL) and we also get an illustration board with the cleaned-up layout, transferred in Xerox upon it. Now this would be what a cleaned-up layout looks like and this is the blue sketch. Are you familiar with any of these?

CF&LR: We've just seen some of them in the morgue.

AD: Well, these blue sketches are just sort of a rough resume of the beginning and the end of an action that occurs in the scene, so it gives us an idea about scale and about who's going to be in the scene and where they're going to be, and what type of rough action they're going to have.

CF&LR: This is done in layout, is it?

AD: This is done either by layout from the animation drawings, or it's traced from the drawings by someone specifically who does this sort of thing: Typical start and finish of action. So it's a guide, more or less, for us. And until we get the color models for each one of these scenes, we have a rough [idea of] how this scene must be painted to support it.

Now, this is the illustration board that we work on and this is what's known as the CL. Then the reason for this is, quite often after this is painted, the Xerox lines on the background are painted out and lost. You know we work with thin, wash-type poster color. It's a thin watercolor, some of it opaques out because of necessity when making changes here and there. So, with the CL over the background, we can replace those lines that are important and remove those that interfere with action or depth.

One might just want the lines only in the foreground where the characters who have the black lines will contact it. So, that's why we have the cel. And we can remove lines where we don't want them, to push it back, back in the distance. We can remove lines with a material that is like a solvent. So all the layouts are dished up like this for us. Most are this size [10½" x 14½"]. It is a 6½-field size. It is generally the format that we all work with. On occasion, we have a special situation that will call for a larger size like the exterior of this church, or interior of the same church. Those are called 10-field. The reason for that is the characters are small in the scene. Now if they were animated for a scale that would work on a 6½ field, they'd be infinitesimal, very difficult for the animator to work that way. So everything revolves around the convenience of the animator, because it's a very difficult thing to get these characters to move properly without the lines becoming huge when blown up on the screen. On rare occasions we've gone bigger than that, but only for an extremely special thing.

CF&LR: Like with Jiminy Cricket in *Pinocchio* you might have?

AD: I don't think we went any bigger than that, except for one scene: the opening scene. The Blue Fairy, as she came across over the countryside and down over the village. That was a rather large one. Then occasionally on some of the space pictures we've done huge backgrounds: the camera can stay real close on a small field and then pull back to get the immensity of the space it's going into. The animation could be bi-packed, which is a way of doing the animation on one strip of film and the background on the other material that keeps its size. You get that on another strip of film and the two are put together in the printer.

These layouts seem very different and very much more schematic than some of the layouts we've seen for earlier films, like *Pinocchio*, for example. Those were completely rendered and done in value, black and white, because the two men who were working on those... Two or three layout guys liked to work on the values and it was sort of a growing business. Now I didn't come here until just after *Snow White*, but the two men who I remember were the mainstays were Hugh Hennesy and Charles Philippi. There were others, too, but they were the principal layout men and they enjoyed doing these full-value sketches. They were a great aid for keeping neophyte painters, as it were (who didn't know a heck of a lot about painting), in line. Consequently, they had to have things pretty well spelled out for them. On *Pinocchio* it was the same way. Quite a few of the layouts were done in very detailed value, and actually I don't think that hurt the picture at all: it had a certain richness because of it. It kept the mood of the picture pretty well under control, so that there'd be 12, 14 people on that picture, just two or three or four laying out, the picture was more consistent.

CF&LR: You worked on *Dumbo* and *Fantasia*?

AD: Yes. I worked on *Pinocchio*, too, and on a lot of shorts. They were fun to do. You'd do them and you didn't have to labor on them forever. And consequently a lot of them turned out a lot more fresh. But the shorts ran about six minutes and they didn't have to hold your interest except to say it clearly and interestingly. That was it.

CF&LR: Who did the backgrounds for the late Donald Duck shorts? There's a very distinctive style we picked up.

AD: Several people did.

It was just a style that was established by the layout artist, I suppose. Sometimes the layout man gives it a direction, but it's usually up to the one who paints it to make it or break it. For instance, if you give a type of drawing to five different people, you're going to get five different approaches. In the case of the short pictures, the background man usually had his own interpretation of it. Unless it was way off the beam, then normally he wouldn't be given the job anyhow. But each person will work his own way from the same set of drawings. A lot of it, especially in the shorts, is variable. You can alter a little bit where it's not too critical, if you feel that you can enhance the scene and that's what we try to do here. Everybody tries to plus the product.

CF&LR: How did you come to get into background rather than animation?

AD: I've always liked to paint. They wanted me to go into animation originally. I came here with a portfolio of paintings and drawings. I had been a commercial artist and I was strong on drawings, strong on painting, but I didn't like the idea of working with a light board. I thought, boy, I'll be blind in a year with that. I liked the idea of moving characters; that was fun. I liked to draw all kinds of things and figures. Painting was more a complete thing because you had to draw and paint. Some think background painting is simple, because it is all drawn for you. All you have to do was fill in between the lines. It's not that easy: it's a highly specialized field and there are probably a handful of people in the world who can do it right.

The whole problem, I guess, is the backgrounds not becoming too obtrusive but still make them so that they are a believable setting for the action to take place in. We have to set the mood, we have to light the characters, make them legible, whether they're in silhouette or lit against a darker background, and we have to make them believable. We have to help the story get across, set the mood. A good example is right here from *Jungle Book*. Quite often in a sequence I'll start out with a few sketches: Woolie [Reitherman] will want to see something, like what we will do about this old dejected place where Mowgli has gone. Turned down, he isn't allowed to stay in the jungle and he runs off to this place, a God-forsaken place, and Woolie thought it ought to have a black waterhole. So, I made (though they're all very close) several sketches with slight variations to pick up that type of mood that he thought it should be. From those ten sketches, I ended up by using for the sequence a combination of two of them.

CF&LR: These sketches were made before any layout of this thing, weren't they?

AD: There were some rough layouts made that the animators were working with. The reason for this is the background artist rarely contributes to the proposed treatment until there's some story work done. Quite often when there's some story work done, there also are some rough layouts that are beginning to develop. In other words, if we can see things that the director has already bought, even though in rough storyboard form, this gives the background artist a clue. Of course, if the background man has a real hot idea, he'll paint it for consideration of all interested parties. I've done several sketches like this at the beginning of *Robin Hood*. If he can sell the preliminary background, it's a timesaver for resolving the final background result. But normally it saves a lot of headaches to take what has been done before and work around that.

CF&LR: How does the mechanics of working with the animators as far as, for example, color is concerned? You're saying that sometimes you'll be dealing with a character that's basically in silhouette—in some cases they'll be light against a darker background. How do you arrive at that decision?

AD: It's a matter of what the mood is supposed to be. For instance, if there's a character working in the shadows, maybe it would be good to have a darker character. You know it's the same one because the silhouette will tell you what he is, and the colors, though subdued, will still identify the character. And then in order to make it read, of course, you have to have the background a little bit lighter behind him. In a reverse situation, where we have a light value character, it will have to work against a darker background. A character is not always one value or one color, you might use three values on him, or even more, but they're either generally a silhouette or generally lighter than the background they're working on. And it depends upon what kind of mood you want, how you paint it.

CF&LR: I see. The animators themselves aren't concerned with the color values, I presume.

AD: They are, quite often. Before we set any models, what we usually do is… The color-model girl will work from character drawings that were taken directly from story sketches, which were done with felt color ink. Rather crude, you know. And the color-model girls will try to interpret that. Then a variety of them are done and they're pinned up, and everybody has their say on them: the layout people, the story men, the animators, the director. I do also. I don't say too much about that at that point, because I know I'm going to change things around anyhow to make it work because what looks good on a white piece of paper is not necessarily going to look good on a background. White will make anything stand out. Just like anything will look good on black.

So, it's started out that way, and everybody has their say, and the reason the animators would like to know is they have to draw these separations for—in the case of a shirt, or say a toga, or a cloak that's going to have a belt around it, and if there's going to be a buckle on that belt, or if it should be a bright belt or a belt that's very quiet and sort of painted so it looks like the jacket, like in the case of Robin Hood and Little John. I make changes in value that have to be made for legibility against the backgrounds. But at least they have a starting point. The animator knows what he has to draw for the color separations, like the collar on the sheriff. Then we'll run a couple of color tests to see if they work out alright on the screen. Sometimes we'll find surprising things, like values will pull apart on the character and the thing that looks real good under our lights, when it gets on film and on the screen: gad, it flies apart! The transition from painted color to projected color through the film is sometimes very startling in value changes. Like things that look white on the screen are unbelievably dull and dark to look at here. Some colors that are too light give very little emulsion on the film and the projection light washes the color out. It becomes so thin, and then drops off. We have to know all this from past experience, apply it, and try to avoid remaking the same mistakes. Retakes are costly.

CF&LR: Are you really working closely with the art director all the time?

AD: There isn't any one person called the art director, per se. Woolie has called me the art director many times. It's a misnomer, actually, because it's a corporate effort, always has been. Woolie has ideas, he has the last word on everything, and Don [Griffith], the layout man, has ideas, and

I do, too. And sometimes the animator gets his licks in as he might think something in the costume's a little bit too bright or not bright enough, or should be more simply drawn. The animators say nothing about the painting, they don't make any waves that way, same as I wouldn't tell them how to do the animating. But between the three of us, we get a meeting of minds, we know how each one of us would like to have it come out and if there's any argument, of course, Woolie always wins. I've had arguments with him, and I, of course, give in because when you're in the driver's seat, what else! But I'll speak my mind and he knows it and he respects that. He likes people to say what they think.

CF&LR: Is Ken Anderson involved at this point?

AD: He is involved, yes. He starts out with the original story. He is the one who starts the whole thing going. He does the characterization, the stimulating beautiful little drawings that suggest idiosyncrasies that could be utilized for each character. His situation drawings and sequence drawings contribute to the whole picture. From there, he also helps out very greatly with the story. In fact, he does an awful lot of situation drawings and he knows layout. They used to have what they called an art director. In fact, Ken *was* an art director. Definitely he would have a lot to say about layouts and quite a bit to say about the color. But in the last analysis, you cannot hold the background painter's hand. You can talk a good background, but the background painter has to paint it to work properly.

CF&LR: Does this present a problem then when you have four or five different background artists working on one movie?

AD: Sometimes it's difficult. We've had as many as 12–14 people, and this can become very top-heavy. But luckily, the last three or four pictures we've been fortunate in being able to keep fewer people to do the picture and actually better qualified people, I think. And people who have worked together. So we try to wear one another's hat and work back and forth and try to pull together what we have done. For instance, I'll start out a sequence and then after I've gotten into it enough and too many layouts are available, then I'll get one other painter to help.

In a case like Bill Layne: he's been a background artist for a number of years and he knows the way we work and the way Woolie likes it to be worked. It's only occasionally that I'll ask him to make a few little changes. Or Don will see some things that might be helpful. Occasionally, I'll make some changes on my backgrounds because I've seen something in his that looks good. This way we work back and forth. And then as we get a little busier, we get another painter in. Now we have four people and we're going to get one more starting tomorrow, and that should be it.

CF&LR: Have working methods changed a great deal since you started out at the studio? You were saying that at one time there was a definite art director…

AD: It's still not any different. I don't think it's any different at all, because I feel that though there was an art director, there was always a director and the director was the one who had the last word. It's the same situation, only one less person with a title. That's what it amounts to. Actually, in a way, it depends upon the director. Like, Woolie has very definite ideas—and he is the director of cartoon features now—and that's all we're doing. In the past, there was Ham Luske and Gerry Geronimi and Wilfred Jackson years ago and a lot of the old timers and Ward Kimball, of course. Ward has very definite ideas, too. He's very easy to work with, though.

He likes innovative things, which is good, and he encourages the painter to look for something new.

It's not quite that way for the features. They have to be almost straight because these pictures can't be dated. When they're re-released every six, seven years, they should retain their appeal and [not] be faddish.

CF&LR: That brings up another point I wanted to ask you about: have there really been any stylistic changes?

AD: There have been. For shorts we used to do it quite often, and they were stimulating and fun. They were short pictures and because they were of 6–20 minutes in duration, people enjoyed the variety of presentation. But an hour and fifteen minutes would be a bore if it was something you didn't get with. The first big feature where we had real stylization was *Sleeping Beauty*. It was a beautiful picture. Eyvind Earle was a very fine designer, and he did his own kind of thing. He did the styling of the backgrounds, and he was the head background man on the picture, and he was also influential in the character design because the characters had to be fitted into this type of stylization.

CF&LR: Pre-Raphaelite.

AD: Yes, almost tapestry-like. And Tom Oreb, who was a character designer here at the time—and a very fine one, too—designed the characters.

As I recall, he did most of them principally from Bill Peet's drawings. Bill draws beautiful straight things, and Tom Oreb redesigned them to fit in with the stylization of the background. Now the whole picture turned out beautifully, but it lacked a really terribly interesting story. It's one example of when you have something that's very beautiful, [but] lacking in story, or something that's even bothersome to the story. Where it becomes so pretty, so beautiful, you are more aware of the art form than what's going on. The story is the thing, it really is. That is why we do it straight.

Now there was another example: *One Hundred and One Dalmatians*. There was another young fellow [Walt Peregoy] who did a very good job of designing backgrounds. This is the first time we used Xerox lines on the backgrounds in the cels, and he had studied with a contemporary in France and he liked to work with arbitrary shapes. He did a very beautiful job, good color. Ken [Anderson] was the art director on that and I thought it was a very interesting picture. I helped out a little on it. I had been working on another project, but when I was through I helped paint in the picture. I thought Walt Peregoy had done a very good job on it with the arbitrary shapes held together by the black Xerox lines of the CL that overlay the painted background. Walt Disney did not like the handling of the backgrounds, like the pattern of colors under the Xerox line drawing. He liked to see things solid and something you could believe, not something that could disturb realism.

Did you see the picture?

CF&LR: No.

AD: It's a very good picture, a very handsome picture. But if you look at it from the average person's viewpoint, it would be a little bothersome at times, because of the arbitrary shapes in the backgrounds.

It seems to me that now, with Xerox in pictures like *Robin Hood* and *Jungle Book*, particularly those two, that the backgrounds are somewhat looser than in the earlier movies.

CF&LR: Maybe it's simply that the edges are less defined, perhaps.

AD: Actually, we try to paint them, let's put it that way. There were few lines used on those backgrounds. If we had used a Xerox line on a CL on them, it would have been too hard a treatment for foliage. Because it would have everything confined with a wire. The architectural things, fine, and say in the case of tree trunks, you can use it all right some of the time. But when it comes to foliage, there's nothing more hard-boiled than leaves with lines around them.

CF&LR: *Bambi* already got away from that.

AD: Oh yes, definitely. That was extremely loose, and it was not really literal. In *Jungle Book*, we tried to be literal up to the point of not being too foreign to the flat character, which had a Xerox line around it. And this was not easy, either. But we made the character work on the softer background without the Xerox line, by using accented lines where needed. We drew them in where we felt that they would be needed to hold the character down. And the rest of the background fell away as the background into the distance, away from the character. So it gave it a little more depth.

CF&LR: Doesn't the softer focus give you, in fact, less depth?

AD: Not necessarily. If you have contrast, you don't loose depth. You can use color perspective and linear perspective and value perspective, and when you have an object or character that is sharp and in focus against something that's out of focus, the character or sharp-focus object is much more apparent. Like, when I look at you, you're rather sharp, but what's behind you is fuzzy. What's behind you is sharp if I look at it and it then becomes sharp. But that's not what you're supposed to do. When you have an overwhelming bunch of material behind the character, if it is there and too noticeable, it can flatten a scene as if the character and background appeared on a two-dimensional surface. This is where *Sleeping Beauty* was at fault.

CF&LR: Right, because everything was in focus.

AD: Too sharp. Though there were some beautiful things in it, everything was too sharp.

This scene in *Robin Hood*, we have Robin Hood in a tree. Now he's necessarily wearing a green outfit because this is what he wore, to blend in with the foliage. Can you imagine how the animator and the whole studio would flip if we filled it full of green leaves and expected the green of Robin Hood to read? My gosh, millions of dollars to animate the thing and you're going to foul it up with a busy green background! We use these characters, both Little John and Robin Hood, with the green costumes against green foliage, but we have to juggle the values and hues.

CF&LR: You put a lot of white in the background?

AD: No, but we must use the right kind of green, the right kind of value and the right kind of intensity and whether it's cool or warm, a different green than his costume, but something that will still work with it. It hasn't been easy, but where we have to use foliage, we have to make it work with proper color and value. This is the problem with backgrounds. And it's been a special one for *Robin Hood*.

Then, too, sometimes we have differences of opinion (put it that way) on whether or not we can change a character now and then in value for a specific reason. We're still with it, we know it's the same character, but he's in a different kind of light. And we try to sell the director on a little different kind of value set-up. He doesn't want to change anything, says it costs more to paint it different colors. Actually, it doesn't. Only the amount of time it takes to make another color model and look at it. Now he's afraid that people will lose the trend if the character isn't always constantly the same, but I don't think that's so. Because, good lord, nobody's ever in the same kind of light. Everybody's always recognizable, whether they're against a window or in the light. But occasionally, we sell a director on the idea of making a little change of pace and it looks good.

CF&LR: Do you always work in gouache?

AD: No, we work with acrylics, too. Only gouaches are much easier colors to work with. We can use them as transparent color or opaque. I did not particularly like these colors when I first used them. I had been away for five years on a ranch doing children's book illustrations and I was used to the designer colors: they're so much richer. They dry very much the same as they are when wet. These colors dry cool and light, and they are made here. They're fine colors. You can use them as transparent or opaque, but because they dry cool and light, it takes a little time getting used to them. They were very milky for a while.

CF&LR: That's why I was wondering whether you used white in the foliage, with green in the background.

AD: It is the overall tonality of the thing, and actually, that won't come out that way on the screen. It loses a lot of that milkiness. What it does: it creates a kind of film of atmosphere, it tends to pull distant things together. As I say, we can't paint paintings. We try to make an overall picture that will enhance the character. Because if you make a painting complete, it would quite often overpower the character.

CF&LR: Some of the backgrounds I saw down in the morgue were done in what appeared to be tempera.

AD: Yes.

CF&LR: Was that used much?

AD: Tempera was used occasionally for short subjects. Years ago, we painted with transparent watercolor. *Pinocchio* was done with transparent watercolor, just layer after layer after layer. And one of the artists, Art Riley, didn't like to work with it, so he decided to add a little bit of white to his transparent paint, which gave it some body. He achieved some very interesting things with this method. About that time, the paint lab ground some good poster color for our use.

CF&LR: Why is it necessary to make all the colors here? Is it unavailable commercially?

AD: I think it's cheaper. I wonder if it is cheaper, though, because actually, I don't think there is a better color made than that [referring to the designer's color]. This is loaded with beautiful rich stuff. You take a green and you squirt some of it out, and you take the richest green we have and it looks chalky by comparison. That's why I have two different kinds here. Frequently, I have to resort to the designer colors if I want something rich and dark. If

I want to change the tonality of something, and I want a transparent rich color, and get a beautiful tint that's bright and not white, then I'll use the Liquitex [acrylic] because it's an extremely brilliant, bright, clear color. You can put on just a small amount and still retain what you have. It is invaluable in warming or cooling an area without destroying the relationship of values. It's like holding a colored gelatin in front of the painting.

CF&LR: What kind of surface do you work on?

AD: It's a very fine illustration board. And before it's shot, it's peeled off the board backing. The layouts are Xeroxed on the illustration board and also on the CL.

It is usual procedure before starting a painting to wet the illustration board on both sides. This removes most oil (from fingerprints) and allows the board to dry flat without a buckling. This wetting and consequent wetting many times before a background is complete causes the board to shrink. As I had said, the illustration and a celluloïd (or CL) each are printed with a duplicate of the cleanup layout drawing. Because of this shrinking of the board, the duplicate images would not register in some cases, and we had a problem until we called for pre-shrunk illustration board before the image was printed on it.

CF&LR: Is there any Multiplane work on *Robin Hood*?

AD: Yes, they have to use the Multiplane camera to shoot these ten-field scenes. Outside of that, there's no Multiplane as such in the picture. The last time we used it was in *Jungle Book* and that was on some of the scenes in the forest, at the beginning and the end.

CF&LR: When you were using the Multiplane more, was the background artist responsible for every level apart from the animation?

AD: I should say so. I had to start out this way: From a reduced drawing of all the levels involved in the scene, I would make a sketch to determine how the assembled scene should look. When that looked possible, I would then proceed to first paint a large background, then continue painting the level next to the background, then the next one away from the background, and finally in this case [Al shows a *Jungle Book* background], these foreground trees were painted on the top or closest level. When the entire sandwich appeared, it would work. We would set up all the elements under the Multiplane camera, light each level, and from that dry run I would make whatever adjustments for color and value that were necessary.

CF&LR: What are the levels painted on?

AD: They're painted on glass. In some cases they're painted on celluloid then mounted on glass, but this is not very good because you can't put a platen down on that celluloid when it's on glass to keep it flat. They're mostly always painted on glass. When there is animation, it is usually on the bottom level on the background. Then there is a platen which will hold it down.

CF&LR: What kind of medium do you use to work on glass?

AD: We used to use oil, but now we find that we can prepare a surface that's going to be painted with black Liquitex and then on top of that we can draw what is supposed to go on that. And we can paint in either Shiva color, which is a casein color, or we can use an acrylic. We can also use some of these, our regular colors, adding an acrylic medium if we want.

CF&LR: Do you have any problem matching colors?

AD: On Multiplane we rarely have animation that will be a direct part of the material that you're painting in the background. Because it's very difficult to get animation on the level that the Multiplane painting will be on, because the animation has to be held down with the platen. That's why they try to put held areas that will go into animation later in the scene on the background level under the platen. Then in that case, if it's going to be part of the animation, like if a wall breaks down or something, that will always have to be on the part that would have a platen to hold things down or else the cels would wrinkle and show up as highlights dancing across the scene involved.

In *Pooh*, all those page turns were done on ten-field cels. This is difficult, because you know when you squash down two or three levels of cels, even though there is a great deal of pressure to the square inch, the darned things can get a little bubble of air and that shows up on the screen.

But I started out saying we paint the level with black Liquitex or black acrylic on the glass, and the reason for that is each level is separately lit. Now when you get a glare from the light below a level, bouncing up, if it's a light value underneath upper level, it will reflect back in to the level down below. So they paint it black, then on top of the black, we paint the scene. It has to be painted black on the back so it isn't reflected on the level below. Many things that we found out were by trial and error.

CF&LR: But there's no reason to use the Multiplane anymore? Is it a question of economy?

AD: Sometimes when there's a special need… I'm not saying that we won't use any for this picture, but I don't see any need yet. They used to go in for production shots, like in *Pinocchio*, where right out of the star comes the Blue Fairy down over the town. That took a long time to be painted. I remember Dick Anthony, who was one of the background men here: great guy. He did a great job making this scene.

We've had a lot of good painters. When I said the layout men did the drawing in full value, that didn't mean that all background people were neophytes. Because there were several who were darned good painters, or they never would have been able to do such fine work. But Dick Anthony painted this, and he worked on it I guess maybe two months off and on. Painted it in oil. And some of the down shots, some of the street scenes took a long time to do.

That was probably the movie that used the most Multiplane. Now, there's less done with production things like that and less need for it, I suppose. There's more characterization, I think, in the last few pictures. Woolie likes to spend his time on the characters and the story part, rather than on the setting. He likes to get the setting over with so he can get down to the business.

CF&LR: How many regular 6½-field backgrounds are there in a feature?

AD: There are a little more than 900: between 900 and a thousand.

CF&LR: How long does each one take you to do?

AD: It varied considerably.

CF&LR: Obviously, with the subject matter.

AD: You might go through and paint a dozen backgrounds and have them done in a week, or a week and a half, or two weeks. And they look great, but then that's not quite what the director wanted. So we will make the necessary changes till he is satisfied. They are usually minor alterations.

CF&LR: Do you often have to return to backgrounds that have already been done?

AD: Occasionally.

CF&LR: Do you work strictly sequence by sequence?

AD: No. I jump all around. But I try to have a helper work in one area on a sequence whenever possible, then it has a consistency within that area. And if there is a difference between that area and another one, we try to get a subtle transition between one set of backgrounds and another so you're not aware of any change. Even though everybody here who's painting for us is good, it's still not easy to get the darn things consistent in color and value because the semantics of painting is not always the same. No one sees things exactly as another person might.

CF&LR: So how far are you into *Robin Hood* now?

AD: I don't know exactly how far. I had a list of how many backgrounds have been done: 400 or so.

CF&LR: So about half way.

AD: Yes, maybe even a little bit more. But, as I say, we have only another year to go. Only!

CF&LR: This is now very different from the old days where you... I mean the length of time you have and the number of people.

AD: True. We have a little longer now than normal because there are fewer people working on it. We have a smaller crew. It used to be that the features had as many as three directors on them. Like Gerry Geronimi and Ham Luske and Woolie: they were all on *Sleeping Beauty*. They each had three or four sequences. They would work more or less independently, but check occasionally. When the sequences neared completion, they would work out the tie-in of each sequence. Of course, they'd go back and forth, and look at what each other was doing to make sure there was a flow.

CF&LR: And then you still had Walt as director-in-chief.

AD: Yes, and he knew what was going on. He did a lot of walking around at night. He had his finger in the pie. He was a smart old boy. A *fantastic* memory. Unbelievable. I was always flattered if he remembered my name, I really was. He had so many things on his mind, and though I'd been here for quite a long time, not as long as many of us. I came here in 1939. Outside of the five years I had gone away... I was working with books for the studio and while I was gone, I'd have to come back occasionally to pick up work. I would be coming up the stairway, and Walt and I would meet unexpectedly in the hallway, and of course I knew who *he* was, I didn't have any problem. But he didn't, either. He called me by name and I darned near dropped over. How quickly the man could remember a name! I hadn't seen him for six months or a year, just enough to say hello, and he'd ask me how the apples were or something. I had an apple and berry ranch up in Santa Cruz county. When I told him I wanted to get out of my contract and take my family on this ranch we had bought, he said, "I wish I could join you." He talked about his days on his father's farm and how he used to ride the apple cart. He was a very human character: real good guy. Too bad everybody has to go. But he made his mark, he really did.

CF&LR: Were you ever involved in the story conferences on the early features?

AD: Rarely, once in a while. Not very often. Background work has always been considered as background work. I've always felt that backgrounding has not been given enough credit for its contribution to a picture. But if it weren't for background painters, I mean good ones, there would not be good-looking pictures because we're the ones who dish it all up for the camera.

It is not too difficult to talk a good background, but when you come down to it, it has to be painted. And if you know what the art schools are putting out today, you know how limited the approach would be: extremely limited to mostly design and abstraction. They don't even teach life drawing or still-life drawing or the basics. They don't teach the scales, as it were. All the kids entering art school want to become prima donnas, be Picasso right off the bat. They forget that he drew realistically and painted realistically before he does the stuff that he does, which I'd just as soon he'd forget. But he's got a great promoter, I guess.

CF&LR: Do you have young background artists?

AD: We're scraping around, trying to find some young people. We've got a fairly young girl in there. We'll have one starting in tomorrow. Very talented girls. Because we're not going to be here forever. I'm not going to be. Unlike other places, we try to tell people everything we know, so we can help people fill our shoes. We like to feel that we can get out of here and leave some of what we have found out behind us. You know, we don't have so many weekends left, and boy, there's a lot of golf to play and a lot of paintings to paint. I do my own paintings, you know, which are not at all like this. But we find art schools do not prepare students that we can use. We went to CalArts, we went to Art Center… I was amazed. I was an Art Center student from way back and they just don't have the type of qualifications necessary now. They're more for design, which is fine; there's a great need for it. But they're more for a commercial thing. For our specialized field, so few people have been taught the academic disciplines. It's the same way in animation. It's a frantic time. I've been screaming for them to get people with talent to bring their samples in for ten years. I said you're not very far-sighted: We're not going to be here forever.

© 2007 Christopher Finch & Linda Rosenkrantz

Walt Peregoy (1925–2015)

Interviewed by Bob Miller in January 1992.

While cartoon characters are brought to life by the animator and his assistants, these characters need a place to live, and it is up to the background stylist to provide that world.

One of animation's most renowned background stylists is Walt Peregoy, who designed the worlds for Disney's *One Hundred and One Dalmatians*, *The Sword in the Stone*, and *Windwagon Smith*.

Born in 1925 in Los Angeles, he studied art at Chouinard Art Institute and joined the Disney Studio in 1943. He served in the U.S. Coast Guard during WWII and resumed his Disney career in 1951. He served as a designer and animation assistant on *Peter Pan* and *Lady and the Tramp*, and did color and background styling for *Paul Bunyan*, *One Hundred and One Dalmatians*, *Mary Poppins*, and *The Jungle Book*. On *The Sword in the Stone* he did background styling, and was lead background painter on *Sleeping Beauty*. Finally, he was one of the four artists profiled on the 1964 Wonderful World of Color episode entitled "Four Artists Paint One Tree".

For six years (1968–1973) he headed Hanna-Barbera's background department, styling such series as *The Perils of Penelope Pitstop*, *Three Musketeers*, *The New Adventures of Huck Finn*, *Dastardly and Muttley in Their Flying Machines*, *Where's Huddles?*, and *Motormouse and Autocat*. He designed the environs for *The Lone Ranger* (1966) and *Emergency + 4*.

Peregoy's original designs have also encompassed architectural environments, sculptures, and theme-park shows and rides, such as Kraft's The Land pavilion and Kodak's Journey into Imagination at Disney's EPCOT Center in Florida.

Walt passed away on January 16, 2015.

Walt and Bob Miller discussed his career in a series of three interviews at Sullivan Bluth Studios; the following is a condensation of these interviews.

Bob Miller: How do you describe your job as a background stylist?

Walt Peregoy: A background stylist is someone who is designing the ambiance, the environment, and the world in which moving drawn characters live. It's very important what that world is.

A background creates a world for animated characters. It's the ambiance. It's not an attempt to make (though it is, now) a live-action representational background that literally looks like a backdrop behind vaudeville animated characters. The characters are not in that particular world.

That's why a stylist is a stylist. You create a world that is compatible with the characters. It isn't that the world is believable because it is rendered realistically, it is believable because of the integrity, the sensitivity, and the awareness of the designer.

But that doesn't exist any more, because producers have no empathy for it and are not interested.

Originally, the difference was Eyvind Earle, Ty Wong, Art Riley, Mary Blair, and myself. We're stylists. We're different artists who have different concepts. The concepts are different because the stories are different. Mary Blair wouldn't design a *Peter Pan* like *The Three Caballeros*. It's not simply because it's set in Latin America. It was a style. It was pastel, whimsical, charming; it was beautifully designed. It was believable.

People believed that Bambi lived in the forest. It wasn't a realistic forest; it was a watercolor forest background. But it fit. That's why it was a good style.

Dumbo was different. *Dumbo* was a hodgepodge of many styles, but it still worked, because there was no fear, and there was no regimentation.

Today, I have the feeling they're trying to say, "Boy, isn't that a great background?" So what? A background isn't anything if it doesn't have characters on it. And it's doing nothing. A background is not something you hang on a wall. People do now, but that isn't the intent. And that's not what they're for. They're not illustrations. It's motion-picture imagery, a world that is filmed. What happens to the artwork is quite special, if you understand it. You don't teach someone to paint this way for film, or use this kind of color. But that's what they do today.

It's important that the stylist be well immersed in the animation film business. And if he has been in the business, he should have empathy for film. Painting backgrounds is a special and unique approach. It's not illustration. It's not painting pictures. It's creating ambiance and a world for the animated moving characters to live in, to work in. The more integrity the backgrounds have, the more integrity the film has. And it's obvious, the more integrity the background stylist has, the more integrity the film will have.

So the background person is a person working under the influence of the personality and style of the background stylist. He is as essential as the animator.

BM: Where and when did you train to become an artist?

WP: I started when I was 17, before I finished my education. I got a job at the Disney Studio with my portfolio, with the education that I had in the Saturday classes (at the Chouinard Art Institute). And this I'm very proud of. I worked for them for six months, in 1943. I quit because I thought it was a factory, and went to work as a cowboy. My first professional job was Disney, my second commission was when I was working as a cowboy, commissioned to do a portrait of the Pauli mare, which was a thoroughbred cutting horse who won the world champion cutting-horse prize at the 1939 World's Fair.

I went back to Chouinard's for one semester. I didn't want to be a commercial artist, so I studied with Don Graham there, who has always been a tremendous influence, a very fine teacher, close to the animation business.

But then I left and went to Mexico, San Miguel Allende, to study, and it was under the influence of Sigueros, Diego Rivera, and Orozco, whom I admire, and still do, very much.

I left after a year, came back to the States, worked for ten months in San Francisco and then the redwood country, in service stations, to get enough money to go to Paris, and went to Paris to study with Fernand Leger. Leger was a very significant artist. An *obus* (that's a shell from the First World War) influenced Fernand Leger's work for the rest of his life, as to the political, the social, and the economic content of his art.

That was the beginning of my art training.

But I will say this: the real training is in the application—drawing. Drawing, drawing, drawing! That is the real teacher.

Drawing in itself—the application, the motivation, and the intent—I find, even at this late date, is more than significant in training! Not just going to school and specializing. The wanting to be an artist is of great significance. And as I say, the conceptual part of why you want to be an artist is how you become an artist, then how you apply yourself; not the schooling.

So now, back I go to work to make a living at Disney's, and this is some ten years later, in 1951, on *Peter Pan*.

I started at the bottom again, as an in-betweener, with as much or more education than most, but no degrees. In other words, I quit high school to go to work for Disney in the 10th grade. So the education was very fortunate, again in hindsight. I'm very appreciative of apprenticing in the animation business with such artists as Marc Davis, Ken Anderson, and there was Ward Kimball, Bill Peet, Bill Tytla, Mary Blair. Others who were influential were Charlie Philippi, Hugh Hennesy, Rico Lebrun, Ty Wong... All very fine artists who had worked in the business. And their work was very available, which was an education itself.

BM: While you were at Disney, did the staff have any influence outside of the studio? In other words, were you looking at other studio cartoons? Was there any influence of those?

WP: The influence, for me, wasn't Chuck Jones or Friz Freleng in the Warner Brothers cartoons. Nor was it Tom and Jerry or Lantz; none of those. The influence other than Disney's was the original UPA group, which at that time was impressive, and was the other side of the coin. They were extremely contemporary, *avant garde*. You could say they were really greatly influenced by the turn of the century, in international art design. That's one studio I never worked for. But I was influenced by them, not so much the others.

I worked at Disney for four years and became a cleanup artist in animation, and then went upstairs (because the background department was on the second floor) to layout and background and became a background painter with Eyvind Earle on *Sleeping Beauty*. I was the first background artist to work right with Eyvind in the beginning of the film, and finished as a background painter, working through *Sleeping Beauty*.

Eyvind Earle was the stylist. He set the styles, and the background artists followed avidly, completely, his direction and his style. A background painter has to adapt himself and his talent and his ability, to whatever degree, to totally mimicking the style of the background stylist. The background stylist on *Sleeping Beauty* was Eyvind Earle. The world in which this film took place was Eyvind Earle's world.

Then I had the opportunity to be the background stylist on *One Hundred and One Dalmatians*, which was a very exceptional opportunity, and was a film that the Disney people were deliberately asserting themselves to do.

They wanted to do something contemporary. So they got a contemporary story, and Walt bought it. Visually, it was a breakthrough. Not as extreme as UPA. It wouldn't attempt to be, but it was a very fine film. And I was privileged to be the background stylist on it.

BM: Chosen by?

WP: By Ken Anderson. That was a great opportunity. These opportunities are rare.

On *One Hundred and One Dalmatians*, my contribution was that world. There were other background painters who worked with me. *One Hundred and One Dalmatians* was better than *Sleeping Beauty*, in this sense, because I had been a background painter, and there was neither the effort on the direction or on my part to make background artists slavishly follow my style. There are sequences in it that drift a little, but that's all right, because the impetus, the direction, the style of the film was set by me, and strongly enough by my design that the film stayed within the direction, but it's not boring! *Sleeping Beauty* is boring. Every scene is identical, every scene has detail, detail, detail, detail. It's all right. It's a good film, but there is a difference.

BM: *One Hundred and One Dalmatians* was the first feature to use Xerography. How did this process affect how you worked?

WP: I had superb layout designers. We had fabulous artists like Ernie Nordli, Ray Aragon, Dale Barnhart. I possibly missed a few, but these were young artists of my generation, and they were damn good. They contributed tremendously to the way backgrounds were. It affected the way I painted because I painted deliberately with the awareness that it was not necessary to go in and render the hell out of a doorknob, or a piece of glass, or a tree.

You can look at *Pinocchio* and it's a very fine film, but it's dated, very dated. *One Hundred and One Dalmatians* will never be dated. It's much like Bruegel of the 1500s. His paintings were as contemporary as anything done today. It's not because of any other thing than he was a superb designer. It's only a two-dimensional surface.

In *One Hundred and One Dalmatians*, the background painter did not highly render the background. I kept Woolie [Reitherman] at bay on *Sword in the Stone*, but his attempt was to gel the Xerox lines against the backgrounds. It became a Ronald Searle affectation. There's no point in that. It's superficial that the films look that way. *Aristocats* looks like a classically painted Disney film with Xerox lines on it. *Jungle Book* is an absurdity in the other sense that it looks like *Aristocats* without the Xerox line and it loses the "crutch". So what you have is neither fish nor fowl that way.

The stylist is the personality. The stylist's personality has as much to come into play in how he works with people, how he has a great deal to do with it.

BM: Did Disney have a say-so in the style?

WP: Oh, no! No, this is one film that Walt didn't have any say-so in the style, and disliked it immensely after it was done. To my being let go after *Sword in the Stone* in 1965 after 14 years: you asked if he [had any influence]; no, he didn't. My wife's comment was, "This isn't going to do you any good." I said, "Why?" She said, "Because the paintings in the backgrounds look too much like you than it does Disney." I take that as a compliment.

When I went on to style *The Sword in the Stone*, Walt did have something to say about the changing of style in the sense that he had Woolie Reitherman who was becoming more authoritarian and had more to say about what the style would be. There ceased to be a stylist after *Sword in the Stone*. I styled *Sword in the Stone*, but as the film progressed, it started to drift backwards, back to what is now known as the classic Disney background style. I feel good about it, but it wasn't the film, background-wise, that *One Hundred and One Dalmatians* was. Nor was it the film, background-wise, that *Windwagon Smith* was. Or films that I did afterwards when I left Disney, where I had complete ability to style the film.

In 1965, after I was fired from Disney, my first real key design job for background was with Ed Graham for *The Shooting of Dan McGrew*, which got an Academy nomination. It was a featurette. There was a very fine director, George Singer, and very fine layout men, Bob Dranko and George Cannata. Dranko and Cannata designed some fabulous characters and layouts. I was asked to style it, so I took the layouts and the characters, and this is unusual because today animators would be incensed to allow a background painter to style the inking of their characters.

Seeing that it was a Robert Service poem that we called *The Shooting of Dan McGrew* in the Klondike time, I thought it was a perfect story and setting to take the layouts and ink them with a quill, with a sketchy line. Just not very accurately, not precisely, but sketched with a quill, with, I think, black ink, and then painted differently from *Dalmatians*, with more arbitrary color behind them. *Dalmatians* had a very Kandinsky-like (if you will) difference between it and *The Shooting of Dan McGrew*. I started on *Sword in the Stone* as painting with arbitrary color behind a Xerox drawing. With *The Shooting of Dan McGrew*, it was very fluid to paint behind it.

I inked the characters myself with this sketchy line. This was when I knew Charley Philippi's wife, Jane Philippi, a Disney inker. She was working for Bill Hanna's sister, Connie. I asked them if they would like to do this project, they would like to take and ink the characters as I had inked them, because I was going to ink the backgrounds. They were delighted. Jane was delighted; Mary Ann was delighted, several others were involved.

This you couldn't do today. Or if you did, you'd be suspect, and I don't know if there's that kind of talent around inking. This wasn't the *Pinocchio* or *Snow White* ink; this was an individual talent each inking girl would use.

I went to work for Herb Klynn, who was the production manager at Format [Studios] who produced *The Lone Ranger*, and he had been the production manager of UPA. It was [for] Saturday morning, but Herb Klynn was a very quality-oriented man.

BM: Is there a difference between feature and television backgrounds? Are the demands the same?

WP: Depending on what era you were in. In 1965, I started with Herb Klynn, and in 1966 we did *Lone Ranger*. As the background artist involved in the styling of the film, I could have taken any one of those pictures and it could have been released by Disney. I'm talking about the backgrounds. And it was absolutely the quality of any film put out by Disney.

On *The Lone Ranger*, I was hired at the conception of the production precisely because I had the experience from Disney's at that time, and because the man who actually had been working with me had no experience in putting this under the camera and putting it on the screen.

The Lone Ranger was an innovative series to do. It's innovative today: torn color paper with black Chinese marking pencil on cel. Powerful for

Saturday morning, but you couldn't say the backgrounds were Saturday morning crap because they weren't. A full-length feature could be made this way and be extremely successful.

After *Lone Ranger*, I was asked to come to Hanna-Barbera to head up their background department, and I believe that was 1967. Being head of the background department also entailed being the background stylist. Prior to my being there, the backgrounds were *Flintstones*, and they were all representational a la *Tom and Jerry*.

When I came on staff they had at the background department, at the time, *The New Adventures of Huckleberry Finn*: live-action animation.

BM: Which was a new challenge for you, because you're integrating live action with the backgrounds.

WP: As I remember, I had no big problem with it. Even though I did the keys on it and painted during the production, I had no problem because the animated part was animation and live action was live action. The mistake would be to try to integrate the animated background, and make the illustration an attempt at photographic realism. Then you'd have trouble because then you're trying to fool, and this doesn't work.

I was the stylist, and head of the background department, supervising backgrounds and styling. Although it was for Saturday morning, Saturday morning did not have a bad name at that time. It was animation production. I would style each series according to the story and the characters, and each one had a style. Some were *Three Musketeers* with the China marker, the grease pencil with painted background, grease pencil-on-cel (but not with torn paper and paint, as it was on *The Lone Ranger*). It was a strong adventure series. The backgrounds on this series had that ambiance and this strength.

Motormouse was more lyrical, as was *Penelope Pitstop*. Color inked lines on cel, rather than grease pencil, against painted backgrounds, which made a big difference: Totally different style.

BM: You mentioned before the importance of the concept stage of a film or TV show. Could you tell me about your involvement as a stylist and how you worked with Hanna-Barbera and the network?

WP: There's the ideal situation and there's the reality of the styling situation. Of course, in comparison to doing pre-production at Disney, the time for pre-production background styling on a Hanna-Barbera Saturday morning series was limited. The time spent is relatively short. I'd say over a period of a month, maybe, at most. And I was given the layouts, and the layouts generally would follow a pattern. They didn't change too much. On something like *Three Musketeers*, which was a period piece, there were layout people who took reference, and for all intents and purposes, [the style] was representational.

Then there would be *Motormouse*, which would be total fantasy. So there was a possibility to go whimsical, and lyrical, and the layouts would have some of that, but then when it came to the styling, we had the prerogative to put it in the ambiance and the character of the story. Of course, we would know what the story was, who the lead characters were, what their personalities were, what the story was in the script. And of course, we'd read the script, which would give an indication.

The background department had the approval of Joe and Bill and Iwao Takamoto, the creative head. When I first was there, I had a lot of freedom to do styling as I saw fit. But there was a time it had to be delivered by the next season, and it would be something like seventeen half-hour shows.

The styling, at first, didn't all have to look like *Scooby Doo* and it didn't have to look like *The Flintstones*. Now it's changed since then. They have a *Flintstones* style and a *Scooby Doo* style and *The Jetsons* style. I am not surprised when young people say to me there is a strange conformity in all of the backgrounds. From studio to studio, they don't change. I would say, in recent times, styling doesn't really exist. It's just a matter of somebody doing key backgrounds, which are not styling, really. They're all similar and all representational, and that pretty well covers it. And also they're illustrations, rather than backgrounds painted for film. That's because in the business there are lots of artists who come from an illustration background and they don't have the experience of the studios in demand. Obviously, an illustrator can fulfill, so that makes it possible for an inexperienced person to be called a background stylist, and it seems as though the demand is for the sameness.

[At Hanna-Barbera] we produced a lot of work. The work was quality work. The backgrounds were as good as any backgrounds for any feature. We didn't go into great embellishment. They were for a series for Saturday morning, but they weren't cheap backgrounds. They weren't in any way limited, especially in their concept. There was a time when background painters didn't get bored, because each series was different.

I hired Dave Wiedman to do *Dastardly & Muttley*: a very fine designer. He had worked for the original UPA group. I said, "Dave, this is your baby, you do it." And he didn't believe it. I said, "Yeah, you can do it. Go ahead." And he did. And it was very different, very handsome, a quality background, art-wise, film.

Gradually, over a period of some six years, Hanna-Barbera fell back in because of their production scheduling, and because of the advent of animation being sent to [overseas] production houses. Originally Spain, and then Australia, then Taiwan, Japan, Korea, Poland, now Russia, now mainland China.

BM: But why did Hanna-Barbera want it to be different at one point and then go back to being interchangeable? Was it economics?

WP: No. Bill Hanna had set up these production houses all over the world, and so they finally got themselves a man who limited himself to the device in formula painting and sent keys that were very easy to reproduce. So they changed, not deliberately, but the whole industry went this way.

Today, the reason why all backgrounds are interchangeable is because, first, there are no background stylists; they're just background painters. And even people who call themselves key background [painters]: I've run into any number of them who have never painted backgrounds for a feature, much less anything else, and they're doing what they call keys, and all they are are illustrations. And most of them have a great facility for copying.

A designer is not somebody who excels in mimicry. There's a great deal of difference.

Before you do a drawing, your attitude toward the drawing is absolutely essential. It's very difficult for a young person to perceive this because they're just attempting to mimic and please somebody else. Fine, this is a learning process. But, in the animation business, because it is a visual-arts medium, everybody's personality comes through.

In other words, we live in windowless houses, and [work for] almost faceless people, and I would venture to say that producers lose sight of the fact that they can control all of the artists, that they can get the film they want. Oh, they do. But they also get the kind of film that is produced in that manner. All that matters is how the film is produced. There's no such thing as making a film that is detached and removed from the personalities of everybody who's working on it.

I know now there are individuals doing background keys who have never even painted backgrounds. This scene is visible in the finished product.

In the late 1970s I was at WED. I was hired by—interestingly enough—the son of [Stephen] Bosustow, who was the head of UPA. His son Nicolas hired me specifically to do a film called *To Try Again and Succeed*, and I was asked to do it because he wanted something different, something original, something creative. Then he proceeded to tell me how to do it, which is normal. I proceeded to tell them, "Well, then, you get somebody else." [They said,] "No, we want you to do it." "Okay," I said, "then I do it."

So that film I'm very proud of. I got design credits on that one, and they didn't call me the background stylist because I designed the characters; I posed the characters in each scene; I laid it out; I painted it; and so I designed it. The film was very good because it was a Sam Weiss-directed film; he was very good. [Bill] Littlejohn had never worked for Walt, but was a hell of an animator. He didn't change my characters.

This had no Xerox lines, no grease pencil: an entirely different style. Different than *The Shooting of Dan McGrew*. And it is, in my estimation, very fine. These eagles really flew. The little eagle, when he's pushed off the cliff, he really falls. Again, it's the integrity of the people, the director, and the animator, the men who wrote the story. And the voice was Orson Welles. You put this all together, you get a fine film.

BM: If background styles are interchangeable today, with little or no difference, do you see any change?

WP: No. No. I don't see any change. But that's not unusual. Because I don't think there's an individual who necessarily has the capacity, the experience, and the sensitivity. I think it takes a very special person to style an animated film. But that person isn't a person who could get financial backing. That kind of person doesn't influence bankers, or producers, or large studios. They think of the artist as a hybrid individual. And they're right.

But if we didn't have those individuals 30 years ago, we wouldn't have had the films we had then. And I can't imagine what they would look like now. They probably would have looked just like they do now, which is over a longer period of time, because they're absolutely interchangeable, absolutely stereotyped. And this is not going to change, unless there—out there that I don't know of—is an entrepreneur who has the desire to do so. And that producer cannot be the one who does it. He cannot call himself a producer if he or she just decides he/she will make the decisions, because he/she doesn't know. That's not very likely, a person with money…

So I don't know yet, but I do know that it can be done. *Don Quixote* could be a fantastic film. There are people to make it, but they truly would need directors now. They need direction. They need motivation. They need security…to produce something of great significance, beauty, pathos, joy, all of that. I don't know. I just don't know.

I speak with great frustration and with a lot of anxiety and a lot of disappointment. And I'm 65; that's not old, but it also isn't young. It leaves very little time for miracles or for that wonderful shot at directing that all of a sudden comes out of nowhere and all of a sudden you've been given the opportunity to do a fantastic piece of work.

It's happened to me on rare occasions, but that has passed, and it wasn't in animation. It was in a theme park. Even in a theme park, that was fantastic work that I did for EPCOT. It won't ever be done in another theme park. The work that I did was all mine. It's very obvious that it's an individual's work, but there are no names.

BM: They don't have a credits list.

WP: That's right. So that means it's impossible for the artist to survive, which is a worse-than-primitive commentary on contemporary art, because art appears where it appears. The fact that some of the best art that I've done in my life is at EPCOT, an amusement park, doesn't mean that it isn't damn good. But it's hidden, you see.

BM: You mean no credit.

WP: No credit. I've talked to young people, and they mention the various series that they enjoy, but you would never have known that. I would never have known that, while I was working there. Nobody ever showed any appreciation for what I did.

BM: Are you talking about the people in the studio or the fans?

WP: The people in the studio. This is a curious part of this business. I did *The Shooting of Dan McGrew*, which received an Academy nomination. Some 20 years later, I was in Germany [working for MS Films]. An animator who had recommended me to Ed Graham came up to me and said, "You know, Walt, I have a letter that Ed Graham wrote me, thanking me for introducing you to him." My reaction was, "Why didn't he write me?" Why didn't he thank me? He got an Academy nomination; I didn't. I styled the picture. It's still unique. I've done so many films that are still innovative 30 years later.

The last film that I designed was *To Try Again and Succeed*. The producer never once really thanked me. I designed a poster for him and failed to sign it. And I had to ask him for a couple of them. He didn't put my name on the brochures that were showing at the museum, where a friend of mine saw it and said, "Oh, Walt. I saw your film. I really liked it. It's very nice. Would you like the program? Well, your name isn't on it." I talked to Nick Bosustow and I said, "Why the hell didn't you put my name on it? You got Littlejohn's name [on it], the animator, he deserves it, and Sam Weiss, Orson Welles. But the guy who designed the film, his name wasn't on it."

So, how can it propagate? How can a film company, through animated film, propagate themselves, if nobody's curious enough to go back and find out who did it? And what's behind them?

Why did *One Hundred and One Dalmatians* look like *One Hundred and One Dalmatians*? Why did it look that way? It wasn't as simple as names. It was because of a lot of people, yes: very fine artists, not just me. But the people who know them ignore the credits. If somebody wants to produce a film, why don't they look up those names? Some of them find out they committed suicide, you know. Great talents. But they don't care. It's not that they don't care; they're so stereotyped even in their own concepts. They're all saying, "Aw, they're not making *Fantasias* anymore." Who the hell wants to? I can make *Don Quixote* not better, but something so different from *Fantasia* but so wonderful it would blow your mind. But they don't want to see it.

My whole intent is to try to influence the industry with innovative, expressive films with the state of the styling of the backgrounds, but it's applicable to everything. The backgrounds, as we've said before, are the world in which the stories take place.

And the fact that they're so mundane and ordinary obviously means that the characters exist in a very ordinary world, no matter how they're styled or how they're designed, fantasy characters or live characters.

BM: Would you blame this on the network or on the studio? When you design a world for a cartoon, doesn't the network have approval first?

WP: Which came first, the chicken or the egg? Originally, networks took *The Flintstones* [from the advertising agencies], and were very successful, and Saturday morning became bigger and bigger and bigger, and yes, networks became more powerful. But that was only because Hanna-Barbera and, gradually, other studios relinquished their right, because of the Nielsen ratings.

It's the sort of thing that you're damned if you do and damned if you don't. It isn't that you can put the blame on the networks; you can also blame the lack of backbone in the animation business.

Jay Ward did *Bullwinkle*. Nobody told him how to do *Bullwinkle*. Nobody told Herb Klynn at Format Studios how to do *The Lone Ranger*. But the advent of production houses and network profit-taking gave the prerogative to the networks.

It's not unlike children. One blames the other. The networks would say, well, you don't have the talent. The producers say, well, the networks make us do it. The background stylist who isn't capable can say, well, the producer won't let me. Everybody blames everybody else.

But it's my opinion that the right to creative integrity has been relinquished.

I'm convinced this industry will survive, but it won't do anything of any real value.

BM: Unless?

WP: Unless they quit looking at it as a product. Why do people say "Saturday-morning quality?" Why should Saturday-morning quality be bad? Can anybody answer that? Why should it be bad?

© 2007 Bob Miller

The Saga of Windwagon Smith

As remembered by Floyd Norman in August 2006.

This text was first published on JimHillMedia.com in August 2006.

We all remember our first job, first car, and certainly our first love. Like everyone else I've got a "first" as well, only mine is going to be a little different. I remember my first animated scene in a Disney cartoon, and how that scene ushered me into the highly coveted position of "animator" at the Mouse House. We'll get to that cartoon in a bit, but first a little Disney history.

Let's go back to the nineteen sixties with the completion of the feature film *One Hundred and One Dalmatians*. Disney's animation department had already suffered a severe downsizing after *Sleeping Beauty*. But now animation was informed it would have to tighten its belt even more.

That meant even long-time Disney animators would be given their walking papers. A painful situation to be sure, but some animators took the bad news in stride. One such animator was Don Lusk. Don, a twenty-year veteran, who showed a sense of humor when informed he was being terminated. Standing before his boss, Don replied: "But I was under the impression this job was supposed to be steady."

I confess I felt guilty seeing many Disney veterans leaving the company. Lowly assistants like myself were spared the ax because we earned considerably less money and could be put to work assisting other artists. Luckily, I found myself a position on a new animated short entitled *The Saga of Windwagon Smith*. Somehow in spite of all the cutbacks, I had managed to survive. Yet I had to put my dream of being a Disney animator on hold. Clearly, Disney had no need for new animators when they had already sent a number of talented veterans out the door.

The Saga of Windwagon Smith was a delightful, folksy short, much like many of the Disney cartoons I saw as a kid. We even had Rex Allen's easy-going drawl for the film's narration. With all the recent cutbacks at the Mouse House, our crew was small, but not lacking in talent. Our director was C. August Nichols, a veteran who had animated on *Pinocchio*. Nick used to joke about animating his favorite character in the film, the evil "coachman" who took the kids off to Pleasure Island where they would eventually be sold as livestock. "He was a mean bastard," laughed Nick, "a real fun character to animate." For layout and production design, we had the talented Ernie Nordli. Walt Peregoy was the color stylist, and if I recall correctly, painted all the backgrounds himself. Finally, Jack Boyd did the effects animation, and the two character animators were Art Stevens and Julius Svendsen. Chuck Williams and myself assisted them. Our crew was small, but more than efficient to crank out a Disney cartoon on a budget.

The film tells the story of a former sea captain who "sails" his modified covered wagon across the prairie much like a schooner crossing the ocean. The film was animated in the stylized technique effectively used by Nick and Ward Kimball in such former films as *Melody* and *Toot, Whistle, Plunk and Boom*. Art and Sven had both worked for Ward Kimball on his Tomorrowland space films as well, where they perfected this animation technique. Though the animation was a little more limited than the average Disney film, it was never short on imagination. The movement was stylized, but even then, it was how and when the characters moved that gave the animation its punch.

I had always admired the animation abilities of Art and Sven. I had been watching their animation since I was a kid in art school. Now, a stroke of good luck had me assisting my heroes. As I inquired about a particular scene one morning, I received an unexpected reply from Art Stevens: "Go ahead and animate it yourself," he said. "You know what to do." I admit I was somewhat taken aback. I had never dared to even request any animation assignments, now here was an opportunity being handed to me. Though somewhat intimidated, I gave it my best shot.

Of course, as in all Disney films the artists are bound to disagree on how things should be done. For instance, the animators continually grumbled about the "foregrounds" Walt Peregoy was painting for the film. They felt their animation was being upstaged by Walt's vibrant color palette. It brought back memories of *Sleeping Beauty*, and the very same criticism of color stylist Eyvind Earle. Meanwhile, we continued to churn out the footage, and my dream of becoming an animator seemed closer than ever. Little did I know at the time that my cartoon future lay elsewhere. In a few years I would be trading my animation disk for a sketchpad, the stock in trade of the Disney story artist.

The Saga of Windwagon Smith turned out to be a pretty good little film. Nothing to write home about, I suppose, but many people have told me how much they enjoyed this little bit of Disney Americana. In many ways it felt like the end of another era at the Mouse House. Many gifted animators had already moved on, and now even our director, Nick Nichols, would be saying goodbye to Disney, where he had worked since the forties. Nick would begin a whole new career as a director at Hanna-Barbera, where he would put in at least another twenty years before his career would come to an end, at, of all places, the Walt Disney Studios.

I remember *The Saga of Windwagon Smith* because one of my favorite animators gave me the opportunity to be more than a clean-up artist. My dream of being a Disney animator seemed just a little bit closer because of my experience on the movie. Yet even with our tiny crew, there were still no screen credits for Chuck or myself. Animation assistants were not deemed worthy of credit until another decade had passed. No matter. I was delighted to have worked on a special Disney cartoon with a very special crew.

Finally, what was that first scene this tyro animator placed on his pegs back in the nineteen sixties? If you remember the cartoon, Windwagon Smith has just roared into town scaring the hell out of everyone, including an old codger sitting on a porch with his rifle. The frightened geezer jumps up and fires his rifle. Ka-blam!

So you see, I got my first shot at Disney animation by having a cartoon character take, you guessed it, his best shot.

© 2007 Floyd Norman

The Making of The Jungle Book

As remembered by Floyd Norman in September 2006.

This series of texts first appeared on JimHillMedia.com in September 2006.

Wolfgang Reitherman and I were alone in the room. Our director had stopped in to look at a sequence being developed for *The Jungle Book*. After the devastating collapse of *Chanticleer* months earlier, the Old Maestro, Walt Disney, had finally given the go-ahead for boarding on a new film. However, this storyboard was not by one of the Disney masters: it was mine.

As Woolie stared at my storyboard for what seemed an eternity, I stood with pad and pencil in hand, ready to take the volume of notes soon to come my way. The tall, imposing director suddenly turned and said, "Let's show the board to Walt." And with that, he turned and walked out of the office. The fact that my storyboard was going to be shown to Walt Disney sent a chill down my spine. What if Walt hated the sequence?

I honestly don't know how I made it into Disney's story department. I did know that story was a coveted position at the Disney Studio. Many friends and colleagues had attempted making the move upstairs, but all were eventually disappointed. So it was ironic that this plum job should suddenly and unexpectedly be dropped in my lap. I did know that story artist Al Wilson was leaving the studio. Al was living in nearby Santa Barbara, and being a golf buff, wanted to spend more time on the links. The rather small story crew on Disney's *The Jungle Book* had an opening.

Of course, I was well aware of the film being in production. My office in 1D-1 was right down the hall from Milt Kahl, and I could hear the soundtrack as Milt ran his animation tests on the Moviola over and over again. I was enjoying a break from feature films, and was content working on short projects where I had the opportunity to assist guys like Ward Kimball. But then one Monday morning my boss Andy Engman called me into his office with some rather startling news. I was being moved upstairs to the story department to work on *The Jungle Book*. News like this would have delighted most artists, but it left me puzzled. Why would they want me in story, I wondered.

So, less than elated, I moved my stuff upstairs to C-Wing on the second floor of the Animation Building. I was well aware of the location. This was Woolie's unit, and the headquarters of Disney's newest feature film. My roommate was story veteran Vance Gerry, a talented, soft-spoken gentleman who had to be the mellowest man in the universe. In those days, the story artists often worked two to a room with their desks facing each other. This gave the story artists opportunity for a continual give-and-take as they went about their task crafting a story sequence.

Still concerned that Disney management had made a blunder, I went about my duties hoping I wouldn't prove too much of a disappointment. Vance told me I would start boarding from an outline by writer Larry Clemmons. Larry was an old guy who had worked in radio in the forties on the Bing Crosby show.[1] In time, Larry found a home at Disney animation, where he became the official writer for many years. Larry would provide the story artists with an outline of each sequence. This was not a script in the conventional sense, rather a rough outline describing the basic theme of the sequence. Working from this bare-bones outline, the story artist would flesh out the sequence. He would develop the ideas and add entertaining bits of business. Once completed, the sequence would be shown to Woolie, and if he approved, your next meeting would be with Walt Disney.

Vance Gerry handed me a handful of grease pencils or China markers. "Draw with these," he said. "Walt likes drawings that are bold and direct. Don't try and dazzle him with draftsmanship, that'll be provided later. For now, it's the ideas that are important." I think this was my first real story lesson. Vance taught me that the job of the story artist is to develop the story—not design the movie or direct the movie—but to tell the story. Vance liked to come up with a drawing that embodied the theme of the sequence and then "dream into it". Allowing the art to inspire the scene is what made Disney films so unique. With all due respect to my screenwriter colleagues, I think this is why the early Disney films were so brilliantly "written".

I confess it took me awhile to adjust to the pace of working in story. Up to that time I had spent my career in the animation department, where working fast was never fast enough. No matter how much footage you could plow through in a week, it seemed you always came up short. Animation artists were always under the gun. There was always a production manager brandishing a clipboard, reminding you that you missed your quota yet again. However, life on the second floor of Disney Animation

---

[1] Larry Clemmons was also a Disney animator in the 1930s and is credited as a writer on *The Reluctant Dragon*.

was blissful. We were all off the clock, and could stroll into work when we felt like it. There was little pressure, and all of us had ample time to complete our work. We met with Walt when he had the time, so that meant waiting for his availability...and that could take weeks. Should we want to view a movie, an assistant would call Warner Bros. or MGM and a print would be messengered to us. We would often sit and chat with guys like Ken Anderson, Frank Thomas, and other Disney heavyweights. Life was sweet, and this kid was finally playing with the big boys.

I remember sneaking upstairs to the third floor to take a look at Bill Peet's boards. Bill had been working away on the story for at least a year before I joined the film. He worked alone in a large office in B-Wing on the third floor of the Animation Building. As always, Bill's sketches were inspiring. Meanwhile, song writer Terry Gilkynson had penned several songs for the movie, and color stylist Walt Peregoy had come up with some bold new ideas for the film's background styling. Downstairs in animation, Milt, Frank, and Ollie were already animating on some of the earlier sequences. Things on *The Jungle Book* appeared to be going well.

Yet, in the midst of all this sunshine, storm clouds began to gather. The Old Maestro had returned from Europe for another look at his new animated film, and he wouldn't be happy.

No doubt, story had a different vibe, and in many ways I missed my animation drawing board. However, I was soon to discover that story came with a whole new set of challenges. Perhaps my old pal Rolly Crump said it best when I asked him about working with Walt Disney. "The closer you get to the sun..." said Rolly, "your chances of getting burned increase." Of course, there are good things as well. Who wouldn't want to work with Walt Disney?

However, working with the Old Maestro was not always easy. Songwriter Terry Gilkyson found this out the hard way when Walt wanted him and his songs removed from *The Jungle Book*. I don't know the details concerning the split with Walt and the tunesmith. But it was enough to trash all of the material Terry had written. All, that is, except one. The Disney master animators loved one particular number and pleaded with Walt to let the tune remain. Eventually, Walt relented. And that's why "The Bare Necessities" is the only Gilkyson song left in the movie.

Next, the Old Maestro turned his attention to Walt Peregoy's background styling. There was no doubt Peregoy was an incredible artist, and his knowledge of color was amazing. Walt—Peregoy, not Disney—had painted a series of color thumbnails that were on display in the hallway on the second floor of the Animation Building. Peregoy intended to use color to push the film in a bold new direction, and those lucky enough to see his incredible color thumbnails were privy to an animation breakthrough.

Unfortunately, this was not the style Disney was looking for. Without hesitation, Disney veteran Al Dempster replaced Peregoy. Never a man to mince words, Walt Peregoy let his boss know how he felt about the decision. Peregoy was one of the few Disney artists who had no fear of getting in the "Old Man's" face. Though they often disagreed, I've always felt Walt Disney truly respected Walt Peregoy for his outspokenness and total commitment to his art.

Walt Disney took great pride in his "storymen"—an outdated term to be sure, but at this time in Disney history it was an accurate one. No woman had ever been given entrée to this famous "boy's club". Of all the story men, no one was more respected than the Disney legend Bill Peet. Bill was always Walt's go-to guy whenever story problems arose. Peet was so trusted by Disney he was one of the few story guys who could handle a film alone. With this in mind, you can understand why this last disagreement was the most painful of all.

As I said earlier, Bill had been working on *The Jungle Book* for nearly a year before I joined the crew, and he had set the tone of the film. However, it was a tone unacceptable to the Old Maestro, and he made his feelings known to his ace story guy. This spat between Peet and the boss drew little attention. After all, Bill had been with Disney since the thirties, and arguing with Walt had become commonplace. We knew once the smoke had cleared, Bill and Walt would have found common ground, and work would continue as always.

Only this time it was different. Peet dug in his heels and refused to back down. Well, you don't challenge Walt Disney without him reminding you that his name, not yours, was on the building. At this point, Peet had had enough. Already a successful author of several children's books, he didn't have to be reminded he wasn't needed. To the shock of every one of us, Walt included, Bill Peet packed up his stuff and headed out the door. Disney's master storyteller would never work on another Disney feature.

During these dark times there were moments of lighthearted fun. If you were lucky enough to have been present on Recording Stage A back in the sixties, you would have seen and heard singer and musician Louis Prima and his band tear up the place. Prima had been selected to be the voice of King Louie, the orangutan Mowgli encounters in the jungle. However, Prima didn't show up alone for his recording session. He brought his band as well. And who could blame them? Las Vegas can be fun. But it can't hold a candle to Disney's cartoon factory.

As Prima went through his number, the Vegas showman couldn't stand still. He was really into being King Louie. With all that energy being expended, the band couldn't help but join in. Of course, you'll never hear this music. Prima's voice was isolated on a separate track so that composer

George Bruns could record final music later. The original tracks recorded by Louis and his band are indeed over the top. I don't exaggerate when I say Prima and his band went ape. The final tracks you hear on the movie's soundtrack have been toned down. And I mean way, way down. Louis Prima at full tilt was more than Disney moviegoers of the sixties would have been able to handle.

By the way, that wonderful scat duet with Louis Prima and Phil Harris was recorded at different times. Because of their busy schedules we were not able to get both Prima and Harris in the studio at the same time. So Phil recorded his part of the song later while listening to the playback of Prima on headphones. Composer George Bruns also recorded a more modified musical backup since Sam Butera and the Witnesses seem to have too much, well, energy.

The story crew of *The Jungle Book* seemed even smaller; not surprising after the loss of a storytelling giant. However, the Old Maestro was undaunted and insisted we push on. With the loss of Bill Peet, we couldn't help but ask the boss a very important question during an afternoon story meeting. "Ahem, Walt," someone sputtered. "What about the story?" Without hesitation, the Old Maestro puffed his cigarette and shot back at all of us, and it's an answer I'll never forget. "Don't worry about the story!" Disney shouted in his gruff voice. "Let me worry about the story! Just give me some good stuff!"

The answer couldn't have been clearer. Walt wanted to be entertained. He knew that if he didn't find the movie entertaining, neither would the audience. Where were the fun, the laughs, and the gags? The charming bits of business that made a Disney film so distinctively Disney? True, I didn't know a lot about storytelling back then, but the Old Man certainly got through to me. From now on, I would approach my storytelling from a whole new perspective. Walt wanted to be entertained, and we darn well better come up with a way to do it.

After a nervous start, I was finally beginning to feel comfortable on the story crew of *The Jungle Book*. After being given an outline by writer Larry Clemmons, Vance Gerry and I began storyboarding Mowgli's second encounter with Kaa the snake. With the sudden departure of Bill Peet, we were all in the process of rethinking much of the movie.

Since Vance and I were busy trying to shape our own segment of the film, I never took the time to check out the Rocky the Rhino sequence being boarded across the hall. Before we knew it, the sequence had been approved to go to reels, and Walt Disney would soon be coming in for a screening. I confess I was pretty relaxed about this screening with The Old Maestro. Walt would be focused on someone else's work, and not ours. If you were a Disney storyman, it always felt good when someone else's butt, not your own, was on the line.

I don't ever recall a morning meeting with Walt Disney. Every meeting I attended was in the afternoon. Maybe the boss felt more relaxed in the afternoon, having gotten the morning's business out of the way. In any event, this meeting would be held in Screening Room 11 on the third floor of the Animation Building. Our director Woolie Reitherman and most of the crew were in good spirits. At last the picture seemed to be moving in the right direction, and Walt had been pleased with our progress. There was a feeling of optimism and confidence this day, but soon all that was about to change.

I arrived late for the screening, and took a seat near the rear of the room. I made it a point to never be in Walt's line of sight lest the Old Maestro might notice me, or God forbid, ask me a question. As the sequence played out onscreen, it was expected that there would be a few shills in the audience with their obligatory laughs. However, there wasn't a sound from Walt, who continued to sit and watch in silence.

For those not familiar with this never-before-seen sequence, it's not unlike many of the other meetings with critters that Mowgli and Baloo encounter on the way back to the man village. Rocky is a dim-witted rhinoceros voiced by radio and television comedian Frank Fontaine. Those old enough might remember Frankie as Crazy Guggenheim on the old *Jackie Gleason Show*. Those even older might remember his radio stint on the *Jack Benny Program*.

In any case, Fontaine did his best voicing the mentally challenged beast as he played out his jungle shtick. The comedian had an idiotic laugh that always garnered laughs from the television and radio audiences, but unfortunately was lost on Walt Disney. The boss shifted uncomfortably in his seat, and muttered under his breath. In short order it was clear that Disney wasn't finding this boneheaded beast all that funny. To be fair, the story artist's drawings were pretty darn funny, and the sequence wasn't all that bad if you watched it with the sound turned off. However, this wasn't a silent movie, and Frankie Fontaine was not amusing Walt.

One might think that all that was needed was a casting change, right? Simply audition another voice actor and voila! Problem solved. Not in this case, I'm afraid. Walt was so annoyed by the moronic rhino that he wanted the beast cut from the picture. This truly disappointed master animator Milt Kahl, who had looked forward to animating the silly critter. He had even completed a model sheet for Rocky the Rhino, a model sheet that would never be used in the making of *The Jungle Book*.

Of course, that model sheet still exists today. On a recent visit to Disney Feature Animation, I saw a young intern working on a scene with the dear departed rhino. He wanted to know why he had a model sheet of a character never used in the Disney classic. I realized he had no idea why the rhino was cut from the film. Unlike the young intern, you now know the rest of the story.

With no rhino to animate, what was poor Directing Animator Milt Kahl to do? Tackle another character, of course. And boy, did we have a character for him! While storyboarding the villainous tiger, Shere Kahn, a question arose: who would voice the smooth, sophisticated scoundrel? I remember both Vance and I said the same name almost instantaneously. George Sanders! Who else but George Sanders?

In big-time Hollywood, no one ever does things the easy way. Why the studio went through a long list of actors they considered for the role I'll never know. In time, even they came back to the obvious choice for the tiger. George Sanders would voice Shere Kahn.

I still remember the scene and the wonderful encounter Shere Kahn has with Kaa the snake. We tried to make our story sketches of the conversation between the snake and tiger entertaining. However, who could have imagined what Milt Kahl would do with our simple sketches? As always, in the old days, the story sketch was simply the starting point. Vance and I simply set things up, and the animators followed through. All that inspired business with the tiger questioning Kaa was the genius of Milt Kahl. Milt developed those scenes and made them his own. Some thirty years have passed, and those scenes still blow me away.

Yet our day of reckoning was still to come and a date had been set for Walt Disney to take a look at our sequence. Like so many others, I began to get the pre-Walt jitters as the meeting date approached. As usual, Vance Gerry was as mellow as always. I don't think it would have made any difference if our meeting had been with the Pope. Nothing seemed to faze Vance as we prepared our boards for the upcoming Walt meeting. Lucky for me, Vance was the senior storyman. So he, not myself, would be pitching to the Old Maestro.

A meeting with Walt was not something easily obtained. Because of his busy schedule, we had already waited a week or two. Now, the outer doors could be heard swinging open, and Disney's signature raspy cough announced his arrival. As usual, Walt attended story meetings alone. No entourage, sycophants, or "yes men" were needed. We were about to hear the verdict on our newest sequence in *The Jungle Book*, and it would come from Walt Disney himself.

A meeting with Walt Disney always guaranteed one thing. After it was over there would be little doubt if you had succeeded or failed. Lucky for me, my teammate was one of Disney's best. Vance Gerry pitched the Kaa sequence in his own casual manner. There was none of the showmanship and pizzazz that some story guys exhibit. Vance simply walked us through the sequence, letting the drawings speak for themselves. Vance knew that

Walt hated being bamboozled. If the story wasn't working, he would know it soon enough. Our office was pretty crowded that day. You'll note I said our office and not conference room. In those days, the meetings were held in the storyman's office. No need to drag storyboards down hallways to a meeting room. I still wonder why this sensible system was abandoned.

The Old Maestro was not known for handing out compliments. I remember songwriter Richard M. Sherman speaking of an incident where he and his brother played a new song for Walt some years ago. Disney listened for a bit, and then said, "That'll work." The Shermans were delighted. That simple statement was a pretty good indication they had "hit one out of the park".

At the conclusion of Vance's pitch, Walt turned to our director Woolie Reitherman and said, "We could use a song here. I'll get the Sherman Brothers to write something for you guys." And with that, the boss excused himself, and moved on to other matters. Woolie, Larry Clemmons, Don Griffith, Frank Thomas, and "the boys" shuffled out of the room delighted that the meeting had gone so well. Vance Gerry had a slight smile on his face. That was pretty much all the emotion my laid-back partner was going to show.

Many years ago, my mom took me to see Walt Disney's *Dumbo* at the Fox Theater in Santa Barbara. Sterling Holloway voiced the stork that delivered little Dumbo to his mom, and it's a voice I'll never forget. Over the years I would hear that same voice in numerous Disney features. Holloway in his own way was a Disney legend. So you can imagine how I felt that day in Recording Stage A as I watched and listened to Sterling Holloway record the song "Trust in Me". The quirky actor sat on a tall stool in a pool of light. There was a music stand in front, and a boom microphone looming above in the large recording stage.

George Bruns scored the music for *The Jungle Book*. Disney, like most film studios of the day, kept creative people on staff, and George had become part of the Disney family. He also played in Ward Kimball's jazz band, the Firehouse Five Plus Two, and I was lucky enough to jam with these talented musicians one Saturday afternoon. I was playing a borrowed saxophone that had seen better days. Whenever the battered horn squawked, Kimball would yell at me, "Play whole notes, just play whole notes!" Today, it was back to business, and Bruns lifted his baton and the music began. Holloway weaved on his stool as he sang. He was quite a sight with his red hair and wide eyes. Sterling Holloway suddenly became Kaa the Snake, and I watched him intently, eager to incorporate much of his mannerisms into my boards. Yet time has a way of moving on, and I did not see the talented actor again until the early nineties when he returned to the Disney Studio to be honored as a Disney Legend. Sterling Holloway passed away in the early nineties. His distinctive voice was replaced by Jim Cummings in *The*

Tigger Movie, a Winnie the Pooh feature directed by Jun Falkenstein. I did story on that film as well, and I'll always regret not getting to work with Sterling Holloway one last time.

While we're on the subject of music, did you know we were going to do a Beatles number in *The Jungle Book*? That's right; the song *We're Your Friends* initially had a rock beat not unlike a popular singing group recently imported from the U.K. As the popularity of this long-haired group continued to soar, we thought, "Why not incorporate this pop style into our film?" However, Walt Disney was no fan of the Fab Four. He saw them as a flash in the pan, and said they would be forgotten in a few years. Walt suggested we stick with something that would never go out of style, such as a barbershop quartet. I confess I didn't totally agree with Walt on this one, but I did get to take home a handful of Beatles albums that the studio had paid for. As for the singing group, I think Walt Disney might have been surprised. Rather than being forgotten, the Beatles went on to achieve some degree of popularity for a few more years.

Finally, there remained the little matter of getting Mowgli back to the man village. That was the all-important scene that wraps up the film. And here we have another instance where the answer is right in front of your face, but you fail to see it. We had gone around and around trying to find a reason that would motivate Mowgli to leave the jungle, but nothing seemed to resonate. "It's simple," said the Old Maestro. "He sees the little girl and follows her." "But, Walt," we sputtered. "He's a little kid. He wouldn't have any interest in girls at that age." "Do it," said Disney. "It'll work!" If you've seen *The Jungle Book*, I think you'll agree with Walt Disney, that it does work.

By the way, the cute little girl at the film's end is the work of Directing Animator Ollie Johnston. It's just plain adorable. Is there any doubt the man is a genius? My favorite line in the movie is when the trio sees the little girl. Baloo warns Mowgli: "Stay away from those things. They ain't nothing but trouble."

I guess I could go on and on with more stories. Frank Thomas animated most of that sequence that Vance and I boarded, and boy, does he make us look good!

On another note, one of the actors doing a vulture's voice in the movie was Digby Wolfe, a producer I would later work for as a writer on the television shows *Laugh-In* and *Turn On*.

Although we didn't think that much of *The Jungle Book* at the time, Vance and I continue to be amazed at how much this film is loved by Disney fans. Many young artists tell me this movie inspired them to seek a career in animation.

Finally, there's the little matter of screen credits. Did you notice that Bill Peet doesn't have a credit on *The Jungle Book* even though he labored on the film for over a year? As a matter of fact, not one story artist (with the exception of Vance Gerry) has a credit on the film. Unlike today, screen credits were not automatic, and one often waited for years to finally see his name on the screen. Many artists never received a Disney screen credit. My first credit was garnered for *The Hunchback of Notre Dame* in 1996, even though I had started at Disney decades earlier. No matter. I was given the opportunity to work with Walt Disney on his final film. That alone is all the reward this animation old-timer will ever need.

I'm often asked the question, "What's your favorite animated film?" For a lot of reasons it always comes back to *The Jungle Book*. Back in the fifties and sixties, cartoon-making was fun. Unlike today, where animated features represent an investment of millions of dollars, we were unimportant, and consequently we were left alone. And being left alone is what allows creators to do their best work. Even a hands-on boss like Walt Disney understood that. When something failed to work, he simply said "fix it," and left us alone to solve the problem. If only today's producers had the wisdom of Walt Disney, and were smart enough to trust their talent.

When I watch *The Jungle Book* today, it's difficult to believe I was ever part of this animation classic. It was so long ago, yet somehow it still feels like yesterday. Most of the "Old Boys" have since passed on, and a new generation of animation artists is hard at work building its own legacy. As these new kids labor over their drawing boards and computer screens at such studios as Disney, DreamWorks, Blue Sky, and Pixar, I can only hope they're having lots of fun.

We sure the hell did!

© 2007 *Floyd Norman*

Bill Evans (1910–2002)

Interviewed by Jim Korkis in Spring 1985.

Morgan "Bill" Evans was born on June 30, 1910, in Santa Monica, California.

His first experience with gardening came from his father's three-acre garden filled with exotic plants. In 1928, Bill joined the Merchant Marine and while he traveled the world aboard the S.S. *President Harrison*, he gathered exotic seeds for his father's garden from distant lands, including the West Indies, South Africa, and Australia.

Bill studied at Pasadena City College, followed by Stanford, where he majored in geology. His education was cut short, however, by the Great Depression. In 1931, he helped transform his father's garden into a business by wholesaling some of these rare and exotic plants to other nurseries. In 1936, Bill and his older brother Jack joined with Jack Reeves to open Evans and Reeves Landscaping, which lasted until 1958.

Their inventory of rare and exotic plants soon caught the attention of Hollywood's elite. Among their celebrity clientele were Greta Garbo, Clark Gable, Elizabeth Taylor, and ultimately, Walt Disney.

In 1952, Bill Evans and his brother Jack were called to landscape the grounds of Walt Disney's Holmby Hills home, including the gardens that surrounded his backyard railroad, the Carolwood Pacific. Walt was pleased with their work and asked them in 1954 to landscape the new theme park he was building called Disneyland.

"We landscaped all of Disneyland in less than a year with a maximum of arm-waving and a minimum of drawings," laughed Bill.

Bill was known not only for using unusual plants, but for using plants in unusual ways, and that was certainly demonstrated by his work on Disneyland. He was eager to import and was an enthusiastic propagator of numerous subtropical species of trees, shrubs, vines, and bamboos.

Unfortunately, his brother wasn't able to completely enjoy the accolades about Disneyland. Jack suffered a massive heart attack two weeks after the opening of Disneyland, was confined to desk work, and was never able to physically return to visit the park. Jack Evans passed away in 1958.

After Disneyland opened in July 1955, Bill stayed on as a consultant, drawing landscape plans, installing materials, and supervising maintenance of the park. Later he was hired by the Disney Company and was named director of Landscape Design, working on Disneyland additions and the master plan for Walt Disney World.

In 1965, Bill wrote *Disneyland: World of Flowers*, a book devoted to the park's horticulture. He wrote many articles on horticulture and landscaping for horticultural publications. He was a Fellow of the American Society of Landscape Architects and served on the board of trustees for the Los Angeles Arboretum. For more than 25 years, he was a member of the Garden Advisory Board for *Sunset* magazine.

In 1975, he was forcibly retired along with other Disney cast members like Yale Gracey and Roger Broggie who had hit the mandatory retirement age of sixty-five, but Bill remained a landscaping consultant with Disney until his death.

In 1992, Bill was named a Disney Legend and in 1996 he was honored by the Landscape Architecture Foundation with a "Special Tribute" award. By then, Bill had garnered an entire roomful of awards from the ASLA (American Society of Landscape Architects). He has also received awards from the American Horticulture Society and almost every other international horticultural, botanical, and arboreta organization.

In a career spanning nearly fifty years with the company, Evans also headed the landscape design effort for the Walt Disney World Resort in Florida. In 1980, he and former partner Joe Linesch created the design for the landscaping at Epcot.

Although he retired in 1975, Bill consulted with Imagineering on the landscaping for every other Walt Disney World park, including Disney's Animal Kingdom, Disney-MGM Studios, and Typhoon Lagoon, as well as Tokyo Disneyland, Disneyland Paris, Disney California Adventure, Tokyo DisneySea, and Walt Disney Studios Park, and he contributed ideas for the landscaping of Hong Kong Disneyland.

He has also consulted on the schematic designs of the Polynesian Resort and Discovery Island at Walt Disney World.

Today, his methods of plant propagation, plant relocation, and recycling are widely used everywhere.

Marty Sklar, now the "ambassador" of Imagineering, said:

> Bill Evans defined Disney theme park landscaping, and trained just about everyone who has created theme park stories in living environments. He was more than a Disney legend—he taught generations of landscape architects how to do their jobs with passion, skill, and tender loving care. A walk through a Disney park with Bill Evans was a lesson in plant history, landscape, storytelling, and Walt Disney dos and don'ts from one of the very few who could truly say, "Walt told me…"

In spring 1985, at a Disney fan gathering in Anaheim, California, Jim Korkis spoke briefly with Bill Evans while other Disney fans swarmed around the animators and other Imagineers in attendance. Jim considers his interview with Bill Evans an example of a "missed opportunity". At the time, Jim was greatly interested in Disney animation and had interviewed several animators. Jim was also interested in Imagineering, but only in those who had designed the actual attractions, and feels he didn't have sufficient background in landscaping nor knowledge of Bill Evans' extensive work. This having been said, there wasn't anything published about Bill at the time and even to this day, we know only of one extensive published interview with him.

Bill had an infectious passion for plants. While he dressed like a jungle explorer, he came across as every inch the gentleman in every sense of the word. He spoke in a consistent rhythm that never betrayed when a wry smile and a joke might suddenly appear. There was also a warm gravelly tone to his voice, like a character who had stepped out of the Old West. Jim found him patient with someone who didn't know much about horticulture.

In the book *The Making of Disney's Animal Kingdom Theme Park*, author Melody Malmberg recounts the three-part philosophy of this master landscaper who influenced so many over the years:

> The first consideration was guest comfort—shade and shelter. The second was screening visual intrusions—creating a berm, a ring of earth and vegetation surrounding the park to hide the real world—or using strategic planting that camouflaged a building or electronics or lighting. The third principle was telling a story through landscaping—creating the right look for the setting, from the mixed broadleaf forest of Tom Sawyer's Mississippi River banks to the serene gardens of Japan.

Bill Evans died on August 10, 2002, at the Santa Monica Hospital at the age of 92. He is survived by his wife, Natalie; son, Pete Evans; and daughter, Barrie Evans-Blattau.

Jim Korkis: I know many of the early Imagineers connected with Disneyland have told me that you were the most under-rated contributor to the park.

Bill Evans: That description is far too generous. I would prefer to say that it was my great privilege to be included in this team of artists that Disney put together.

JK: How did you become involved with the Disneyland project?

BE: The way Disneyland went together, the whole thing was a teamwork effort, a teamwork project. I wouldn't be there in the first place if it wasn't for my brother, Jack, who struck up a great friendship with Walt through a mutual friend. Of course, we were involved in landscaping Walt's home. We had a little preview of what Walt had in mind on a much larger scale, without knowing it at the time, not having the vaguest notion that we would be invited years later to do all this on a full-scale basis at Disneyland. Walt had that little scale railroad that he used to tour the neighbor kids on, one kid to a car. He wrapped it around his home two or three times. In late 1951, we were planning railroad berms and trestles and railroad tunnels.

JK: How did Walt describe his concept of Disneyland to you?

BE: Disneyland existed in Walt's mind for a great many years before the first shovel of earth was turned. Walt's idea of a park was to build an outdoor entertainment facility where the adults would have every bit as good a time as the children. I think today they outnumber the kids substantially. Fortunately for us, he wanted a lot of green plant stuff. That was one of the elements Walt felt would separate his park from the Coney Island format. This was to be a park that would be clean and beautiful and colorful and a very pleasant place to be. We kept this in mind when we set about to put a green frame around all those adventures and rides, and all the great imagination that Walt brought into being with the help of those people on his team.

JK: Walt brought you in right at the beginning in 1954.

BE: My brother and I hiked the area with Walt. The early days when we arrived, the site was still producing a commercial crop of oranges. Every square foot was planted with either oranges or a little patch of walnuts or a little patch of avocados. There was a public street, Cerritos, that ran right through the middle of the land and that eventually disappeared. We were in charge of "greening it up" from a jungle to a Victorian scene to a Missouri River bank to something as contrived as the Storybook Land landscape.

JK: What was the first thing you did?

BE: We superimposed a drawing on an aerial photograph of Disneyland and endeavored to salvage whenever possible the existing orange trees. We did this because they represented to us the equivalent of about five hundred dollars a tree, which was a lot of money in 1954. Wherever the grade remained at the original elevation, we could keep the trees. If we raised or lowered the grade, we lost some trees. We opened the show with a whole lot of the original trees in place. We started with an orange grove and did selective removal. There was a grove of windbreak eucalyptus. We preserved those. You still see those when you take the Jungle Ride. Those eucalyptus trees are what separate you from Main Street.

JK: Tell me more about the orange trees you salvaged. Where did you use them in Disneyland?

BE: Do you remember the old stagecoach ride? We used some of the trees there. The illusion of pounding through stagecoach country was not enhanced by a crop of oranges. So we had to spend a lot of time picking all the fruit off of those trees. We did the same thing in the Jungle Ride, picking oranges off the trees to avoid the smart cracks of the ride operators who would have loved to see an orange tree when they came round the bend. We festooned those trees with all kinds of tropical vines that grew vigorously to the ultimate dismay of the orange-tree hosts. All those orange trees ultimately died under the blanket of those tropical vines.

JK: Were you also able to relocate some of the walnut trees?

BE: Some of the walnut trees were subjected to the indignity of being truncated and inverted because Walt had another role in mind for them. We selected some because Harper Goff, who was art directing the jungle, had the inspiration of turning them upside down to get a kind of a mangrove effect onto which we grafted the top half of the orange tree, truncated also to get branches. It gave a pretty good illusion. I believe there are one or two left. They were cast into the concrete lining of the river.

JK: I understand you also saved trees that were on the path of the new freeways being built.

BE: The freeways, which were penetrating the suburbs around the Los Angeles area, made possible the salvage of a lot of trees that we could not otherwise have found. We literally snatched them from the jaws of the bulldozer the day before they were to be demolished. We'd box 'em out and haul 'em down to Disneyland. When I'm at Disneyland, I can tell you tree after tree. This one was from the Santa Monica freeway and that one was from the Pomona freeway and so on.

There are some queen palms flourishing in the jungle ride. They faced a much grimmer fate because they were squarely in the path of the Santa Ana Freeway and were destined for the dump. We jumped in on time to salvage them and transport them down to the jungle, where they were very welcome and thanks to our need they are still with us. The jungle has a horticultural mix from all around the world.

JK: As a kid, the Jungle Cruise ride was my favorite attraction.

BE: That two-acre man-made jungle is the best darn jungle this side of Costa Rica. What we were attempting in this jungle was to try to bring forth the illusion of a jungle. Perhaps what the armchair traveler might have in mind. Turns out when you really plod through an authentic jungle, you are apt to travel for a day or two and the scenery doesn't change much, maybe one or two species without interruption. We were trying to capture this and get all kinds of textures and all kinds of effects: The palms, the tree ferns, the philodendrons. You get a kind of "man-eating" atmosphere. The giant bamboo was not actually a jungle denizen, but it fills a role conveniently. You might discover a rather pedestrian castor bean plant, but the effect is good and it adds to the textures. We picked material from Brazil, material from Africa, material from India and Asia and Malaysia. We pushed it all together. It's all quite compatible in the sense that it all has that lush, vigorous growth. Really strong growth. What we attempted to do in planting the jungle was to make it look as though we had nothing to do with it. We were working on a pretty tight budget.

JK: So you mixed the real with the stuff that looked real?

BE: In the jungle, a lot of those trees are native to tropical Africa, India, South America. They are interspersed with things not truly tropical, but they have a tropical aspect like that bamboo we use from China that grows 40–50 feet high. You are not aware it isn't tropical. You see it as part of the jungle texture. We take a bit of the real stuff and we interlace it with something else.

JK: I've been told that the soil at Disneyland wasn't good for planting.

BE: The soil at the site was sand. It was almost ball-bearing sand. You could have used this stuff for a good grade of concrete. It wasn't contaminated with any soil. It was just sand. That isn't the best prescription for horticulture, but we made do. We got satisfactory results by pouring a lot of liquid fertilizer on this stuff. Not that many years later, with a lot of water and a lot of fertilizer and this southern California climate, it didn't take a long time to get a lot of growth.

The sand was totally lacking in any nutrients. Actually, it was the best possible in hindsight. The easiest thing to put into the earth is fertilizer. The hardest thing is to correct the lack of drainage and we had perfect drainage. We made out very well. The evidence is the growth you see at Disneyland.

JK: Creating a berm around the park was unique at the time.

BE: The purpose of the berm that wraps around the park was to exclude the freeways and the neon signs and the 20th century through which you travel in order to arrive at Disneyland. Walt didn't want that intruding on his illusions inside. So the solution was to build this berm of sand, which was anywhere from ten to twenty feet high, and then garnish it with all the vegetation we could lay our hands on to complete the screening and shut out the Edison transmission towers, freeway interchanges, and high-rise hotels. That back berm had some very young pine on top of it that within the first ten years grew to thirty- to forty-feet high.

JK: I saw an unusual picture of planting the berm. What type of machine was that?

BE: That was a tree-planting extender. [Laughs] That's just a plain, ordinary, garden-variety front-loading tractor, but it wouldn't reach where we had to go, so we took a couple of pieces of water pipe and a chain and put a handle on the front of the tractor so we could put the trees up on the berm. In those days we didn't have hydraulic cranes that are so convenient today.

JK: It sounds like you did a lot of work to try to get everything green by the opening of the park.

BE: Walt liked to have the scene complete when the curtains were drawn open. He wanted that landscaping to being as close to full scale and mature as possible. He didn't want to wait five or ten years for young trees to grow up and produce shape. We scampered around the country to try to find all the mature trees we could and it didn't take long to exhaust the budget. The park was built on a very modest budget.

JK: Is the story true that Walt told you to put Latin names on weeds?

BE: Yes, absolutely. I had to tell Walt by the time I got around to the back berm that we had run out of money and plant material and were scraping the bottom of the barrel. Walt said, "I notice you have some head-high weeds out there. Why don't you put some jaw-breaking Latin names on them?" So we did as he suggested. The weeds were growing almost as high as trees, so we put some fancy names on them. Walt got such a kick out of it that he mentioned it at the cast celebration for the tenth anniversary of Disneyland.

JK: As a kid going to Disneyland, it never occurred to me that the Matterhorn wasn't a real mountain, but actually just a building with real plants on it.

BE: Let me tell you the prescription for planting a reproduction of a Matterhorn. The formula is to fill a cement bucket on the end of a 125-foot boom with some planter mix, and then plop down a few plants, and a tree, and on top of the pile plop down a gardener on top of the plants and then hoist the whole thing up in the air about a hundred feet. Find some place to dump the soil and plants and stomp them into place. And go back down for another load.

That's how the planting was done. The area was equipped with a plastic irrigation and drip system and some rather conventional plumbing to make sure that everything drained. We had a sophisticated system of feeding those plants. [Laughs] We had an old 50-gallon oil drum on the top of the Matterhorn connected to the irrigation system, and we dumped some fertilizer in that and periodically it dribbled down on the plants.

I think the Matterhorn was about 1/100th scale, so it wouldn't do to put fir trees or pine trees up there because they would be totally out of scale. We found some old stunted pinyon pines on the edge of the Colorado Desert and brought those in. They were three to six-feet high, but much more in keeping with the scale. Very short needles. But in intervals of every three or four years they get replaced.

JK: So many things have changed since Disneyland opened.

BE: It was characteristic that areas changed at Disneyland, not excepting the berm itself. We pushed the berm aside three different times, sort of like loosening your belt to accommodate greater girth. We had to push the railroad track out in order to let the park expand. That finally became impractical. And now, the rides penetrate the berm and railroad track. When you are in the Haunted Mansion ride or Pirates ride, you are outside the railroad. The structures that house the rides were built there. You get there by going through a tunnel underneath the railroad track.

Nature's Wonderland is an example of something changing. It was where the Stagecoach Ride was. We were pushing the sand around and picking up trees and putting them elsewhere using a reasonably broad inventory of plant material: lots of pine trees and maple trees and such. When it all became Big Thunder Railroad we weren't able to save the beaver dam stuff because it was an entirely different environment, and that was a shame.

The entrance to Tomorrowland changed drastically from opening. The point I'm making is that scenery often changes at Disneyland. Almost like a play where scene one is a drawing room and scene two is a country village street or something. It meant in many instances we'd sweep aside four or five acres of landscaping and shuffle things around because we didn't want to lose all those years of growing. So we looked to see what we could salvage every time something changed.

The show goes on and the trees go on, too. When we built Small World, we didn't want to lose the green-tree skyline, so we put the trees in boxes and put them on the roof where they are all maintained by a drip irrigation system. The effect is when you are approaching Small World, you are seeing a continuous green backdrop even though there is a section in boxes.

Even the front door has been changed. You can't even get into the parking lot the way you used to. There is a whole new entrance now. We used to keep that flower crop in front rotated. We replanted four or five times a year. For your first introduction to Disneyland, when you arrived at the parking lot, we always had that nice carpet of color to welcome you. Throughout the park something like 500,000 plants are replaced every year, and those plantings are scheduled at least ten months in advance. Every crop is programmed and sequenced.

JK: Is there something you particularly miss at Disneyland today?

BE: We're grieving for things long gone at Disneyland. One of the things I really miss are the mermaids they used to have at the Submarine Voyage.

Those young ladies were very proficient. They were equipped with a Naugahyde tail section and they had to learn to swim in dolphin fashion. They were pretty good at it. But they couldn't get out of the lagoon. There were always lots of volunteers to help them out. [Laughs]

JK: I understand you had to come up with a pretty innovative way of moving trees at Disneyland.

BE: Necessity is the mother of invention. We occasionally had to move trees around and couldn't use the accepted practice of putting a large box around the root system because sometimes the weight would have been more than we could have handled. That big coral tree in Adventureland would have weighed about twenty tons, but this way it comes out to about two-and-a-half tons because it doesn't carry any real estate with it. We propped the tree up so it wouldn't fall down and with a fire hose we washed all the sand away from the roots. Then we put a steel pin through the trunk to give us a handle. Hooked a crane onto it and unceremoniously removed it from its happy home and replanted.

Those young pine trees we planted on the original berm eventually grew to some thirty-five feet and the time came for us to move them. We didn't want to lose the progress we had made in their growth. We used the same method. Most horticulturists or nursery men would be horrified at the idea. We had no means of knowing whether we would be successful or not, but we thought it was worth a try because the circumstances were such that we either had to throw the trees away or try to move them in this undignified manner. Again, we drilled holes in the trunks and put a pin in the trunk as a handle. We used a big front-loader to ease the tree out of the ground and then we'd pick it up.

We'd pick the trees up and the earth equipment picks up the real estate and puts it all in a new location. Progressively, we denuded one berm and then...say, can you "nude" a berm? [Laughs] Well, that's what we did. We moved the trees from the old berm to the newer berm that was farther out. We could salvage about eighty percent of the trees at twenty percent of the cost, so this was a process we found very useful to us.

When we went down to Florida to build Walt Disney World, we moved 2,000–3,000 trees to the profound amazement of the professionals by drilling holes through the trunk of the thing. When we replanted like that, we would spray the area. You see them doing that on the freeways. We put together a little grass seed, a little fertilizer, a little insecticide, a little fungicide, and throw in some flower seed, too, and then we spray it on just like painting the wall of a house. And in a matter of months you get growth.

JK: Walt certainly gave you a lot of challenges, everything from the Matterhorn to those miniatures in StoryBook Land.

BE: Take a look at Geppetto's village. The trick there was to somehow get some kind of association between the Alps that are very much more miniaturized than the village. We picked a bunch of plant material with very small leaves and they were growing in small two- to three-inch pots, and we kept them in the pots and plunged them in the earth. If they started to grow, we pounced on them and pruned them back a little bit. We didn't let the roots get out of the pots and had kind of a bonsai effect on them and stunted their growth. Once in a while we had to change a few, but for the most part those trees lasted for years. They were in sync with the structures, if not with the Alps. All scaled down and stunted by the simple process of containing the roots. We simply planted the plant and the pot.

JK: I never realized before how much landscaping can fool the eye.

BE: Landscaping isn't just what you see, but what you don't see. At the Submarine Voyage, you don't see a big reinforced building over an acre in extent, about the size of a parking garage. Instead of seeing an acre of concrete roof, what you see is all these trees. The biggest trees there are growing in 4–5 feet of sand that was heaped on the top of the roof. When you ride through the monorail or PeopleMover, you are moving through a forest, but a surprisingly brief distance below the surface is a concrete roof. This is a roof garden, a different kind of roof garden.

JK: You're right. It doesn't occur to you when you are going through that area.

BE: In Tomorrowland, around the Autopia and the monorail, Walt wanted a lot of green stuff because it adds to the experience. When you ride through there on the PeopleMover, the monorail, or the kids on the Autopia, you have the sense of moving because you are going by the trees all the time and you don't always see what is around the corner until you get to the corner. That's the adventure.

JK: So you always tried to have the landscaping support the story?

BE: You pick from a spectrum of plants that range from cactus up to pine trees and maple trees to tropical banana trees. You try to choose the material that enhances the illusion the art directors are seeking. You try to back that up with plant material that extends the illusion, that is simpatico with the scene.

In the Painted Desert, the Joshua trees we used are the real McCoy. We brought those in from the desert areas. It gives a sense of reality that you are actually in that location. However, the most successful element in that setting was some of the cacti. We never had any trouble with those because they were made out of fiberglass. [Laughs]

The trees on the Missouri River shore are either the real McCoy or such reasonable facsimiles that they are compatible. There are native sycamores that grow in Missouri. We don't use those same sycamores. We use the native California sycamore, but it makes the same contribution to the scene. The pine trees are not the same species, but you don't recognize the difference

JK: How did the idea for topiaries at Small World originate?

BE: Walt had been to Europe and had seen some fine topiary. He was suitably impressed with the artisans who had fashioned this material. Conventional topiary goes back some 3,000 years. The plant material customarily employed to produce topiary figures was very slow growing—yew trees and such. It takes years and years to respond to the desired effect.

Walt was a bit too impatient for that. "Let's get some topiaries in the park in a year or two," he said. He didn't see any point in waiting twenty years. So what we did was get plant material of suitable size. The artists would do illustrations that they wanted. We blew them up to full size, and then took a lot of reinforcing rods and warped it around into the shapes we needed. In effect, we built a kind of skeleton out of steel.

We persuaded these plants that they should grow to correspond to that skeleton. You bend them a little bit in January and a little bit more in February and a little bit more in March until you get the bones of the plant around the basic shape, and finally you get to what you want. We managed to get a good handle on it in two years' time. The difference in doing this short-order topiary is that this stuff grows fast. That is a great advantage for the opening, but it is a great disadvantage in the long haul. That European topiary is hundreds of years old. This stuff isn't going to last a hundred years. We can get maybe ten years out of it. We have to have stand-ins behind the scenes ready to come aboard because this stuff outgrows and we can't hold it down indefinitely. Both California and Florida have back-up topiaries. We borrow from Florida because it grows faster down there.

The earliest ones at Disneyland were animal characters like the hippos from *Fantasia*. At one time, Walt was even thinking of putting them on turntables that rotated so it would look like they were dancing.

JK: I'm impressed by the different varieties of trees and such at the park.

BE: If you tour Disneyland, there are some really remarkable trees in there. Not the least interesting fact is that many of them are there because we were trying for instant landscaping and wanting to have shade and scale for openers. Like the topiary, you have to be careful those trees don't rapidly outgrow their usefulness. Fortunately, all the major trees in the public area are still there. They have changed places. We moved them around like checkers on a board. The only ones we had to remove were the ones on Main Street.

When we tried finding just the right tree for that area, we were trying to find something that didn't have a distinctive personality that was readily recognizable. We didn't want a magnolia or a pine in there. What we were trying to get was something Mid-America. But we don't want them to be bare in winter.

JK: I know you constantly keep adding new trees to the park.

BE: There was this one tree that had nineteen trunks. It's a palm native to West Africa. I think it is the best specimen in southern California. We found the tree up in Santa Barbara in an old estate that was about to be subdivided. We boxed that tree up. We broke all the ordinances hauling it down. It weighed twenty-two tons and I think we got twenty-two tickets from the highway patrol. [Laughs] We finally got it into Tomorrowland where it remains today.

For a great many years what was good about Pershing Square in downtown Los Angeles were these ficus trees that cast their shade on the turf of the area. The city decided they needed the space for an underground parking garage. They salvaged about two-thirds of the trees that were boxed and moved to one side. There were eight trees they decided were too big to save. They were in the process of demolishing them with a chainsaw. I got there after they had chopped one tree down. "Oooooh, woodsman, really spare that tree! What gives?" So they said they had a contract to demolish and haul them away for $150 apiece. I said, "Okay, I can top that. If you promise to take your chainsaw home and forget about demolishing them, I'll give you $50 a tree." We went in and scooped up those trees and brought them down to New Orleans Square. We gave them a whole new lease on life.

JK: With all this expertise, did it make it any easier landscaping the Magic Kingdom in Florida fifteen years later?

BE: In Florida, we had a perfectly miserable experience in the theme-park area down there because the Florida terrain. The site of Disney World is a big piece of real estate, almost fifty square miles. Walt wanted that kind of dimension in order to separate himself very thoroughly from the neon jungles that surround Disneyland. That was the plus side. The minus side was most of that site had an elevation, I think, the fall in ten miles was only ten feet. There weren't any hills on the property, although they were described as hills by the local surveyors.

As an example, I wanted to start a tree farm to start producing some of the material we needed. A surveyor said, "There is just the place for it. There is a hill over on the West Side that would be just fine. Not that many trees on it." He drove me over. There wasn't a bit of road. We were pioneering that country. It was pastureland and swamp, and exceedingly poor pastureland at that. We finally arrived at the spot and he said, "How do you like that? What do you think of that?" And I said, "Where?" "Why, it's a hill!" he said.

Boy, you could have fooled me. There was a place out there about maybe six or eight feet of freeboard before you ran into the water table.

"I'll walk up there, but catch me if I fall. I don't want to roll all the way to the bottom." [Laughs]

That's where we put the tree farm.

When we built the theme park, we had to lift the elevation of a hundred acres a maximum of 15 feet and a minimum of 10 feet. In order to get some freeboard to build the biggest basement in Florida, you had to raise the elevation. The process was to dig a 250-acre lagoon and the yield from that spoil is what built that site.

If you look at the soil profile in that part of Florida, it is kind of like a Danish pastry. There is a skinny layer of sand on top and then there's some peat muck, maybe something else, and underneath all of that, some blue clay and underneath that pink clay and then brown clay and gray clay. All the colors of the rainbow, but all clay.

When you move the earth, you take off this layer and put that over somewhere else and this layer on top of that, all of this abominable soil. You could dig a hole in that and fill it with water. It was absolutely impervious to water. You had just as much water in there a week later.

That's still a problem today.

When we built Epcot, we were able to convince the engineers that no matter what it cost it would be a great economy to ignore that kind of source and go find a sandy source for soil. We have a very congenial environment for the landscaping at Epcot. No clay.

JK: Tell me about Walt himself.

BE: My brother Jack and I took great pride in the fact that Walt would never hover over us like he did the art directors. He really trusted us. He would say something like, "Bill, I'm putting in a skyway, make it look like it's in the Alpines," and it was up to us to make it a reality. He didn't talk things to death. One of the amazing things about Walt was that he knew the tremendous contribution landscaping could make.

Here's a story about how Walt communicated. If you read anything about Disneyland, you've heard of Admiral Joe Fowler, who was a retired admiral who had done more than his stint in the service. Walt heard about him and went up to meet him in northern California and persuaded him to climb back into harness. He was the vice-president in charge of construction for a great many years all through Disneyland and all through Walt Disney World. He was actually my boss. I reported to the admiral. Admiral Fowler translated Walt's directions.

When we were building Disneyland, we used to make a tour of the site every Saturday. Once a week, Walt would hike the whole site. We really thought we had outdone ourselves when we got these big trees for the hub. They were really big trees: eight tons each in six-foot boxes.

Along came Saturday; we had planted them a couple of days earlier so I thought I would really impress both my bosses: Walt and Admiral Fowler. I think Walt liked those trees. Those were good trees. But his way of liking them was to turn to Joe and say, "Where did Bill get the bushes?"

Walt was not given to extravagant praise. He had the best in terms of artists and technicians and engineers. He had the best. They all performed. They all put out for Walt. And it wasn't because he slapped them on the back and said they were doing a great job. I don't think anybody ever heard him say that. You just wanted to do the best you could. Actually, you ended up doing better than you thought you could. You felt supported so you could experiment and take some chances.

JK: Just listening to you, I can see that you are very passionate about horticulture.

BE: I certainly feel that trees are living, breathing individuals. They're alive and respond to the elements. A building doesn't yield to the breeze. I can see the life in the trees by the way they move. We have some giant bamboo in the jungle that grow to a height of 30 or 40 feet, and in the breeze, you get an effect like a ballet dancer. When I first started working on Disneyland, I planted a eucalyptus tree when it was about the size of my little finger in caliper, and now that tree is 50-feet high or better with a massive trunk, a really handsome tree. I mean, it has dignity. This is a beautiful tree. This is something that wasn't in Anaheim thirty years ago, and look at this tree now. I literally wrapped my arms around the trunk of that tree. I love that tree. It's a beautiful tree. It has embraceable bark, I should point out. [Laughs]

JK: You certainly got the opportunity to work with a lot of different plant material working for Disney.

BE: To overly simplify, we pick from a very broad spectrum. It just so happens that in this area of southern California you have a wider choice of plant material than anywhere else in the United States. In Miami, they can grow a few tropicals that we can't. As a trade-off, we can grow a dozen plants they can't grow in Miami because it is too hot and humid for them. You can't grow a white birch tree in Miami, but we can do it here.

One of the great pities is professional designers don't avail themselves of this wide choice of material. You have to go to someplace like the Arboretum or the Huntington Gardens to really see choice trees and plants, but they could be in any residential garden.

JK: What's in the future for Bill Evans?

BE: Even though they seem to keep calling me back on new projects, most of us are old now. We've all graduated and are getting a little long in the tooth for Disney. They've got a lot of young bright-eyed, bushy-tailed people. The landscaping is in capable hands. There is a young fellow who was my assistant in the days when we built Walt Disney World who is now the chief landscape architect.[1] I think he'll keep things going. I've still got a few old hands in that landscape crew at Disneyland that I brought down in 1954.

I'd like to underscore the fact that the reason Disneyland and Disney World are really good from a landscaping standpoint is that they have the very best maintenance. It doesn't make any difference how carefully you contrive the planning or how good the material is or how efficiently it is all installed. The whole thing depends on maintenance and those people are doing a first-class job.

JK: Thank you, Bill. And thanks for not using a lot of jaw-breaking Latin names for the plants. I don't think I would be able to spell them correctly.

BE: My pleasure. If you get into horticultural names, it doesn't mean much to a general audience. Walt was never trying to educate people about landscaping or anything else, but he believed people would know the difference between good landscaping and bad landscaping, and Disneyland was the best.

© 2007 Jim Korkis

---

[1] Paul Comstock.

Jack Bradbury (1914–2004)

Interviewed by Alberto Becattini from 1987 to 2004.

We met Jack Bradbury in *Walt's People: Volume 3*. Klaus Strzyz's interview in that volume focused on his career as a comic book artist. Here is the story of his life as an animator.

This interview results from conversations and letters dating from 1987 until briefly before Jack's death on May 15, 2004. It originally appeared in *Comic Book Marketplace* #103 (Gemstone Publishing, June 2003).

Alberto Becattini: How did you become interested in animation?

Jack Bradbury: In the summer of 1934, Disney's *Three Little Pigs* was causing quite a sensation in my home town, Seattle, and I rushed to see it. I couldn't help but be impressed and interested. One of the Disney directors, Ben Sharpsteen, was visiting friends in Seattle that summer, and through them I heard that the Disney Studio was planning to enlarge its staff in preparation for bigger things, the first of which was to be a feature picture, *Snow White*. I immediately wrote to the studio and sent samples of my work. The answer I soon received was encouraging: "Come down for a two-week try-out period and see if you are capable of doing this kind of work." So, at age 19, late in October 1934, I left Seattle with a one-way bus ticket to California with about $50 in my pocket, and appeared several days later at the old Hyperion Avenue studio in Hollywood. I started out as an in-betweener, filling in drawings in-between other drawings done by animators and assistant animators. By the end of my two-week period I had mastered it well enough to be put on the payroll and start working at the magnificent sum of $15.00 a week. Not much money, but happily it didn't take much for a young cartoonist to live alone on in those days.

AB: What was the atmosphere like at Disney in those days?

JB: It was great. A wonderful, light-hearted spirit prevailed throughout the studio, and along with the fun and frolics, there was the sincere desire of everyone to make Disney cartoons the very best seen on the theatre screens today. As beginners, we were all working in a large room together, doing in-betweens and breakdown drawings. Along with this daily work, we were privileged to take part in a training program. Several times a week we spent part of our day in an art class, drawing from a live model, and one full morning a week was spent at the zoo, sketching live animals. All this was done under the expert, watchful eye of a very fine instructor, Don Graham.

AB: What were some of the early Disney cartoons you worked on?

JB: Among the first ones I worked on there was a Silly Symphony cartoon, *The Tortoise and the Hare* [released January 5, 1935] and a Mickey Mouse cartoon, *The Band Concert* [released February 23, 1935]. I recall we were asked to put on considerable overtime on that, which was rewarded with vouchers for a dinner at Leslie's, a little restaurant on Vermont Avenue in Hollywood. By the beginning of the next summer I had apparently improved enough to be offered a seven-year contract, which also called for definite raises every three months for the first few years, then every six months after that. In late 1935 I became an assistant animator. For a year, I was assistant to Robert Wickersham—whom we called "Bob Wick"—on several shorts, including *Thru the Mirror* [a Mickey Mouse cartoon, released May 30, 1936] and the Oscar-winning *The Old Mill* [a Silly Symphony cartoon, released November 5, 1937]. When Bob decided to leave Disney and go with the Fleischer Studio, I was reassigned with two other assistants, Don Lusk and Ken Hultgren, to assist animators Milt Kahl, Eric Larson, and Jim Algar on *Snow White*. These men were to animate all the animals in the picture, and in some scenes there were as many as thirty active little creatures on every drawing.

AB: Was it during that period that you became a full-fledged animator?

JB: Yes. Nearing the end of our assignment on *Snow White*, a number of the young would-be animators were given one scene each to animate in a short titled *Farmyard Symphony* [released October 14, 1938]. My scene was a short one of a bull adding his voice to a chorus of other animals singing, more or less harmoniously, in a barnyard group. Actually, I became a full-time animator after doing a try-out scene of one man's awkward efforts at playing tennis. I showed it to Ham Luske, a top animator who had recently become a fine director on *Snow White*. He liked my effort and with Perce Pearce, a story director, showed it to Walt. The result was my becoming an animator full time, my first assignment being on a short, *Ferdinand the Bull* [released November 25, 1938], directed by Ham Luske. I animated the young bulls butting and slamming each other around to show off and impress the men who staged the bullfights, then I did the scene where the full-grown Ferdinand saunters overs and blithely sits down under a tree...on the stinger of an angry big bee. He takes off, bellowing with surprise and in pain.

AB: Later on you animated on *Pinocchio*, *Fantasia*, and *Bambi*. Which sequences did you work on?

JB: On *Pinocchio* [released February 7, 1940] I did some of the animation on Figaro, Geppetto's cat, again for director Ham Luske. I did enough footage to deserve screen credit [as John Bradbury]. After finishing my work on *Pinocchio*, at the time when we were moving to the new, larger studio in Burbank, I was working again for Luske, animating flying horses, centaurs and centaurettes for Beethoven's "Pastoral Symphony" in the next feature, *Fantasia* [released November 13, 1940]. I now had an assistant of my own, Wilbur Streech, a graduate of UCLA. After *Fantasia*, we began work on *Bambi* [released August 13, 1942]. I did the fight sequence, wherein Bambi and Ronno battle over the doe, Faline.

AB: Why did you leave the Disney Studio in 1941?

JB: The Disneys were in big financial trouble because of the huge debt incurred building a grand new studio. Also, the income from the animation features was not coming in as well as expected, as the war had ended Europe's lucrative market for US films, and the revenue from showing the films in all remaining markets was not enough to support a studio that size. Soon there were rumors of impending layoffs, and when they started laying off animation department people first, those Disney employees who had become union members decided by vote to strike the studio. I had gotten married in December of 1940, and in the early summer of 1941 found myself out on strike, with no income and our first child on the way. Five animators and their assistants from our unit, 1F, all went out, everyone but Eric Larson, the supervising animator of our group. The strike lasted two dreary months [from May 28 until July 28, 1941], and was finally settled by outside mediation. I received a telegram telling me to return to work. I had hardly had a chance to get started on my next assignment, *Wind in the Willows* [later released as part of *The Adventures of Ichabod and Mr. Toad* (1949)], when I got another notice that I had to leave. Art Babbitt, one of two top animators who had also gone out on strike [the other one being Bill Tytla], got his notice the same day and we walked out together.

AB: Then you went to work at the Warner Bros. animation studio?

JB: Not immediately. A number of ex-Disney employees found work at MGM and Warner's, but several studio friends and I, somewhat weary and fed up with studio problems, were offered an opportunity to do something else, and we took it. America was at war, and the yards were turning out cargo ships as fast as they could. These were known as Liberty ships, and our group was soon among the crews painting the darn things in the shipyards down in San Pedro: quite a change from making animated cartoon movies, although we made almost as much money as we had at the studio. I had hardly started working there when I received an animation job offer from MGM, but decided not to take it. However, about nine months later, when I got a second chance to go back to animation, this time to work with Friz Freleng at Warner's—which was then known as Schlesinger's—I left the shipyard and returned to studio work.

AB: Although you worked at Warner's for about two years, from 1942–44, you only got screen credit on three shorts, as far as I know…

JB: They had a weird system there regarding screen credits. Warner's had four separate units, each with its own director, story and layout men, background artist and six animators. When a unit completed a picture, only one animator received screen credit for that picture, though all six had worked on it. I don't recall why it was done this way, except perhaps six names might have cluttered up the opening title too much. As for my first screen credit at Warner's, here's an odd but true little tale. When I started working for Friz Freleng's unit, he put my name on his animators' screen-credit list, and the first time my name came up, it was put on a picture on which I'd not done even one drawing. [*Jack-Wabbit and the Beanstalk*, a Bugs Bunny short released June 12, 1943. The other two Warner cartoons Bradbury got screen credit for were *Meatless Flyday*, released January 29, 1944, and *Stage Door Cartoon*, released December 30, 1944].

AB: What was it like to work at Warner's, compared to Disney's?

JB: Friz was a great director to work for, and his group of artists [including story man Mike Maltese and animators Dick Bickenbach, Ken Champin, Gerry Chiniquy, Manuel Perez, and Virgil Ross] were a fine bunch to work with. Actually, I went through a difficult time at first getting on track, for I hadn't even lifted a pencil for well over a year. Besides, most of the animation I'd done for Disney had been four-legged, life-like animal action. Here at Warner's, all the animal characters, like Bugs Bunny, Sylvester the Cat, Porky Pig, etc., were humanized animal characters. We also worked on a cartoon series with a bungling GI character called Private Snafu. These pictures were done for the Army and were supervised by Major Ted Geisel, better known as Dr. Seuss.

AB: Were you still working at Warner's when you started drawing comic-book stories?

JB: Yes. In 1943, one of the animators I knew in another unit, Gil Turner, introduced me to Jim Davis, a friend for whom he was doing some comic-book work in his spare time. These comic books consisted of animated animal characters, done very much like those we'd been doing at the studios. Ken Hultgren was also working for Davis at that time, at home. Jim represented Sangor Publications [a.k.a. Editorial Art Syndicate, or Cinema Comics], a New York concern run by Ben W. Sangor and Richard Hughes which packaged comic-book titles for various publishers, including Creston [a.k.a. American Comics Group], Standard, and National/DC. Sangor and Hughes had their own artists in New York, mainly animators from the Paramount/Famous Studios like Dan Gordon, whereas Jim was in charge of the West Coast branch, buying stories and artwork done by Hollywood animation artists and writers. This comic-book thing looked pretty good to me, so I thought I'd give it a try. Jim told me to go ahead, rough up a story, and let him see it. I did a little twist on the old Tortoise and Hare tale and he okayed it for me to draw up and ink.

AB: So you left Warner's to do comic-book work full time...?

JB: Well, yes and no. I had just started drawing comics for Jim when he offered me quite a bit more money to leave Warner's and work for Carey-Weston, the small animation studio he was in charge of. Anyone not in the service during wartime, but receiving a deferment doing war work, could not change jobs without first appearing before a draft board. A friend, Ray Patin, who was at that time president of the Screen Cartoonists Guild and also worked at Warner's, decided to leave and go with Jim also. We appeared before the board together, accompanied by our guild business agent, who explained for us the reason for our making a change and the board okayed our move. Ray and I then began our work for Davis' outfit, both animating on their defense film [*The Inside Story of Seaman Joe*] and doing comics on the side. We later did a parts manual for the Lockheed P-80 fighter jet, which was also considered deferrable war work. My brother Ed, an engineer at Lockheed at that time, was paid well to supervise our bumbling efforts several evenings a week, and somehow we got through the stuff. After the Lockheed manual was finally completed, Jim somehow managed to find us an animated cartoon picture to do for Cathedral Films, a religious film company. The war over and our Cathedral film done, most of us were now planning to work at home on comic books full time. No one intended going back to the studios. Several months passed with each of us working at home, then Jim, Al Hubbard [former Disney and Warner storyman], Hubie Karp, and I decided to share an office together. First it was a real-estate office in Glendale, where I lived, then we moved to larger accommodations in Montrose, a nearby town. From Montrose we moved again, this time into an office in downtown Glendale. Owen Fitzgerald, a layout artist, was there for a while, too. Ken Hultgren still worked at home, but he and writer Homer Brightman came around nearly every day to lunch with us.

AB: Were you all working for the same comic-book titles?

JB: Yes. We were doing strips for such titles as *Ha Ha*, *Giggle*, *Coo Coo*, and *Happy*, published by the American Comics Group, in which both Sangor and Hughes had an interest, and by Standard, who bought the stories from Sangor. Hughes, who served as editor in New York, would send in his comments every week or two, but it was up to Jim Davis entirely whether stories were acceptable or not, and he always seemed pleased with my work. Some of my own characters were Footsy Hare (which was my first comic-book strip for Davis), Tuffy the Cat, Bagshaw Bear, Humphrey Hummingbird, Butch McSparrow, Stanley and Homer (a horse and a dog), Li'l Thomas Hippopot, Rufus and Goofus (two Dachshund dogs), Pansy the Chimp, Fremont Frog, Hucky Duck (a Huckleberry Finn-type character), Gooligan (a tough dog), "Doc" E. Z. Duzit (a little gnome-like doctor who treated the forest animals), Clem McHedgehog, Boar Brummel, and probably a few others I cannot remember.

AB: Did you do the drawing as well as the writing?

JB: I wrote, penciled, and inked most of them. I didn't do the lettering, though, which was done by Mel "Tubby" Millar, a former story and story sketch man at Disney and Warner's. I also did quite a few strips that I did not write, like Snoozer, Billy Bull, or Spencer Spook, which was written by Hubie Karp and by Hughes, I think. Occasionally, Hughes would request a special idea be developed, like the Hepcats, written by gifted Cal Howard and drawn by me. Then, sometime in 1948, the bottom fell out of the independent comic-book business, and our work for Sangor came to a rather abrupt end. Jim Davis had been doing the *Fox and Crow* comic himself for about three years [for DC/National Comics], and still had that to do, but the rest of us were now basically out of work. Luckily, Lynn Karp [Hubie's brother and a former Disney animator] and I were told that Standard Publications wanted us to do some work for them. For the next couple years [1949–51] I wrote and drew seven issues of a series called *Spunky—Junior Cowboy and His Talking Horse Stanley*. I enjoyed very much doing these, for again I was free to write and draw whatever and whoever I liked.

AB: Then you went to work for Western Publishing?

JB: Well, I'd first gotten in touch with Western in about 1947, when the animated comics with Jim Davis were already slowing down. Western, which published [under the Dell imprint] Disney comic books, as well as several other titles featuring licensed characters from animation, movies, and TV, had offices out in the Beverly Hills business district, and Tom McKimson, whom I'd known as an animator at Warner's, was art director there. I heard that work was available for me if I wanted it. Yet the thought of doing work for Western was not too enticing, as I would no longer have the freedom I'd had when working for Sangor. It meant using stories from their storymen, plus drawing an eight-panel page (for Sangor we had only six panels per page), and having to bear down and draw all Disney characters. Not to mention the pay, as they offered about $18 per page, drawing and inking, a far cry from the $25 per page we had been getting at Sangor's.

So I mulled it over very carefully for a bit, then decided to take a fling at magazine cartoons first, something I'd always wanted to try. A number of Disney men had gone into magazine work and done very well at it: Virgil "Vip" Partch, Don Tobin, Claude Smith, Dick Shaw, and Roy Williams, to name a few. There was a large market for magazine cartoons at that time and so once again I worked for a while at home, writing gags and doing up rough sketches to mail to the magazines. As these were returned and continually sent to other magazines, who rejected them in turn, I began to realize selling cartoons was not that easy. My drawing was probably too Disney-ish, not distinctive enough. The successful magazine cartoonists had each been able to develop an individual style, far different and away from the Disney influence. I, unfortunately, had not.

AB: So you eventually decided to go with Western?

JB: Right. After keeping at it [magazine cartoons] diligently for several months, I decided I'd fooled around long enough. I had five mouths to feed—we had now three sons—and I needed to start making some money again. I called Tom McKimson and made an appointment to see him. Tom was very cordial and I came away with a ten-page Donald Duck story to pencil in [published in *Walt Disney's Comics* No. 113, February, 1950]. They also furnished their artists with all the fine Strathmore paper needed. From a slow start, I gradually worked into their way of doing things. Pencil it in, take it over for an okay, then ink the thing, deliver it, and pick up the next story to work on. At first it was taking me twice as long to do the work, with all this driving back and forth, but slowly I picked up speed.

AB: Were you still working in the Glendale office at that time?

JB: Yes, I was. But after I felt I was pretty well set at Western, I packed up my family and two dogs and left town. We moved south about 60 or 70 miles, to the lovely coastal beach town of Balboa, in the Newport Beach area. That was in 1951, and we would live there for the next 17 years.

AB: I suppose you were assigned to draw the Disney characters because you had been a Disney animator, right?

JB: Yes. I was already quite familiar with most of the Disney characters, having done so many of them in my early days as an in-betweener. I also did a few stories with the Warner characters for a while—Bugs Bunny,

Porky Pig, Elmer Fudd. Later on [1959–66] they had me draw quite a few stories starring the Walter Lantz characters—Andy Panda, Oswald the Rabbit, yet from the early 1950s onwards I worked mostly on the Disney gang—Donald Duck, Donald's nephews, Mickey and Minnie, Goofy, Pluto, the Seven Dwarfs, the Li'l Bad Wolf—you name it, I worked on it. I also did some stories starring Uncle Scrooge, that wonderful brainchild of the gifted Carl Barks, whom I'd see occasionally out at the Western offices. You know what? I never liked drawing the Disney ducks that much, whereas I enjoyed other characters like Mickey and Goofy. I never thought I was that good as a Duck man.

AB: Well, I think your Ducks were great!

JB: Thanks, but that won't make me change my mind. My own sons told me they preferred Barks' Ducks to mine, and I certainly couldn't blame them for that!

AB: You also drew several issues of *Beany and Cecil*…

JB: Sure. Beany and Cecil, the Seasick Serpent. I enjoyed doing quite a series of comics and coloring books starring them. I had known Bob Clampett at Warner's, where he had directed cartoon shorts. He was the creator and owner of the popular TV show, *Time for Beany*.

AB: Of course, all of these you drew anonymously, as that was the policy at Western…

JB: Yeah, of course I wasn't able to sign any of the stories I drew for the comics, but they gave me a credit line on the children's books and coloring books I drew, mostly with the Disney characters, but a few Bugs Bunnys, too. When the illustrations were done in wash, I would be penciling only, the color art being provided by someone else [e.g., Campbell Grant or Gene Wolfe]. I drew and inked several large Disneyland coloring books, with ideas taken directly from the world-famous theme park itself.

AB: Have you ever tried doing a syndicated strip?

JB: I have, but to no avail. In 1939, when I was still working at Disney's, Hank Porter, who was head of the publicity art department, and I did a speculative comic strip for Edgar Bergen, the famous ventriloquist. I did the drawing from photos Bergen had given me and Hank followed right behind inking them. We did two weeks of dailies in three days and delivered them to Bergen's office, then we waited weeks while Bergen and the syndicate haggled over satisfactory financial terms. But unable to come to an agreement, the strip died a-borning. Shortly after, it did appear as *Mortimer and Charlie*, drawn this time by Chase Craig and Carl Buettner, both of whom later worked at Western. It didn't last long in the paper we took, the *Los Angeles Times*, nor, we heard, in the rest of the country. Hank and I had considered our work on the strip purely speculative, but when the problem between Bergen and the syndicate proved unsolvable, we received apologies for the interminable delay and $200 for our work. Later on, in the 1950s, I was asked by Western to draw two syndicated strips on speculation: *Beany and Cecil* [probably written by Vic Lockman] and *Bozo the Clown*. Unfortunately, neither one was sold.

AB: Did you write any of the stories you drew for Western?

JB: Not for many years. As I said before, they had their own storymen at Western, talented people like Del Connell or Carl Fallberg, who did their scripts in storyboard form, as they had previously worked in animation themselves, just like the guys who wrote stories for Jim Davis. Yet I did write some of the stories I drew for Western and for the Disney Studio later on. Indeed, most of the stories I did from 1963 onwards were never published in the USA, as they were produced for the overseas market.

AB: *Hundreds* of them were published in Italy and in most other European countries, as well as in South America. Were these done for the Disney Studio?

JB: For a few years, I drew them for Western, then directly for Tom Golberg at the Disney Studio, from about 1967 until 1978. I did the Ducks, Mickey Mouse and Goofy, Gyro Gearloose, Chip 'n' Dale, and the Li'l Bad Wolf, among others. I usually penciled these, the inking being done by studio artists [Ellis Eringer or Steve Steere]. Late in 1973 or early in 1974, I went back to doing stories for Western, too. Phil DeLara, the resident artist on Chip 'n' Dale, had died, and they asked me to take over the strip, which appeared monthly in *Walt Disney's Comics and Stories*, which I did, penciling only, for a couple years. Then, for a short while, due to my deteriorating eyesight, I quit drawing and did story writing only, but not with any great success. It didn't matter, I was about ready to quit working anyway, and in 1978, at age 64, I retired, although occasionally I'd still do some work for Western on the larger coloring books.

AB: Actually, you wrote one more story in 1987, which was drawn by Dave Bennett...

JB: Oh, sure. That was a Spencer Spook story that Ron Frantz published in a reprint series he did. It was fun working with Dave, my friend and foremost fan, who is a fine cartoonist/layout man/animator and director in southern California. Dave has collected over 5,900 pages of my comic-book work. That's a frightening amount of stuff and today it fatigues me just to think of it. However, if Dave says I've done that much, I must believe him, for he has it all in his collection at home. By the way, Dave did a beautiful drawing of Mary Jim and me when we got married in 1984. I'd known Mary Jim for many years, as she had been married to Bob Karp [Lynn's and Hubie's brother], who wrote Donald Duck and other Disney-syndicated newspaper strips for 37 years until his death in 1975. Mary Jim and I lived in Santa Rosa until recently, when we decided to move south to join her son's family. With us both well into our 88th year, it won't be too long before we need a little help.

AB: Looking back at your great career in animation and comics, what would you like to say?

JB: I can only say that I am grateful for having spent those early years in the old Hyperion Avenue Disney studio. It was a blast! I am not sorry I left animation and got into comics, for my first love, before going to Disney, was comic strips. The syndicated newspaper kind, of course, but comic books were pretty close. And comic books were good to me, enabling me to support my family comfortably and allowing me to work on my own time and live where I wished. To have worked in the early days of both animation and comics has been a privilege and a pleasure for me. In both cases, I feel I was awfully lucky to have been there and at that time. So, I rest my case, and put down my drawing pencil for good. Like Ferdinand the Bull, I'd like to just sit now, and smell the flowers.

© 2007 Alberto Becattini

Lynn Karp (1905–1992)

Interviewed by Alberto Becattini in Spring 1984.

Lynn Karp is one of the many Disney animators of the golden age of cartoons who made the transition to comics. In this interview, which was conducted by mail in the spring of 1984, Lynn speaks about his years at the Disney Studio, as well as about his comics efforts, also mentioning his brothers Bob and Hubie, who worked in animation and comics as well.

Lynn Karp died in Lancaster, California, where he had lived for several years, on August 8, 1992.

Alberto Becattini: Let's start with a classic question: when and where were you born?

Lynn Karp: I was born Theodore Lynn Karp on September 8, 1905, in Minneapolis, Minnesota.

AB: Did you have any formal art training?

LK: Yes. I attended a painting class at the Art Institute of Minneapolis, and later at the Chicago Art Institute. I had some excellent teachers: Robert Brackman, Glenn Miller, Walt Lee, and Ralph Love.

AB: What was your first professional job?

LK: I worked as a staff artist for the *Minneapolis Journal* until 1936, when I moved to California in search of greener pastures.

AB: Tell me about your work as a Disney animator.

LK: I was hired at the Disney animation studio on Hyperion Avenue, Hollywood, on August 8, 1936. I was there for seven years, both on features and shorts. I had screen credit on *Pinocchio* (1940), *Fantasia* (1940), and *Bambi* (1942).[1] As for shorts, I contributed to such Silly Symphonies as *Farmyard Symphony* (1938) and the Oscar-winning *The Ugly Duckling* (1939), as well as to a very nice Mickey Mouse cartoon, *The Pointer* (1939). [Karp is also credited with animating on at least two other shorts: *Mickey's*

---

[1] JB Kaufman notes: "Karp did work on *Bambi* but didn't get screen credit. Nobody got screen credit on *Fantasia*." (But credits, including Karp's, were printed in a program book.)

Surprise Party (1939) and *Donald's Vacation* (1940)]. Along with the daily animation work, we would take part in a training program, drawing from a live model or sketching live animals. We had a very fine instructor called Don Graham. That lasted for six and a half years, most of the time I spent at the studio.

AB: Among the people you worked with at the Disney Studio, who do you remember more fondly?

LK: Oh, there were so many talented guys there. Among the directors I worked with, I recall Clyde "Gerry" Geronimi, Jack Cutting, and Jack King. As for animators, I was good friends with Jack Bradbury and Ken Hultgren. Jack, Ken, and I worked together on the "Pastoral Symphony" sequence of *Fantasia* for director Ham Luske, as well as on *Bambi*, where I did the quails. Like me, they would later become comic artists. And they were damn good at that, too. Another friend, Carl Barks, worked for Western Publishing after leaving Disney's at about the same time I did. I knew him well in the old days, although, of course, he worked in the story department.

AB: Why did you eventually decide to leave Disney?

LK: In the end, there got to be too much footage pressure, and on May 18, 1942, I left for other fields. I wanted to work on my own, and drawing comics allowed me to do that.

AB: What about your early work in comics?

LK: I guess I started around 1944. Jim Davis, a fine animator I'd first met at Disney's when I started there in 1936, was recruiting animators from the Hollywood studios to create funny-animal comics for a New York-based outfit called Sangor Studios. So I started writing and drawing comic-book stories for such titles as *Ha Ha Comics*, *Giggle Comics*, and *Goofy Comics*, and had quite a lot of fun doing them. Sangor had a publishing outfit called Creston or American Comics Group, but they also provided stories to such publishers as Standard, National [aka DC Comics], and probably others yet.

AB: Do you remember working on any specific series or characters?

LK: I worked on a whole lot of them, and it's hard to remember them all. Among those I wrote and drew were the Gopher Boys, Boogie Beaver, Zomby and Bomby (a kangaroo and a koala), Little Billy Bear, Cookie, the Kilroys—but I also worked on Little Chief Breezee, Spencer Spook—oh, there are too many to mention. And I created Witch Hazel for the Sangor comics—now, this was before a similar character appeared in a Disney cartoon short [Donald Duck in *Trick or Treat*, 1952].

AB: Did your brothers Robert and Hubert also work on the Sangor strips?

LK: Yes, they did. Hubie wrote a whole lot of them, including several of those I drew. He'd previously worked for the Disney Studio and written the *Mickey Mouse*, *Silly Symphony*, and *Jose Carioca* syndicated strips while there. Then he went over to Warner's, but quit animation writing for comics in the mid-forties. Unfortunately, he died of a heart attack when he was just thirty-four years old.

As for Bob, his main occupation was writing the gags for the *Donald Duck* syndicated strip, which he did for about forty years [1938–75], until he passed away. But he also wrote a few comic-book stories on the side. By the way, I drew a strip that Bob wrote called *The Middles*. It was syndicated to Australian papers during the latter half of the forties [1944–55]. My brother-in-law, Don Gunn, also worked for the same Sangor titles as I did. Don had been a Disney animator himself in the late thirties [1936–39], then he moved to New York and went to work for Kay Kamen on Disney merchandising, and later on he did a lot of comic-book work for Sangor and Western Publishing. He died in the street of a heart attack in Rochester, N.Y. [in 1972, at 56 years old].

AB: How did you come to work for Western Publishing?

LK: As I recall, by the late forties the Sangor Studio was fading away. Some of the best artists left at about that time and most of them went to work for Western, which was publishing all of the "animated comics" under the Dell imprint. Jim Davis, though, had been doing *The Fox and the Crow* for DC Comics, and would keep that account for another twenty years. I think it was in about 1948 when Standard, one of the publishers Sangor had been selling his stories to, told Bradbury, Hultgren, and me that they wanted us to work directly for them. So I did, for about four years, and then went over to Western. Actually, I had done some work for them before, but by 1953 I was freelancing on a regular basis. I think I started there by working on the Walter Lantz strips—Woody Woodpecker and Andy Panda. I also did a lot of stories starring the MGM characters: Tom and Jerry, Mouse Musketeers, Spike and Tyke, and Barney Bear. Toward the end, in the early sixties, I was mainly working on the Hanna-Barbera characters: Ruff and Reddy, Yogi Bear, Huckleberry Hound. As a matter of fact, I remember drawing several stories for a weekly comic produced by Western that was published in Britain [*Huckleberry Hound Weekly*], which I worked on for quite a spell.

AB: Didn't you ever draw any Disney strips while at Western?

LK: Yes, I did, although I didn't do that much. I remember drawing Mickey Mouse [for a 1947 Cheerios Giveaway entitled *Mickey Mouse Meets the Wizard*], the Three Little Pigs [for *Donald Duck Beach Party*, 1955], and

Chip 'n' Dale. [Although Karp says he did, no Chip 'n' Dale stories appear to have been drawn by him.]

AB: Did you also write your own stories at Western?

LK: Only occasionally, as Western had their own writers—excellent ones like Del Connell, Carl Fallberg, and Don Christensen, who had also worked in the animation field and were able to write their stories in storyboard form. Anyway, I did write a few stories myself, from time to time, with Andy Panda, Oswald the Rabbit, and the Hanna-Barbera characters.

AB: Did you always ink your own pencils? If not, who was inking?

LK: Yes, I did, except for the last few years at Western, when I was often penciling only. As for inkers, I remember Steve Steere did quite a lot of work in those days. But there may have been others.

AB: It appears that you stopped working for Western in 1962. What did you do after that?

LK: I did *Dennis the Menace* for Hank Ketcham for a couple of years—the comic book, not the newspaper box. [The *Dennis the Menace* comic books were published by Hallden/Fawcett until 1969. Owen Fitzgerald and Al Wiseman drew most of them, but Karp was evidently on the art staff for a while.]

AB: That means you left the comics field in the mid-sixties. What have you been doing since then?

LK: After leaving comics, I worked in the commercial art field for several years. For the last fifteen years, I've been doing landscape painting. I'm proud to say that I've done well at it, and now get as much as $4,000 for a painting. My favorite subjects are the Pacific Coast, the Sierras, Canada, and other scenes of particular interest in the colorful West. My paintings are displayed in several art galleries throughout the States, and have earned me quite a few awards. Next birthday, September 8, 1984, I'll be seventy-nine, but I'm still working eight hours a day and doing more than most men do at fifty. Besides that, my wife Ann and I have traveled a lot: Ireland, England and Europe, all of the Hawaiian Islands, Alaska, and New Zealand.

© 2007 Alberto Becattini

Dave Michener (b, 1932)

Interviewed by Didier Ghez on May 10 and May 23, 2006.

Having worked as an assistant to Milt Kahl for seven years and as a co-director on *The Great Mouse Detective* along with John Musker, Ron Clements, and Burny Mattinson, Dave Michener is among those key artists at the Disney Studio that were instrumental in passing the baton to the "new generation".

Dave was born on November 5, 1932, and joined the studio in 1956, animating on *The Mickey Mouse Club* and soon becoming Milt Kahl's assistant. He had a hand in every Disney animated feature from *Sleeping Beauty* to *Oliver & Company*.

In 1983, he took the enormous job of producing and directing all of the character animation for the pavilions at EPCOT Center, and then performed similar duties for Tokyo Disneyland's Meet the World attraction and for a PSA pre-show on the history of aviation at Disneyland.

Dave retired from Disney in 1987 and moved to Hanna-Barbera, where he supervised the animation of *Jetsons: The Movie* and acted as the supervising director on *Once Upon a Forest*, before deciding to retire for good.

This interview was transcribed by James D. Marks.

Didier Ghez: Maybe we can get started in a very traditional way, which is, could you tell me when you joined the Disney Studio?

Dave Michener: I was going to a school called Chouinard Art Institute in Los Angeles. I was given a four-year scholarship there. Walt Disney used to make regular visits to that school because he was financing a lot of it. All those teachers in that school were working professionals. My drawing teacher worked at the Disney Studio, too, and taught artists there. I guess Walt Disney had seen my artwork on one of his trips to Chouinard's. He was impressed with my drawing. He went to my drawing teacher and asked about me. I didn't know any of this, of course. My drawing teacher came to me one day in class and said he wanted me to come out to Disney for an interview.

DG: Who was your teacher? Was it Don Graham?

DM: Yes, Don Graham was my teacher. He was, in my opinion, the greatest art teacher that ever lived. He was just superb.

Don had me get my best artwork together to show him. He then sent me out to the Disney Studio for an interview. I went out there and had my interview. They never even opened my portfolio or looked at my artwork. I came home and I was in tears. I was crying. I told my wife—we were just newly married—I said, "My God, they wouldn't even look at my artwork." I must have really "laid an egg". I didn't find out until the next day in school. They came and told me they had a telephone message from the Disney Studio. I went to the phone and they asked me to come to work. What I didn't realize was Walt Disney had already told the personnel department if this fellow shows up, you take him. That is why they didn't look at my artwork, which I didn't know, of course. It took me months before somebody told me that's what happened. It was quite an adventure. I started there in 1956.

DG: Had you always wanted to work for the Disney Studio?

DM: If I was going to work in the movie business I wanted to work for the Disney Studio. I was very young then. I thought, there are all kinds of things I can do, but if I work in a movie studio, that is where I would like to work. That is why I was so upset when I came home and they wouldn't look at my artwork. They did later, of course. I didn't realize Walt had sort of given me the inside track. It all worked out fine.

DG: What was your first assignment at the Studio?

DM: I started on *The Mickey Mouse Club*.

DG: Who were the artists with whom you were working at the time?

DM: The animators? Or what?

DG: The animators. Of course, you were working with Bill Walsh, the show's director. Yes, the animators.

DM: Oh, gosh, there were a whole bunch of them, probably two dozen animators. I think they are all gone now. All these men were 20 to 25 years older than me. They put me right into a key position as soon as I started at the studio with what they considered to be their top men. I guess it was in, oh golly, probably around 1960 when they closed the television unit and the "shorts" unit. They used to call it that. They made 15-minute "shorts" for theaters. They laid off hundreds and hundreds of people and kept me. They cut the department down from 1,500 people to less than 100. Walt decided at that point in time that he just wanted to do an animated feature every few years. So an awful lot of people were let go. My first feature that I ever worked on was *Sleeping Beauty*. Prior to that, I worked on *The Mickey Mouse Club*, when that was going. I worked on *Paul Bunyan*, which was a featurette. I worked on *Donald in Mathmagic*

Land, which was a featurette. I did lots of commercials. I did about a dozen Donald Duck shorts. Then the roof fell in on that department and they just wanted to do features. After they got done laying everybody off, they moved me over to *Sleeping Beauty.*

DG: Before we talk about *Sleeping Beauty*, can you remember some of the artists with whom you worked, either on the shorts or on *The Mickey Mouse Club*? Did you work with Jack Hannah on the show?

DM: I worked with Jack Hannah. I worked with Les Clark. I worked with Ward Kimball.

DG: Any special memories of those artists? Any stories you can remember about them?

DM: They were all directors at that time. They were directing television and the shorts. Most of the animators didn't make the transition from shorts and television into feature animation. It was a very rough time. A very upsetting time to see so many of your friends being let go. I made new friends very quickly. Again, I think my strength in drafting was what kept me from getting laid off and got me onto feature animation.

DG: You worked with Les Clark. Not a lot of people talk about Les Clark. How was he as a director? What were his peculiarities or his style as a director as compared to working with Jack Hannah?

DM: Les Clark was a rather quiet man. He wasn't very outgoing. He wasn't an extrovert. Of course, Kimball was and Hannah was. Les Clark helped me with my career a lot. He was very helpful in showing me things and teaching me things in the brief time I worked with him. I think he, too, was let go, not too long after that big shake-up happened. Wolfgang Reitherman was my director for years and years and years. I worked with Ward Kimball on a couple of feature films, *Bedknobs and Broomsticks* was one. Jack Hannah was kind of the Donald Duck guy. I must have done about a dozen shorts with him. He was a very interesting man, a whole lot of fun to work with. I had good times working with all of them, actually.

DG: How was Jack Hannah as a personality? How was he as a person? As an artist?

DM: I never knew much about his art. I had never seen any of his artwork. He was a very nice man. We had a lot of fun together. We used to take nude sunbaths, on the roof of the studio, on our lunch hours and "chew the fat". [Laughs] The studio had what they called the "Penthouse Club" which you became a member of if you wanted to, and if they accepted you. They had their own barbershop, a masseuse, and steam baths. We used to lay around on the deck up there on the roof and catch some sun rays. He was a very interesting man. Very entertaining.

Those guys were all 20 to 25 years older than me. In fact, they always called me "the kid". If it was a miserable job that nobody wanted to do, they said, "Give it to the kid. He'll do it."

DG: What was the worst thing they gave you to do?

DM: I guess the hardest thing I ever did was I animated in *Winnie the Pooh and the Blustery Day*, which actually was my first screen credit. I animated what they called the heroes' party. It was a birthday table and every character in the movie was in that scene. Nobody wanted to do it because with so many characters it just multiplied your pencil mileage. You couldn't make much footage. You always had a kind of a footage commitment at the studio. They wanted you to animate so many feet a week. If you fell below that, then they would call you in and ask you why. Have a little conversation about it. I think the reason I was given that scene was that it had every single character in the picture in that one scene. Therefore, the film mileage was pretty slow coming out. Every character you do just doubles the work. There were probably eight or nine characters in that scene. So it was just a tremendous amount of work. It turned out okay. It is the one they used in their trailers and everything, and had stills made out of in the art department for a long time.

I was very excited about that movie. I animated an awful lot of Tigger. I was actually a junior animator working with Milt Kahl on that project. I think they consider him the number-one animator in the history of the studio. He liked the way I drew very much, too. He wanted me for a key assistant job. He let me animate when I had time, and could, on my own time. I was pretty excited, not only to work with him, but it was the first thing I got screen credit on. It won the Oscar that year. That was pretty exciting, too. I still have a picture of that in my studio here, at my animation desk, with the Oscar. You know, they are all a group effort. The Oscar wasn't given to me specifically; it was given to the film. Like all of our films, they are group efforts. Everybody contributes.

DG: So you worked as a key assistant to Milt Kahl?

DM: Yes, key assistant and junior animator.

DG: What are your own specific memories of Milt? Do you have any stories of him getting mad at the other artists?

DM: Milt was a very explosive personality. He was very combustible. He didn't fool around with people too much. I mean, if he thought you were a shit head, he told you right to your face you were a shit head. He never pulled any punches. He never got involved in politics. He was very straightforward. The reason I enjoyed working with him so much was he helped an awful lot. He treated me like his son. But again, I think he had the reputation of being the strongest, most powerful draftsman in the studio. He, like Walt Disney, loved the way I drew. It was a very good relationship. I had worked with Frank Thomas prior to that. When the position with Milt came open, he came and grabbed me very quickly and wanted me to work with him.

DG: How was it different to work for Frank Thomas compared to working with Milt Kahl? What was the difference in style between the two?

DM: Frank Thomas, again, was a superb animator. Frank Thomas was a rather quiet man, but he knew what he wanted. He knew how to do it and he did it beautifully. I worked with him on *Mary Poppins*, on the penguin sequence. He animated most of the penguin sequence. Again, there were multiple characters in the scene. He would rely heavily on me to animate some of the other characters. He would do the principal characters. I enjoyed working with Frank. He had a very analytical mind. That is why his animation was always so superb. He knew how to analyze movement down to the "nth" degree. It shows tremendously in his work.

DG: Do you remember some specific scenes you worked on for Milt? Maybe things he told you? Or things he really liked?

DM: Well, do you mean feature? Or featurette?

DG: Both.

DM: Both? I animated a lot of Tigger. Milt liked the way I animated. He was sort of famous for giving me two or three key drawings in a scene and letting me animate them. Then when I animated them and got a pencil test of them, I would show them to him. They usually had very minor corrections on them. When we were working on that movie, of course, his wife died. He came to me one morning and he said he had to take some time off work and get away. He gave me I don't know how many scenes of Tigger and Pooh to animate. He told me to animate them, but hold on to them until he came back and he would look at them, which I did. He didn't make any changes on any of them. It thrilled me beyond all belief. As I've said, he treated me like a son. He really, really did like me and I liked working with him. He pushed my career very hard.

I had always wanted to do story sketch. Do storyboards. Finally, I got an opportunity to do story sketches and I remember he was very upset that I was going to leave the animation department and do storyboards. He patted me on the back and said, "You know it is your career and your life. You should do what you want." So I went into story sketch. Then I went into story development and did that for a long time. Then they made me a director. Then they made me a director and a producer. I figured I did that for quite a while and decided that is about as far as you can go. So I took an early retirement. I had had a heart attack and open-heart surgery. I just figured I didn't want the stress and everything that went with the position.

DG: If we come back for a few minutes to the beginning of your career, during the time where you were working on shorts, who were your friends at the studio?

DM: Animators?

DG: Animators, directors, and artists.

DM: Oh, gosh, I was friends with everybody. Plus I was responsible for creating the volleyball court for lunchtime activities. I played tournament volleyball as a young man for years. Two-man volleyball, doubles on the beaches in southern California for years. I had always wanted a volleyball court so we could go out on our lunch hour and blow off steam. I was just friendly with everybody. I loved everybody. My God, I was so lucky to work with such incredible talents. Volus Jones, Jerry Hathcock, who I worked with when I first started there, Earl Combs, George Nicholas, George Goepper, and Hal King.

DG: Let's talk two minutes about Hal King because that's going to help Pete Docter with his project. Who was Hal King? What kind of a person was he?

DM: Hal King was again a sweetheart of a man. He worked in a different part of the building from me. I worked in the part of the building that was called the "ivory tower". [Dave laughs] All of the key animators, Walt's original animators, were in that one wing of the building. Hal King was about two wings away. He worked a lot with John Lounsbery, who was another man I loved very much.

He was probably 20 to 25 years older than me. I liked him because he smoked a pipe. It looked good in his face. He was actually quite a good-looking man. He had a wonderful, wonderful beach house down in Laguna Beach. Again, that is probably another reason we got along so well because I have always loved the beach. We still live very close to the water, not only this house but our other house. I try and spend time between both houses. Actually, I do two weeks here and two weeks there up north. Both houses are close to the ocean. I'm a water baby.

DG: I just published an interview with Volus Jones. Did you work with him at all?

DM: Not closely, no. Again, he was part of, I think, the Jack Hannah group. You had the three big directors, or four. You had Woolie Reitherman, who was the feature film director. Ward Kimball, who was the top director. Then you had the shorts and featurettes who were Les Clark and Jack

Hannah. I never worked closely with Volus at all. He was in another part of the building. He was just somebody I got a "kick" out of.

He was the other way, he was quite an extrovert. He was a lot of fun to always talk to. He was always kidding around, treating things pretty light.

Eric Cleworth was someone else I loved very much. I never worked closely with him, but he was just a super man. He of course died many years ago. He was an awfully, awfully wonderful person. Again, he always looked out for me because I was so much younger. They all kind of treated me like I was their son. I just felt so honored and privileged to be able to work in that group in what I guess you would have to call key talent that Walt Disney had. It was a once-in-a-lifetime experience. I never had any trouble going to work. I went to work early and I left late. I worked way over 40 hours a week. I just got into it where it was exciting to me.

I remember one time when I had first started there, I had only been with the company about six months. I was sitting on the bench at lunchtime in front of the Animation Building and Walt Disney walked over and sat down next to me. He put his arm around me and he said, "Well, what do you think, Dave, how are you going to like it here?" I looked at him and I said, "Walt, I haven't been here that long, but I have gone through every room in this building and I have never seen such incredible artwork in my life. It is just fantastic. I can't even imagine why you would want me to be part of your club." He patted my knee and he said, "You'll be okay, you'll be okay."

I was really impressed with all the artwork that I had seen, the backgrounds and the model sheets. Later on, because Milt was the top animator, I did do most of the model sheets on the features. A lot of them have my name on them, as a matter of fact. Milt being the key animator, he not only made model sheets for people, but the other animators would have to bring their scenes of animation to you and you would make drawings for them. That is one way where you kept good quality control. That was another one of my many duties for many, many years.

DG: When did you move into story or doing story sketches?

DM: My first story?

DG: Yes.

DM: That would be on *The Fox and the Hound*.

DG: No, sorry, I meant the first movie to which you contributed story drawings or story sketches.

DM: I think that was *The Fox and the Hound*. No, I take that back. My first story-sketch job was on *Robin Hood*.

[About Winnie the Pooh.]

Walt Disney was the one who wanted to do the Pooh stories. After he died, it was decided, probably by the producers, that there wasn't enough story content to make a feature film. That is when they decided to make a bunch of featurettes. Walt Disney was always very fond of the Pooh stories. The first one we made was my first animation credit, as an animator. It won an Oscar. I think Walt would have been thrilled.

DG: To move back to when you started working on *Sleeping Beauty*: what do you remember of the production of that movie?

DM: I was moved on that movie, as I've said before, at the time they were laying off and breaking up the departments on television animation and shorts. Those of us who survived, which weren't many, moved on to feature. Again, I think my drawing ability got me started on that. I went in and sat right down with the top animators as a key assistant. I had been a key assistant for many years before that. At that time it was decided that *Sleeping Beauty* had been in work too long. They wanted the film finished and out in the marketplace. It was supposed to be the Rolls-Royce and the Cadillac of all animated films that were made. I don't personally think it turned out that way. It was an incredibly expensive film. A very hard film to work on.

[About *One Hundred and One Dalmatians* and *The Aristocats*.]

DM: On *One Hundred and One Dalmatians*, the animators I worked with in that were Hal Ambro and Blaine Gibson, who were dynamite animators. We worked on Roger going through the park with the dog on the leash. I think that is where Pongo, the male dog, met Perdita, the female dog. I spent an awful lot of time on that. There was a great amount of footage in that sequence. I was very proud of that movie, even though I didn't get screen credit.

For *The Aristocats*, I animated the opening of the movie: the horse drawing the cart across the bridge. That was the first time I had ever animated a four-legged animal. The legs were mostly covered up anyway by the bridge. I was proud when that movie opened and the horse-drawn carriage went across the bridge. I had done that!

DG: Do you remember any specific sequences on which you worked on *Sleeping Beauty*?

DM: On *Sleeping Beauty*, actually, I didn't do animation. I was a key assistant.

DG: What was the most difficult thing you had to do on *One Hundred and One Dalmatians*? Do you remember any specific stories on the production of that movie?

DM: When I worked with Milt Kahl on that movie, I was responsible for putting spots on the dog.

DG: For putting what?

DM: For putting the black spots on the white dog. That was a terrifying job. I knew if one of those spots ever jumped or jittered or jerked, there would be hell to pay. That was a very difficult job, along with my other duties. That was another thing Milt Kahl demanded from me. He did not like the special-effects department. I animated most of his special effects for years.

DG: Really, I had no idea. That is very interesting. Why did he dislike the special-effects department?

DM: I can give you a direct quote of his. He said, "If you ask for a cup of water, they give you a bucket."

DG: You did some of Kaa the snake in *Jungle Book*.

DM: Yes, and also Shere Khan. Again, I was responsible for putting the stripes on the tiger.

DG: *Robin Hood* is the movie on which you moved to story, isn't it?

DM: Yes, it is.

DG: What were your first assignments in story? Do you remember some of your contributions on *Robin Hood*?

DM: On *Robin Hood*, there were a number of things I enjoyed. I did Prince John when he was dictating a phony love letter to Maid Marian. The snake was the scribe writing it down. He was playing a harpsichord and singing. The snake was writing down what Prince John was saying. I did work on that.

DG: Do you remember some sequences in *Robin Hood*, some story ideas that you had and liked very much, but in the end were discarded?

DM: I actually storyboarded an entire sequence in that movie that was thrown out.

DG: What was it?

DM: It was this storyboard where Prince John was playing on his harpsichord dictating his phony love letter for Sir Hiss to write down. It was a rather lengthy sequence. The sequence was well received, but it was decided that the picture was running long. I think they did a cutaway to Prince John.

Another sequence I did in there that was wonderful was part of that, too, but there was a carrier pigeon in there. That is when the snake took Prince John's letter to the post office to mail it. There was a carrier pigeon who was the mailman behind the counter. The way he used to deliver the mail is, he had a catapulted chair that he would sit on. He would pull a trigger and shoot himself through the air. They just cut from Prince John to the snake going down the hall and sticking the note under Maid Marian's door. I have that whole sequence framed and up in my house up north.

Every time I would start a new project, I would put all the old sketches in cardboard boxes and tie them up. I would call the morgue to come and pick them up and store them. I remember on a couple of occasions the morgue would just say, "Dave, we have so much crap down here, can't you do something with that stuff?" I said, "Sure." So I ended up with a pretty good handful of original artwork. That is stuff that I had done. Stuff I had framed and put in my homes. I am very proud of it and happy to have it.

DG: I can imagine that. Did you work on projects that didn't get released, like *Musicana*? Or *Catfish Bend*?

DM: *Catfish Bend* was one I worked on that was never put into work. Since you brought that up, one of the very last things I did for Disney was in 1985, when they made me an executive writer. I wrote the first treatment on *Beauty and the Beast*, the very first treatment. By now there was all-new management at the company. I submitted the script for *Beauty and the Beast* and they called me into the office. They said they liked it very much, but they didn't want to do any more classic fairy tales. They wanted to do films that were "right now", like *Oliver & Company*. They thanked me very much and thought my treatment was excellent. I retired a few years later. They just shelved the script. I have the original script. I had wanted to direct that movie, too. I thought that would be my "swan song". I ended taking an early retirement.

DG: Was the final version very different from what you had suggested at the time?

DM: Yes, there were a lot of parts of it that were completely different from what I had envisioned. Probably for the better. Mine was based on the classic French film.

DG: What were some of the ideas that you had suggested that you really liked that didn't appear in the movie as it is today?

DM: I liked my opening. I had a storm. All these people on horseback were galloping down to the wharf to observe the ship at sea in trouble trying to make port. It was having a lot of trouble getting to port. But it did. To me, it was what they always called, in the movies, "the hook", something that grabs you right off. I always felt that starting the movie with this action scene, of this ship trying to get into port, would be a very good hook to get you into that movie.

DG: What about the project *Catfish Bend*, did you work a lot with Ken Anderson on that one?

DM: Ken Anderson and I worked together on that. When I went into story, again, they sat me down with one of their top men. Ken Anderson and I had adjoining rooms the whole time I was on story. He and I worked very closely together for years. Ken taught me an awful lot. I loved working with him. That experience to me just made my career in story because he was so goddamned good at it. I used to listen to every single word he said. At night, when he would go home, I would go next door to his office and look at the drawings. I would try to figure out why in the world they were so great and why couldn't I do things like that. He was just a marvelous, marvelous story man.

DG: What were the main lessons that you got from him?

DM: He always told me to be sure that my story sketches were easy to read and they weren't confusing to look at. You should be able to understand the thing at a glance. He also taught me the value of using magic markers, colored pencils, and things for mood and atmosphere. I think those two things were the main two things he taught me. I got to the point, actually, where we had worked together so long that it became very difficult to tell his work from my work. I remember one of my dearest friends, in layout, Don Griffith. He was the head of the layout department. We became lifelong friends. Don came to me one time and he took all of the storyboards out of my office and down to the director's office to look at. Don told me one day, "You know, they were looking at those story sketches down in Woolie's office." Woolie said, "You know that Ken is getting better and better and better." Don said, "Those aren't Ken's drawings. Those are Dave's." He said, "You should go down and look in his office." And he did. He came down. He also came down with Ron Miller, who was the CEO of the company at that time. I think it was not even a week later I received the biggest raise I'd ever gotten in my life. It was just incredible. Don Griffith was a very dear friend, a superb artist. I just loved his work. We got along famously because we both drove Corvettes. [Laughs] Anybody who drove a Corvette, in those days, was a friend of mine automatically.

DG: I heard that the story of *The Rescuers*, the first one, evolved quite a bit from what it was originally to what it ended up being in the end. That it was a story about communists or spies or something like that. Do you remember that first version of the story?

DM: No, I don't. I may not have even been on the project at that time.

DG: Same question on *The Rescuers* as on *Robin Hood*. Were there ideas that you contributed that you liked and were cut in the end?

DM: Oh, yes, there were two scenes in there that I contributed to very much, story-wise, that I liked. I did probably most of the story work on

Medusa and her swamp mobile and her getting around in that thing. I did the story work on Medusa coming down the gangplank of the ship with the two crocodiles, Nero and Brutus. When the little girl took off, she wanted the crocodiles to get her and bring her back. The other thing I liked very much was when Bernard and Bianca were on Orville's back. They had gone down to the swamps in Florida. It was a back view. Bernard put his arm around Bianca and his finger is walking along the back of the seat. The other thing I worked so hard on is when I did the whole sequence in story sketch when Medusa put the girl down the well into the black hole to find the Devil's Eye, which was the big diamond that was hidden down there. It was a scary place for a small child. I thought the thing that would make it even more scary would be to stick the diamond in a human skull down there. We would put the diamond in the eye socket. So I developed that whole thing. That's when the thing glittered and she hollered up, "Medusa I found it." Medusa said, "Bring it up. Bring it up." I developed that whole sequence in story.

DG: Are there things that you really liked and didn't make it to the screen?

DM: One of my personal experiences was with *Beauty and the Beast*, which didn't make it at that time. It made it later, of course.

DG: I think at the time you worked on story, there was a young artist called Pete Young.

DM: Pete Young was somebody I loved very much. He was a good deal younger than me and he worked in the art department when he started with the company. He wanted to do story sketch. I mentioned to people that I thought he should have a chance. When Pete got his chance to come into story, they put him up with me for a while, to work with me in the same room. We worked together for quite a few months. Then they moved him to another part of the building. Somewhere along the way, they threw us all out of the Animation Building anyway and put us in a warehouse in Glendale. Jeffrey Katzenberg was then head of the movie department. Michael Eisner was the CEO. Again, any number of people left the studio because they saw they weren't being treated properly, stuck in a warehouse over in Glendale. Pete died very young. He did wonderful sketches.

DG: What was he like? What was his artistic style? What ideas did he contribute? Can you remember?

DM: He was very quiet, very soft-spoken and very emotional about his work. I know he took criticism very hard. I used to work with him on that. To learn to get some calluses. In story you are always going to get some lumps. It wasn't anything personal. It was just different people having different ideas. That was just the nature of the territory. He died after we had all been moved over to the warehouse in Glendale. Literally across the street from what used to be the Tokyo Disneyland building. Which is actually when they made me a producer/director. They put me over to WED on special assignment. I directed the animation for all the parks worldwide. I spent almost five years doing that.

DG: Oh, really? I didn't realize that. What were your most interesting assignments? The assignments you liked best?

DM: I enjoyed working on all of them. They all had different problems. Tokyo Disneyland was a wonderful experience. I did all the animation for that park. I also did a show called *Meet the World* which I produced and directed. It was animation and live action combined. That was the theater in the round. The whole audience rotated. Not the screen, but the audience physically rotated from screen to screen in the theater. That was a history of Japan. I have some of those paintings from that movie, too. I have framed them. It was like a thousand years of Japanese history in twenty minutes.

DG: Yes, that must have been quite a challenge.

DM: It was great fun in Burbank. The Japanese would send a group over every few weeks to look at everything and discuss it. They would have me make any changes they wanted. Then when the show was ready and I put it all together, it was done on a soundstage at the Burbank studio and accepted there. Then the company sent me to Tokyo to help put it in place. It was all done on 70mm film. Some of those 70mm screens were done to match a point. The screen was like 180 degrees. It was a tremendous undertaking. That was fun, too, because when I was producing and directing, the animators that were working with me on that spoke no Japanese. So I invented a way, when I made the exposure sheets out, to make them out in English like I normally do. Then I can write next to it the Japanese words. So my animators animated what was being said, but they lip-synced to the Japanese word.

DG: Was it animated by American animators?

DM: Oh, yes, I had a studio within a studio at the Disney Studio in Burbank. I had my own unit for almost five years, where we did Tokyo Disney and EPCOT and the World Showcase, also the Disneyland park in Anaheim.

DG: Did the Japanese team that came to see the project ask for a lot of changes?

DM: No, not too often. Not too many.

DG: Do you remember specific stories of working with them? Or fun things that might have happened?

DM: There were a number of background paintings I needed for that. I had to hire an illustrator. They were all based on famous Japanese shoji screens. In museums, like in the Louvre in Paris, you are not allowed to photograph them because of the flash-bulb damage they are afraid of. I had to research everything very carefully. I hired a couple of people from UCLA to work with me part-time, when they could. My funny joke on that is the Japanese would come over and say, "No, no, no, Mr. Michener, more blue, more blue. No, no, no, Mr. Michener, more red." They had to be authentic reproductions of very famous Japanese screens. I have any number of those in my movie collection. I was very grateful to have those. Those were the types of things nobody wanted anyway when you were done with a project. So, I kept them.

DG: Pete Docter is writing an article right now about John Sibley.

DM: I worked with John when I was in shorts and television. John worked on shorts. He was Jack Hannah's number-one animator. In my television and shorts days, I worked with Sibley off and on. He was a character also. He was so darn good at actions and broad movement. That showed in everything that he did.

DG: How did you meet Pete Docter?

DM: Pete Docter was a student of mine at CalArts. When I retired early, Roy Edward Disney, who had always been a good friend of mine, was very upset about that. He thought I should stick around there and teach the young people at the studio. Not through him, but through other people in the studio I was asked to go out to California Institute of the Arts and teach the animation classes. California Institute of the Arts was a Disney-endowed school. A lot of the artists from Disney taught out there, off and on, on a freelance basis. Occasionally when someone retired, they would go out there and work full time. That is what they asked me to do. They asked me to come out since I was going to retire early. They asked me if I would go to CalArts and teach the young people, which I did for a number of years. It was in 1994, or 1996, I can't remember. I received a phone call, and they asked me if I would come out and run the department out there. Peter Docter was a student of mine at CalArts when I was teaching there. A wonderful one at that, a very talented man. I was tremendously amused with him. He was just a super person, too. I have had a fortunate career in the movie business. I am very lucky. There are very few people that I disliked or couldn't get along with. I did very well.

DG: You did work on *The Great Mouse Detective* and *Oliver & Company* from the screen credits?

DM: Yes, I did. On *Oliver & Company*, I was in development and story.

DG: Very early on.

DM: Yes, right from the start. That movie was one that management wanted to make. It was a right-now kind of a movie. It wasn't a fairy tale. I worked in development and did some writing for it. I didn't actually work that long on it. The people who worked on that were people that were from my EPCOT unit when I had my own producing and directing unit for the parks. George Scribner, who directed that movie, was actually someone that I had hired to work for me on the EPCOT unit. There were a half a dozen fellows that were that way. I had a very good unit. Everybody loved that unit. Everybody loved working on it. In fact, I just got a phone call the other day from a friend that I haven't seen for years who worked on it. He said, "You know, Dave, that is the most fun I had there." That is quite a compliment.

DG: Do you mean the EPCOT unit?

DM: Yes.

DG: What were you doing on that project?

DM: I was the producer and director. I had my own animation unit. I did all the animation for all of the parks.

DG: In EPCOT specifically, can you remember the best projects you worked on or the ones liked best?

DM: One that I worked on that isn't there anymore is the Kodak pavilion. It was a ride-through and there was a purple dragon that I created for that ride. It was supposed to intimidate the audience when they drove through.

DG: It was called Figment.

DM: Figment, a figment of your imagination.

DG: Did you work with Tony Baxter on the creation of that ride?

DM: Tony Baxter and I did work together. In fact, I met him not too long ago. I am still a member of the Motion Picture Academy. I saw him at the academy theater one night. He was the one who told me the Figment character was no longer there. I used to get a belly laugh out of that because the animation I did for the parks ran for years. I said, "Well, guess what? My animation has the longest runs of any animation in the world." [Laughs]

That was a joke.

DG: You co-directed *The Great Mouse Detective*.

DM: Yes.

DG: How did that story evolve? Were there big changes made?

DM: Not really. The working title was *Basil of Baker Street*. When the movie was almost done they renamed it *The Great Mouse Detective* because they thought *Basil of Baker Street* didn't have the interest that it should have. It was called *Basil of Baker Street* because Basil Rathbone in live action played that part[1] for years. I don't think there were big changes. I thought that one went through rather smoothly.

DG: Were there things that you liked that didn't make it to the final version?

DM: No, like I say, I was one of the directors on that. I thought it went through pretty much the way we had laid it out. There were four of us directing on that.

DG: Yes, there were John Musker, Ron Clements, Burny Mattinson, and you. How did you split the work among all of you?

DM: Usually, we would just take a sequence. A lot of times we would get together and talk to each other and say, "Well, I would really like to do this particular sequence." That happens. If somebody is low on work, and the sequence is ready, it goes to that director. Usually, you sit down and talk about it and break it up the way you want to do the things you want to do. You come to an agreement on how it is to get done. It is never a problem. It is just that certain people want to do certain sequences.

DG: Did any of you have any specialties like funny sequences? Or emotional sequences or something like that?

DM: I preferred doing personality stuff between characters. Emotional stuff. I was probably less interested in chase sequences. I never got all that excited about chase sequences.

DG: Did any of the other directors like doing chase sequences or action sequences?

DM: With Ron Clements and John Musker, I don't think it made much difference. I think they enjoyed doing any of it. I did, too. It is not that I would ever turn down a chase sequence or wouldn't do it. I had done them; it just wasn't my favorite thing to do.

DG: Did you sponsor any artists so they could enter the studio? Did you identify artists that you thought were so outstanding that they had to join Disney?

DM: No, I never got involved in that with people that came to the studio. I was on the review board at Disney for many years. New talent was the part of the review board to go over and hire or not hire. There were people I thought the studio should have gone out of their way to keep and not let them get away from them.

---

[1] The part of Sherlock Holmes.

DG: Like who? Who are the artists that most impressed you during those years?

DM: Tim Burton was one that came as a very young man. He did wonderful, wonderful things. He didn't stay very long. I don't think the studio gave him much of a break. John Lasseter, who is now the head of Disney Animation. He was somebody I always admired and I hoped the studio would hang on to and not let get away from them. Those were two of the people, no question about it in my mind. I had a tremendous amount of respect for their abilities.

DG: I have just a few more questions for you. The first one, coming back to your animation years, did you have any specific characters that you particularly enjoyed animating? Or specific types of characters?

DM: You always have favorites. In our first discussion, I said my first animation credit was on *Winnie the Pooh and the Blustery Day*. It won an Oscar that year. I was part of a team on that. I loved animating Tigger and I did a lot of animation on Pooh Bear. I guess those were my two favorites. I had a lot of fun with those.

DG: Were there some characters that were particularly challenging or that you really didn't like to draw, for some specific reason?

DM: No, I don't think so. I always got my head into it pretty good. There weren't characters I disliked drawing at all, I don't think. There were characters I thought were an awful lot of work. I just didn't mind drawing them; they were just very difficult for me to do.

DG: Like which ones, for example?

DM: Madame Bonfamille in the *Aristocats*. Oh, I guess Edgar the butler. He was very difficult. But, again, Milt Kahl set the standard on that. He was just one incredible draftsman. Probably the greatest draftsman the studio ever had. If he wasn't, he was certainly right up there with them. Like Marc Davis and a couple other people. Milt always set the standard for character design and everything.

DG: Yes, Milt Kahl, being famous for always getting the toughest characters to animate and you being his key assistant, you probably handled quite a few challenges.

DM: Milt always laughed because he said, "They always give me the human figures to do because they are so damn hard to do." He set the standard. He treated me, as I've said before, like a son. If he had scenes that had two or three characters in them, he would do the principal character and pose the animation in the ones that were less important in the scene. He would let me animate those. It was an experience of a lifetime for me. When he asked me to work for him one day, I just couldn't even believe it. It was quite an experience.

DG: How did that happen? Did he just come into your office and come right to your animation desk and ask you if you wanted to work with him?

DM: I was sitting right across the hall from him, and at that point in time I was one of Frank Thomas' assistants. We were coming to the end of a project. I had my room filled with drawings of my children. I was making pen-and-ink drawings of my children and putting those up in my room. He walked into my office one day and looked at the drawings I had made of my children, on the wall. He asked me, "You know, I am going to have to have an assistant. Would you be interested in working with me?" My teeth almost hit the floor. I said, "You're kidding." He said, "No, I'm not kidding." So I said, "God almighty, I will travel across the hall and work with you. What an honor."

DG: Was it as easy as that? What did Frank Thomas say at the time? Did Frank Thomas not fight to keep you?

DM: He had his own personal assistant for many years. Usually, at the end of a picture when the workload became so heavy and production deadlines and everything were looming on the horizon, these animators would pick up another assistant animator to help them or another two assistant animators to help them. You worked in basically what we called a unit. I wasn't about to take Frank's… His key assistants had worked with him for a great number of years. I don't think that was ever a problem at all.

DG: Who was Frank's key assistant at the time?

DM: Dale Oliver. Dale and I were very good friends for years and years and years. He was a very quite soft-spoken, wonderful person.

I think I mentioned before, at one time or the other, I had worked with just about all of the Nine Old Men. But to sit down and work with Milt Kahl on a one-to-one basis, that was incredible. We worked together and we made a very good team for a great number of years. He is the one who made me a junior animator and gave me animation. He looked after me. It was a very responsible position, because him, being the key animator, made me the key assistant. It was a thrill of a lifetime for me.

DG: Are there some artists at Disney that you particularly admired? Whose art or style or work you particularly admired?

DM: Oh, sure, lots of them. All kinds of them. Don Griffith was the head of the layout department there for numerous years. He became a very dear, close friend of mine. He was actually kind of a mentor of mine. We socialized together quite a bit. He was just a superior artist and a wonderful friend. I greatly admired his layout work. He was the key man, the key layout man on everything that went through there, feature-wise. Milt, of course, I admired tremendously. I admired all of those guys: Frank Thomas, Ollie Johnston, Eric Larson, Marc Davis… I was always flabbergasted that I was even associated with those people.

DG: When did you work with Marc Davis?

DM: I think he was the very first one of those "big shot" animators I ever worked with. Marc Davis was also teaching school at Chouinard's when I was a student there. I didn't have him for a teacher, but he was there. So I knew of him. I knew that Marc liked my work, too. Oh, golly, I can't remember on what movie I worked with him. It could have been *One Hundred and One Dalmatians*, but I'm not sure.

DG: What was specific about Marc's style that influenced you? What were the things that you greatly admired in Marc Davis' work?

DM: Marc was a "right-from-the-shoulder" draftsman. It never seemed like work to him or to me. I never thought his stuff looked like it was work. It looked like it came out of him easily. Marc was a very friendly, respectful person. I know Marc liked the way I drew very much, too. He told me so. Marc got along beautifully with everyone.

DG: Were there some people in the story department that you would consider not as creative as others? People that were outstanding story artists?

DM: Well, I had my favorites. Ken Anderson, of course, who I worked with closely for a number of years. He was considered the top man in story, at that point in time. Vance Gerry was another story man there, who actually was at Chouinard's when I was there. He was older than me. He left before I did. Vance was one of their very top storymen.

DG: Can you tell me a little bit more about Vance Gerry? What kind of a person he was?

DM: Vance had a very dry sense of humor. Going back to our art-school days, I guess he was in the service in WWII. He was quite a bit older than me. He was a very quiet person. He was very intense. I loved Vance like a brother. I got a big belly laugh out of him every time I talked with him because of the dry sense of humor of his. He would just come off the wall with these things and he would just "crack" me up.

DG: Do you remember some of the ideas he contributed? Or some anecdotes about him?

DM: Vance Gerry, when I was starting in story, was, I think, Woolie's top storyboard artist. Ken Anderson was the top story-development man. Ken also did storyboards. Right behind Ken Anderson, Vance Gerry was the next top story man. Again, I was always in very good company and learned an awful lot from everybody. When Vance was in story, I was an animator. I came into story quite late, actually. I moved through the system very rapidly.

DG: Did you work with Julius Svendsen?

DM: I did. Julius Svendsen was another animator I worked with. He and Art Stevens, I think, were roommates. I had left the studio for a couple months. When I came back they put me with Julius Svendsen as his assistant. Julius Svendsen was a marvelous draftsman, too. Another big man. A very big man, but very quiet, very pleasant, and a good sense of humor. I did a lot of Ludwig Von Drake. I worked with him probably for a couple of years directly, as his assistant.

DG: In the '50s? Or '60s?

DM: That would have been, I think, probably the '60s. Julius had a very tragic death.

DG: What happened to him?

DM: I think he took vacation with his sons and had a boating accident. That was very hard for me to take because he was somebody that liked me very much, too.

DG: Much later in your career you worked with a newcomer named Steve Hulett.

DM: Yes, Steve, I think I mentioned before, was Ralph Hulett's son. Ralph Hulett was one of the very top background painters. Steve Hulett came on board as a writer. Steve and I worked together for a long time. Steve was always a very good friend. Then I think he just happened to get a very good job working for the union. He still works for the union.

DG: Did he have a particular style? Do you remember some things that happened with him?

DM: I remember he had been published in an edition of the *Los Angeles Times* newspaper. I can't remember for what, but I do remember it was quite a prestigious honor.

DG: Who were the story artists that you interacted with most. Vance Gerry? Burny Mattinson?

DM: I think probably Ken Anderson. As I mentioned before, Burny Mattinson came into story later than I did. He and I were roommates. We interacted because we shared the same room for quite awhile. Vance and I never worked together in story, but we were always good friends. Burny and I did work together.

DG: Who was the most fun to work with? Who sparked the biggest number of ideas for you?

DM: Ken Anderson was a big help in moving my career along. I knew he was considered the top man in story development. I listened very carefully to what he told me. I studied his work very closely. Probably on a one-to-one basis I was closer to him than anybody I had worked with in story before.

Burny, of course, I had worked with for years. He came out of animation also. While I was still in story, he became a director and went on from there. Then we came back and worked together on *The Great Mouse Detective*. I think he was producer/director on that, if I'm not mistaken. He would always explain why he wanted something changed to me. It always made perfect sense. It was just the way he wanted it and the way he looked at it. It was the way he thought it should be. My job was to give him what he wanted. I never disagreed with him. I could always see his point of view.

DG: Do you think there were some really specific things he was looking for in a movie? Could you define those?

DM: Well, I guess entertainment is the number-one word. He was always looking for "how do you get the most entertainment out of this?" But he was also very pragmatic. He wanted it to make sense, and not be just frivolous. I enjoyed working with Woolie.

DG: I think one of the last projects in animation you worked on in story was *Oliver & Company*. Did you actually like working on *Oliver & Company*?

DM: No.

DG: I am not completely surprised. Okay, why not?

DM: It was a movie I felt just wasn't going anywhere. I had been used to working on classic fairy tales and things like that. *Oliver & Company* was not. *Oliver & Company* was the choice of top management. I think I mentioned before they wanted to make movies that were kind of "right now". They didn't want to get involved in classic fairy tales that much anymore. They changed their mind very quickly. *Oliver & Company* is not a memorable movie. I can't even remember working on it that much. It just wasn't that interesting a film to me.

DG: Yes, I would have to agree with that. That was the time when management changed, when Eisner and Frank Wells came on board.

DM: Yes.

DG: What was the mood in the story department when that happened? Was it joy? Was it despair? How would you define it?

DM: I think it probably took awhile for anything to sink in on that because there wasn't that much relationship between management and animation. I first became concerned for animation when they actually threw us all out of the Animation Building in Burbank. They put us all in a warehouse in Glendale. They wanted the office space. To me that was kind of the beginning of the end. I still have pictures of that at home where we all had our pictures taken in front of the Animation Building when we were being moved. We all in animation thought this is the end. The roof caved in.

I started working long, long hours for the studio. When I left the studio in 1987, a lot of people wanted me to go to CalArts and teach animation, which I did. I found that experience invaluable. All my years of teaching for the city school system here in Los Angeles, years earlier, along with being a professional artist for Walt Disney, helped me immensely at CalArts. Of course, that is where I met Pete Docter and a lot of other wonderful people. That really helped me along, at CalArts, and my experience as a teacher.

DG: Why did you stop teaching at CalArts?

DM: I had taught there for quite awhile. I took a part-time job at Hanna-Barbera in animation. Bill Hanna had heard that I had left Disney, I guess, that is the only thing I can figure. Anyway, I went and talked to him one day and he wanted me to come and work. I told him I couldn't. I was teaching school. I could come after school and weekends, which I did. Then in the summer time, I worked full time for Hanna-Barbera when school was out. Then when school started again, he said, "Well, me and Joe are going to retire." They had had tremendous success in television, but they hadn't really done a super feature film in animation. They wanted me to stay on and direct that. I said, "I can't. I have got to go back and teach." They offered me a salary that was pretty nice. So I gave up the CalArts job after three or four years.

I directed the retirement show, *Jetsons: The Movie*. I was the supervising animation director on that. Then they sold the company to Ted Turner, I think it was. I was the supervising director on *Once Upon a Forest*. Then I decided enough is enough. It is time to smell the flowers. So I put in a couple of years with Hanna-Barbera. I had a lot of fun there. Bill Hanna, I worked with directly, and he was just a marvelous gentlemen. We got along very well. He was not very happy when I was leaving.

DG: My last two questions relate to your career. When you started working for the parks, do you remember, aside from the Meet the World project, other specific projects you worked on?

DM: Meet the World came later. I actually started on the World Showcase in EPCOT Center. Then I did the character animation for the General Motors pavilion. I did the character for the Kodak pavilion. Those stick out in my mind. I worked with Tony Baxter on those. I believe he was the art director on that stuff.

DG: Yes, on the Kodak pavilion that is for sure.

DM: At that point in time I was considered producer/director. The four-and-a-half years I spent working for Marty Sklar and WED Enterprises, which is now Disney Imagineering, I was a producer and director.

DG: Who were the most talented artists that you had in your team at the time?

DM: Well, there was Joe Ranft, who died recently. He worked for Pixar.

DG: He was working for you at the time?

DM: Yes, I hired him.

DG: Wow!

DM: I shouldn't say I hired him. I wanted him hired. He was assigned to me. Mike Giaimo was assigned to me, too. He was a story guy. Ed Ghertner, a very young man, was assigned to me for layout. Greg Shepard was assigned to me as an assistant director.

DG: You had an amazing team.

DM: There was Jim Mitchell. Actually George Scribner was an animator for me in my unit. He was the one who became the director in *Oliver & Company*. Chuck Harvey was another animator who worked for me. I never did know what happened to him. He just wandered away one day.

DG: Really?

DM: I never knew why. That was a wonderful unit I had, just a wonderful unit. I still get phone calls from a couple of people who worked with me back in those days. They say, "You know, Dave, it was the best time I had in that company." I was thinking after I talked with you, not only did I have very young people, but I had had people who had been around there for years. They were just never given a chance and I gave them chances. You never saw grins on people's faces so broad in your life. I had one fellow come to me who worked in the effects department. He said he was looking at something on the movie I was working on and he thought, "Gee! That looks like it would be fun to do." I said, "Well, take it and do it!" He gave me this real funny look and he said, "Are you serious?" I said, "Of course, I'm serious." So he left, and about two hours later he came walking back and said, "I just want to let you know that I've worked for this company for over

20 years and nobody has ever given me a chance. You are the first person. I will never let you down." It just brought tears to my eyes. I started to cry.

DG: What was the project?

DM: I don't remember the specific project. I used to sit on what they called the review board, which is where the key artists in the studio would look at new artists' work that were applying for jobs. That is where I gained some of my employees, people I worked with in the EPCOT unit. I had that unit almost $4^{1/2}$ years. I was looking at a copy of the memo that Marty Sklar sent me when we finished everything. It is the most incredible thing I'd ever read in my life. I framed it and put it in my house. It was just a glowing memo. So I finished the EPCOT thing after almost five years. The EPCOT unit was then disbanded and everybody was reassigned to other things.

DG: Do you have specific memories of the World Showcase project or the General Motors project? Any things that you remember vividly?

DM: I did animation as the audience rode through in these cars. There were these huge Grecian vases. I never saw the thing completed, actually. I had the hieroglyphics on the vases that were animated. As the audience rode through, these two big vases were animated as you approached. That was sort of interesting. They were kind of challenging things.

In Tokyo Disneyland, in *Meet the World*, a show I produced and directed, it was the first time I had ever worked with 70mm film on giant screens. There were two 70mm projectors together, almost a 180-degree view. It was like the old Disney theater in the round. The whole audience rotated. It was a four-act thing. It was a combination of live action and animation. That was sort of challenging. I had never worked with 70mm film. That was an experience.

DG: What is the big difference when you work with 70mm film? What creates the challenge?

DM: The size of the film. You know we did everything in 35mm film; 70mm film was much bigger than CinemaScope. It was much bigger than that. It was the biggest film that I had ever seen in my life.

DG: Did you travel to Japan for the project?

DM: When I was all done. Everything I did was moved out to a sound stage on the Disney lot, and it was run out there for everybody involved to make sure it was good and correct and was working the way it should work. Then when all the film was done for Tokyo Disneyland, they sent me to Tokyo with a group to just make sure the stuff was being projected there the way it was conceived back in Burbank and there weren't any problems with it. I did go to Tokyo for a couple of weeks.

DG: My last question will be, what is your best memory of your whole career at Disney?

DM: I would have to say working with Milt Kahl. He really pushed my career. I couldn't get anybody better to do it than him. It seemed like he was always just very understanding and on my side. We hardly disagreed on anything. On occasion we would. I had an immense amount of respect for him because of his position and reputation. I was probably more careful with him because of his reputation. Milt had a very explosive personality which anybody in that studio would tell you about. I always admired people who could draw well. Milt was the premier draftsman in animation, just like Ken Anderson was the premier story guy and story-development guy. I studied their drawings and tried and learned as much as I could. I would stay after work sometimes and Xerox stuff and try and redraw it myself. I would try to figure out why these people were as great as everybody said they were. They were role models for me. They were people I looked up to and had an immense amount of respect for.

© 2007 Didier Ghez

In Memory of Vance Gerry

As written by John Musker in 2005.

I've known Vance for over 25 years. Wse first worked together on *The Black Cauldron*. I can still see Vance with his saddle shoes and a sweater casually draped over his shoulders. His limpid eyes were constantly bemused at the absurdities that swirled around the story department, and his throaty laugh filled the room along with his amazing drawings. He reminded me of William Windom, who played James Thurber on the sitcom, *My World and Welcome to It*. Windom played Thurber with wry and offhand charm, qualities that typified Vance as well.

Make no mistake, though. Despite Vance's quiet and genial exterior, he was a man of powerful artistic convictions, and a masterful draftsman and designer of tremendous elegance and charm. If you're unfamiliar with his work, check out his concept art for *The Sword in the Stone* in *Treasures of Disney Animation Art*. He did a beautiful color sketch of a vine-entwined sword embedded in an anvil, which dwarfs a tiny figure of a boy in the background. Brilliantly staged, it is moody, dramatic, full of big, bold values and graphic power. Take a look also at Frank and Ollie's *Illusion of Life* book, where they reproduce wonderful pen-and-ink studies for *The Rescuers* of Penny and Rufus in the orphanage, full of warmth and drama. Or, if you work at Walt Disney Feature Animation, check out the third floor, where boards are filled with splendid drawings for projects that may never see the light of day, but are blessed with the distinctive Vance touch.

Through the years, I've also marveled at another demonstration of his art not as many are familiar with: His stunning caricatures. I remember a particularly brilliant one he did of John Lounsbery that Henry Selick was in awe of: "It's like… a Picasso!"

In the early '80s, I was developing an early version of *Basil of Baker Street* (before it received its new and "improved" title of *Great Mouse Detective*). It ran afoul of Ron Miller, its producer, who found it strange and odd. It was Vance who revived the movie with his drawings and story ideas (as did Burny Mattinson also). Vance's sketches radiated appeal and charm. Like everything Vance did, the effortlessness of the drawings was stunning. I can still hear Vance "pitching" his writing and drawing of Basil's demonstration of his deductive powers to Dawson: "You've sewn your torn cuff together with the Lambert stitch, which of course only a surgeon uses." I don't remember if the Lambert stitch was Vance's invention or if he got it from Doyle, but to this day I think of Vance when I hear it. The drawing of the Lambert stitch was not only stylishly drawn, but beautifully calligraphed in that distinctive Vance script.

Vance was a mentor to many young, developing, brilliant story artists like Pete Young, Ed Gombert, and Joe Ranft. He was a mentor, too (although that word is too high falutin' for Vance, whose picture appears in the dictionary next to "self-effacing"), to some novice directors like Ron Clements and myself. Even as recently as a few weeks ago, his words of encouragement to me meant a great deal, and were a warm fire on a cold night.

Vance was a conduit to the Walt Disney Studio's past for us young'uns. It was he who, when we were developing *Little Mermaid*, brought to our attention the legendary illustrator Kay Nielsen and the drawings he did for a proposed animated version of Andersen's fairy tale that were gathering dust in the archives. Without Vance, we would never have known those fantastic drawings existed, drawings which helped inspire the handling of the storm sequence among other things.

"Inspiring" is a word that applies to Vance as well. He was a gentleman and a gentle man. He was centered. He had passionate interests outside the confines of the studio walls. He was an oasis of calm and professionalism in a stormy sea of story changes and strong personalities. His brilliance as a draftsman, designer, stager, and colorist was exceeded only by his own modesty. In a world (and a studio) where tooting your own horn was not uncommon, Vance took the road less traveled. He didn't campaign. His horn remained "tootless". What he did was draw and paint prolifically, and he spoke volumes with those countless gems.

Joe Ranft related the other day that years ago on *Oliver & Company*, Vance, with whom he was sharing a room, told him about a dream he had the night before. In it, Vance was in a large story room, stacked floor to ceiling with a vast number of storyboards crammed with sketches. And every single drawing, Vance wryly noted, needed, "just a little change". Vance would have made those changes without complaint, done them all with his usual offhand wit, charm, and skill.

I'll miss you, Vance. You're a great talent and an even greater man.

John Musker
Director, Walt Disney Feature Animation

© 2007 John Musker

Vance Gerry (1929–2005)

Interviewed by Charles Solomon in October 1993.

Born in Pasadena, California, in 1929, Gerry studied at the Chouinard Art Institute before joining Disney on May 16, 1955. He began his career as an assistant in-betweener. Moving on to layout artist, he contributed to such Disney television shows as *The Goofy Success Story*, *Goofy's Cavalcade of Sports*, and *How to Relax*, and such featurettes as *The Truth about Mother Goose* and *Donald in Mathmagic Land*. As a layout artist, he also worked on the features *One Hundred and One Dalmatians* and *The Sword in the Stone*.

Gerry exhibited his talents for storytelling beginning with the 1967 Disney classic *The Jungle Book*, and went on to be a major contributor to such other Disney favorites as *The Aristocats*, *Robin Hood*, *The Rescuers*, *The Many Adventures of Winnie the Pooh*, *The Fox and the Hound*, *The Black Cauldron*, *Oliver & Company*, and *Hercules*. He received a story adaptation credit for the 1986 Disney feature, *The Great Mouse Detective*. For *Fantasia 2000*, he worked on the conceptual storyboards for the "Carnival of the Animals" sequence.

From 1995 on, Gerry turned his attention to visual development and character design. In those capacities, he contributed to such later features as *Pocahontas*, *The Hunchback of Notre Dame*, *Tarzan*, and *Home on the Range*.

In addition to his activities at Walt Disney Feature Animation, Gerry also operated his own letter press, The Weatherbird Press, which published many fine print graphic books.

Vance Gerry passed away on March 4, 2005.

Charles Solomon: When and how did you join the studio?

Vance Gerry: In 1955. It was where I could get a job. I wanted to be an illustrator, but I couldn't quite make that, so I was going to go to work as a printing salesman. The understanding was that I could use my designs, which I'd learned at the Chouinard Art Institute, to design printing. That seemed like a reasonable idea, but Don Graham, who was a teacher at Chouinard and one I greatly admired, said, "Forget it. You've put all this time in going to art school; you go over to Disney. They're hiring people." He more or less ordered me to do it. Disney to me was not anything special at that time. As a kid, I'd always wanted to work for Walt Disney, but as a grown-up I'd forgotten Disney.

It was because of television that they hired me and a bunch of others. I was hired to work on television, on the *Disneyland* show.

CS: How did you come to the story department?

VG: The directors always had to redo the storyboards in order to make them filmic. They always would use their layout personnel to do it. They were going to draw the final layouts, anyway, so why not have them restage the storyboards the way the director wanted them, the way he saw them? That was how I got into story: I had done some story drawings on *Dalmatians* which were pretty successful—people seemed to like them. After Walt died and we developed the stories ourselves, I was working exclusively on story sketches.

CS: How did the stories originate?

VG: The stories were always developed with drawings, usually by Ed Penner, Joe Rinaldi, Bill Peet, and a bunch of others. Walt developed the stories with the story artists. The directors were not involved until Walt felt he had something. Then he would assign a director, the director would pick up the storyboards, take them to his room and then try to make a film out of them. Of course, Walt supervised that, too. That was generally the way we did it.

There were a lot of big layoffs in the late '50s, early '60s. I imagine the studio was cut as far as about 75%. There were only about 25% of the people left who had originally been in animation. A lot of the story people went except for Bill Peet. Bill was the only one left that I recall who did feature work. He and Walt developed *Dalmatians* all by themselves; they developed *Sword in the Stone* by themselves. Bill started *Jungle Book*, then there was a disagreement of some kind and he left. We were stuck because there were no storymen, so Walt had Woolie develop the stories. Eventually, we got a writer named Larry Clemmons. We worked with him on a script, which we would send to Walt and he would say yes or no. When we got the script down, we'd make the storyboards, which was absolutely the wrong way to do it, but Walt was busy, I guess. I don't know why, but that was the way we did it.

There were a number of revolts along the line, people didn't like it, they didn't think that was the way to do stories, with scripts. Animated cartoons should not be written, they should be *drawn* and that's the way they should be developed. But, practically speaking, that was the way we had to work.

Clemmons was very good with talent. He was very good at getting voices and talent and very good at writing. But everyone accused him of being a radio writer, because he *was* a radio writer. He wrote in terms of radio and it was difficult to make cartoons that way.

CS: At what point did the story sketch artist come into the process?

VG: After the boards were given to the director or directors. I think *Dalmatians* had two or three directors, and their layout men would develop the story for the film under the directors' supervision. That's when I would do it. Whatever I did would eventually be carried into the layouts. Ideally, you would use what you did on the storyboards, but it didn't work that way. By the time you got to layout, you did something entirely different—whatever the director wanted.

We would get the finished boards. Peet did beautiful boards and we loved them, but they were storyboards. They didn't have much to do with the film, really. That's what a storyboard should be: there's a big difference between a storyboard and a film—at least the way we worked.

CS: Talk a bit about Peet's drawings.

VG: He was just a master at staging and mood, and all done very simply. He didn't use color, or very seldom. He just drew with a grease pencil.

The animators had their ways, too. If you were an important animator, you generally developed it your own way. Frank and Ollie and Milt and those fellows always pretty much planned out the cinematic scheme themselves. The director could argue with them if he wanted to. Those animators, including Woolie himself when he was an animator, pretty much directed their own sub-sequences. Of course, this is my view of the process—someone else might see it all differently.

CS: How did you work with Walt?

VG: There was really an aura about him: when he came into the room, you really felt it. You wouldn't see him very often, but when you did, you got his full attention. He worked very closely with the characters and what they would do and what they would say. It was very easy for him to change his mind, which he did. But he was always looking for something better. He could really freewheel into the stuff, but if he was in the right mood, people would be very excited: he would excite them by how he would act things out or by suggestions he would make.

He knew what he wanted and that's why the whole business was so successful, why Walt Disney animation was successful. Because he knew what he wanted, even before the animators were able to do it. In my case, which was in his later years, as far as I know, he still worked just as hard, even though he may have had a lot of other projects like EPCOT or Disney World or the live-action pictures.

Walt did have a lot more things he was working on. The director would call a meeting when he felt he was ready to show Walt what he had, which would be a story reel or animation or an animated sequence or a storyboard sequence. Even though the director made the storyboards into the film, many times we had to show the boards to Walt. I can't remember exactly why—maybe we had gone astray or we'd tried something different or he'd asked for something different along the way.

CS: Could you talk about Walt's death and the transition at the studio?

VG: Everybody who was anybody there had been developed by Walt himself. But nobody seemed to have, or to have ever had since, the ability he had to know what he wanted. You could say Ralph Bakshi was a guy like Walt who knew what he wanted. His pictures had his mark on them, he was sort of talented. But Ralph didn't have the appeal or the taste to appeal to a large audience.

We were in the middle of *Jungle Book* when Walt died. He had already finished the picture as far as he was concerned—he'd told us the ending. God, we had maybe five or six boards of our version of the ending which we were going to show him—twice we tried to do this. The second time, he didn't even bother listening to the storyboards. Larry would start and Walt would interrupt. Finally, Walt sat back and told how he wanted the ending—which is the way it is in the picture—exactly.

You know, if anybody had told me that ending, anybody else, I'd have told 'em they were nuts. But it's the perfect ending for that picture: The boy sees the girl and it's the girl that makes him go back—it's nature that makes him go back to the man village.

CS: Several artists have told me that the sound of Walt's drumming on the arm of his chair was the death knell for a board.

VG: Or the sound of the change jingling in his pocket. On *Sword in the Stone*, he sat behind me, and it was a sequence where they give a lot of exposition about how there's going to be a tournament and how you have to do this and that—an introduction to the tournament. It was a long, long, long bunch of talking, and I could hear Walt's change jingling. Of course, we thought it was pretty good; we worked on it. But he could tell. He didn't get that close to things; he didn't want to get that close to things, so that he could see it fairly fresh. His change was jingling—I can hear it now—and we cut the sequence down.

CS: After Walt's death, the studio seems to have ossified, with people asking, "What would Walt have done?"

VG: I know Woolie would go with something he knew would work, rather than go out and try to invent something new—which has a lot to be said for it, if you've been through the process of trying to make something out of nothing. My feeling was you had to have Walt or somebody like Walt to have a point of view that he formed of what he definitely wanted to do.

Now it was divided among all these workers, so the focus was diminished soon after Walt died. About the time we started *Aristocats*, there was some kind of committee system that involved the live-action people. Not a lot, but it involved live-action people on some management level, so it was not just in the hands of the animation people.

I remember Frank [Thomas] was a little upset once: the management was called in to hear what Robin Hood's voice would be. Some people were on one side, some people were on the other side; the management said, "No, this is what we want," and Frank said, "That's the end of an era—the management now tells us what we should be doing." He was very unhappy with that.

CS: You worked on the ill-fated *Chanticleer*.

VG: I was very excited because *Chanticleer* was the picture I got on in development, while Ken Anderson was working on it. We had George Bruns as the musician; Mel Shaw worked with us every day. It was a musical, it was really exciting, especially for me, as I was practically a newcomer: to work with those guys—and Walt, because he would come in frequently, as it was a project he was excited about. We had Marc Davis, who had done all those fantastic drawings, and he was sitting right next to me and making even more fantastic drawings! So I really felt like I was in a really special place.

At the meeting where someone just said, "You can't make a character out of a chicken," I think I was the only who didn't realize that Walt was dumping the picture. Afterwards somebody kept saying, "Didn't you understand, he's not going to make the picture?" I think there was another reason he didn't want to make it, but it seemed like such a great thing at the time. Ken was especially let down because he had put so much of himself into it. Woolie, I really can't tell you. They've pulled the thing out probably ten times since then, and it always just gets put back on the shelf.

CS: Could you talk about the post-Walt era?

VG: I'm sure it was terribly depressing to those guys who'd been with him for so long. He wasn't that close to me. He did know who I was, but I wasn't one of his boys, he hadn't personally developed me. It always seemed such a darned struggle to make these pictures, anyway; I figured it was just going to be more of a struggle.

CS: The bright spot in that era is *The Rescuers*, which you worked on. I gather there were three different versions of it, the first of which had Bernard and Bianca rescuing an imprisoned poet in the USSR.

VG: It wasn't supposed to be the Soviet Union, but it looked that way, didn't it? That was what killed it, I think. Walt had Bill Berg develop that and

Joe Rinaldi did all these beautiful drawings. Everybody was excited; they thought it'd be an interesting picture, and if you read the books, it was. But Walt put the kibosh on it because somebody said it was too dark—too many boots and troops stomping along. Maybe it was the Soviet Union, maybe it was politically incorrect before anyone was politically incorrect.

I think the people who held the poet were just supposed to be some people off in a dark, dark country. The way Joe had drawn them actually made them look like they might be German, or in German uniforms. But since the Cold War was very hot at that time, everybody assumed they were Soviets, and I think in the book they were.

CS: The second version involved a rescue from a zoo.

VG: There was a version they hired a young fellow named Fred Lucky to work on. He was one of the very first young guys they hired in the development of young people. They kind of let him go on that *Rescuers* idea. He and Ken Anderson and a couple of other guys, but mostly Fred, worked on that picture for a year in development. I had left the studio at that time, but when I came back, I came back on the day that Woolie had decided not to go with Fred Lucky's version. He said, "It's too complicated. I want a simple story: A little girl gets kidnapped and the mice try to get her back, period." That's the story, so Ken began working on villainesses. He did a lot that were like Cruella and a couple of others, so that's when it shifted.

In the third version, we had a bear who lived in the zoo and was a friend of the little girl. He performed, and there was a big song in there that he performed for the little girl. By this time, he had become an Italian; he was a bear with an Italian accent. I think Louis Prima was going to be the bear. I don't know if Louis Prima had an Italian accent, but everybody who told the story told the bear's part with an Italian accent. The bear was eventually cut out, and you just see the sequence where the two mice go into the zoo, then very quickly come out of the zoo.

CS: What's it like at the studio now?

VG: Jeffrey [Katzenberg] likes to work with a script, but I forgive him, because he's given us so much work. My personal thing is that he doesn't understand drawings all that well—neither does almost anybody else in the business. But Jeffrey works so closely with us on these animated pictures. He's great; he gets right in there and digs in and catches us where we're off, and he's right every time.

CS: What differences do you see in the young artists, as opposed to the older ones?

VG: They sure work a lot faster now. The animators especially have to work a lot faster. There was the golden era at the studio and there was the leaden era; that was the one I worked in. Even in those days, the animators would see something on a storyboard and get excited. They would *petition* to get that scene. They'd want to do it so badly, they'd do anything. Nowadays, the animators don't have time to even do that. They just get the scenes and do them as quickly as they can, although I'm sure there're exceptions to that.

I'm one who always looks to the past, and no way do I ever see us duplicating the beautiful work that was done during the '30s and '40s. I don't see anyone else doing it, either. But in spite of that, I think our pictures come out really looking good; when the whole picture gets on the screen it's really kinda beautiful—and comes pretty darn close. Maybe if you take the films on their own and don't compare them to the pictures of the past, they're excellent.

I just think these guys didn't get enough opportunities; they didn't have Walt to develop them and tell them what he wanted. In the '30s, Walt was discovering an awful lot that was brand new to the animators; I don't see any of that. I think the animators today don't have as broad a view of animation as the guys at the end of the '30s. I think they tend to see animation as something that moves correctly, rather than emphasizing personality and character. That's really easy to say, because you know how hard character animation is to come by. I'm often contradicted by the pictures you see on the screen, though.

© 2007 Charles Solomon

Vance Gerry (1929–2005)

Interviewed by Christian Renaut in 1998.

Christian Renaut interviewed Vance Gerry in 1998 for his book on Disney heroines. Christian had just spoken with Joe Grant and Burny Mattinson. In fact, the three old-timers were working very close to each other; their offices were near and they met about once or twice a week at the studio. Early on, Vance told Christian he had difficulties remembering things, but after some time, he did. Here are the most important excerpts. Most of the interview focused on kids in Disney pictures.

Christian Renaut: The first time I came across your name in the credits was on *One Hundred and One Dalmatians*. But I'm sure you were there before…

Vance Gerry: I started on *Sleeping Beauty*.

CR: Were you in story then?

VG: No, I was in layout.

CR: On *One Hundred and One Dalmatians*, who designed Anita? Milt Kahl?

VG: Yes, it was Milt. Prior to that, it was done much more like rotoscope and as the feature progressed, it seemed to fit in less and less, so Milt redrew her and it was a shock to us.

CR: What was shocking?

VG: It was less realistic, much more drawing.

CR: People who worked on that picture all agree on how great it was to work on it.

VG: It was the last time I remember a lot of excitement. You know, many young men including myself were brought in the layout department. There was a new artistic approach and we were going a new way, introducing the Xerox. And the backgrounds were going to be treated in an entirely different way. The layout men had a lot more to do with what came up on the screen. Woolie was very excited about it because it was a modern, up-to-date, contemporary story, not a fairytale, and it had modern contemporary characters, of which Cruella was the most successful. So it was quite an exciting time. But Walt didn't like the treatment. He liked the picture, but not the treatment. So we began to make it less attractive, and there began a sort of competition between the artists, the animators, and the storymen, so excitement withered and of course a lot of people got laid off.

CR: Regarding *The Jungle Book*, which seems to be the next picture that also got the artists very involved, I heard that Walt Disney was not around very often and even didn't seem to pay much attention to the ending.

VG: For two years we had a very different ending.

CR: Tell me more about that first version.

VG: It was something like the boy got to see his mother. He went back to the village to see his mother after the big fight with Shere Khan. But Walt told us he thought about that ending with the little girl. I thought it was a crazy idea: it was so foreign to what we had been thinking, but obviously it was the right one. So we started working on it and Ollie made it work. It was all Walt's idea, but Ollie pretty much designed the character.

CR: Mowgli doesn't really look Indian. Did they go for a more Indian look to start with?

VG: They tried to make the very early Mowgli look Indian, but I think people felt, "We don't want any controversy," and it was also for a mostly Western audience. We just wanted to make him cute.

CR: More about children: would you agree that the main feature for drawing kids is the bigger forehead, like with Penny, for instance?

VG: Oh yes, it was a formula they worked out in those days. With Penny, Ollie did that very accurately, too.

CR: When you were working on *The Aristocats*, after Walt's death, weren't you concerned about the similarities with the plot of *Lady and the Tramp*?

VG: I don't remember that it was ever much of a point. I don't think people felt, "We're doing the same thing over." I don't recall any discussion about that.

CR: Any remembrance about the female character, Duchess?

VG: Eva [Gabor] did a very good job and animators liked her. Duchess was difficult to draw. I remember they had a terrible time trying to draw that cat.

CR: Did any artist go to Paris to draw any inspiration as they do now?

VG: I don't remember them making a special trip to Paris.

CR: The heroine in *Robin Hood* is Maid Marian…

VG: She was a very forgettable character. This picture was the most difficult that I worked on. The story wandered round and round and round, and we thought the prince and the snake were much funnier then than they are today. People don't see how funny we thought they were then. Many people didn't like the picture, but we worked on it as hard as on any other picture. I wouldn't say it was a bad picture, but it certainly wasn't terrific. And, you know, the best guys were on it!

CR: It seems the story development on *The Rescuers* was particularly hard with things revolving around a political issue.

VG: It went through a very long period of development until finally Woolie said, "We're gonna make it simple: it's a kidnapping, that's it, that's all there is to it." And the guy was right. Yes, there was a bear at the zoo, and it was quite well developed. He had a song and everything. Quite a lot was put into it, and I think Frank and others said, "I don't know if we should get rid of that nice piece of entertainment that we've got just to make the story work better." Woolie [himself] was reluctant to give it up because a lot had gone into it.

CR: Are kids tougher to manage in stories or in animation?

VG: I don't see any particular difficulty, as long as you get the right voice. The animators pretty much picked up the voices they wanted to animate.

CR: It must be rather hard to direct children when they do the voices...

VG: We had a guy named Larry Clemmons who was a writer and who was very good at directing kids. I don't think it was much of a problem directing kids. I wasn't always there, so I can't tell you, but I know Larry was very good at it.

CR: How did you share tasks on writing the story on *The Rescuers*?

VG: Ken [Anderson] was very much the leader. We all followed him. The story was really developed by the director, the animators, and Ken. There were a lot of people working on the story. Gee, I worked on the whole picture, but people jumped around from one sequence to another in those days. You worked on a sequence for a while, then the director would put someone else. No sequence became your own.

CR: How different would you say are Penny in *The Rescuers* and Jenny in *Oliver*?

VG: I would say Jenny was much more aware; she had been around.

CR: As for *The Black Cauldron*, I've been told that Eilonwy didn't live up to the storymen's expectations after all.

VG: There was a little worry that she might have been too argumentative all the time

CR: But she was that way in the book.

VG: Yeah, but maybe she would lose some appeal that way. She was a girl who was very influential on the story. She was 50% of it.

CR: What did you work on after that?

VG: I worked on it for about eight months in story, then I went into production and came back to work on the ending part of *Black Cauldron*, and then on *The Great Mouse Detective*.

CR: You also worked on *Hunchback of Notre Dame*, didn't you?

VG: On *Hunchback of Notre Dame* I mostly worked on story development. I did some storyboarding. Sometimes Gary and Kirk would ask me if I had any ideas. And actually Esmeralda came closer to my drawings than any other character I ever worked on.

© 2007 Christian Renaut

John Musker (b, 1953) and Ron Clements (b, 1953)

Interviewed by Clay Kaytis on August 23, 2005.

It is obvious that when fifty years from now historians will look back at the new golden age of Disney animation, which reached its peak between 1989 and 1994, a few names will always appear in their texts: Jeffrey Katzenberg on the executive side, Andreas Deja and Glen Keane on the artistic side, and Ron Clements and John Musker as far as movie direction is concerned. Is it any wonder that all the artists that we mentioned in this list learned their trade directly from Walt's people, carrying on the flame for generations to come? Clay Kaytis' in-depth interview with Ron and John proves that is not.

This interview originally appeared on Clay Kaytis' AnimationPodcast. com and was transcribed by James D. Marks.

Clay Kaytis: You could describe John Musker and Ron Clements, without exaggerating, as monumental characters in the landscape of modern animation. I feel like anyone who has enjoyed any success in feature animation over the last 20 years owes a great deal of gratitude to Ron and John. Because if you trace the current popularity of animated movies back far enough, you will find that it all began to build with a little film they directed that showed Disney was still capable of solid storytelling called *The Great Mouse Detective*. After that, they took us under the sea in *The Little Mermaid* and on a magic carpet ride in *Aladdin*. To the top of the mountain of Mount Olympus in *Hercules* and an interstellar voyage to *Treasure Planet*. I don't know if many people know this, but last Friday [September 9, 2005] was the last day Ron Clements and John Musker worked at Disney feature animation.[1] At their farewell party last week so many people showed up to say goodbye and thank them for what they had done for animation that the event had to be relocated outdoors. I was lucky enough to have

---

[1] John Musker and Ron Clements rejoined Disney on March 6, 2006.

worked with Ron and John on *Hercules* and *Treasure Planet* and I know many people share my sadness to see them leave Disney. But we also know that Ron and John will continue to make great films no matter where they go. So, definitely, my hat's off to you guys. Thanks for everything. Without taking anymore time I will let them introduce themselves.

John Musker: I am from the Midwestern heartlands, which, actually, Ron is from, too. I have more of an accent, although I've lost it.

CK: So you are from Chicago, John?

JM: Yes, I am from Chicago. I was born to a big Irish Catholic family back in Chicago. Most of them are still back there. I grew up there. I didn't actually come out to California until I came to school here at CalArts. I'd never been to the state of California, even, when I came out here. I actually went to college back there. I didn't get out here until I was 20 or 21. I went to CalArts after I had already gotten a degree in English back at Northwestern University in Evanston, Illinois.

CK: You, Ron, are from Sioux City, Iowa?

Ron Clements: I am from Sioux City, Iowa. Yes, I grew up there and I was never in California until, I think, 1973, when I first came out. I worked at a TV station in Iowa, in Sioux City, while I was going to high school. I was interested in animation so I talked them into… I had made some Super 8 films that I showed at the TV station… "We can do animation." So we rigged an animation stand and set it up at the TV station. I did a few animated commercials for the TV station. Then I did my own film because I wanted to do a film. Someone from Los Angeles, who knew someone at Hanna-Barbera, saw that film. I brought the film out. I worked at Hanna-Barbera for a few months. I found out about the talent development program at Disney and got into that around 1974.

JM: Ron used to do exciting things like courtroom drawing. Didn't you?

RC: At the TV station I did all kinds of things. Once I did a big murder trial that had been moved there. I did courtroom drawings and tried to figure out how to do that…

JM: That prepared him for his eventual career at Disney, dealing with murderers and trial lawyers.

RC: [Ron laughs] I did little things for the station IDs. I would draw the things for station identification—little graphic things. The big thing was the news because every day, you know, I didn't know what stories would come in. They would kind of know the stories about three in the afternoon. The newscasts there would go on about 6:00pm. So I had a few hours to do the little graphic things that went behind the newsmen. When they talked about a fire, I had to draw a fire. When they talked about a car accident, I could do a car, sort of looking like a shred.

JM: That was another era, I'm afraid.

RC: That was high pressure to get those graphic things done.

JM: In the early days those were actually carved in stone tablets behind people's heads.

RC: It was a new deal, actually. It was chromeakey with the blue screen. The newscaster would have a blue screen behind him and you could put anything you wanted behind him.

JM: Jokes and things.

CK: You guys didn't meet, actually, until you were at Disney?

JM: Right, even though we are the same age. Despite my wise appearance, I'm actually six months younger than he is. We didn't meet until I started at the studio.

RC: I was here before John. I actually started before the character-animation program at CalArts, which started a couple years after I started at Disney. But I think the first time I met John was just as they were getting into the character-animation program and John was interning for the summer.

JM: Yes, I was interning during the summer of 1976 after one year at CalArts. I was sort of invited because they had liked my tests. I got to work with Eric Larson for six weeks during the summer. So that was great. I got to do my own personal test with Eric and was introduced to the whole thing. I was obviously interested in Disney because that's why I came out here. I had heard of CalArts. I had actually sent my portfolio, after I got out of Northwestern. I majored in English. I was an editorial cartoonist for the paper. I was interested in cartooning. I hadn't really taken many art classes because I thought drawing was mostly self-taught and you couldn't learn that much going to school anyway.

Then I heard Disney was... When I was a kid, like seven or eight years old, I was interested in being a Disney animator. Then as I got older that kind of fell away. I got more interested in other things, like editorial cartooning and comic books—still drawing-related things but not so much animation.

Then a couple of things happened. I heard Richard Williams talk at a Chicago film festival in 1972. He had just finished *The Christmas Carol* that he worked on with Chuck Jones. I thought that was so cool. He talked about animation and it was so intriguing. It sort of reawakened my interest in animation as a possible career. Then Chuck Jones came out to speak at Northwestern as part of an animation festival. Again, he spoke so well about animation and it sounded intriguing. Right about that time the Christopher Finch book came out, about the art of animation. You actually attached faces and names to these characters. He talked about a training program for Disney. I really became more orientated to that, so I put together a portfolio that I sent to Disney when I was getting out of Northwestern. I thought, *What am I going to do?* I really didn't want to go to graduate school because I was afraid I would become a permanent student and never leave school. I've got to get out in the real working world. So I sent a portfolio to Disney. They said they wanted drawings of animals and that sort of stuff. At first I was trying to draw and it was the winter, because I got out in the middle of my senior year. I got out a little early because I got some credits. I'm trying to draw these animals and I'm out in the freezing cold in Chicago. Like in the early spring. It was so bad. I thought, *I can't do this.* So I went to the Field Museum in Chicago, which is the natural history museum like the one here in Exposition Park. Of course the animals are in dioramas. They are stuffed. So when I sent my portfolio to Disney, they rejected it. They said, "You don't draw well enough, and go away." One of the things they said was, "Your animal drawings are stiff." Well of course they are stiff! They're not stiff, they're stuffed! I managed to capture that immobile quality that they had. Anyway, they rejected them. Then a week or two later they sent me a letter. It said, "Maybe you meant to send this to CalArts?" I had never even heard of CalArts.

CK: Oh, really?

JM: CalArts? What's this thing? So I sent for information on the school. I resubmitted the same portfolio. It turned out they accepted me to be in, literally, the first character-animation program that Disney was more involved in and where Jack Hannah was in charge of the program. The teachers included Ken O'Connor, who was one of the great art director layout guys here; T. Hee was caricaturist and director; and Bill Moore, a great design teacher from the old Chouinard School and more recently the Arts Center. So I wound up applying there. I went to school at CalArts for two years. In my class that first year were Brad Bird and John Lasseter, who was my suitemate, kind of, in the dorm, and Darrell Van Citters, Nancy Beiman, Jerry Rees, Joe Lanzisero, Bruce Morris, and Doug Lefler.

RC: Tim Burton.

JM: Tim Burton was in the second year, yes. And Mike Giaimo and Chris Buck were a year behind us. So we learned a lot from each other at CalArts. That was a great experience for me as it turned out. I learned more from people like Darrell and Brad and Jerry than I necessarily learned from Jack Hannah, although he was a nice guy. They knew more about animation. I really didn't know much at all about animation itself. Some people from the studio saw my work after the first year and invited me to be an intern.

After the second year I actually started working here. So I started at Disney in May of 1977. Which was three or four years after Ron was here, actually.

CK: Ron, you had already worked on *Pete's Dragon*, right?

RC: The way it worked when I started, you had to submit a portfolio to get into the talent development program. It was only started after *The Jungle Book* was a huge success in the 1970s. The way I heard it, the studio was thinking of maybe shutting down animation after Walt died. The animators, who were still there, like the Nine Old Men, were getting close to retirement. They were thinking of closing it down and then *The Jungle Book* was this huge success. So they thought, *We actually want to keep it going*. And they started looking for and recruiting people. They hadn't done this for years and years. When you got in the program you weren't hired permanently. You were hired for four weeks to do a personal test, working with Eric Larson, who was in charge of all the young people. You could animate anything you wanted for four weeks working with Eric. At the end of that time the review board, which was mostly the older animators, would look at your test and decide if they thought you had potential or not. If you made it through the first four weeks, you went another four weeks. Same thing again, if you made it through eight weeks, then you were actually hired, on a more permanent salary. My first four weeks were really shaky because I was really, really nervous. But I did better the second four weeks. The first project I worked on as an in-betweener and an assistant was *Winnie the Pooh and Tigger Too*. While I was working on that I did another personal test, on my own time, which everyone was encouraged to do, with Cruella De Vil, which they liked a lot. After I did that test, Frank Thomas asked me if I would apprentice under him as an animating assistant, a trainee animator.

CK: Wow.

RC: Which was a huge, huge opportunity. I said, "Let me think about it." [John laughs.] No, I was really excited about that. I worked with Frank on *The Rescuers*. That was the first feature that I worked on. I think I worked on it for about two-and-a-half years, working with Frank Thomas. I would animate and I would show him my animation. He would do drawings over my animation and talk about what was good and what was bad. Just kind of mentor me, which is really, I think, a good way to teach animation. That is probably one of the best ways to learn it, to work with an experienced animator who can just point out the way to do it. After that I was an animator on *Pete's Dragon*. Then I was a supervising animator on *The Fox and the Hound*. Then I moved out of animation into story.

CK: What character did you do on *The Fox and the Hound*?

RC: The character I was assigned on *The Fox and the Hound* was Big Mama.

JM: It was typecasting, because she was a "Pearl Bailey". She was kind of a big entertaining black woman and they thought of…

RC: They thought of me….

JM: It was soulful and kind of breezy…

RC: I was a natural. It was a perfect fit.

JM: Because he is so sassy.

RC: On *The Rescuers* I had worked on mice and swamp folk. But I researched owls. I looked at owls. I studied footage of owls. I studied footage of Pearl Bailey. I had a little trouble with the character. It always seemed to me that she wasn't really in the story. She was outside the story, sort of commenting on what was happening all the time. So at a certain point I wanted to try another character. Then I did some of Tod and a little bit of Copper. Tod and Copper.

JM: You did some of the fox, didn't you? He won't ever change. You're forgetting some of your best scenes.

RC: Oh, yes, I did some stuff with the little fox and the owl together, where she is singing to him.

JM: That character was originally going to be a crow in *The Fox and the Hound*. Pearl Bailey was to play a crow. They were thinking a little bit of *Dumbo*, maybe, but she was like, "I am not going to be a crow." Okay, so they changed it. Didn't they? From a crow to an owl.

RC: Yes. That was really fun. I went to recording sessions with her and watched her. I enjoyed animation a lot and animation was fun but I was always interested in story as well. Early on, on *The Fox and the Hound* I had sort of wanted to get into story, but I actually stayed on *The Fox and the Hound* until the end before I did move into story. Then I moved into story on *The Black Cauldron*. I knew John. John worked on *The Fox and the Hound* also. He was a Dinky animator.

JM: Yes, Boomer and Dinky and Squeaks. You are forgetting Squeaks: a little caterpillar-like character. It was me, Brad, Jerry, and Cliff Nordberg who were doing a lot of that. Cliff Nordberg was an older animator who had worked under Woolie Reitherman. He was a very cartoony sort of animator. He wasn't considered in the ranks of like Frank and Ollie. He was more intuitive, in a way. He would just think, this seems funny to me, and kind of go with it. It wasn't the angst of, "I spent hours worrying about Sir Hiss and his back story." Cliff would be like, "What does he do in the scene? Let's do it kind of funny."

CK: He had been around awhile?

JM: He had been around awhile. I think he started in the '40s and worked on *Ichabod* and did some great scenes. He worked on some scenes in Woolie's unit. He was known as more of a comic-action animator.

RC: Frank was really the opposite of that. Chuck Jones once called Frank the Laurence Olivier of animators. For Frank, animation was this unreachable goal. He once said that in his whole career he thought that he only did like three scenes that he felt really turned out right. Frank was anguished, but that was the part he enjoyed about it: the torture of animation.

JM: Nordberg just kind of rode it out. He just had fun with it. He had worked with Ward Kimball and John Sibley, Woolie, and people like that.

RC: People with no rules.

JM: Yes, people with no rules. Or very loose rules. When I would show Cliff stuff, he would say, "Ward used to say, 'There is a funny picture in this scene. Make sure people see the funny picture.'" A tableau, almost, that was comic and that sort of thing. He literally would work over my scenes. Actually, I was working on *The Small One*, which was the first thing I worked on, which was this Christmas featurette. Originally, Eric Larson was going to direct. Glen Keane had done some designs on it. It was thought of as the young peoples' movie, where they were going to get training to work on the featurette. But then I think Don Bluth wasn't happy about the direction it was going. He was, in a way, kind of the leader of the young people, except the CalArts people were a weird offshoot that he really hadn't anticipated. I don't think he was a huge fan of them, particularly. So we wound up being assigned to *The Small One*. We thought, great, we are going to work with Eric and work on these Glen Keane designs that were kind of cartoony. But anyway, one day we came in and Eric was off the movie. Don Bluth was now in charge. John Pomeroy had redone the designs to look more like Mowgli in *Jungle Book*. "Wait a minute, what happened?" Cliff Nordberg was doing this auctioneer character, so I did the scenes that Cliff didn't do of that character, who sort of looked a little bit like Tony in *Lady and The Tramp*. When they designed him they sort of pulled out the model sheets.

RC: I've seen them.

JM: When I was at CalArts I'd done some scenes of Tony because I thought that was a cool design that John Lounsbery had done from *Lady and the Tramp*. I got to work on that and again Cliff really helped me with scenes trying to make them clear. You know, with timing and all that kind of stuff. He was my mentor at that time.

RC: When I started, as I've said, it was before CalArts, and there weren't that many trainees that came before the whole CalArts generation. The group when I started there was Don Bluth, Gary Goldman, John Pomeroy, Dale Baer, Dick Sebast, and then Andy Gaskill. Then Glen Keane came shortly after I started. And then Randy Cartwright and Ed Gombert. That was kind of the pre-CalArts group. Then the character animation started at CalArts, and then from that point on I think the majority of people that came were from CalArts.

JM: Did you go to CalArts?

CK: No, I didn't. All of my best friends did.

RC: Don Bluth was kind of the leader of the pre-CalArts group. Although I would say there was more of a schism between Don and the CalArts group. Even though I wasn't part of the CalArts group I think I was friendlier with…

JM: He was kind of the black sheep of the Bluth group. He didn't drink the Kool-Aid that other people had. So he was not part of the religion. Ron was brought up in Catholic school, as I was, and I still am a practicing Catholic. Ron very early in his upbringing developed a strong streak of both stubbornness and questioning authority and resisting attempts to make him toe the line which he developed in Catholic school, I think. Questioning like, "Why are we doing this?" He was sensitive to feeling when someone he thought was perhaps manipulating him or something. So early on, even when we were there, he was, in his own quiet way, sowing the seeds of revolution against…

RC: Revolution against the revolution.

JM: Yes, that's true in a way because Don was trying to lead a coup or revolution, too. I think in a way, Don was thinking films aren't that great the last few years. "I'd like to get it back to *Pinocchio* if I can." I think some of us from CalArts would support that idea in the abstract, that, yes, they were better before and they had kind of run off the rails. Production values and story had gone down. The films weren't as good as the classic first ones through the gold and silver ages of animation. They had become mundane. The animation wasn't as good. The production value wasn't as good. The storytelling wasn't as good. Everything seemed like it had declined.

RC: Right. When I started, the thing being held up as the Holy Grail was a film that was projected pretty far into the future, but it was already in the works. It was called *The Black Cauldron*. *The Black Cauldron* was going to be the new generation's *Snow White*. It was going to be a kind of pinnacle. It was going to bring back classic Disney in a way that may have been eluding the studio for a while. I think ultimately it didn't turn out that way.

JM: Mel Shaw, a veteran artist who had worked on *Bambi*, did these beautiful pastels and sort of laid out the story. We'd go down the halls and see it. We'd go, "Wow." It made it seem like it had more meat and substance.

It was darker. The books it was based on were really good. It seemed like a pre-Harry Potter.

RC: It had really good characters. It was kind of a *Lord of the Rings*, but a little younger take than *Lord of the Rings*. It had great themes and great characters. Great visual possibilities, but…

JM: There was a schism in its development. Again, the studio was fracturing in the '70s a little bit with the CalArts people going one way and the Bluth people going another way. Some of the older veterans who had been kind of suppressed under Frank and Ollie and Woolie and the Nine Old Men regime, they finally had their day in court or they wanted their day in court on *The Fox and the Hound* and even on *The Black Cauldron*. So there was just lot of things colliding at the time.

RC: I think *The Fox and the Hound* is a good movie in its own way. I think it had a higher potential. It is also interesting in terms of the old generation and the new generation and where things were and where things went. Everybody worked on *The Fox and the Hound* in some way. That included the older animators like Frank Thomas, Ollie Johnston, and Woolie Reitherman, who worked on it for a while. The Bluth people worked on it early on. It is the first film that the CalArts people like John Lasseter, Tim Burton, Chris Buck, and John Musker sank their teeth into.

So everybody it seems like Bill Kroyer, Henry Selick…

JM: …Dan Haskett…

RC: So many people that went on in animation in all kinds of different areas somehow all kind of met during *The Fox and the Hound*, for a brief moment.

JM: Mark Dindal, too.

RC: Yes, Mark Dindal. It was the crossroads.

JM: It was the crossroads. And then out of that different paths.

RC: Bluth broke away during *The Fox and the Hound* and started his own studio.

CK: Working with Frank and Ollie, was there pressure? You know what I mean? Like they were working on it for so long and you were working on the same show as them?

RC: Yes, I always felt a lot of pressure. Milt was there, too. Milt didn't actually mentor people because I think he didn't have a temperament for mentoring people, but he was there and he looked at your stuff. Milt was extremely critical and just knowing he was going to see what you had animated made you feel nervous.

And certainly working with Frank, who was a perfectionist, who had extremely high standards. I loved working with Frank. One of the greatest things in my life was that I got a chance to work with Frank and look over his shoulder a little bit. But sometimes, I have to admit, I envied people who worked with Ollie Johnston because there was a different approach, I think. Ollie, it seemed to me, just made animation look easy. It wasn't easy, but he made it look or seem easy. Frank made it seem impossible. As I say, "the impossible dream," like something he had been striving for his whole life and never felt like he had achieved his goal. To me that was daunting, I would say.

JM: Yes.

RC: Certainly daunting.

JM: Yes, Ron really worked with Frank. We knew they would look at your stuff and we always felt the weight, not only of them but of the past Disney films: that's kind of like a legacy. Those are so great and if your work was going to be up against them, how are you going to measure up?

RC: Anyone who comes here feels that. Certainly I think we both were really inspired by the Disney films as kids, and particularly *Pinocchio*, I think, was a film we're kind of overwhelmed by. *One Hundred and One Dalmatians* for me also was a film I just sort of went crazy about. So I aspired to work at Disney since I was a kid. I had read about Disney and anything I could find on Disney, so I had some sense of who those people were and what they had done. So it was intimidating.

JM: I'm packing up my offices right now and I am finding some of my animation drawings from *The Fox and the Hound*. I haven't animated in a long time and I'm hoping some day to get back to it. When I see these drawings, I'm like, "Wow, this is bad." I really feel like if I had stayed with it, I think I would have gotten a lot better. I certainly had room to grow.

RC: I was just getting into it a little bit, and of course we're talking about 2D drawn animation, which is a thing future generations never will quite understand. The animators actually held pencils in their hands and they actually made drawings on paper that then were photographed or painted on cells.

JM: You are saying this for posterity?

RC: Saying this for posterity. Most people think of animation as drawing. You talk about the drawing. A lot of people were overwhelmed by the amount of drawings you had to do. That seemed to be the thing people were amazed about in animation. You actually had to do thousands and thousands of drawings. But the emphasis at Disney wasn't so much on the drawing. That was almost something that you needed to master or try to master and get past, because the emphasis was totally on the acting and the performance.

Even someone like Frank Thomas, I think, would say he was not a superb draftsman. He forced himself to become a good draftsman just by hard, hard work and dedication, unlike people like Milt Kahl and Marc Davis, who were naturally superb draftsmen. Frank was a superb actor and there was so much emphasis about acting and character. Getting into the character. Getting inside the character. Making the character seem like he is thinking and having the audience know what the character is thinking all the time. That's really what the emphasis was on. Even among the newer generation there were excellent draftsmen and there were struggling draftsmen. I certainly was a struggling draftsman. I never felt like I could draw at all to the satisfaction that I wanted to be able to draw.

JM: People like John Pomeroy, Andy Gaskill, and Glen Keane were really good draftsmen.

RC: Yes, you would always try to get drawings from the better draftsmen to help you if you were struggling with your drawings.

JM: Now that is kind of out of the equation almost completely.

RC: I don't have any way of knowing this, but I think that Frank Thomas would have been a good CG animator and might have really enjoyed that. He was analytical. He was a great musician. And the way he thought and the way he approached drawing. The drawing was frustrating; it was something he had to work past.

A guy like Milt Kahl would have been a little like Andreas Deja is now. The drawing is so much a part of it for him. I don't think he would have enjoyed it at all.

JM: Ollie Johnston, his drawings were so effortless... Mark Henn in some way was somewhat a modern-day Ollie Johnston, in some ways that he drew loosely but really powerfully and effectively. But when you move it to the CG world, that effortlessness doesn't necessarily translate. So it would be frustrating for those people, I would think.

CK: On *The Black Cauldron* you went into story as well, right, John?

JM: I did. I was part of the younger generation. In the meantime Tom Wilhite, an executive who was under Ron Miller, had come in. He was trying to give the young people a voice in animation. He was kind of their advocate. He was only a few years older than we were. He was trying to bring those people along. Knowing that *The Black Cauldron* was looming, he wanted to get a younger director in there. Because on *The Fox and the Hound* even, there were some clashes between the old guard of Art Stevens, who was a veteran who got his chance to finally direct a feature, and some of them. Ted Berman was a veteran story man, again, who got a chance to do a feature and yet was maybe out of touch with some of the sensibilities of the CalArts-type people. So they drafted me to be a director on *Cauldron*. I was sort of imposed on these other directors. Here, we are going to throw this younger guy in with you as a director and they didn't want…

RC: I think John was picked because even among the CalArts people he was kind of a natural director. People would show their test to him and always try to get input. He was always just good at constructive kinds of notes, just helping you to make your scene better.

JM: I think, more so than that, was the fact that my animation wasn't that good. So they didn't want to take away someone who really was a powerful animator. By default, almost, I sort of got elected. So I didn't necessarily aspire to it at all. I literally did get drafted into it. I thought, *Well this will be sort of interesting*. But, because I was imposed on those guys, we were totally out of sync creatively.

RC: The other three directors would have meetings and not tell John about the meetings.

JM: Yes, it was like that. I would find out they had a meeting. "They did?" Or even the character design. It was a crazy time because Joe Hale was elected. So they brought me on as a younger director. Joe Hale, who had worked with some younger people and Henry Selick, and what not, on *The Watcher in the Woods*, I think, and worked well with them. Tom Wilhite said, "Well, here is Joe Hale. Here is a guy; he is willing to give younger people a voice." So Tom had Joe produce *The Black Cauldron* partly because he said he is going to include [the young guys].

RC: Ron Miller as well, I think.

JM: Ron Miller was really the executive that Tom was answering to, Walt's son-in-law who was running the studio. I think that they said, "Well, this makes sense get some younger people in there." But Joe was completely torn because it was almost like a conservative/liberal or left wing/right wing thing.

For example, Tim Burton was in development on *The Black Cauldron* partly because he did these drawings and sketch books that were really great. John Lasseter, when I was about to swing over on to *The Black Cauldron*, said to me, "You know who you should really get doing stuff on this? Tim. Have you seen his drawings?" I had seen some of his drawings, but not that many. "You've got to see his sketch books." So I looked at Tim's sketchbooks where he has sketched people in line for the ride for the *Rocky Horror Picture Show* at that time. Anyway, he had these great fantastic concepts and observations and style and all that stuff. I talked to them about getting Tim to do visual development on the movie. Joe was very supportive of it. So Tim did all these characters that were very Tim

Burton for *The Black Cauldron*. I thought they were great and Joe thought they were great.

But Art Stevens and the other directors said, "This isn't Disney, this is so out there. This is too bizarre, this is something else. You are going down a totally wrong path." There was very much a schism there. It was a schism even in terms of the development of the story. Pete Young was working on the story. Ron was working on the story. I was working on the story. Steve Hulett was working on it, too. But we were out of sync with the directors: What we thought, what was good about the books, and what we were trying to do. How old Taran the hero should be. We kind of favored a younger guy like the books. No, he should be more like a Luke Skywalker. He should be like a 15–17-year-old young man. We were like, no, he should be 12 or 13. Joe was getting pulled in different directions at the same time. He went to Ron Miller and said, "Which way do you want me to go on this?" He came back and told me this. I wasn't privy to the conversation, but I believe he said, "We can go this kind of new way and kind of break out and do this kind of different, this UPA thing, that Tim sort of thing over here. or we can do the traditional Disney, classic Disney approach. Ron said, 'I want the classic Disney approach.'" I remember Joe's comments to me at the time. He said, "Ron Miller said, '*Lady and the Tramp*, we just released it over in Europe right now. It is doing great. Why would I want to change that? That's what I want to go with.'"

When Joe was telling me this, I was thinking to myself in its own way we are talking about *Lady and the Tramp* here. Even though, yes, superficially it looks more different, but in terms of heart and story and all that we're actually trying to throw it back earlier.

RC: So *The Black Cauldron* kind of split in half. Out of that a small satellite was created, *The Great Mouse Detective* (or *Basil of Baker Street*) which was Tom Wilhite's way of saying, "Well there is a certain amount of people who just don't seem to be adjusting to *Cauldron* or aren't really working…"

JM: It was the island of misfit toys that we sort of went to. Ron was the one who pitched *Basil of Baker Street* at the time to Joe Hale. He went to Joe Hale and said, "I've got this book that I think would make a good movie."

RC: Principally because I was a huge Sherlock Holmes fan. I was looking for something. I felt you could do something with Sherlock Holmes in animation.

JM: Joe liked it and it wasn't much. There weren't "gong shows". There wasn't any development process that codified in any way whatsoever.

RC: Out of that someone made a drawing. I don't remember who made the drawing. Could it have been Vance Gerry? Or it could have been Mel

Shaw? I don't remember, but someone made a drawing. Joe showed that drawing to Ron Miller, and Ron Miller said, "Yes, make that."

JM "Yes, let's start cooking on that one."

CK: Were you one of the misfit toys?

JM: I was one of the misfit toys, so they came to me and said, "You go off on this movie."

CK: That's when you guys paired up?

JM: That's when we sort of paired up. We had sort of been working on *Cauldron*, but not mutually in sync with the directors.

RC: We bonded a bit on *Cauldron* because we were in sync with each other and not in sync with the directors.

JM: I think Ron had definite ideas on the story of *The Black Cauldron*. I thought, *Yes, that is the way to go*. I'm behind that. Graphically, I was pushing it in just a different direction. I did storyboards for different sequences. They never used my ideas or boards. They never saw the light of day.

RC: We both have credits on *The Black Cauldron* on additional story. What additional story means is a story that never got used in the movie.

JM: They didn't like it and didn't use it. It never even made it to the cutting-room floor. So we worked together on *The Great Mouse Detective*, then called *Basil of Baker Street*, for a while. Ron Miller's new idea was that he was going to be the actual producer of that movie. He had never been strictly the producer on one of the animated films before. He said, "I'm going to sort of get in there and work with these young people and we are going to get something out of this."

As we worked on it, what happened at the same time, though, was that the studio came under the threat of a takeover. Ron Miller, who was the producer, would disappear for months at a time because he was besieged. Saul Steinberg, this money guy, wanted to greenmail the company to take it over and sell it off. He was buying up stock. So there was a big thing, like is Disney going to get fractured and shattered? It was a big distraction. Months would go by and nothing would happen. In the meantime, before that, just to back up... I don't know if you want the excruciating details.

CK: Yes.

JM: When I was first assigned *Basil of Baker Street*, I started developing it in a way that I sort of liked. Joe Ranft was working on that earlier version. Joe was one of the great people on this planet and in this business and in the medium: A wonderful story guy. He did these great boards on the movie. But in general the tone that I was pushing on that was not the tone that wound up in the movie, although there were flavors of it, but it was a little more Monty Python-ish. Well, I thought at the time, a mouse... Sherlock Holmes is just too mundane... Can we do a spin on it? It was a spin on maybe the clichés of Holmes even. People just said, "You are going too far out in left field."

For example, in our version, Basil played a mouse-size version of a tuba instead of a violin. When he wanted to think, he would bring up this tuba. It was sort of a parody of these Holmes-ish elements. In our version of Dr. Dawson, Ed Gombert had done this great drawing of this very myopic but really overweight guy. We said he is kind of hideous, but he is this lady's man and is attractive. Everywhere he goes, women are attracted to him like flies to honey. So it was kind of bizarre. It was a left-field version of the thing.

We spent six months working on that thing. We showed it to Ron Miller. He was completely nonplussed. Like, what the hell is this? Joe Ranft did a very funny drawing. I still have it up on my board to this day, where Ron Miller looks kind of like Frankenstein and he is saying, "Where is the goddamn warmth?" He felt that it didn't compute at all. "I thought you were doing a mouse show? This guy doesn't look that appealing to me." So at that point they brought Burny Mattinson on to work with me.

RC: He had been doing *Mickey's Christmas Carol*.

JM: He had been doing *Mickey's Christmas Carol* and had finished that up. This is about 1982. They said, "Okay, Burny, you work with John and you do this." So I really backed off because I felt my approach is out of sync with them. In the meantime, I kept thinking I don't know if I really fit in here. I'm ready to leave. I'm going to be gone. There are other projects outside that I'm hoping to get going. Brad Bird was trying to get *The Spirit*, the Will Eisner story, off the ground as an animated feature at that time, with Gary Kurtz up in San Francisco. I was like, "Hey, Brad, you get that going and I'm there in a week. You know I'll be there."

RC: John Lasseter was trying to get *The Brave Little Toaster* going. There were various projects. Tim Burton was doing live-action, Super 8 films. Strange little films, that nothing would ever come of, obviously. *LUAU*, was it?

JM: *LUAU*. I was technical advisor

RC: It is a beach movie. A kind of a parody of the Frankie Avalon beach movies.

JM: Have you seen it? Tim played it. It was great to see everybody.

CK: Yes, I've seen it. It was great.

RC: Tim played the head from outer space that got in the surfing contest.

JM: "I'm the most soulful man in the universe." So after that, Burny sort of took over. Vance came in… I don't think Vance had worked on the first version.

RC: I think Pete Young was still involved.

JM: I think Vance, more than anybody, sort of righted the ship in that he found a way of making it warmer and more appealing.

CK: Ron, were you involved in any of this?

RC: I was involved with both versions.

JM: He sort of went along with the first version. The second version you were in sync with, too.

RC: The main thing, in the second version, which I did like, was pushing the villain more, which was Professor Ratigan from the book. But, there were things I liked in both. There were things that carried over, but more subtlety. I was doing story and story went on a long time. *Cauldron* was the film that most of the animation staff was working on. *Cauldron* was a long production. I think it went on for four years in production, which is a long time for any animated film. So we had this kind of leisure. We had a lot of time to do boards on *Great Mouse*, but no animation. It spent a lot of time gestating in story. Then this thing happened. Suddenly we heard about Saul Steinberg. We heard about the takeover. Nobody knew what was going to happen…

JM: I was in Hawaii at the time on my honeymoon—not my honeymoon, my anniversary. This was in 1984, the summer of 1984. I remember sitting in the airport as we were about to fly back and seeing the headlines in the newspaper: RON MILLER OUT…MICHAEL EISNER IN. I looked at my wife and said, "I am going back there, but I don't know if I'll have a job when I get back. I don't know what is going on."

RC: The weird thing was, Ron Miller was actually the producer of *Basil of Baker Street*. Then Ron Miller disappeared. He was gone. So we had no producer. It is like the teacher is gone and the kids are in the classroom. Michael Eisner came over. Roy Disney brought Michael Eisner over, but nobody really knew we existed. There was a question like, should we tell anyone? Or should we just keep doing this and not tell anyone.

CK: Did you continue? Or did you wait and hold back?

RC: Burny talked to Roy. Roy Disney was to find out that there was this project that had been going on for a while. Then Roy brought in Michael Eisner, who we had never met, and Jeffery Katzenberg, who we had never met. We had to sort of pitch *Basil* to them, to those guys.

JM: We had been working on it for two-and-a-half or three years, which seems unbelievable now. It was that long, just meandering around the story and being reworked. At that point it was at a crossroads. He could have just said, "No, forget it." So there were literally boards up in the hall like an outline of the story that we pitched to him. Not even continuity boards. It was more like a general board. And he's like: "You've got the comedy and the adventure."

RC: But where is the goddamn emotion?

JM: Was that it?

RC: Was it the emotion? But fortunately, they liked it. The main reason they liked it was they had been developing a project at Paramount, which they had just come over from: a young Sherlock Holmes. This had pretty high similar elements, so they did okay it. Michael Eisner said, "How much do you think it will cost?" *Cauldon* had cost nearly $50 million dollars, which was an enormous amount of money for an animated film at that time. We thought *Great Mouse* or *Basil* could be done for half that. Michael said, "I want it for $12 million. Or $10 million." Or something like that. Then he said, "How long will it take to do?" We thought it would take like maybe two more years to do. He said he wanted it in one. So the budget and the time schedule were immediately cut in half. It was exciting that they were going to make it.

CK: You guys were ready to go, basically?

RC: We were ready to go.

JM: A little more warmth.

RC: A little more warmth. So it got into this sort of accelerated thing, from this long-term story development into a very fast production period on the film. The other weird thing, in terms of me being a director, related to Ron Miller leaving. John was a director on that film. Burny Mattinson was a director. A guy named Dave Michener was a director, but Ron Miller was the producer. When Ron Miller left, they decided Burny would become the producer. But Burny didn't feel that he could still direct while focusing on what he needed to focus on as a producer. It opened up a spot for another director. So I was considering that. I was thinking I might want to move into directing. I liked story. I have always been interested in story, but in directing you have more control over the story than you do as a story person. So I asked John and Bruce Morris what they thought. They seemed to think it was a legitimate idea. So I asked Burny to consider me for that slot. That's how I moved into directing.

CK: Wow. Just ask for it!

JM: Well, that sort of happened with me, too, with Ron Miller. I can't remember, maybe it was on *The Black Cauldron* where he first talked to me about directing. I was sort of hemming and hawing. I was sort of noncommittal and I had to come back to him like in a few days and say, "Actually, I'm interested in that."

RC: So John and I were both directors on that movie and we both did a lot of story work. Even though we were both directors, we weren't actually a team at that point.

CK: You weren't Ron and John yet?

RC: No, we weren't that yet. That really came about as we got into production on *The Great Mouse Detective* and Michael Eisner had a "gong" show.

JM: The first of the "gong" shows here, which was in January of 1985. He brought the "gong" show here.

RC: Bring 3, bring 5 ideas…

JM: There was a table, only a dozen people at that one, including Jeffrey and Michael. This was before Peter Schneider was here. So people brought their ideas and Ron pitched *The Little Mermaid* at that "gong" show, as well as *Treasure Planet*.

CK: I was going to ask you how many of your ideas were ideas you brought or ideas they said, "Make this movie?"

RC: Actually, I had three movies that I sort of suggested because I did sort of pitch *Great Mouse*, though it was sold more by this one drawing that somebody did. The drawing was better than the pitch. Then I did a pitch at that first "gong" show: I pitched *The Little Mermaid* and what I called, at that time, *Treasure Island in Space*. They were both gonged at the "gong" show.

JM: Which means rejected.

RC: Which means rejected. All I remember was, either Michael or Jeffery, they thought it was too close to *Splash*.

JM: They were going to do a sequel to *Splash* at that point. *Splash* had come out a few years before. They were going to do a sequel. They said, "No, we are going to do that next!"

RC: *Treasure Island in Space*, they said, was really similar to the next *Star Trek* movie that's coming out. They were involved in that with Paramount. The next *Star Trek* movie that came out was actually the one where they went back to save the whales. So I've never quite known how that was so similar.

JM: Well, you know how live-action development was. It probably was *Treasure Island* at one point.

RC: I was particularly bummed at that point. Particularly about *The Little Mermaid*, because I really thought that there was a lot of potential in that.

I remember that evening with my girlfriend who became my wife. She wasn't my wife then.

JM: She was posing as your wife.

RC: I had written a two-page treatment on those two projects and three others because they wanted five ideas. Jeffrey Katzenberg sort of called me a day or so after that. They actually had read all the treatments. He sort of went down the line on each one. Then he said, "We really like *Mermaid*. We want to put it into development." So it was "gonged" and suddenly it was back. It went into development for a while. I worked with Bruce Morris, who was at the studio then, and Doug Lefler was doing some stuff on it.

About that time one of Michael Eisner's mandates, and Jeffery's as well, in terms of animation, was they wanted to see scripts on everything. The weird thing which almost no one could comprehend was before that time there were no scripts really on the animated films. There were writers involved, but there weren't actual scripts. They worked from outlines and storyboards. Things would be boarded and then dialogue would be added. It was the way it worked under Walt. It certainly worked under Walt. It was effective. Michael wanted to see scripts. They were looking for a writer for *The Little Mermaid*. At one point it looked like Michael Cristofer, who wrote *The Witches of Eastwick* and I think was a Pulitzer Prize winner, was going to write *The Little Mermaid*. I actually met with him briefly, but he pulled out at a certain point. He felt his take would be just too dark for Disney. They just wouldn't go for it. At that point I had written a live-action script that was done on a very low budget for The Disney Channel which was just getting started. I had done some writing and I was interested in writing. I knew something about writing. John is a good writer and he...

JM: I kicked in some dialogue on *The Great Mouse Detective*. I was an English major in school, so I had actually written a full script.

RC: So I asked John if he would be interested in collaborating on a screen play for *The Little Mermaid*. We had gotten along well in terms of working before, and he said yes. So we wrote the script together. The script turned out really well. At that time also, the thing that was going on, the studio had contacted Howard Ashman. I think David Geffen was really high on Howard and had suggested Howard to the studio.

JM: To Jeffrey.

RC: To Jeffrey. While we were finishing *The Great Mouse Detective* we flew to New York to do some press on *Great Mouse*. We met with Howard for the first time. He was doing a musical called *Smile*. Howard expressed interest in *The Little Mermaid* when he heard the studio was exploring the project. He was a big fan of Hans Christian Andersen and had written a musical called *Andersongs* or something like that earlier. So he read our treatment. We started with a 20-page treatment on *The Little Mermaid*, which we had expanded from a two-page treatment. He read that and suggested ideas where the songs might go and what the songs might be. We had a crab in the treatment that was kind of the court conductor. He suggested that the crab should be Rastafarian. We sort of questioned that at first. Then he explained why he wanted to bring the Calypso music in and things like that. So we actually met with Howard before we wrote the script. We had an idea of what the songs should be even though they hadn't been written yet. Then we wrote the script and turned it in, and they liked it very much. Jeffrey was very positive on that script. Yet we were both directors on *The Great Mouse Detective*. So it made sense, since they liked the script, that we direct the movie. We weren't necessarily going to direct the movie until they actually read the script. That's kind of what led to that.

JM: I think *American Tail* helped propel *The Little Mermaid* along because that came out and it was a success.

CK: *The Great Mouse Detective* is considered the turning point, the start of good things.

JM: I remember it got really good reviews and everything. The day it came out Jeffrey called us up and said, "Congratulations, we just love these reviews." I said, "Well, I hope it turns into the box office... I hope it does well. What do you think it is going to do?" I still remember what Jeffrey said. "I'm telling you: you'd have to carry yourself out of here on a stretcher if I told you how much money this thing was going to make."

This, in hindsight, I realized, was his way of avoiding the question. He really didn't know. He didn't want to be quoted in any way or attach a number to it. As it turned out, it didn't do all that well at the box office. In terms of critically, and even from an audience point of view, it seemed like it did help get things moving in a direction where younger people here had a voice in the movies. Certainly people like Glen Keane and...

RC: People really had fun on that movie. We had fun on that movie. Animals in clothes are more fun to animate. It is easier. That was part of the selling point of the movie. Why it could be done cheaper. Had we done, certainly *Cauldron*, everyone had been scared by how much that movie cost. It didn't do very well. So with *Great Mouse* it was sort of pulling back in a lot of ways in terms of budget, still a young, talented staff. It was something you could just have fun with. *Cauldron* was kind of a tougher thing to have fun with the animation. It did bring a little more spirit back into the place and at least paved the way a little bit for what was to come.

CK: You guys have written four films together, right?

RC: *The Little Mermaid* was the first, then *Aladdin*, *Hercules*, and then *Treasure Planet*.

CK: Has your process stayed the same pretty much or changed over the years? How do you guys approach writing?

RC: It has stayed pretty much the same.

JM: The way we write a script is we generally try to work together on the treatment or the outline. We bandy ideas back and forth in terms of characters. We do notes on just what appeals to us about the subject matter. We have read the source material if it is adapted from something. We do that independently. Then we get together and bounce ideas off each other and say, "Yes, I like that. I don't like that. That is an interesting avenue to go down." Then we've kind of done the ground work. Then we actually start writing a script. Usually the way we do it is, I go first and write, just sort of ad lib on paper, improvising and writing the same scene four or five different ways. I feed pages to Ron, and he takes them and edits them and rewrites them. He may use part of it or inject his own thing. I don't see the script until... I'm feeding him things as I go along. He fashions it, but he doesn't show me anything until he is done. So I see a completed script from him based on what I've written and what he has rewritten. Then I say, "Why did you do this? Why did you use this part?" He says, "You wrote that!" I'm like, "I did?" By that time I can't even tell or remember.

RC: He usually doesn't remember... He kinds of reads it fresh.

CK: It is like writing two different scripts, but it is the same script.

JM: Really it is the same script, but I have some distance from it because I've been trying different things. We have an outline. We have a roadmap. It isn't like I'm going off in a completely different way. There are different solutions to the different scenes. Then he makes choices and adds things. In *The Little Mermaid*, if I'm remembering right, the way the whole inter-cutting in the middle where the crab is on the dinner table and the chef is in the kitchen. It seems to me that was all Ron's interweaving of that thing. I can't remember what I wrote. I may have written just a little piece of that... So it was really kind of fun to read it, the way it worked back and forth from the kitchen scene to the dinner table. "Yes, that seems like a movie. That's cool." But there were other sections where there were things that I had actually written. Then I make notes after I've read his thing. I think this is a little clunky or whatever and we go back and forth at it. We turn it into a script. Maybe we bounce it off some friends of ours, whose opinions we respect, to get some objectivity. Then we turn it in to the executive types who have to read it. In the case of *The Little Mermaid* it seemed to be well received even at that point. We didn't have songs, as

I recall, because Howard was too busy doing other songs.

RC: We described the songs.

JM: But we didn't have the lyrics for the songs.

RC: The songs had already been spotted. We just, kind of, have a description of the songs and a rough idea of what would happen.

JM: But in the case of *The Little Mermaid*, Howard was able to take our script and when he did the witch's song, he took some of the scenes we did in dialogue and threaded them through the music. Even the name: "Poor souls." Was that a name he gave? Did you come up with that?

RC: It might have been in the script.

CK: *Poor Unfortunate Souls*?

JM: Then he worked the material into the scenes.

RC: We wrote little intros. Howard actually liked our intros into the songs, which I was sort of pleased about.

CK: You mean like the dialogue leading into it?

RC: Yes, like the dialogue leading into it. He said that stuff is hard to write and a lot of people don't do that. He thought we did good intros. That was a nice compliment.

JM: Howard came out and worked. He lived in New York at the time. But he came out and spent three weeks out of every four, here in the building, working on the other songs. We would show him storyboards. He had ideas on that. We'd show him character designs and the whole thing. So he was really actively involved in the development.

RC: In the whole process on *The Little Mermaid*, there were certain low points where everything looked like it might fall apart. But for the most part that was a very exciting kind of period. Most people were genuinely excited about the movie.

JM: They loved the music.

RC: With *Cauldron* we kind of felt it had potential, but it could have been this thing that didn't turn out. Whereas with *The Little Mermaid*, there was this sense that because we were going back and doing a classic fairy tale with a whole new group of people, everything just kind of felt like it was coming together. So there was a lot of excitement about the movie and a lot of hope for the movie and I think a lot of enthusiasm.

JM: *The Incredibles* had a similar thing, when people were working on that.

CK: I was in high school when *The Little Mermaid* came out. I was a high-school kid and I wasn't an animation geek or fan or anything at that time. It was a great movie.

JM: You weren't?

CK: No, that was later.

JM: It was fun even when we were done. And they were sort of previewing it and it played well. I was in a conversation with Jeffrey Katzenberg before the movie came out where he was on the phone with Michael Eisner and he was saying, "Yes, it is getting there. It needs some punching up, but we are getting there." He sat down and told myself and Maureen Donnelly, who was the associate producer. She was really getting the movie done, "You know this movie isn't going to do as well as *Oliver & Company*. That is okay because it is a girl's movie. Those movies don't do as well as guy's movies. Why, I don't know." *Cinderella* had come out the year before and made a certain amount of money. "That's just the way it is. That's okay. We don't expect more out of it than that."

RC: Their expectations were not super high for the movie until our first preview, which was good. The first preview kind of took everybody by surprise. It played well. The numbers—they always look at the numbers—they were really, really high. Some of the best they had ever gotten. Now they were like really focusing on this movie that had been slightly under the radar. Jeffrey, I think, kind of had the idea. He noticed that the adult reaction was extraordinarily high. We actually had another preview, that they had never done before, where the film was previewed with just an entire adult audience. No families, no kids, just young adults. I would say it played even better at that preview. So then Jeffrey felt there was potential in the movie beyond what he had thought. We needed to try to market this for adults as well as kids and bring in a wider audience. This could actually expand the audience for a Disney film. It did. It sort of opened up possibilities.

JM: We just had this discussion the other day with a person who is in the corporate end of Disney, nowadays. He said he was at an early screening of *Mermaid* down in Florida before it was really released. One of the other financial types who worked at Disney, who doesn't now, leaned over to him after the movie was done and he said, "Write-off." [Ron and John laugh] I hadn't heard that before, but I believe it. There were these people who said, "What is this animation thing?"

RC: When Michael and Jeffrey first came to Disney, they were not animation fans. I don't think even as kids. I think they kind of looked at this thing, like what is this Disney animation thing? They sort of warmed to it and I think they became supportive of it. But I know there were other people, not them so much, who really had a very bottom-line mentality. They felt what they needed to do was farm out the animation. Have it all done overseas. Have it done much cheaper. They even felt that you could make an animated film, at that time, for two million or three million. Then even if you made like, say, 20 million, you'd be very successful. There were definitely people who felt that that was the way to go.

JM: Funny how that thinking has now come around again.

RC: Then there were people like us who loved animation and loved the Disney films and wanted them to go the other way to make them better, and felt if you could make them really good, that you could actually compete with live action and have bigger audiences. And make even more money if that's even possible. It ended up sort of going that way. It could have gone the other way, too.

JM: From our point of view, maybe I shouldn't speak for you, when we were making *The Little Mermaid,* we felt we were making a fairy tale. We had a tradition to live up to, of these great films. I don't think we thought of it as this commercial thing. We were trying to make a good movie.

RC: At that time, I think we weren't married. We didn't have families. I know for me it was always frustrating that the films…

JM: No, I was married.

RC: Oh, you were married?

JM: I got married in 1979. I've been married for a long time.

RC: He's been married a lot longer than me. But basically it was frustrating in the sense that I felt like when I talked to people who I knew, no one had ever seen the Disney movies. They were family films. They were kid's movies. Why would young single people have seen the movies? It just sort of felt frustrating. I felt like…

At that time we had a tradition among those of us who weren't married. A big group of us would go to Westwood like every Friday and go see…

JM: The lonely guys.

RC: The lonely guys. We would go and stand in line and see the new big film coming out. There was just this sense of wanting the films to be seen by a wider audience. It was not a question of box office. We had the feeling they had the potential to be seen by a wider audience. I never really thought of the Disney films as being kid's films. Certainly…and I'm talking about the early films like *Pinocchio, Bambi, One Hundred and One Dalmatians,* or whatever. You can watch those films as an adult. They are totally entertaining, they don't play down. They are not something just for kids. That's how we always looked at what we were doing. We weren't just making films that were just for kids. Yet I felt like the audience wasn't recognizing that, at least the American audience. The interesting thing was the films also played around the world. They played in Europe and Asia. In some of those places, like France and even England, those films actually did play to adult audiences. There was an adult audience for animation. I think we felt frustrated because animation at that time seemed so limited in terms of the audience.

CK: Did you have any idea that it would be successful? You knew it probably was a good movie.

JM: The previews had gone well, so we hoped. We were sitting in a room with Peter Schneider in his office and he said—because I think Spielberg had seen it—"Spielberg says this is going to make $100 million." He said that to us. This was before the movie came out. I said, "Oh, really? Spielberg said that? Oh, that sounds cool."

RC: That was quite a compliment.

JM: I was always disappointed because domestically it didn't make $100 million.

RC: $87 million.

JM: Yes, it was close. What does he know!

RC: It was the highest-grossing animated film that had been made up to that point. At the same time *Mermaid*, when it played over Thanksgiving weekend, did like $8 million, which was really good, once again. But that same weekend *Back to the Future II* did $45 million.

JM: Wow!

RC: So it wasn't like a phenomenon by any means. Certainly for animation it was very successful. We were very happy. Totally happy with the way *The Little Mermaid* did. It wasn't really until *Mermaid* that they actually made a decision, which we actually questioned at the time. They made a decision to put it on video the following May or something like that. They had never done that before with a recent film.

JM: Roy Disney didn't want them to do it. We didn't want them to do it. But they said, "We are doing it anyway." I think Bill Mechanic, in charge of home video, felt they could really make a killing with it.

RC: And they did. In video it was better than any video that had come out at that point. And merchandising, which they are very interested in, started to take off. So ultimately I think the film became hugely profitable beyond even what you would think, even with the $85 million take, which transformed things very significantly at the studio in many ways, in very good ways. But ultimately there were some things out of that that were not so good. I guess there is good and bad that can come out of anything that is successful. Certainly what is not so good is the desire to try to repeat that success.

CK: You guys are answering all my questions. I don't have to say anything. Yes, how do you leave one movie and think of the next project, knowing how successful you just were?

RC: For us, we wanted to do something very different after *The Little Mermaid*.

JM: They talked to us about *Beauty and the Beast* at the time.

RC: They had talked to us about this shortly after, or just as *Mermaid* was coming out, about directing *Beauty and the Beast*, which was still in story stages.

JM: I was actually open to the idea, but Ron… We were at Musso and Frank Grill, or somewhere, with Peter Schneider and having lunch. Ron says, "I need a break. I can't possibly go into something like this." I said, "Well, maybe…" He was like, "No way!" I said, "Okay. Forget it." I mean, I would rather not have done it, except it was Howard Ashman again and there were things that were appealing. But jumping right into it again, he was like, "I've got to recharge the batteries." Okay, so we will recharge the batteries.

RC: We could have done *Beauty and the Beast*, is what he is saying, if not for my stupidity. We were also, then, after a bit of recharging, we had actually pitched doing *We're Back*, the dinosaur thing. We both liked those books and thought that would make a fun animated film. Then we found out Spielberg was already doing *We're Back*. So the Studio pitched, at this time, three ideas to us to do as our next movie after *Mermaid*. One of these was a project called *King of the Jungle*. We also turned that down.

JM: Which mutated into *The Lion King*. We didn't see any future in that movie. It is obviously a no-brainer. Lions? Africa?

RC: Another one was *Swan Lake*, which was once again a little like *Beauty and the Beast*. We felt that's just too much like *Mermaid*. We wanted to do something a little different. Then the third idea they pitched to us was *Aladdin*, which Howard Ashman already developed earlier while he was working on *Mermaid*. He had developed the treatment on that and some songs. We really liked the idea of *Aladdin*. We turned down *Beauty and the Beast* and *Lion King*, but if we hadn't turned those down, we would not have gotten to do *Aladdin*. We liked doing *Aladdin*.

CK: When I saw *Aladdin*—and like I said, I wasn't a huge animation guy—I was like, "Wow, a Disney movie in a totally different style." I thought animation would be a cool career when I saw that movie.

JM: Glad to hear that.

CK: Thanks, guys.

JM: We didn't steer you wrong.

RC: That was the idea behind it: to do something a little different. I would say that it didn't necessarily stem from a commercial instinct so much as a primary thing. Both of us had a similar thing early on as we were doing stuff. Somehow with *Mermaid* we never had to find an animation hook in terms of that movie. We felt it was a natural for animation. The fish are going to talk. It would look stupid in live action. You could do *Mermaid* in live action, but not at all in the way we were thinking. But *Aladdin*, we felt just looking at it and reading it, that that was very legitimate for live action. We were trying to figure out a way to do *Aladdin* that couldn't be done in live action. That there would just be no way you could do it in live action.

We were both fans of Robin Williams and we had talked about him actually a little bit on *Mermaid* of doing a voice on that. Robin Williams had done this thing for the parks called Back to Never Land. When we wrote the script on *Aladdin*, we wrote it with the idea of Robin Williams doing the genie, wrote it in kind of his style. That was primarily to make *Aladdin* really well suited for the animation medium, along with exploiting the flying carpet and the monkey and stuff like that. That almost dictated that it be more of a comedy than anything the studio had done.

CK: Making fun. Like *Pinocchio* is in there.

JM: That was an ad-lib that Robin had done. We recorded a lot of stuff. Eric Goldberg was the directing animator. He would listen to all the takes, as would we. We would pick our favorites. We would kind of reconstruct the scene a little bit. Eric would say that part where he does *Pinocchio*. I would say, "What part is that again?" He would say, "Don't you remember the part where he went... Woops... Like the nose growing long." Did everyone get that? I'm lengthening my nose as I'm sitting here. I went, "Oh, yes." Even though we had written it for Robin, we encouraged him to improvise and ad-lib the things that cracked us up. Eric would see visual possibilities...

RC: Even though we wrote the script with Robin in mind, Eric took it a step further than we were even thinking. We thought of the genie as a shape-changer. That he would be transforming and doing visual things. Eric was really the one to actually have him turn into the celebrities.

JM: He pulled us into that. Originally we were like, there have to be certain rules. We don't want to date the film. So when he does an Arnold Schwarzenegger voice, he can make him look like a strongman but don't make him look like Arnold. Eric would say, "Come on, if he does Jack Nicholson, he has got to look like Jack Nicholson. Let me try and just show you." He would show us, and once we saw it, of course that's how to do that.

RC: The way we got Robin for *Aladdin* was we wrote the script with Robin in mind. But we had never talked to him or met with him. We had no idea if he would be interested in doing it or if they could convince him to do it.

CK: Did you have a backup?

JM: At one point the contract sort of semi-fell apart. Jeffrey came to us and said, "Who is your number-two choice?" We had no number-two choice. Let's hope they get Robin.

RC: Eric was the first animator on that film because he came from outside the studio. He had his own studio in London. We were familiar with Eric's work. John was good friends with Eric. He knew him from before. So he seemed like he was a great animator and this would really be something that would be up his alley. When Eric was at the studio, we took an old comedy album of Robin's where he did a comedy routine, and Eric did a couple of tests where he did animation to Robin's comedy routine. Then we brought Robin in and showed him storyboards and showed him that test. He seemed to get it right away.

JM: Yes, both in the case of *Mermaid* and *Aladdin,* because production was heavily going on at that time, Peter Schneider was going, "If you want to develop some animation credit, you have to go outside the studio. We need these people who are working on the movies right now."

RC: Everybody else was working on *Beauty and the Beast.*

JM: In the case of *Mermaid* it meant we got Duncan Marjoribanks back, because Brad had recommended him, having worked with him on *Family Dog* and knowing him from before that, when he worked on H&B. He said Duncan is a good animator. Based on Brad's recommendation, we talked to Duncan and brought him in to do the crab on *Mermaid*. Dan Haskett, whom I had known from early days at the studio, had helped on the development of Ariel on *Mermaid*. We couldn't use Glen Keane and those people because they were busy. It happened again on *Aladdin*. Okay, you can develop something on this, but you have to find somebody outside of the studio. Charlie Fink, a development executive, told us, "Eric is available. You could get Eric Goldberg." We thought that would be a coup. We really liked his animation.

RC: A perfect fit.

JM: Not only a perfect fit but kismet, like in that we needed somebody, and he was interested in coming here. They were trying to get him and it all fell together in a serendipitous way.

CK: Everyone that rolled off *Beauty and the Beast* came to *Aladdin*, right? That was the last movie that had everybody who was a top animator.

JM: Yes, it was before they developed the overlapping pictures.

RC: It sort of had to be. It wasn't so bad for us because we skipped a film. But for the people who didn't skip movies, it was bad. People went from *The Little Mermaid* to *The Rescuers Down Under* to *Beauty and the Beast* to *Aladdin* without a break. I mean it was pretty much the same staff doing those movies, one movie after another.

JM: *Lion King* was a year and one half after *Aladdin* because they had story issues and they sort of back-burnered it. They couldn't keep up.

RC: *Lion King* and *Pocahontas* were the first where the staff split into two. Some of the people went on to *Lion King*. Some of the people went on to *Pocahontas*.

CK: Was that a hard thing to deal with?

RC: Certainly with *Aladdin* it was grueling for people. I know that we were just hearing these stories about people. They were having carpal tunnel and burnout and various things. From, I would say, *Oliver & Company* through *Aladdin* it was one a year. It wasn't that the whole film was made in a year, because the development and story were done by different units. But basically the animation staff was making one of those things a year, which always had been talked about but never achieved before. It was achieved for a period there, but it almost killed some people at the same time.

© *2007 Clay Kaytis*

Further Reading

Below you will find additional reading material that is indispensable for completing the portraits of all the artists interviewed in this book. We tried to select only those sources that give very in-depth knowledge or a different perspective on the artist's work and career.

Hugh Harman

Barrier, Michael. "The Careers of Hugh Harman and Rudolf Ising." *Millimeter*, vol. 4, no. 2, February 1976.

Barrier, Michael. *Hollywood Cartoons: American Animation in Its Golden Age*. Oxford University Press, 1999.

Bertino, Tom. "Hugh Harman and Rudolf Ising at Warner Brothers," p. 105–109, in: Perry, Gerald and Danny Perry. *The American Animated Cartoon*. E.P. Dutton, 1980.

Burnes, Brian, Dan Viets and Robert W. Butler. *Walt Disney's Missouri*. Kansas City Star Books; 2002.

Friedwalk, Will. "Hugh Harman 1903–1982." *Graffiti*, Spring 1984.

Hanna, Bill. "East Meets West," p. 19–32, in *A Cast of Friends*. DaCapo Press, 2000.

Kenworthy, John. *The Hand Behind the Mouse: An Intimate Biography of Ub Iwerks*. Disney Editions, 2001.

Merritt, Russell and J.B. Kaufman. *Walt in Wonderland*. Edizioni Biblioteca dell' Imagine, 1992.

Ward Kimball

Amidi, Amid. *Cartoon Modern*. Chronicle Books, 2006.

Amidi, Amid. "Remembering Ward Kimball." AnimationBlast.com/view/wardkimball, November 14, 2002.

"At Ward Kimball's House." *The E-Ticket*, number 39, Spring 2003.

Ghez. Didier (ed.). *Walt's People: Volume 2, 3*. Theme Park Press, 2015.

Kredel, Bob. "In Profile: Ward and Betty Kimball, Pioneers in Preservation." *Locomotive & Railway Preservation*, March/April 1995.

Welbaum, Bob with Fr. Ron Aubry. "A Visit with Ward Kimball (Parts 1–4)." Laughingplace.com, Sept. 23, 2004, to January 3, 2005.

Erwin Verity

Shale, Richard. *Donald Duck Joins Up*. UMI Research Press, 1976.

Winston Hibler

West, John G. *The Disney Live-Action Productions*. Hawthorne and Peabody, 1994.

Bill Anderson

Tytle, Harry. *One of Walt's Boys*. ASAP Publishing, 1997.

West, John G. *The Disney Live-Action Productions*. Hawthorne and Peabody, 1994.

Bill Walsh

Bowles, Jerry. *Forever Hold your Banner High*. Doubleday, 1976.

Keller, Keith. *The Mickey Mouse Club Scrapbook*. Grosset and Dunlap, 1975.

Petersen, Paul. *Walt Disney, Mickey and Me*. Dell, 1977.

Santoli, Lorraine. *The Official Mickey Mouse Club Book*. Hyperion, 1995.

Watts, Steven. "Bill Walsh: Make Sure People Go to See It," in *The Magic Kingdom, Walt Disney and the American Way of Life*. Houghton-Mifflin, 1998.

Williams, Roy. *Secret World of Roy Williams*. Bantam Books, 1957.

George Bruns

Care, Ross. "George Bruns." *The Cue Sheet: The Journal of the Film Music Society*, Volume 18, No. ¾, July–Oct 2002.

Tietyen, David. *The Musical World of Walt Disney*. Harry N. Abrams, 1990.

Buddy Baker

Danly, Linda. "Buddy Baker: An Appreciation." *The Cue Sheet: The Journal of the Film Music Society*, Volume 13, January 1997.

Eastman, Tish. "Buddy Baker, Creating Music Magic for the Disney Theme Parks." *Disney Magazine*, Spring 1996.

Eastman, Tish. "Composer Buddy Baker and the Disney Sound." *Disney Magazine*, Spring 1996.

Eastman, Tish. "The Story Behind Buddy Baker's Score for the Haunted Mansion." *Persistence of Vision*, number 9.

Fess Parker

Anderson, Paul F. *The Davy Crockett Craze*. R&G Productions, 1996.

Cotter, Bill. *The Wonderful World of Disney Television, A Complete History*. Hyperion, 1997.

Parker, Fess. *The Real-Life Story of Fess Parker*. Dell Publishing, 1955.

West, John G. *The Disney Live-Action Productions*. Hawthorne and Peabody, 1994.

Walt Stanchfield

Walt Stanchfield's drawing class notes can be found at: www.animationmeat.com/notes/waltstanchfield/waltstanchfield.html

Marc Davis

Ghez. Didier (ed.). *Walt's People: Volume 1, 4*. Theme Park Press, 2015.

Alice Davis

Solomon, Charles. "Alice in Disneyland." *Disney Magazine*, Spring 2004.

Surrell, Jason. *Pirates of the Caribbean: From the Magic Kingdom to the Movies*. Hyperion, 2005.

T. Hee

Beiman, Nancy. "Memories of T. Hee." *Cartoonist PROfiles*, No. 81, March 1989.

Beiman, Nancy. *Prepare to Board!* Focal Press, 2007.

Justice, Bill. *Justice for Disney*. Tomart Publications, 1992.

Thomas, Frank and Ollie Johnston. *Disney Animation: The Illusion of Life*. Abbeville, 1981.

Tytle, Harry. *One of Walt's Boys*. ASAP Publishing, 1997.

Maurice Noble

Furniss, Maureen. *Chuck Jones: Conversations*. University Press of Mississippi, 2005.

Morse, Scott. *Noble Boy*. AdHouse Books, 2006.

Schneider, Steve. *That's All Folks: The Art of Warner Bros. Animation*. Henry Holt & Co, 1990.

Walt Peregoy
Amidi, Amid. *Cartoon Modern*. Chronicle Books, 2006.

Floyd Norman
Ghez. Didier (ed.). *Walt's People: Volume 3*. Theme Park Press, 2015.

Bill Evans
Evans, Bill Morgan. *Disney World of Flowers*. Disneyland, 1965.
"Creating the Disney Landscape: Interview with Bill Evans." *The E Ticket*, #23, 1996.
Rollins, Bill. "Disney's Landscaper." *Los Angeles Times*, July 24, 1983.

Jack Bradbury
Bennett, Dave. "An Interview with Jack Bradbury." *The Adventures of Spencer Spook*, No. 4, March 1987.

Vance Gerry
Canemaker, John. *Paper Dreams: The Art and Artists of Disney Storyboards*. Hyperion, 1999.
Hill, Jim. "Remembering Vance Gerry (1930–2005)." JimHillMedia.com, March 8, 2005.
Thomas, Frank and Ollie Johnston. *Disney Animation: The Illusion of Life*. Abbeville, 1981.

Ron Clements and John Musker
Beiman, Nancy. "Interview with John Musker and Ron Clements." *Cartoonist PROfiles*, January 12, 1993.
Culhane, John. *Disney's Aladdin, the Making of an Animated Film*. Hyperion, 1992.
Kurtti, Jeff. *Treasure Planet: A Voyage of Discovery*. Hyperion, 2002.
Rebello, Stephen and Jane Healey. *The Art of Hercules, the Chaos of Creation*. Hyperion, 1997.
Wickham, Rhett. "Great Animated Performances: Profiles of Modern Masters (Parts 1 and 2)." Laughingplace.com, March 11 and 12, 2004.

Other Great Resources

Magazines
Animation Blast
Cartoonist PROfiles
Disney Magazine
Disney News
Disney's Twenty-Three
Funnyworld
Hogan's Alley
Persistence of Vision
Storyboard
StoryboarD—The Art of Laughter
Tales from the Laughing Place
The Carl Barks Fan Club Pictorial
The Disney World
The "E" Ticket
Tomart's DISNEYANA Update
WD Eye

Websites and Blogs
Walt Disney Family Museum: waltdisney.com
The Disney History Blog: disneybooks.blogspot.com
The Disney Book and History Network website: pizarro.net/didier
Disney History Institute: disneyhistoryinstitute.com
Michael Barrier: michaelbarrier.com
Andreas Deja: andreasdeja.blogspot.com
Animation Podcast: animationpodcast.com
Jim Hill Media: jimhillmedia.com
Cartoon Brew: cartoonbrew.com
Daveland: davelandweb.com and davelandblog.blogspot.com
Animated Views: animatedviews.com
The Blackwing Diaries: blackwingdiaries.blogspot.com
Mayerson on Animation: mayersononanimation.blogspot.com
Animation Animagic: animation-animagic.com

David Gerstein's Ramapith: ramapithblog.blogspot.com

Michael Peraza: michaelperaza.blogspot.com

Floyd Norman: web.mac.com/floydnorman/Site/Blog_/Blog_.html

Vance Gerry Memorial blog: vancegerry.blogspot.com

Harriet Burns: imagineerharriet.com/harriet

Claude Coats: claudecoats.com

Gustaf Tenggren: www.gustaftenggren.com

Hans Bacher: one1more2time3.wordpress.com

2719 Hyperion: 2719hyperion.blogspot.com

Disneyville: kayaozkaracalar3.blogspot.com

Kevin Kidney: miehana.blogspot.com

A Film L.A.: afilmla.blogspot.com

Jim Fanning's Tulgey Wood: jimattulgeywood.blogspot.com

The Cartoon Cave (Pete Emslie): cartooncave.blogspot.com

Laughing Place: laughingplace.com

Stuff from the Parks: matterhorn1959.blogspot.com

Gorillas Don't Blog: gorillasdontblog.blogspot.com

The Pickle Barrel: perkypickle.blogspot.com

Animation World Network: awn.com

Micechat: micechat.com

Harry-Go-Round: harrymccracken.com

Michael Sporn's Splog: michaelspornanimation.com/splog

Animation Who and Where: animationwhoandwhere.blogspot.com

Disney Comics Mailing List: nafsk.se/pipermail/dcml

Alberto Becattini's Animators' List: alberto-s-pages.webnode.it/animators-until-1970/

Theme Park Press: themeparkpress.com

Acknowledgments

Walt's People: Volume 5 was, again, a collaborative effort and would never have seen the light of day without the critical support of Disney historians and enthusiasts.

Jim Korkis is the godfather of *Walt's People: Talking Disney with the Artists who Knew Him*. He suggested the very concept of the series while providing his interview with Bill Evans for Volume 5.

A few of those historians, Christopher Finch and Linda Rosenkrantz, Richard Hubler, Clay Kaytis, Jérémie Noyer, Dave Oneil, and Rick Shale, are new to the project team.

Along with them, my heartfelt thanks go to the other historians who allowed me to reproduce their interviews in this volume: Michael Barrier, Alberto Becattini, John Burlingame, Harry McCracken, Bob Miller, Christian Renaut, Charles Solomon, Dave Smith, and Christian Ziebarth, as well as Bob Welbaum and Percy Willis, who did the most precise editing job I have ever seen, and the talented Pete Emslie, who designed the cover images for this new volume.

I am also indebted to Robin Allan, Amid Amidi, Paul F. Anderson, Donald Ault, Byron Baker, Teresa Barnett, Alberto Becattini, Jerry Beck, Nancy Beiman, John Cawley, Ross Care, Sandro Cleuzo, Becky Cline, Pete Docter, Sébastien Durand, Maureen Furniss, Howard Green, Katherine and Richard Greene, George Griffin, J.J., Kelly Haigh, Reg Hartt, Jim Hill, Jud Hurd, Jerry Jenkins, J.B. Kaufman, Hans Kiesl, Cathie Labrador, Andrew Leal, Jenny Lerew, Mike Lyons, James D. Marks, Mark Mayerson, John Musker, Josh Noah, Floyd Norman, John Province, Craig Richardson, Timo Ronkainen, Randy Scott, Germund Silvegren, Tom Sito, Michael Sporn, Alva Stevenson, Robert Tieman, Emru Townsend, Darrell Van Citters, and Faye Wolfe who all contributed directly or indirectly to the project.

Finally, without the love, patience and help of my wife, Rita, it would have been difficult to find the energy to put together this fourth volume of *Walt's People* in a timely fashion.

Announcing Walt's People: Volume 6

If all goes according to plan, I should be releasing *Walt's People: Volume 6* by October 2008, at the latest.

The contents of Volume 5 promises to be even more exciting than the current volume. It will contain interviews with Ken Anderson, Roger Broggie, Claude Coats, Larry Clemmons, Marvin Davis, Diane Disney Miller, Edna Disney, Lillian Disney, Roy O. Disney, Sharon Disney, Joe Fowler, Joe Hale, Bud Hester, Steve Hulett, Dick Irvine, Wilfred Jackson, Fred Joerger, Ollie Johnston, Milt Kahl, Ward Kimball, Izzy Klein, Eric Larson, Ron Miller, Ken O'Connor, Frank Reilly, Carl Stalling, Iwao Takamoto, and Frank Thomas, among others. As ever, those interviews were all conducted by the most prominent and knowledgeable Disney historians.

To be kept informed of the release date, availability, and precise content of this exciting new volume, please check the Disney History blog: disneybooks.blogspot.com

About the Authors

MICHAEL BARRIER began interviewing people who worked for Walt Disney in 1969 when he was editing and publishing *Funnyworld*, the first serious magazine devoted to animation and comic art. He interviewed hundreds more before the publication, in 1999, of his book *Hollywood Cartoons: American Animation in Its Golden Age* (Oxford University Press), a critical history of Disney and other Hollywood animation studios. He is now researching and writing a biography of Walt Disney for the University of California Press.

ALBERTO BECATTINI was born in Florence, Italy, in 1955. He lives there with his wife and a few tons of books and comics. Although his main occupation is teaching English in high school, he has been into comics since he learned to read. As a comics scholar, he specializes in Disney characters, U.S. syndicated strips, and comic books. From the 1970s onward, he has written hundreds of articles and essays, as well as a few books. Since 1992 he has been contributing to Disney magazines published by The Walt Disney Company-Italy, writing articles, and translating stories. He has also translated several Italian Disney stories for the U.S. comic books published by Gladstone, and has written for such U.S. magazines as *Comic Book Marketplace*, *Comic Book Artist*, and *Alter Ego*. He wrote books about Milton Caniff, Floyd Gottfredson, Bob Lubbers, Paul Murry, Alex Raymond, and Alex Toth, among others. His other passions are animation, classic American illustration, paperback cover art, and pin-up art…and the Fiorentina football team.

PETE EMSLIE has been a professional cartoonist for over 25 years. He was hired by Walt Disney Canada in Toronto in 1984, which led to an offer in 1990 to transfer to Walt Disney World in Florida. Pete left Disney in 1994 and returned home to Canada, where he now lives the life of a freelance artist working primarily with Disney and its licensees to illustrate children's books and other character merchandise. He is also currently teaching part-time in Sheridan's animation program providing instruction in character design to first year students.

CHRISTOPHER FINCH is the author of *The Art of Walt Disney*, *Walt Disney's America*, and *The Art of the Lion King*. He has written two dozen books on art and popular culture, including *Rainbow: the Stormy Life of Judy Garland, Of Muppets & Men, Jim Henson: the Works, Sotheby's Guide to Animation Art* (with Linda Roenkrantz), and *Gone Hollywood* (with Linda Rosenkrantz). His monograph devoted to the work of the artist Chuck Close was published in 2010.

DIDIER GHEZ has conducted Disney research since he was a teenager in the mid-1980s. His articles about the parks, animation, and vintage international Disneyana, as well as his many interviews with Disney artists, have appeared in such magazines as *Persistence of Vision, Tomart's DISNEYANA Update, Animation Journal, Animation Magazine, StoryboarD,* and *Fantasyline*. He is the co-author of the art book *Disneyland Paris: From Sketch to Reality*, runs The Disney Books Network web site (www.pizarro.net/didier), and serves as managing editor of the *Walt's People* series.

JIM KORKIS is an award-winning teacher, a professional actor and magician, and a published author with several books (all of them through Theme Park Press) and hundreds of magazine articles to his credit. He is an internationally recognized Disney historian and his original research on Disney heritage has been used by the Walt Disney Company for a variety of projects. He taught animation at the Disney Institute and animation history for interns at Disney Feature Animation Florida.

BOB MILLER is an animation professional who has written extensively about the industry for *Starlog, Comics Scene, Animation Magazine, Animato!, Animation Planet, Comics Buyer's Guide,* and *APATOONS*.

JÉRÉMIE NOYER, Ph.D, is a French teacher, lecturer, journalist, and musician. His articles have appeared in such publications as *Cinefonia Magazine, Lucasfilm Magazine,* and *Fantasyline*, and on the web. As such, he's been conducting Disney research for more than ten years and has interviewed several hundred Disney artists, including composers, directors, producers, scriptwriters, animators, actors, and imagineers. He has also written the booklet of Disneyland Resort Paris' Official 15th Anniversary Album

CHRISTIAN RENAUT is neither a journalist nor a writer, but a teacher whose passion for Disney has been a major occupation for about 35 years. He had always dreamt of going to see the Disney studio and meeting the artists. It's against all odds that he stubbornly got over hurdle after hurdle to eventually be one of the rare researchers from Europe accepted at the Disney Archives. Thanks to Philippe Videcoq (who dubbed many Disney features), Frank Thomas, and Ollie Johnston, who personally introduced him to the powers-that-be and their former colleagues, the dream came true in 1987. It took him 14 years to see his first book, *From Snow White to Hercules*, published by Dreamland in 1997. The foreword was written by Frank Thomas and Ollie Johnston. The congratulations he received from Roy Disney and Michael Eisner opened even more doors for another project, *The Disney Heroines*, published in 2000 with a foreword by Glen Keane. His work is based on about 100 personal interviews from the old-timers to the new generation of Disney artists. In 1988, he was the only outsider ever accepted to visit the Disney/Spielberg studio in London during the making of *Who Framed Roger Rabbit?*

LINDA ROSENKRANTZ is the author of 17 books, including a history of the telegram, a childhood memoir, and a series of bestselling books on baby names. With Christopher Finch, she co-wrote a social history of the movie colony in the golden age, *Gone Hollywood*, and *Sotheby's Guide to Animation Art*. She also writes a weekly syndicated column on collectibles.

RICK SHALE is a professor of English at Youngstown State University, Youngstown, Ohio, where he teaches courses in film study and screenwriting. He is the author of several articles on film and popular culture. His previous books include *Donald Duck Joins Up: The Walt Disney Studio During World War II*, three books on the Academy Awards, and two books of local history. He is a Phi Beta Kappa graduate of Ohio Wesleyan University and earned master of arts and Ph.D. degrees in American culture from the University of Michigan.

DAVE SMITH, the ultimate authority on all things Disney, founded the Walt Disney Archives in 1970 and served as its director until his retirement forty years later.

CHARLES SOLOMON, an internationally respected critic and historian of animation, has written on the subject for *The New York Times*, *TV Guide*, *Newsweek*, *Rolling Stone*, the *Los Angeles Times*, *Modern Maturity*, *Film Comment*, the *Hollywood Reporter*, *Millimeter*, the *Manchester Guardian*, Amazon.com, and *National Public Radio's Day-to-Day*. His work has also appeared in publications in Canada, France, Russia, Britain, Israel, the Netherlands, and Japan. His recent books include *The Prince of Egypt: A New Vision in Animation* (Abrams, 1999), *The Disney That Never Was* (Hyperion, 1995), and *Enchanted Drawings: The History of Animation* (Knopf, 1989; reprinted, Wings, 1994), which was a New York Times Notable Book of the Year and the first film book to be nominated for a National Book Critics' Circle Award.

More Books from Theme Park Press

Theme Park Press is the largest independent publisher of Disney, Disney-related, and general interest theme park books in the world, with dozens of new releases each year.

Our authors include Disney historians like Jim Korkis and Didier Ghez, Disney animators and artists like Mel Shaw and Eric Larson, and such Disney notables as Van France, Tom Nabbe, and Bill "Sully" Sullivan, as well as many promising first-time authors.

We're always looking for new talent.

In March 2016, we published our 100th title. For a complete catalog, including book descriptions and excerpts, please visit:

ThemeParkPress.com

From Bambi to The Lion King

Mel Shaw's incredible career as a Disney artist and animator began in 1937 when Walt Disney offered him a job during a game of polo. Packed with nearly 400 illustrations and photos, including exclusive Disney concept art, *Animator on Horseback* is the story of Mel's life, in his own words.

themeparkpress.com/books/animator-horseback.htm

The Studio Life of a Disney Legend

Eric Larson, one of Walt Disney's famed "Nine Old Men", went to work at the studio in 1933 and left in 1986 He knew everyone at Disney who was anyone, and he kept a diary of the personalities, the pranks, and the politics. This is his warm, witty story.

themeparkpress.com/books/50-years-mouse-house.htm

Disney History— Written by You

Who writes the Disney history you love to read? A select group, immersed in the history and culture of Disney, from films to theme parks. Now these authors reveal their inspirations, their methods, and their secrets. Why just read Disney history when you can write it yourself!

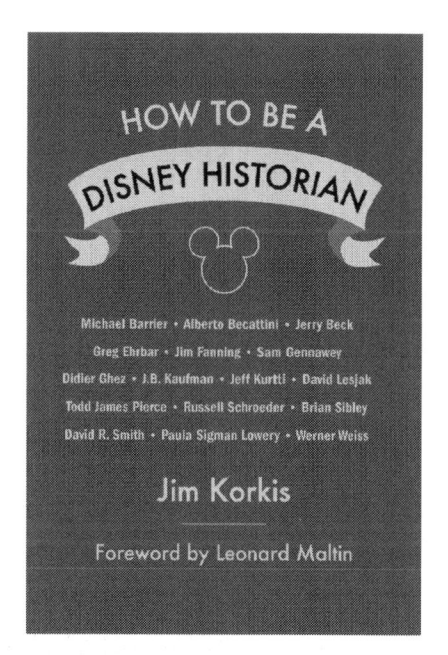

themeparkpress.com/books/disney-historian.htm

On the Road with Walt

Join Walt Disney on a whirlwind tour through Europe at the dawn of Disney's Golden Age of Animation. Didier Ghez follows in Walt's footsteps on a "vacation" that set the stage for Disney's classic films and influenced everything from Disney animation to its theme parks.

themeparkpress.com/books/disneys-grand-tour.htm

Walt Disney and the Pursuit of Progress

Think "Walt Disney" and you come up with animation and theme parks and Mickey Mouse. But Walt's real passion was technology. Documentary filmmaker Christian Moran (along with Rolly Crump, Bob Gurr, and others) provides a fascinating history of how Walt shaped the future while entertaining the masses.

themeparkpress.com/books/great-big-beautiful-tomorrow.htm

Disney History from the Source

The *Walt's People* series is an oral history of all things Disney, as told by the artists, animators, designers, engineers, and executives who made it happen, from the 1920s through the present. In this volume: Harper Goff, Jack Hannah, Frank Thomas and Ollie Johnston, and many more.

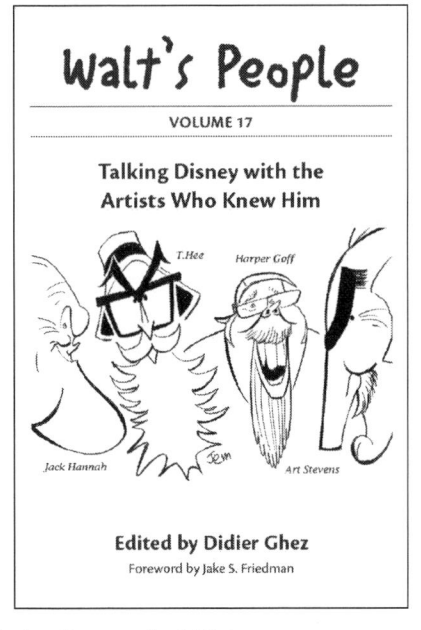

themeparkpress.com/books/walts-people-17.htm

Printed in Poland
by Amazon Fulfillment
Poland Sp. z o.o., Wrocław